RELIGION, CULTURE, AND HISTORY SERIES

SERIES EDITOR
Jacob N. Kinnard, Iliff School of Theology

A Publication Series of
The American Academy of Religion
and Oxford University Press

AMERICAN ACADEMY OF RELIGION

Schleiermacher on Religion and the Natural Order

ANDREW C. DOLE

OXFORD
UNIVERSITY PRESS

2010

OXFORD
UNIVERSITY PRESS

Oxford University Press, Inc., publishes works that further
Oxford University's objective of excellence
in research, scholarship, and education.

Oxford New York
Auckland Cape Town Dar es Salaam Hong Kong Karachi
Kuala Lumpur Madrid Melbourne Mexico City Nairobi
New Delhi Shanghai Taipei Toronto

With offices in
Argentina Austria Brazil Chile Czech Republic France Greece
Guatemala Hungary Italy Japan Poland Portugal Singapore
South Korea Switzerland Thailand Turkey Ukraine Vietnam

Published by Oxford University Press, Inc.
198 Madison Avenue, New York, New York 10016

www.oup.com

Oxford is a registered trademark of Oxford University Press.

Library of Congress Cataloging-in-Publication Data
Dole, Andrew, 1966–
Schleiermacher on religion and the natural order / Andrew C. Dole.
    p.   cm.
Includes bibliographical references and index.
ISBN 978-0-19-534117-1
1. Schleiermacher, Friedrich, 1768–1834.   2. Religion—Philosophy.
3. Philosophical theology.   I. Title.
BX4827.S3D65 2009
210.92—dc22   2009005272

9 8 7 6 5 4 3 2 1
Printed in the United States of America
on acid-free paper

for Bob and Marilyn

Acknowledgments

I owe thanks to many people for assistance in bringing this book to completion. The book itself is a descendant of my doctoral dissertation. Schleiermacher is a historical figure who can profitably be read from any number of angles, and I have been fortunate enough to have had guides into his work who represent a variety of academic disciplines. One of the remarkable things about the Yale program in religious studies is that it allows for a high degree of communication between scholars of religion (including theologians) and philosophers. I acquired an interest in Schleiermacher from Robert Adams, who offered a graduate seminar on Schleiermacher's theology in the philosophy department at Yale during his time as chair. Robert Adams would eventually supervise my work for the dissertation, along with David Kelsey and Nicholas Wolterstorff. I owe the beginnings of my awareness of Schleiermacher's importance for the contemporary discourse of religious studies largely to Dale Martin, who strove to impress upon my cohort of graduate students the importance of familiarity with current work on the methodology of the study of religion. I received financial assistance in the form of a dissertation fellowship from the Charlotte W. Newcombe Foundation, and from Yale University in the form of a John F. Enders research grant.

During and after my years as a graduate student I have benefited from conversation with many of my fellows, in particular Corey Beals, Andrew Chignell, Jesse Couenhoven, Chris Ganski, Jeff Hensley, Sam Newlands, and Stefano Penna. I owe to Todd Buras a particular debt of gratitude for several years' worth of in-depth discussion, not only on Schleiermacher and theology but also on philosophers from Locke to

Lewis and beyond, during commutes from New Haven to Middlebury. Westover School in Middlebury served as an idyllic home base during my graduate years, and I fondly recall conversations on academic and nonacademic subjects with Joanne Dexter, Janis Gilley, Tom Hungerford, and Chris Sweeney.

Various persons at Amherst College have been of help in ways both obvious and subtle during the composition of the book proper. My colleagues in the religion department—Robert Doran, Jamal Elias, Maria Heim, Susan Niditch, and David Wills—have applied a variety of methods of encouragement over the past four years, and I am grateful for their perspectives, correctives, promptings, and examples. Jason Carbine was a source of humor and support during his year at Amherst. Christian Rogowski and Sigrit Schutz assisted both with a few tricky bits of Schleiermacher's German and in locating translation proofreaders; I am thankful to Markus Gerke, Matt Stumpf, and Hannah Winnick for looking over my translations, and to Amherst College for funding their work. I also owe thanks to Amherst College for a Trustee Faculty Fellowship, which made possible the final stages of the book's composition.

Consistent encouragement and assistance with the project has come from the broader community of Schleiermacher scholars, many of them members and associates of the American Academy of Religion's Schleiermacher Group. These include Richard Crouter, Francis Fiorenza, Christine Helmer, Jeffery Kinlaw, Jacqueline Mariña, Lori Pearson, Brent Sockness, Terrence Tice, and Walter Wyman, Jr. Thanks are also owed to Terry Pinkard and Wayne Proudfoot for their input on important issues related to my arguments; to Wolfgang Virmond for assistance at the Schleiermacher Archive in Berlin; and to John Rupnow at the Edwin Mellen Press for bibliographical help. Special thanks are owed to Paul Capetz and Ted Vial, who read the entire book in manuscript form and offered valuable feedback.

I owe thanks to Jacob Kinnard and Cynthia Read at Oxford University Press for giving the book a chance, and for being forgiving with such issues as deadlines and word counts. Anonymous readers for Oxford contributed valuable correctives and suggestions; Carol Hoke and Liz Smith have done their best to make my prose readable.

My deepest gratitude is reserved for my wife, Sarah Buteux, who has followed the composition of the book with interest and sympathy from the very beginning. Her support for my studies and research has been unflagging, her patience endless, and her criticisms gentle yet firm. Her character and remarkable abilities have made our life and work together limitlessly rewarding, and I could not have completed this book without her help. Our son George was born just in time to put the final drafting of the manuscript into a healthy perspective. Finally, my parents, George and Lois Dole, have stood behind my education and my activities as a scholar; their efforts and their lives are the real source of whatever positive qualities my work possesses.

I dedicate the book to Robert and Marilyn Adams. They and their work exemplify the scholarly virtues of exhaustive historical research, careful and charitable exegesis, clarity of expression, and argumentative rigor. It is painfully clear to me that my work falls short of their own in each of these respects; but I take comfort in imagining that I have learned something of scholarship from them.

Contents

Schleiermacher on Religion and the Natural Order

Introduction

He who is bound for Halle will return either as a pietist or an atheist.
                    —A common saying in eighteenth-century Prussia

1 *Schwärmer* or Unbeliever?

In the spring of 1806, newly admitted to the rank of Professor *ordinarius* of theology at Halle, Schleiermacher commenced work on a second edition of *On Religion: Speeches to Its Cultured Despisers*. The process of revision, which occupied his attention between March and July of 1806, occasioned no little anxiety on his part. After spending a month on the first speech, Schleiermacher confessed in a letter to his friend Joachim Christian Gaß that he still found himself conflicted about the entire project. In fact, "I would almost wish to no longer have it be printed at all," he wrote. "It has now been seven years since it was written, and it seems to me that so much has changed since then that the whole construction of the book is now no longer suitable."[1] Apart from the difficulty of adapting the contents of his earlier writing to the changing times, Schleiermacher was aware that his original text contained both "unnecessary difficulties" and also "no few burdensome inducements to misunderstanding." He was determined to remedy these defects without changing the original tone of the book, although as he began work on the crucial second speech he confessed that he had "no firm conception" of how to accomplish the former without risking the latter.[2]

In September 1806 the second edition appeared in print with a dedicatory letter to Gustav von Brinckmann, in which Schleiermacher took note of his hope that the "inducements to misunderstandings" present in the original text, "so varied as to be entirely miraculous," had been remedied. But he also called attention to one particular kind of misunderstanding that he hoped the revised edition would *not* eliminate:

> Nothing, however, would make me sorrier than if those great misunderstandings at which we have often amused ourselves should no longer arise in the way in which this book will be judged anew: namely that with our way of thinking we are always taken by unbelievers to be zealots (*Schwärmer*), but by the superstitious and those in slavery to the letter, to be unbelievers. If my book no longer bore this character, then rather than improving it, I would have completely deformed it.[3]

The tumultuous reception the original edition of the *Speeches* had received was not entirely unexpected. Upon coming to believe that his mentor and ecclesiastical supervisor Friedrich Samuel Gottfried Sack had been assigned as the official censor of the book, Schleiermacher had written in February 1799 to Henrietta Herz, in whose salon the *Speeches* had originally been conceived, of his worries regarding the work's prospects. Of particular concern was the last part of the second speech, where Schleiermacher had praised Baruch Spinoza as a man "full of religion and full of the holy spirit" and had described the idea of God as a product of religion rather than as its source: "[W]hether we have a god as a part of our [religious] intuition depends on the direction of our imagination (*Fantasie*)."[4] Sack had once expressed to Schleiermacher his opposition to the confiscation of "atheistic books." However, to deny the imprimatur to such a book in the official capacity of a censor might be a different matter, and his remarks regarding the idea of God, Schleiermacher thought, "will certainly strike him as just as good as atheism."[5] Although Sack did not in fact serve as the book's censor,[6] Schleiermacher's fears were partly realized, for on learning the identity of its author Sack wrote to Schleiermacher that in his considered judgment the work was "no more than a spirited apology for pantheism, a rhetorical presentation of the Spinozistic system," that its underlying theory was "the most desolate as well as the most pernicious," and that he could in no way understand "how a man who adheres to such a system could be an honest teacher of Christianity."[7]

Accusations of pantheism and atheism were serious matters for an aspiring Prussian intellectual in the context of the early nineteenth-century "crisis of theism."[8] Memory of the *Pantheismusstreit* that had unfolded during Schleiermacher's youth and centered around Gotthold Lessing's alleged fondness for the philosophy of Spinoza were still very much alive, as Sack's remark demonstrates, and the *Speeches* had been composed in the heat of the *Atheismusstreit* surrounding Johann Gottlieb Fichte, whose unorthodox views in the end cost him his position at Jena.[9] Schleiermacher's invocation of Spinoza and reduction of God to the status of a religious epiphenomenon could not but invite controversy; in reviewing the work for the *Neue allgemeine deutsche Bibliothek*, for example, Jakob Christoff Rudolf Eckermann opined that the understanding of religion presented therein comported all too naturally with "atheism and the view of the mere necessity of the world in its entirety."[10] The reputation as a radical which the work's reception afforded Schleiermacher followed him to his first academic post, when word reached him in the summer of 1804 that his former teacher Eberhard had remarked that "this is how far things have come: an open atheist is called to Halle as a theologian and preacher."[11]

In revising the *Speeches* Schleiermacher's response to these accusations of atheism was twofold. He was concerned to make it clear that the accusation that he was, in his person, an unbeliever was false, and his attempts to mollify his orthodox critics extended to substantive changes to the most controversial sections of the text. Revisiting the topic of the idea of God, Schleiermacher systematically obfuscated the radicalism of the second speech by dropping claims describing God as an actually existing intentional object of religious states of mind and indeed as a *cause* of 'pious feelings' into the text—precisely the type of claim that he had taken pains to avoid in 1799.[12] While this may have been a wise move by a younger scholar in a heavily policed intellectual climate, Schleiermacher thereby replaced his earlier radical but clearly stated view with an internally inconsistent set of claims regarding God's relationship to the phenomenon of religion. The conceptual incoherence of the *Speeches* in its later editions, particularly when compared with the original, is in part a result of this editorial activity, and it is on grounds of the greater coherence of the 1799 *Speeches* that this edition is preferred by Schleiermacher scholars.[13]

Schleiermacher also, however, prefaced the republication of his work with a declaration that he was pleased at having been taken for an atheist: More precisely, he declared himself pleased at the fact that diametrically opposed types of readers had drawn diametrically opposed conclusions concerning the posture of the book and its author toward religion. In each case the *Speeches* had been received as a product of the "enemy camp," and it was this aspect of the work that Schleiermacher hoped the revised version would retain. I suggest that Schleiermacher found the pattern of diametrically opposed criticisms to be a sign of success because it indicated that he had succeeded in demonstrating a simultaneous commitment to both of two positions commonly thought to be incompatible. One of these was a commitment to the Christian faith sufficiently robust to cohere with the duties of a preacher or an academic theologian; the other, a willingness to side with Enlightenment philosophers such as Spinoza, for whom the natural order, including the "human order," constituted a single, organized totality of causes and effects the details of which might be known by means of natural philosophy. Schleiermacher was well aware that for many religious conservatives both his embrace of determinism and his willingness to locate the origin of the idea of God in, roughly speaking, human psychology rather than revelation would be tantamount to atheism, and similarly, he was well aware of the tendency of religion's "cultured despisers" to associate any degree of fondness for religion with a suspension of all higher intellectual operations. If he protested against these associations and thus against being labeled either a zealot or an unbeliever, he nevertheless credited those who produced such claims with grasping something important about his work.

When five years later Schleiermacher published his first treatise on the methodology of academic theology, *Brief Outline of the Study of Theology*, he formalized the notion of a dual standpoint by describing theology as comprising multiple subdisciplines, some of which view Christianity from within and some "from above." A generally favorable review of the work by his occasional correspondent Ferdinand Christian Schwarz called particular attention to this aspect of Schleiermacher's proposal:

> The theologian is supposed to stand above Christianity, and at the same time in its midst; he is supposed to regard it as an outsider (*Exoteriker*) with all the skepticism and coolness of a critic, and at the same time as an insider (*Esoteriker*) be inspired by it to the greatest warmth; in the generalities of Christianity he is supposed to perceive clearly the variations in their distance from the idea, and is supposed to belong to his particular ecclesiastical party with his entire soul; from his lofty standpoint he is supposed to regard everything which pertains to a party-spirit, indeed all of Christianity itself, as a single form amidst many forms of religion, and at the same time this same theologian is supposed to bear the fullness of Christian feeling in his spirit and perhaps work as a cleric in the lowest form of ecclesiastical service with enthusiasm, and should the need arise with polemical fire.[14]

The notes of incredulity in this passage should not mask the fact that Schwarz saw correctly what less charitable interpreters of the *Speeches* had missed: Schleiermacher's ambition to keep a foot planted in both the confessional and critical camps and to recommend this posture as the appropriate one for the academic theologian.

2 Schleiermacher, Religion, and Religious Naturalism

In broadest outline, my aim in this book is to present a reconstruction of Schleiermacher's account of religion. I aim to fill a notable, even remarkable, lacuna in the scholarly literature: There is at present no monograph in English that is dedicated solely to discussion of Schleiermacher's account of religion, and no extended treatment of the subject that is not ultimately concerned with questions of theological import.[15] My intention is to focus on Schleiermacher's description of religion as a natural phenomenon—as a collection of human conditions, practices, and artifacts that can be understood as constituting a coherent whole, with its own distinctive nature and propensities. It should not be controversial in the least to claim either that Schleiermacher grounded his best-known texts, the *Speeches on Religion* and *The Christian Faith*, in an account of religion in this sense or that this account is of importance for the history of the academic study of religion. However, the details of his account of religion and as a result the nature of his historical significance are matters of dispute. My focus in this book is for the most part on Schleiermacher's texts, but it will shortly become clear that my reconstruction is intended to oppose a view of Schleiermacher that is widespread within the English secondary literature and so is intended as an intervention in the history of effects.

My opening anecdote is intended to set the stage for the project of reconstruction by calling attention to a deep-seated characteristic of Schleiermacher's writing. Long before "religious studies" was envisioned as a specialized discipline, academic discussions of religion prominently displayed a tension between two tendencies that can be described roughly as the "confessional" and the "scientific." The first of these terms connotes some measure of adherence (or perhaps, better, commitment) to religion; the second connotes the desire to pursue reliable knowledge (including knowledge of religion) through the best means available. As the epigram with which this introduction opens suggests, by the time Schleiermacher enrolled as a student at Halle in the latter part of the eighteenth century the university had come to symbolize in the popular mind the tension between these tendencies, due in no small part to the prominent controversy early in the eighteenth century surrounding the work of Christian Wolff.[16]

Schleiermacher's earliest writings reveal a young man determined to stand on both sides of this divide, immersing himself in the works of Spinoza and Leibniz and siding with the most theologically controversial of their views even as he developed his skills as a preacher and prepared for his theological examinations.[17] His first period of residence in Berlin in the late 1790s found him in the company of a genial set of religiously disinterested cosmopolitans who were mystified by the combination of Christian conviction and intellectual curiosity that he displayed, and *On Religion* was in effect a response to their request on his twenty-ninth birthday that he explain how this combination was possible.[18] The project of *On Religion* was to offer an attractive, even seductive, portrayal of religion to an audience suspicious of not only ecclesiastical authority but also pious otherwordliness in general.

Thus Schleiermacher, partly as a result of historical accident and partly by choice, found himself at the opening of his public career working at the intersection of the confessional and scientific impulses as these were represented in the debates of his day. And if, as I have suggested, his ambition was to demonstrate that it was possible to do justice to both impulses simultaneously, this stance brings Schleiermacher's work into conversation with a long-standing family of approaches to the study of religion. In publicly stating that he found it gratifying to be labeled (wrongly) an unbeliever, I take it that Schleiermacher was signaling that some of his readers had correctly perceived that in the *Speeches* he had attempted to occupy what he would later describe as a standpoint "above Christianity"—a standpoint, that is, that did not take the traditional stock of Christian doctrinal claims, particularly those regarding God and the supernatural, as foundations for reflection on religion but rather treated these claims as themselves part of the phenomenon under investigation.[19] This standpoint is a hallmark of what is commonly referred to as the perspective of *religious naturalism*. Locating Schleiermacher in relation to religious naturalism is one of the aims of my reconstruction of his account of religion.

In this book I will not be speaking of religious naturalism in the sense of a negative ontological commitment—commitment to the nonexistence of anything other than the natural order—as, for example a contemporary, self-described religious naturalist such as Wesley Wildman uses the term.[20] Nor, like D. Jason Slone, do I take the term to refer to the position that religion is a "product of human nature," although Schleiermacher fairly clearly qualifies as a religious naturalist in this sense (according to this criterion Tylor, Frazer, Freud, and contemporary evolutionary-psychological theorists of religion are religious naturalists, while Marx, Durkheim, and other sociocultural theorists qualify as nonnaturalists).[21] The sense in which I will be using the term is rather that reflected in J. S. Preus's *Explaining Religion: Criticism and Theory from Bodin to Freud* (1987). Preus described a "naturalistic paradigm" in the study of religion, with roots in the "theological wars" of the sixteenth century, which attained its first clear articulation in the works of David Hume. According to Preus, the distinguishing mark of this paradigm at its origin was that "religion could be understood without the benefit of clergy—that is, without the magisterial guidance of religious authorities—and, more radically, without 'conversion' or confessional and/or metaphysical commitments about its causes *different* from the assumptions one might use to understand and explain other realms of culture."[22] Preus described a gradual "maturation" of this paradigm up to the point where, as a reflection of the Enlightenment's "aspiration to explain everything," "the same procedures for explanation that seemed accurate and fruitful in the realms of nature and social institutions were now applied to religion itself."[23] For him the naturalistic paradigm in relation to religion had to do above all with the *explanation* of religion by way of the identification of its *natural causes*; in the context of early modern European intellectual culture this project naturally assumed the form of a search for the historic or prehistoric *origins* of religion but from Comte on (according to Preus) expanded to include explanations of religion's continued *survival* as well.[24]

The idea that Schleiermacher was a religious naturalist in this sense is not new. Twice within the last generation his writings on religion have been positively associated with religious naturalism by authors writing in English.[25] In 1989 Peter Byrne, in *Natural Religion and the Nature of Religion*, discussed Schleiermacher as a theorist who inherited several of the distinct streams of religious naturalism operative within the tradition of deism.[26] Following Friedrich Max Müller, Byrne traced the origins of religious naturalism to the attitudes of pre-Enlightenment Christian theologians toward non-Christian faiths: Where Christianity itself was taken to be grounded in revelation, these others were taken to be "merely human" affairs with purely natural causes. For the deists, however, whose project was the construction of a religion based only on materials available to all regardless of their relationship to any purported theophany, this distinction ceased to function. According to Byrne, "the elevation of natural religion to the status of *true* religion entails a naturalistic stance on all religion: it is not a naturalism which denies the existence of divine beings, but one which gives a human origin to all thought about the divine."[27] The ruling assumption of this sense of naturalism, then, is that "all religion must have a human origin and be explicable by reference to mundane powers and facts."[28] Thus the deists understood religion to have a human origin and explanation: "Though a divine being is its object, it is not generated by that being but rather by mundane capacities of mind directed upon mundane facts."[29] Schleiermacher, according to Byrne, fully embraced this form of religious naturalism, but in contrast to the deists' attempt to construct a natural religion shorn of historical and cultural accretions, Schleiermacher argued that historically and culturally specific forms of religious belief and practice—*positive* religions—are the locus of true religion. Thus, since he offered a favorable account of the intersection of the 'essence of religion' and the contingencies of history, "[t]he effect of Schleiermacher's description of the nature of religion is to tie living, worthwhile religious expression to cultures."[30]

Six years later Walter Capps devoted a section of his ambitious *Religious Studies: The Making of a Discipline* to Schleiermacher.[31] Capps presented Schleiermacher as one who worked entirely within the "Enlightenment paradigm" for the investigation of religion as this had been articulated by Kant. According to Capps, this investigative paradigm had two distinct steps. The first step, *reductio*, involves the identification of the "first principle" of religion, under the controlling assumption that "religion is rooted not in divine revelation or some form of ecclesiastical authority, but in something eminently natural and human." The second step, *enumeratio*, is aimed at "recuperating whatever might have been lost in shifting religion from revelation to natural grounds." Applied to a particular religion such as Christianity, this two-stage procedure allowed Enlightenment figures "to claim that nothing of substantive or spiritual importance had been lost in the reconceptualization of religion on a natural base."[32] Schleiermacher, according to Capps, diverged from Kant not with respect to the basic framework regarding how religion was to be understood but with respect to the question of what human capacities should be identified as those most fundamentally associated with religion: Where Kant had located the core of religion in practical reason, Schleiermacher opted "to define religion as a kind or quality of feeling."[33] Capps regarded this choice as Schleiermacher's contribution to the history of the study of religion: It amounted to a shift in the understanding of religion from an ethical to an "aesthetic mode."[34] For Capps, Schleiermacher's *Speeches* and its "sequel," *The Christian Faith*, represented a serial execution of the Enlightenment paradigm: The first reconceptualized religion on a natural base, and the second offered a positive accounting of actual, historical Christianity in terms of that base.

My reconstruction of Schleiermacher's account of religion stands in continuity with the treatments of Byrne and Capps with respect to the question of Schleiermacher's relationship to religious naturalism. On my view, for Schleiermacher, doing justice to the scientific impulse required regarding religion as a phenomenon whose existence and characteristics can be accounted for by means of knowledge not of the supernatural but of the natural order. It was his ambition to reconcile the confessional impulse with this particular construal of the scientific impulse—thus to reconcile religious *adherence* with religious *naturalism*. So while my primary aim is simply to present the content of Schleiermacher's account of religion, an interest in making clear the respects in which this account was intended to serve the cause of 'mediation' between the scientific and confessional impulses constitutes the overarching framework of my project.

3 Friend or Foe of the Study of Religion?

The positions of Byrne and Capps regarding Schleiermacher's relationship to religious naturalism do not represent the majority report of scholars of religion working in English. Discussion of recent trends in the reception of Schleiermacher will hopefully make clear the reason there is a point to a book such as this one at present.

For more than a century it has been a common practice to refer to Schleiermacher's corpus as an important precursor to various strands of empirically oriented scholarship, whether this be *Religionswissenschaft* in the classical sense, the historical study of religion or historicism more generally, or the study of religion as an aspect of human culture.[35] Particularly in view of his role as cofounder of the University of Berlin, flagship institution of Prussian scholarship and model of the modern university, Schleiermacher has been credited with championing the advance of the sciences in their various forms in the face of significant opposition from both ecclesiastically and politically connected forms of religious conservatism; most recently Thomas

Albert Howard, for example, has portrayed him as an enthusiastic agent of the nineteenth-century *Verwissenschaftlichung* not only of Christian theology but also Prussian academic culture more generally.[36] Schleiermacher's writings on religion are also associated within the history of effects with radical criticism, an association grounded historically in Ludwig Feuerbach's claim that Schleiermacher, "the *last* theologian of Christianity," represented "an essential buttress and the de-facto confirmation" of his own theory of projection.[37] Indeed, the neoorthodox view that practically dominated scholarship on Schleiermacher for much of the twentieth century highlighted his entanglement with extraconfessional modes of inquiry, assigning him a crucial place in the post-Reformation apostasy of theology and the drift of European culture away from orthodox Protestantism.[38]

At the present time, however, there is one sector of the field of contemporary scholarship wherein a very different estimation of Schleiermacher holds sway: the sector that comprises discussions of the history and methodology of the academic study of religion by North American scholars, particularly where a sharp distinction between the *study of religion* and *theology* is taken to be a prominent feature of the academic landscape. Within this area of scholarship Schleiermacher is widely regarded not so much as a forefather of the academic study of religion as something of a patron saint of resistance to it. While the reception of Schleiermacher generally has a long, fascinating, and frequently depressing history,[39] the most recent and most relevant period in the Anglophone reception of his work is that inaugurated by the publication of Wayne Proudfoot's *Religious Experience* (1985).[40] Proudfoot's intent was not primarily to exegete Schleiermacher on the topic of religion but to employ both historical and philosophical reflection in the service of criticizing prominent patterns in the treatment of religion by contemporary scholars. His primary target was the idea that religion is to be understood as a kind of experience radically different in kind from the sort that can be evaluated and criticized by ordinary means. According to him, the practice of appealing to "religious experience" arose as a response to the corrosive effects of Enlightenment criticisms of traditional religious doctrines and apologetic arguments and by the late nineteenth century had blossomed into a well-developed "protective strategy" that incorporated not only claims about what religion is but also a principled resistance to the project of explaining religion in naturalistic terms.

On Proudfoot's account it was Schleiermacher who initiated this protective strategy by claiming that religion is "an autonomous moment in human experience and is, in principle, invulnerable to rational and moral criticism."[41] Crucial for Schleiermacher's strategy, according to him, was the notion that religious experience owes nothing to the contingent and the historical: "For Schleiermacher and for the tradition that derived from him, descriptive accuracy is to be obtained and reductionism is to be avoided by insisting on the immediacy of religious experience, and on its radical independence from beliefs and practices. It is a moment of experience which remains unstructured by, though it is expressed in, thoughts and actions."[42] In the early twentieth century this approach was adopted by scholars such as Rudolf Otto, Joachim Wach, William James, Ernst Cassirer, and Mircea Eliade.[43] Moreover, its influence persisted, on Proudfoot's account, during the century's penultimate decade:

> Schleiermacher's approach continues to inform much contemporary religious thought and philosophy of religion, even among those who think of themselves as having broken with that tradition. If they disagree with the claim for the autonomy of religious experience viewed as a sense of the infinite or the feeling of absolute dependence, they employ similar arguments to defend the irreducible character of religious experience construed as the experience of the sacred, or as limit experience, or of religious language, practice, or doctrine. In each of these cases, despite considerable differences, the autonomy of the religious life is defended in order to preclude inquiry and to stave off demands for justification from some perspective outside the religious life. The result is a combination of genuine insights into the ways in which religion ought to be studied and protective strategies which serve apologetic purposes.[44]

All in all Proudfoot associated Schleiermacher with two important developments in the history of the study of religion. The first of these is the rise of claims as to religion's experiential nature or core specifically calculated to combat "reductionism"; the second, the insistence that religion is a matter to be *understood* rather than explained, which Proudfoot traced to the influence of Schleiermacher's lectures on hermeneutics (although he acknowledged that it was Dilthey who first "carried the theory beyond application [in Schleiermacher's work] to written texts and employed it for the interpretation of all cultural expressions"[45]). The combined effect of these two developments, on his reading, was to shield religion from the sorts of scrutiny that might delegitimate it by explaining religious beliefs and practices as the results of factors operating within the natural order. As he put the point in his summary chapter, "The program that Schleiermacher inaugurated with his portrayal of religious belief and practice as expressive of an autonomous moment of human experience has been extremely influential for both religious thought and the study of religion during the past two centuries. The felt quality of an experience from the subject's point of view is considered to be the only legitimate account that can be given of that experience, and the result is a protective strategy that serves apologetic purposes."[46]

In spite of the fact that Schleiermacher was not the primary focus of *Religious Experience*, Proudfoot's treatment has had a greater impact on the Anglophone reception of Schleiermacher than any text since Richard R. Niebuhr's

Schleiermacher on Christ and Religion.[47] This is due at least in part to the fact that Proudfoot's diagnosis of a split within the academy between those interested in the project of *explaining religion* in naturalistic terms and those interested in *protecting religion* from such explanation gained the book a considerable following. At its publication *Religious Experience* was received by at least some readers as a polemic against "theologizing tendencies" in the academy: Carl Raschke, for example, greeted it in the pages of the *Journal of the American Academy of Religion* as a welcome entry in the struggle against "a cultic dogmatics that masquerades as a theory-neutral phenomenology" and against the threat of the academic study of religion "becoming subtly enthralled to a new sort of militant, politically motivated theosophy that mystifies the marginal and forbids normative reasoning."[48] The idea of a class of scholars who in the interests of religious "protectivism" combined appeals to an experiential ground with an insistence that religion requires *interpretation* rather than *explanation* came to be reflected in pronouncements by a wide range of scholars, including Robert Sharf:

> The strategy of privileging experience on the one hand, while leaving the term unexamined on the other, has proven particularly opportune to those who envision their mission as one of combating the pernicious and ever-present threat of reductionism in the study of religion. By situating the locus of religious signification in phenomenological "inner space," religion is securely sequestered beyond the compass of empirical or social-scientific modes of inquiry. Wayne Proudfoot, who has undertaken an extensive analysis of this particular exegetical strategy, has argued that the category "religious experience" is of relatively recent provenance, and that it was "motivated in large measure by an interest in freeing religious doctrine and practice from dependence on metaphysical beliefs and ecclesiastical institutions." As a consequence of the desire to shield religion from secular critique, the modern study of religion was thought to require the development of specialized hermeneutical tools sensitive to the irreducible experiential foundation of religious phenomena.[49]

Tomoko Masuzawa's casual reference, at the close of her recent book, *The Invention of World Religions*, to the project of "round[ing] up sundry varieties of crypto-theology scurrying in the tribunal of science" is a recognizable descendant of this perception of a deep-seated division within the ranks of scholars between those dedicated to the pursuit of knowledge of religion and those who stand in the way of this project.[50]

Proudfoot's claims about the contents of Schleiermacher's understanding of religion appear to have spread along basically the same vector as his general diagnosis of the threat of theoretical protectivism. In spite of the subsequent appearance of Byrne's and Capps's very different portrayals of Schleiermacher, in the decades following the publication of *Religious Experience* Proudfoot's characterization of Schleiermacher reappeared in a number of prominent locations. These include Stewart Guthrie's *Faces in the Clouds* (1993),[51] Terry Godlove's contribution to the collection *Religion and Reductionism* (1994),[52] Grace Jantzen's *Power, Gender, and Christian Mysticism* (1995),[53] and Sharf's entry on "Experience" in *Critical Terms for Religious Studies* (1998).[54] Claims to the effect that Schleiermacher was a religious protectivist, a theorist of autonomous religious experience, and one who insisted that religion cannot be *explained* but only *understood* but whose authors do not cite Proudfoot specifically have also been common; some examples are Preus's passing references to Schleiermacher in *Explaining Religion*,[55] Hans Penner's entry on "interpretation" in the *Guide to the Study of Religion* (2000),[56] and any use made of Schleiermacher by Russell McCutcheon.[57] The themes emphasized by Proudfoot—above all, Schleiermacher as an opponent of the reductive naturalistic explanation of religion and as one motivated by an apologetic, protective intent—are strongly in evidence in both documented and undocumented references within this literature. The spread of this portrayal of Schleiermacher throughout a literature wherein a commitment to the naturalistic explanation of religion is the most important mark of scholarly credibility has led to pronouncements like that of Robert Segal:

> [A] naturalistic account, however inadequate, is more adequate than a
> religious one, which amounts to the litany that religion originates as
> a response to the transcendent. Feuerbach, Freud, and Durkheim
> provide a host of processes and entities like projection, wish
> fulfillment, complexes, collective representations, and symbols to
> account for how and why religion originates and functions. Friedrich
> Schleiermacher, Rudolf Otto, and Mircea Eliade, their religious
> counterparts, provide nothing.[58]

4 Hermeneutical Partisanship and Schleiermacher Interpretation

Claims by Proudfoot, Segal, and others that Schleiermacher stands on the wrong side of a crucial methodological issue are reminiscent of charges advanced at earlier points in history from a very different standpoint. Schleiermacher's remarks to Brinckmann concerning the reception of the *Speeches* constitute the first in a long series of observations on the tendency of his writings to attract criticism from "both the right hand and from the left."[59] His writings on religion have from the beginning been notably vulnerable to what might be labeled *partisan interpretation*, and partisan interpretation not only informs much of the history of the interpretation of Schleiermacher's work but also plays a significant role in the ways in which contemporary scholars of religion construct the history of their field. A partisan interpretation, as I will be using the term, is concerned above all else with locating a text or an author on a discursive map that distinguishes sharply between "us" and "them," orthodox and heterodox, sound and unsound, friend and foe. A "hermeneutical partisan" is interested primarily in a text's display of signs of loyalty to the friendly camp or, conversely, of overt or covert signs of sympathy with the enemy; and for the sufficiently partisan interpreter the discovery of clear signs of commitment to the platform of the enemy effectively obviates the need for further investigation, for it provides sufficient grounds for rendering a judgment concerning the merit of the work in question.

It should be obvious why Schleiermacher's texts, if they generally have the character that I have described, have historically invited partisan interpretation. For if the primary interpretive task is to uncover signs of membership in the enemy camp, his texts provide a rich source of material for partisans on both sides of the disputes with which he concerned himself. This vulnerability to partisan interpretation across a wide range of divisions is, it seems to me, the primary reason that so much of the history of Schleiermacher interpretation has been, according to Richard Niebuhr, "so often nothing more than the noise of 'schools' and parties clashing, rather than an intelligent consideration of the issues and the first principles involved or of the real intentions motivating the other's thinking and molding his style." I suspect, moreover, that it is also the primary reason Schleiermacher has been "of all major European theologians the most caricatured," as Edward Farley has succinctly put the point.[60] Most relevantly for my purposes, this feature of his work also helps us understand why, according to Richard Crouter, "especially in North America and the U.K. the study of Schleiermacher reflects the stresses and strains that delineate the line(s) between religious studies and theology."[61]

The mediating character of Schleiermacher's writing also, however, offers the opportunity for changes of heart considering his party affiliations. Probably the most famous of these changes took place within the heart of Karl Barth and is reflected in the distance between his 1923–1924 Göttingen lectures on Schleiermacher and the "Concluding Unscientific Postscript," which he appended to these in 1968. The early Barth in particular is for my purposes a sterling example of a hermeneutical partisan in virtue of his policy of zero tolerance for the contamination of Christian theology by extratheological scholarship, which was the source of his strenuous opposition to the "scientific theology" of scholars such as Troeltsch and von Harnack.[62] In the Göttingen lectures Barth objected to Schleiermacher's presentation of Christianity as one example of the genus "religion," whose nature can be grasped otherwise than from within: "[T]o determine the nature of Christianity, one does not go to Christianity itself but to a court which stands over against both it and similar structures, and which quite apart from Christianity knows what is what in matters of religion and the church."[63] In Schleiermacher's work Christian theology was "secretly betrayed and sold to the methods of empirical scholarship"; if his work did, *per impossibile*, represent the completion of the work of Luther and Calvin, then "the right thing to do would be to become a Roman Catholic again," and in historical retrospect Schleiermacher's influence constituted "a wrathful judgment on Protestantism which invites it to repentance and conversion instead of continuation."[64] Revisiting the content of these lectures during the final year of his life, however, Barth was willing to entertain the possibility that Schleiermacher might have been attached to extratheological modes of inquiry only "accidentally, extrinsically, and unauthentically," while "necessarily, intrinsically, and authentically" committed to Christian theology (he did not raise the possibility of an "authentic" commitment to both). More important, Barth was willing to wonder whether in the end his questions concerning Schleiermacher's theological bona fides were the right ones to ask, such that answers to them would "be sufficient for a substantive judgment (positive, negative or critical) about the standpoint he represented."[65]

If Schleiermacher's intention was to combine perspectives commonly seen to be irreconcilable, then the partisan interpretation of his texts is at risk of a particular kind of interpretive blunder that, it should be noted, Barth himself evaded. The risk in question arises when the mediating project drops entirely out of sight and attention is focused only on those aspects of his work that for the hermeneutical partisan signal membership in the camp of the enemy. This outcome represents a danger not because interpreters stand under any obligation to acknowledge the validity of the project of mediation: Indeed, for the partisan this project is likely to be regarded as either impossible or illegitimate and will thus be either irrelevant to the interpretive project or itself grounds for criticism, as was the case for Barth. The danger lies rather in the possibility that the interpreters, in focusing only on those parts of the text that to them signify membership in the enemy camp, will miss the fact that the text also contains elements designed to represent the position they favor and proceed to advance as a *corrective* to Schleiermacher's writings a proposal that they already contain. This is particularly embarrassing in cases where Schleiermacher is also accused of espousing this very proposal by members of the opposite camp.

This state of affairs is reflected, I think, in the characterizations of Schleiermacher that circulate within the contemporary Anglophone literature. Polarizing descriptions of the field of religious studies—with interpretive-protective "theologians" or "religionists" on the one side and explanatory-critical religious naturalists on the other—lay the groundwork for the project of reading Schleiermacher's texts with an interest not in understanding the details of his positions but in establishing his party loyalties. Moreover, if Karl Barth's extensive familiarity with those texts prevented him from losing sight of Schleiermacher's attempt to do justice to both the scientific and the confessional impulses, the same cannot be said for contemporary scholars, some of whom seem entirely unaware that his work represents an attempt at mediation between religion and science.

Besides having a fairly specific history, the view of Schleiermacher that appears most frequently in Anglophone discussions of the history of the study of religion is also remarkably disconnected from the Schleiermacher scholarship of the last forty years. Revived scholarly interest in Schleiermacher in Germany in the wake of the decline of neoorthodoxy dates more or less to the establishment by Martin Redeker of the Schleiermacher *Forschungsstelle* in Kiel in 1967, followed by the establishment of a corresponding institution in Berlin in 1979. Under the leadership of Hans-Joachim Birkner during the 1970s these research centers were the center of efforts to produce a new and badly needed critical edition of Schleiermacher's writings (the *Schleiermacher Kritische Gesamtausgabe* or KGA), volumes of which began appearing in 1980.[66] Important monographs and essay collections on Schleiermacher appeared from the early 1970s on, several in the dedicated series *Schleiermacher-Archiv*, and while initially Schleiermacher research continued to be occupied with the influential criticisms lodged by Barth and his followers, in 1993 Christian Albrecht declared not only the time of "sweeping, ideologizing condemnation" but also the period of the rediscovery of Schleiermacher closed and announced the beginning of a "new, unbiased phase" of research.[67] During the intervening years Schleiermacher has been the object of intensive historical and systematic investigation in German that has touched on every area of his corpus, including the production of a full-length biography by Kurt Nowak in 2001.[68] Two consistent features of these recent discussions are directly relevant to my reconstructive project. First, it is now standard practice to locate discussions of Schleiermacher's writings on religion, as well as on theology, within the framework of his architectonic of the *Wissenschaften* as this developed during the first two decades of the nineteenth century. Second, Schleiermacher's lectures on ethics, the "science of the principles of history," have regained for a substantial number of scholars their status as "the crux of Schleiermacher's philosophy" and one that provides a crucial theoretical background for his writings on religion.[69]

The impact of this second Schleiermacher renaissance on English-language scholarship has been significant but selective. One of the primary reflections of renewed interest in Schleiermacher has been a steady stream of translations of previously unavailable primary texts. The appearance of Richard Crouter's translation of the first edition of *On Religion* in 1988, for example, marked the opening of a new chapter in English-language work on Schleiermacher by supplanting for scholarly purposes John Oman's 1893 translation of the third edition. This text joined a growing body of contemporary translations that have made Schleiermacher more accessible to readers of English at present than at any time since his death. For my purposes the most important of the recent translations are Schleiermacher's open letters to Lücke prefacing the publication of the second edition of *The Christian Faith*, his early essay on freedom, and his later lectures on ethics.[70]

A noteworthy feature of secondary scholarship in English during this period is that it has been almost exclusively those affiliated with Christian theology who have taken notice of either the German literature or the recently translated primary texts. Discussions of Schleiermacher's understanding of religion that are conversant with these two sources have appeared in recent years, written by both scholars long active in the field (Gerrish, Crouter) and more recently (Capetz).[71] However, for two reasons the location of this material within the disciplinary framework of theology has been unfortunate. The first is that most recent discussions of Schleiermacher's account of religion in English are either explicitly or implicitly oriented toward questions of confessional import, whether this is couched in terms of "theological adequacy," fidelity to Reformation or Reformed tradition, or the persistent chestnut of religious epistemology, "knowledge of God."[72] The second is that these discussions have had little impact on the work of scholars of religion who hold Christian theology at arm's length. Whether this is a reflection of how specialized those who work in the area of "theory and method" have become or indicates a principled resistance among such scholars to reading works associated with theology I do not know. Either way, the results are striking. At least in English, between those who work directly on Schleiermacher and those concerned primarily with the history and methodology of the study of religion a great gulf appears to be fixed. A remark by Crouter in 1992 has lost none of its force since it was penned: "When we leave the archival world of Germany and turn to the more familiar landscape of recent English-language work, we see that a more complex Schleiermacher is badly needed."[73]

5 Three Framework Issues

To round out this introduction I discuss three areas in which my investigations are significantly informed by the history of Schleiermacher reception and by concerns representative of the naturalistic tradition in the study of religion. The three subjects I discuss constitute, in a sense, the main parameters of my reconstruction of Schleiermacher's account of religion, and by the close of the discussion it should be fairly clear how I understand my project to relate to the currently available literature.

a "Inwardness" and Religion

Suppose an early twenty-first-century scholar set herself the task of extracting an account of religion from the writings of an author from an earlier period.

Suppose, further, that these writings were informed by the followin
istic: The author consistently spoke of religion as something int
human mind or spirit, a purely cognitive, emotional, or otherwise n
and consistently denied that anything "outward"—gestures or dis........,
trine or ritual, community or tradition—could be considered as part of religion.
However, suppose, further, that this author had offered an account of the relationship of religion to ostensibly religious discourse, ritual, community, and
institutions—an account, let us say, that explained how these public and observable phenomena arise and persist within history—while nevertheless maintaining that these are *not* part of religion. If we suppose that our reconstructor
does not herself share in the idiosyncrasies of this historical author and considers religion to include public and historical phenomena, it should be apparent
that she faces an important choice regarding the scope of the term *religion* in
the reconstruction. Whose sense of the term should be employed: her own or
that of the subject of her investigation?

There are two paths open to our reconstructor. The first would allow the
sense of "religion" in her work to be dictated by the historical author's view of
the subject. The account of religion that results from taking this option will be
an account of a purely inward or mental phenomenon and will not extend to
the discussion of such matters as ostensibly religious discourse or historically
extended tradition. The reconstructor will, it seems to me, want to make it clear
that the reason she does not discuss these is that they were intentionally
excluded from religion by the historical author, and she may even want to discuss the ways in which the author took notice of these and ultimately decided
to excise them from religion. However, given that the reconstructor decides at
the outset to limit her reconstruction to religion as the author understood it,
this need not be a major locus of discussion.

The second path would allow the sense of "religion" to be dictated not by
the historical author's but by the reconstructor's view of the subject. In this
case the reconstructor will be interested in the ways in which the author
accounts for those public and observable phenomena that the *reconstructor*
takes to be part of religion. She will want to make it clear that religion, as the
term figures in the reconstruction, differs from the way the term was used by
the author and may want to discuss the reasons for this, but given that she
decides at the outset *not* to allow the terms of the inquiry to be dictated by the
author's view in this regard, this need not be a major locus of discussion.

What our reconstructor should *not* do is to limit her inquiry to religion as
understood by the historical author as a purely inward phenomenon and then
criticize the author for *ignoring* or offering no account of religion's public,
social, or historical dimensions. In actuality, the author, in the case as I have
described it, did not ignore these. Rather, he took notice of these phenomena
and offered his own account of them on his understanding that these do not
constitute part of religion, for religion, as the author used the term, has no

public dimensions. The reconstructor who proceeded in this way would be giving the term *religion* different meanings in two different contexts and would thus be committing the fallacy of equivocation.[74] In the context of the historical author's understanding, religion has no public or historical dimensions to ignore, but as it figures in the reconstructor's critique, religion has such dimensions that must be taken into account.

I offer this thought experiment as a way of prefacing what I refer to in this book as the "standard interpretation" of Schleiermacher. According to the standard interpretation—the interpretation that, as the moniker suggests, dominates the secondary literature—religion according to Schleiermacher is "a sense and taste for the infinite"; it is "an intuition of the universe"; it is "a feeling," "a matter of feeling," or "a feeling of absolute dependence upon God." Each of these phrases is a citation or paraphrase of a claim by Schleiermacher, and those familiar with his texts will recognize their provenance: the second of the *Speeches on Religion* and the opening sections of *The Christian Faith*.

A serviceable example of the standard interpretation is found in Claude Welch's *Protestant Thought in the Nineteenth Century* (1972). Welch described this two-volume project as an attempt at a transnational history of Protestant theology from the publication of the *Speeches on Religion* to the first World War; he divided this span of time into three periods, the first of which roughly coincided with Schleiermacher's public life (1799–1835) and came to a close with the publication of D. F. Strauss's *Life of Jesus Critically Examined*.[75] Of the twenty-five pages that Welch dedicated to the exploration of "Schleiermacher's theological program," approximately four were reserved for discussion of Schleiermacher's conception of "the nature of religion." Although Welch did not limit his discussion to the second of the *Speeches*, he did identify that text as "undeniably the locus classicus for Schleiermacher's new definition of religion."[76] Welch summarized Schleiermacher's conception of religion by noting that "[r]eligion is, in [Schleiermacher's] famous phrases in the first edition of the *Speeches*, 'a sense and taste for the infinite,' an 'intuition and feeling of the infinite,' of the universe," noting in the same connection Schleiermacher's talk of "utter dependence" as the essence of piety in *The Christian Faith*.[77] Welch took note of the importance of the term *Gefühl* for the later Schleiermacher but resisted the notion that religion is a *kind* of feeling; rather, "'feeling' designates the place in which religion is to be sought. This is to say, in the language of romanticism, that the locus of religion is the innermost realm of human existence."[78] Schleiermacher's association of religion with "immediate self-consciousness" Welch understood as entailing that "religious awareness is irreducibly also self-awareness"—not, however, merely subjective self-awareness but rather awareness of the self's "determination by what it is not."[79]

So far forth, on Welch's description it would seem that religion according to Schleiermacher is something restricted to the realm of human interiority and a matter of purely individual consciousness. In fact this was not Welch's view, and in the final paragraph of his summary he called attention to Schleiermacher's claims that religion is unavoidably *particular* as opposed to abstract, *historical* as opposed to unchanging and atemporal, and *social* as opposed to individual (indeed, on his view Schleiermacher's high esteem for the church stood in considerable tension with his Protestantism). Welch said little, however, by way of reconciling these claims with his description of Schleiermacher's "definition" of religion: little, that is, by way of explaining how a "sense and taste for the infinite" could be *particular, historical,* and *social.* In his concluding remarks he suggested that "one may even view the discussion of the nature of religion in the second speech as an abstract formula, a description of that which is *presupposed* in the empirical actuality of religion," but the actual content of the notion of the "empirical actuality of religion" was left unstated.

In attributing to Schleiermacher the view that religion is a "sense and taste for the infinite," Welch was following a common and rarely questioned practice in Schleiermacher interpretation. Simply put, it has seemed obvious to many that the second of the *Speeches on Religion* and the corresponding paragraphs of *The Christian Faith* present Schleiermacher's earlier and later *definitions of religion.* It has thus seemed obvious to many that a sufficient answer to the question "what is religion according to Schleiermacher?" can be obtained from those texts without recourse to the remainder of his writings. Now Welch did not limit his exposition entirely to these sources: The idea that religion is particular, historical, and social is premised on material found not in the second but in the fourth and fifth of the *Speeches on Religion* and not in Schleiermacher's remarks on the "essence of piety" in *The Christian Faith* but in the extended discussion of "pious community" which frames these remarks. However, by mentioning Schleiermacher's insistence on the historical particularity of religion without resolving the tension between this claim and the idea that religion is just a "sense and taste for the infinite," Welch effectively reduced consideration of the "empirical actuality" of religion to an addendum or footnote to Schleiermacher's *definition* of religion.

Among contemporary scholars it has been Russell McCutcheon above all who has repeatedly recycled the characterization of Schleiermacher as a proponent of a purely interior religion. In the edited volume *The Insider/Outsider Problem in the Study of Religion* (1999), for example, McCutcheon ascribes to Schleiermacher the view that "religion is a highly personal feeling, an immediate consciousness, of absolute dependence on something other than oneself."[80] In keeping with the major concern of the volume, the moral McCutcheon draws from this observation has to do with the question of who is in a position to study religion. McCutcheon concludes from the fact that (according to him) "Schleiermacher firmly placed religion within the interior, private, and personal realm of experience, emotion, and feeling" that the study of religion can be executed only by the religious:

The implication for the insider/outsider problem is that religious feelings are preeminently a matter for the insider; any attempt to translate, or reduce these private feelings and emotions to such exterior causes as politics or psychoses is bound to misinterpret and misconstrue them. The essence of religion, this feeling of being absolutely dependent on God, can therefore only be understood from the inside, through a direct intuition. The outsider, the one who emphasizes the role to be played by rationality, simply misses the point if they think that one can study religion objectively from afar.[81]

The point of the thought experiment with which this section opens is that even if the standard interpretation is correct—even if religion for Schleiermacher was just "a sense and taste for the infinite" or "a feeling of absolute dependence"—it does not follow that the contemporary reconstructor must allow these statements to determine the limits of the project. The option is open for the reconstructor to allow her own understanding of the extent of religion to determine the parameters of the reconstruction and so to include what, if anything, Schleiermacher had to say about the topics of religious discourse, religious practice, and religious institutions.

Fortunately, however, there is one respect in which the analogy between our thought experiment's historical author and Schleiermacher fails. There exists within the secondary literature, far more prominently in German than in English, a substantial minority report regarding the question of what religion is for Schleiermacher. Trutz Rendtorff gave concise expression to the defining characteristic of this minority report in his discussion of *On Religion* in *Kirche und Theologie* (1966), an English translation of which appeared as *Church and Theology* in 1971: "[I]f we were to cut a cross section through Schleiermacher's theory of religion, rich as it is in motifs, we might uncover a single characteristic running through his treatment of religion: religion is described as a particular way of communication, religious communication."[82] Rendtorff's engagement with Schleiermacher took place within the framework of a broad investigation of the role played by the notion of "church" in post-Enlightenment theology, with the specific conviction that the rise of historical consciousness in the nineteenth century was intimately connected with the "revitalization and strengthening of the sense of the church as a social organism."[83] Rendtorff presented Schleiermacher as an inheritor of Semler's distinction between public and private religion: The former refers to officially sanctioned institutional teachings, and the latter to the free development of religious conviction within the individual. Schleiermacher's *Speeches* were oriented toward private religion in Semler's sense—that is, religion "defined by its possession of its own possibilities independent of the church's theology and its system."[84] However, Schleiermacher crucially included among these possibilities a capacity of religion to develop *socially* and thus *historically* along lines in accord with its own nature rather than institutional sanction. "If it is to be successful, the reconstruction of the concept of religion must provide information about the way in which religion has a life of its own open to development, and the scope to compete materially with the positive historical reality of the church, mingled as it is with other elements and subjected to critical examination. The reduction of religion to a merely abstract entity, a principle, etc. is insufficient. Rather, Schleiermacher's thesis is oriented to a religion capable of concrete life."[85]

For Rendtorff, then, the "necessary sociality" that Schleiermacher claimed for religion was not an addendum to his definition of religion but was itself a fundamental defining feature. Thus, for him the fourth of the *Speeches* was no less important for understanding Schleiermacher's conception of the nature of religion than the second. The identification of religion's essence as a "way of relating to the universe" represented only the first step of Schleiermacher's own reconstruction; the fourth speech complemented the second in that "the positive theory of the church recapitulates in its basic traits the essence of religion as a structure of reciprocal impartation."[86] Religion for Schleiermacher is everywhere and always a social affair in that the most basic religious activity is the "reciprocal impartation" of that which constitutes "inward religion," and since it was Schleiermacher's aim to propose an account of the social embodiment of religion that could constitute an alternative to the actually existing churches of his day and above all as an alternative to state-sponsored religion, he "carrie[d] the discussion into the realm of society in its nonpolitical form" and thus "produce[d] implicitly with his theory of the church a concomitant theory of society."[87]

For the minority report, a satisfactory answer to the question of what religion is according to Schleiermacher *begins* with reference to religion's "necessary sociality" and "positivity." Roughly, according to the minority report, "religion" refers not just to a form of consciousness but also to a set of *activities*—paradigmatically, communicative activities—which Schleiermacher understood to lead naturally to the formation of particular kinds of *social organizations* (churches). Rendtorff's analysis of Schleiermacher's understanding of religion as ineluctably social is symptomatic of the renewed interest in Schleiermacher's social-theoretic writings that has marked the last half century of Schleiermacher interpretation, enjoying a kind of heyday during the 1960s and at present constituting one of the main lines of work for Schleiermacher scholars.[88]

My intention in what follows is to side firmly with the minority report and to lay out the case for the claim that "religion" for Schleiermacher refers not to an abstract and ahistorical condition of human subjectivity but to historically extended and culturally embodied sets of human attitudes, activities, practices, institutions, and artifacts. One of my aims in this book, in fact, is to break the hold that the standard interpretation has over the secondary literature in

English and to do so on straightforwardly textual grounds. To that end I allow the paradigmatic interests of the minority report in questions of religion's social and historical embodiment to drive my activities as a reconstructor. Thus, I spend relatively little time discussing the terms that stand at the center of Schleiermacher's account of religion, 'intuition' and 'feeling' (*Anschauung* and *Gefühl*). For my purposes, understanding the content of these terms in fine detail is less important than understanding their role within the phenomenon of religion as Schleiermacher understood it. The most important point of all is that religion, according to him, is *not just* an intuition, a feeling, or some combination of these; religion extends beyond human subjectivity and into the interpersonal and historical realm.

It is important to note, however, that there are good reasons for scholars to continue to be interested in the topics within Schleiermacher's writings that constitute the standard interpretation. Interest in religious epistemology and specifically knowledge of God in the construction of human subjectivity and in Schleiermacher's relationship to transcendental and idealist philosophies of his day are still with us, and these continue to motivate important work by Schleiermacher scholars, which repeats many of the themes of the standard interpretation. It is certainly possible, however, to focus at length on these themes in connection with Schleiermacher's account of religion without claiming that they exhaust the content of that account, as Peter Grove has recently demonstrated in his substantial work on Schleiermacher's philosophy of religion.[89] Grove's interest in religious epistemology dictates a tight focus on Schleiermacher's various discussions of the essence of religion, on his theory of subjectivity, and on the relationship between his dogmatics and his lectures in philosophy (*Dialektik*); he brackets entirely discussion of religion as a historically and culturally diversified and socially embodied phenomenon, treating it rather as a cognitive affair that can appropriately be discussed in the singular in abstraction from all particularization while at the same time acknowledging the selective and partial character of this treatment.[90]

b Actual and Ideal Religion

Returning for a moment to the thought experiment proposed earlier, suppose that our twenty-first-century scholar faced a different problem in reconstructing a historical author's account of religion. Suppose the subject of the scholar's investigations had described as religion a phenomenon that was strictly *ideal* in the sense that it involved nothing but the most praiseworthy types of human thought, feeling, and behavior. As described by the historical author, religion has nothing to do with dogmatism, intolerance, violence, politics, willful ignorance, or any abusive or coercive use of power; rather, religion is tolerant, peace loving, apolitical, open to the advance of knowledge, and so on. However, suppose, further, that this author had addressed the subjects of ostensibly religious intolerance, politicization, and coercion, describing how these emerge and are sustained within actually existing ostensibly religious institutions and communities—while consistently maintaining that precisely because these are not ideal, they are in fact *not* part of religion.

It should be apparent that our reconstructor, inasmuch as she is not inclined to restrict her own understanding of religion to the realm of the purely ideal, faces the same problem of scope as in the previous section and that analogues of the two paths described above are available. She can choose to limit herself to her author's understanding of religion and thus produce a reconstruction that discusses only the ideal; alternatively, she can approach the subject through the lens of her own understanding of religion and incorporate within the reconstruction the ways in which the author accounted for the nonideal aspects of religion. Either way she may want to call attention to the specificity of the author's understanding of religion and its relationship to the nonideal aspects of religion as she understands it. Again, what the reconstructor should not do on pain of equivocation is limit herself to discussion of religion as an ideal phenomenon and then criticize the author for ignoring or offering no account of religion's involvement in coercion, politics, and violence.

As this second thought experiment suggests, in my view the issue of normativity—more precisely, the relationship between the ideal and the nonideal—constitutes an important theme for the project of reconstructing Schleiermacher's account of religion. It should not be controversial to claim that Schleiermacher's writings on religion present an idealized version of religion, one characterized by tolerance for internal and external diversity, a love of knowledge, and so on, nor should it be controversial to observe that his conception of "true religion" was intended to represent a point of contrast to actually existing religious belief, practice, and institutions and so to serve as a principle of criticism and a basis for religious reform. However, if it was Schleiermacher's position that "religion" and "true religion" were synonymous—if, that is, anything that falls short of ideal religion is *not religion at all*—then there is a considerable distance between his usage of the term and that which is likely to seem natural to a contemporary scholar of religion. Moreover, if this is the case, then the point of the second thought experiment is that the contemporary scholar has the option of construing the task of reconstruction so that it extends to what, if anything, Schleiermacher had to say by way of explaining why actually existing religious traditions, communities, and institutions have the less than savory characteristics they do.

This might seem a trivial point, but failure to note a distinction between Schleiermacher's various discussions of the characteristics of true religion and his account of the actual condition of religions has significant consequences. The most common way to fail to observe this distinction is to simply mistake Schleiermacher's account of true religion for an account of religion as it actually exists. This conflation leads to the attribution to Schleiermacher of a remarkably strong doctrine of religious autonomy, according to which religion is immune not only to the corrupting effect of politics but also to the conditioning effects of culture and even of language itself. So understood, Schleiermacher can be interpreted as claiming that the historical life of religions owes nothing to historical contingency of any kind—that religion *in the actual course of events* maintains a stringent purity from nonreligious factors.[91] This view of Schleiermacher's understanding of religion as absurdly ahistorical makes him out to have been massively uncritical of actually existing religion. Indeed, if this was his position, it would be difficult to understand how he could ever have been taken to be either a religious reformer or one whose influence diverted the scholarly investigation of religion down broadly historical channels.

The textual case for interpreting Schleiermacher as one who held "religion" and "true religion" to be synonymous is, however, stronger than is the case for characterizing him as a proponent of a purely inward religion. In certain passages in the *Speeches* Schleiermacher labeled as "not religion" phenomena that fail to display the characteristics of his ideal religion— for example, his claim that the practice of keeping a "wondrous chronicle of the descent of the gods" represents "empty mythology" rather than religion, as well as his ascription to the members of the "common church" "not religion but merely a little taste for it."[92] My view is that the restriction of religion to the realm of the ideal in the *Speeches* is a rhetorical artifact that was effectively supplanted later by talk of "diseased conditions" of religion, a notion that appears in the *Speeches* but was elevated to the status of a technical notion in the *Brief Outline*. Thus, only a highly selective exposure to his corpus can sustain the view that "religion" denoted for Schleiermacher an ideal phenomenon unsullied by history. However, even if this were not the case, the point of the second thought experiment would stand: A reconstructor facing the description of chronicles of the descent of the gods as "not religion" is not constrained to allow such a passage to mark the boundary of her reconstruction.

In the chapters that follow I keep the distinction between the ideal and the actual firmly in view, and my efforts are oriented toward a reconstruction of Schleiermacher's account of *actual religion*—his account of how and why actually existing forms of piety, doctrinal traditions, religious communities, and institutions have come to have the characteristics that they do. As in the case of inward religion, I argue that Schleiermacher's account of true religion constitutes one area of his broader discussion of religion in toto and that interpretations that limit themselves to his ideal religion miss an entire sector of his writings. I also argue, however, that "ideal religion" was not only a normative notion for Schleiermacher. Clearly, ideal religion is meant to contrast with the actual condition of religion and thus serve as an indication of how religion *could* and *should be*. Nonetheless, it will become apparent that discussion of ideal religion also played an explanatory role for Schleiermacher, in no small part because of the developmental character of his overall account. Because actually existing religion represents the outcome of a developmental process that has deviated in ways large and small from what would yield ideal religion, understanding how religion *could have* and *should have developed* constitutes part of the project of understanding how religion *has in fact* developed.

c Explanation and Understanding

Consider a remark by Hans Penner, which appeared in 2000 under the heading of "Interpretation" in Braun and McCutcheon's *Guide to the Study of Religion*:

> Schleiermacher is important to the topic of interpretation for three reasons. First, he established the beginnings of a new "science," the "science of understanding." Second, this science is obviously different from the search in the natural sciences for explanations by causal laws. Third, his emphasis on religion as a feeling of absolute dependence, an experience different from physical or moral feelings, marks the beginning of a general study of religion that is not reducible to ethics, aesthetics or natural law.[93]

Penner attributes to Schleiermacher seminal influence in the development of the "hermeneutical tradition," whose significance for the contemporary study of religion can be summarized under three points: First, the task of the scholar is to grasp the "lived experience" of his subjects; second, this experience is "thoroughly and radically historical"; and third, "interpretive theory since Dilthey views the history of science with suspicion" and thus prefers to deal in "pluralism, dialogue and discourse" rather than "analysis, comparison, universal rules and unity."[94] According to Penner, Schleiermacher's definition of "religion as a feeling of absolute dependence" requires an approach to religion that is different from the search for explanation by causal laws. Penner's remarks echo those of Preus, for example, who noted that the "so-called hermeneutical tradition," "associated with the names of Schleiermacher and Dilthey, has typically been seen as an alternative to explanation, explanation being rejected as a procedure inappropriate to, or unworthy of, religion."[95] For both Preus and Penner, the trajectory imparted to the study of religion by Schleiermacher's work leads away from the project of explaining religion through the identification of the causes that account for its origins and persistence. This understanding is reflected as well in the writings of McCutcheon, who in *The Insider/Outsider Problem* defended his preferred methodology in the following terms: "Contrary to the tradition represented by Schleiermacher, which presumed that humans are fundamentally different from other parts of the natural world, this [naturalist] tradition models itself after the natural sciences in attempting to generate universal theories of human behavior from the analysis of specific cases."[96]

The historical basis for this view lies in Dilthey's appropriation of Schleiermacher's work on hermeneutics for his own account of the nature and method of the human sciences. For Dilthey the difference between the subject matter of the *Naturwissenschaften* and the *Geisteswissenschaften* required a corresponding difference in method. The natural sciences in his understanding were dedicated to the study of "facts that enter consciousness from without" and the human sciences to "facts which enter consciousness in an originary way from within"; the understanding of the former required "inferences that add to the given by way of a combination of hypotheses," whereas for the latter "the coherence of mental life, as something already given, is everywhere their basis." Thus, in Dilthey's classic phrase, "we explain nature, but we understand mental life."[97] Dilthey regarded Schleiermacher's description of the process of textual interpretation as a crucial component of the procedure whereby this understanding could be attained; he credited Schleiermacher's lectures on hermeneutics as "the origin of a general discipline and methodology of interpretation," which in historical retrospect constituted "a vital link between philosophy and the historical disciplines, an essential part of the foundation of the *Geisteswissenschaften*."[98]

The historical importance of Schleiermacher's work on hermeneutics for Dilthey and, through him, the 'hermeneutical tradition' is clear. But the brief mentions of the subject by Preus and Penner elide the fact that Dilthey's insistence on the centrality of hermeneutics for the *Geisteswissenschaften* took place by way of a drastic expansion of the range of that science in relation to Schleiermacher's understanding.[99] The question of how *Schleiermacher* understood the methodology proper to the investigation of those phenomena constituted by human activity does not arise in their remarks, and thus neither does the possibility that *Schleiermacher* might have had a view of how religion, for example, is to be investigated that differs from that of more recent devotees of the hermeneutical paradigm.

This subject is one on which the renewed interest in Schleiermacher—and in particular, the prominence of Schleiermacher's lectures on ethics—has made a significant impact. Gunter Scholtz's *Ethik und Hermeneutik: Schleiermachers Grundlegung der Geisteswissenschaften* (1995) is a prominent attempt to recover Schleiermacher's distinctive understanding of the study of humanity from beneath the weight of the hermeneutical tradition.[100] For Scholtz the common practice of restricting attention in contemporary discussions of the *Geisteswissenschaften* to Schleiermacher's hermeneutics is an "almost grotesque distortion" of the historical record, as it ignores his own discussions of the varieties of scientific investigation.[101] Scholtz's concern was not with theory of religion but the hermeneutical tradition in philosophy more generally; for him, "It is one-sided and askew when today a 'line' of 'hermeneuticians' ['*Hermeneutiker*'] Schleiermacher-Dilthey-Heidegger-Gadamer is constructed and it is then claimed that in this theoretical sequence the problem of understanding was increasingly acknowledged as universal, and made more profound."[102] Lost in this construction of a hermeneutical tradition as the culmination of the historical trajectory of the *Geisteswissenschaften* is Schleiermacher's own understanding of what was involved in the *wissenschaftlich* investigation of humanity.[103]

Schleiermacher's distinction between *Physik* as the "science of outward nature" and *Ethik* as the "science of spirit" indeed prefigures Dilthey's *Naturwissenschaften-Geisteswissenschaften* distinction. However, Schleiermacher did not conjoin to this distinction in subject matter a corresponding distinction in methodology. Rather, his discussion of the forms of inquiry proper to the various sciences maintained a strict parallelism across this central division. Schleiermacher distinguished between "empirical" and "speculative" subdisciplines within both *Physik* and *Ethik*. The empirical subdiscipline of *Physik* is *Naturkunde*, dedicated to gathering information about the material world; its counterpart within *Ethik* is *Geschichtskunde*, dedicated to the same task in relation to human activity.[104] In addition, where "speculative physics" is dedicated to identifying the laws operative within physical being and testing these against the deliverances of *Naturkunde*, "speculative ethics" has a precisely parallel task in relation to the study of history. Thus, in general *Ethik* is, in Schleiermacher's well-known description, the "science of the principles of history," dedicated to the discovery of the laws that account for those "activities of reason" that constitute human history, above all those activities in which reason's "imprint" upon nature is made manifest in the formation of human culture in all of its varieties.[105] Furthermore, as in other areas of his thought, Schleiermacher took the relationship between the speculative and empirical branches of each wing of *Wissenschaft* to be one of mutual enrichment: According to Scholtz, "*Ethik* as a general theory of culture is already based upon experience, and scientific 'facts' become such only with the assistance of theories."[106] Hermeneutics figures for Schleiermacher as a subdiscipline of *Ethik*, a "technical science" oriented toward a specific area of human activity; neither *Ethik* considered as a whole nor its other subdisciplines, including those concerned with religion (*Religionsphilosophie* and the various branches of theological study), are characterized by an interpretive methodology.

The point of calling attention to the restricted role for Schleiermacher of interpretation as a methodology within the human sciences is to make it clear that his own approach to the topic of religion cannot without further ado be assimilated to that of later hermeneutical theorists. Far from anathematizing the project of explaining religion, Schleiermacher in his various discussions offered claims as to the *human capacities* operative in religion, the *events within history* that mark the beginnings of particular religious traditions, the *developmental tendencies* that can be observed in the history of religions, and the impact of extrareligious factors that contribute to the flowering or decay of particular religions. Schleiermacher's treatment of religion (with the notable exception of claims that he advanced in his capacity as a Christian theologian, a topic pursued below in chapter 4) in fact fits neatly into the causal-explanatory paradigm whose historical development Preus pursued in *Explaining Religion*.[107]

The historical irony of Schleiermacher's assimilation to a hermeneutical tradition hostile to the project of explaining religion lies in the fact that particularly during the 1820s Schleiermacher attracted a considerable amount of ire for his stance on the propriety of *wissenschaftlich* investigations of religion. Some of the most noteworthy aspects of his work on the second edition of *The Christian Faith* constituted a sharp response to the rise to prominence of "awakened" pietism, a deeply conservative, culturally aggressive, and politically connected movement for the leaders of which *Wissenschaft* represented little more than a "surrogate for religion."[108] Not only Schleiermacher's call for an "eternal covenant" between religious faith and science but also his defense on the right of "the leaders of science" to mount whatever investigations of "both piety itself and the community pertaining to it" they saw fit stood in sharp and intentional contrast to the positions expressed by this movement. Schleiermacher's scathing remarks in his *Sendschreiben* to Lücke about "those gloomy creatures who regard as satanic all research beyond the confines of ancient literalism" and the "complete starvation from all science" that their growing influence threatened to bring about endeared him to neither those of his contemporaries who were interested in "protecting" religion from scientific investigation nor their patrons within the Prussian state and aristocracy, although for later generations of liberal scholars these remarks constituted a prescient foreshadowing of the cultural and political dominance this movement attained as the nineteenth century wore on.

This is not to say, however, that all responses to Schleiermacher's stance on the importance and propriety of the *wissenschaftlich* investigation of religion were negative. In an extensive review of the first edition of *The Christian Faith*, which appeared in 1824, Friedrich Wähner declared Schleiermacher "completely correct" in arguing that the essence of Christian piety could be determined only from a standpoint "above" Christianity, "and indeed it cannot be said how it could be otherwise. For if we take our standpoint within Christianity in order to compare it with other kinds of faith, we inevitably presuppose that which according to our declared intention we are trying to find, and we soon entangle ourselves unfailingly in a petitio principii."[109] Wähner in fact celebrated Schleiermacher's "attempted equalization between the claims of ecclesiastical certitude and the demands of the scientific drive" as a welcome counter to the present day's "growing attacks of obscurantism and apoplectic incursions of bigotry, the epidemic evils of the impotence of reason (*Verstandesimpotenz*)."[110] Schleiermacher's work heralded for Wähner the birth of a new "scientific treatment of the various forms of faith": "What has to this point not come to pass may perhaps yet succeed in the future, for in our time learned, farsighted men have raised the study of external nature to the rank of a science through a rounded systematic approach; why could not the same claim be advanced, by means of an analogous procedure, for the multifarious organizations of piety?"[111]

6 Overview

My first chapter is concerned not directly with religion but with a preliminary issue of considerable importance. Schleiermacher's youthful essay "On Human Freedom" demonstrates that early on he was an enthusiastic proponent of a comprehensive doctrine of causal determinism. In this early essay Schleiermacher sought to develop a compatibilist understanding of human freedom, one that would show that ordinary moral practices such as holding each other accountable for our actions, feeling remorse for past action, and resolving to act morally in the future make sense within the context of an understanding of all of human activity, including such inward events as moral deliberations, as the causally necessary result of previous events. The essay cannot be described as an unqualified success, but both the notion of freedom as a matter of inward determination and the tensions that Schleiermacher explored between the thought that one's actions are predetermined and the feeling of moral agency reappear in his later writings. He would eventually describe the relationship between freedom and necessity as a "relative antithesis" in the lectures on *Dialektik*, the point being that from a vantage point "above" this distinction it is possible to say that "everything in the realm of being is just as free as it is necessary."[112] I then offer some remarks on the difference determinism makes for understanding Schleiermacher's later texts, focusing in particular on the *Speeches on Religion*; I also defend the claim that Schleiermacher retained his commitment to determinism after the early 1790s from the challenge presented by Jacqueline Mariña's recent exposition of the *Monologen* of 1800. Finally, I turn to Schleiermacher's 1824 Academy address on the difference between ethical and natural law (*Sittengesetz* and *Naturgesetz*). There I argue that Schleiermacher clearly envisioned that the study of the "activity of reason," the science within which the study of religion is to be located, would yield the discovery of a body of ethical law that governs human activity in the same way as natural law governs the activity of inorganic bodies. Overall, Schleiermacher's determinism constitutes an important parameter for the account of religion that the following chapters present: for over and above specific claims about that phenomenon, Schleiermacher, as I understand him, was committed to the position that everything that occurs within time, and thus every constituent part of the collection of human activities commonly known as religion, is the result of the operation of causes within the natural order, which are potentially knowable.

In chapter 2 I take direct issue with the standard interpretation of Schleiermacher's account of religion. Beginning with an examination of the *Speeches*, I argue that an answer to the question "what is religion?" is not in hand until it the structural significance of the term *essence* is understood. I argue that a statement of religion's essence does not define religion but does provide the crucial element in the "formula" by which religion is defined: Properly understood, religion is defined as a set of phenomena that stand in an *appropriate relationship* to religion's essence. The idea of an "appropriate relationship" is intentionally vague, as I use the term to summarize claims by Schleiermacher about the connection of a variety of religious phenomena to religion's essence. However, the dominant component of this idea seems to me to be that of development: Phenomena such as acts of discourse, social organizations, and artifacts are part of religion if they arise as developments out of religion's essence. In accordance with Schleiermacher's discussion of the term in *The Christian Faith* I ascribe to religion a concentric structure, with both inward and outward religion counting as developments out of this essence. I also locate the term *piety*, which plays a central role in both later editions of the *Speeches* and in *The Christian Faith*, in relation to this structure, resisting the common perception that the terms *piety* and *religion* are interchangeable. In this chapter I also discuss the difference between ideal and actual religion: With respect to both inward and outward religion Schleiermacher distinguishes between the forms religion would assume if left to develop according to its own principles from the forms it tends to assume when exposed to the contingencies and contaminations of history. Finally, I call attention to one theoretically significant ramification of Schleiermacher's manner of defining religion. Since religion is defined by relation to a central essence rather than by a boundary, it does not come to an abrupt end at a certain developmental distance from its essence but "trails off" as this distance increases. Religion does not cease when one passes, say, from feelings into beliefs or from inner spiritual states to outward activities and circumstances; rather, a wide range of conditions and activities can be or become part of religion by being or coming to be related to religion's essence in the appropriate manner.

In chapter 3 I take up Schleiermacher's discussion of religion's "necessary sociality." Part of the reasons this aspect of his work has for the most part eluded scholars who have had access only to the *Speeches on Religion* and *The Christian Faith* is that although the theme of religion's social dimension figured prominently in these texts, it was in Schleiermacher's ethical writings that human sociability was discussed at greatest length. Following a brief overview of the corpus of these writings, the earliest of which predate the *Speeches*, I offer a reading of the fourth of the *Speeches* which unpacks the argument of the speech in terms of the structure of religion described in chapter 2. I consider the fourth speech to be at least the equal of the second with respect to overall importance for understanding Schleiermacher's account of religion, for it is the fourth speech that describes how religion's essence catalyzes the formation of religious community and the various ways in which the propensities of human nature and the forces of history influence the careers of such communities.

I then turn to Schleiermacher's ethics lectures, which contain the substance of his mature reflections on religion as a matter of social formation. The core of the discussion of religion in these lectures is Schleiermacher's description of how religious activity (specifically, religious communication) results in the formation of "common feeling" among the members of particular communities. This idea is significant for two reasons. The first is that by the early 1800s "feeling" (*Gefühl*) had come to represent for Schleiermacher the most inward, most personal, and most particular aspect of human existence— literally, feeling is "nontransferable" (*unübertragbar*)—and yet in religious activities feelings become the object of a common discourse that results in the "inward formation" of religious individuals at the level of *Gefühl* in accordance with the character of the overall community. The second is that in this regard religion represents one example of what Schleiermacher describes as "the ethical process," whereby social groups and the individuals who constitute them come to be formed; thus, the manner in which religion takes shape and develops historically is described by the same laws that also describe other exemplifications of human sociability. I also discuss Schleiermacher's understanding of material religion (i.e., ritual practice and the production of religious artifacts) and his treatment of the historical conditions that bear on the formation of religion. Schleiermacher understood the history of religions to be rooted in the characters, geographical conditions, languages, and "folk traditions" of the populations within which particular religions develop; he also sketched a typology of historical-social forms of religion, beginning with family religion and progressing through a tribal or patriarchal stage and a civic or political phase in which religion and the state are intertwined. In historical perspective, the formation of institutions dedicated solely to religion and distinct from the organs of the state was for Schleiermacher not the natural but the *ideal* social condition of religion, one whose realization represents the culmination of religion's historical-social development.

Chapter 4 focuses on Schleiermacher's dogmatics, *The Christian Faith*. Along with much of the interpretive tradition, I take this text to represent Schleiermacher's mature attempt to showcase the compatibility of the confessional and the scientific impulses. I frame my discussion in terms of the "eternal covenant" between religious faith and scientific inquiry which Schleiermacher proposed on the occasion of the republication of *The Christian Faith*. I argue that one prominent interpretation of this eternal covenant, according to which it amounts to the proposal that theology and science withdraw into distinct spheres of influence and that each respects the other's claim to its particular territory, is mistaken. Properly understood, Schleiermacher's ambition was to propose an arrangement for the constructive appropriation of the deliverances of the unimpeded scientific investigation of religion by theology and to promote a willingness on the part of adherents of Christianity to understand themselves and their religion as fully integrated into the natural order.

The account of Christianity presented in *The Christian Faith* was intended to model the kind of religious self-understanding this covenant would require. I argue that this account incorporates an initial naturalistic understanding of Christianity—one that does not presuppose the existence of anything outside the natural order—within a broader set of theological claims about God and the world. I claim that the successful mediation between religion and science in this case would require that the initial presentation of Christianity constitute a viable common ground for both the scientifically and the religiously minded and that Schleiermacher's broader theological "overlay" on this presentation not contain claims likely to be disproved by the advance of scientific knowledge. Like many interpreters, I do not believe that this attempt at mediation was entirely successful and I call attention to what seem to me to be the points of greatest tension between Christian doctrines as rendered by Schleiermacher and the deliverances and demands of the sciences. But it is more important for my purposes to describe the project and make clear the respects in which it informs the argument of *The Christian Faith*, and the points where the success of the project is most questionable highlight the lengths to which Schleiermacher was willing to go in the cause of mediation.

Finally, in chapter 5 I present a summary statement of Schleiermacher's understanding of religion and its place within the natural order. I begin with a series of answers, in descending order of length, to the question "what is religion according to Schleiermacher?" I then discuss three themes that have emerged from the previous chapter and constitute loci of interest for contemporary theorists of religion: the question of the historical or temporal origins of religion, religion's relationship to the political, and the question of how religion as Schleiermacher understood it might figure as an object of *wissenschaftlich* investigation. I conclude with remarks on Schleiermacher's significance within the history of the academic study of religion and on the possibility of regarding his writings on religion as a historical resource for contemporary nontheological scholars of religion's understanding of their vocation.

I

Schleiermacher's Determinism

Although the principle of determinism is firmly established in the physical and natural sciences, its introduction to the social sciences began only a century ago, and its authority there is still contested. The idea that societies are subject to necessary laws and constitute a realm of nature has deeply penetrated only a few minds.... As regards social things, we still have the mind set of primitives.

—Emile Durkheim, *The Elementary Forms of Religious Life*

If I again observe the eternal wheels of humanity in their progress, then this vast interaction, where nothing movable is moved by itself alone and nothing moving moves only itself, must put me at considerable ease about your complaint that reason and soul, sensuality and ethical life, understanding and blind force appear in such separated proportions. Why do you see everything individually, which surely does not function individually and for itself? The reason of one person and the soul of another affect one another as deeply as could only happen in a single subject.

—Schleiermacher, *On Religion*

1.1 Introduction

Sixteen years after Schleiermacher's death, his former student August Neander inaugurated the journal *Deutsche Zeitschrift für christliche Wissenschaft und christliches Leben* with an essay surveying the past half century's developments in Christian theology. Much of the essay is given over to praising the importance of "the blessed Schleiermacher," whom Neander credited with initiating "a new creative epoch in German theology" by describing and advocating a relationship between religious faith and scientific inquiry intended to provide for the full development of both.[1] On one point, however, Neander decisively parted company with his mentor. He could not agree that a "feeling of absolute dependence" provided the "fundamental tone" of the entire religious life; but more important,

> something that we must characterize as a fundamental error of the
> great man hangs together with the one-sided elevation of this
> moment, something that belongs particularly to that which needed to
> be expelled through the subsequent development of the Christian-
> theistic principle in theology: whenever Schleiermacher's principles
> lead to determinism, whenever he denied creaturely freedom as an
> independent factor in a real sense and posited evil (*das Böse*) as
> something necessary in the process of human development. Here,
> however, we must sharply distinguish the system and the man from
> each other.[2]

Its consonance with Reformed orthodoxy notwithstanding, Neander found Schleiermacher's embrace of the doctrine of determinism—the doctrine that all events take place of necessity—to be the mark of a failure of internal consistency and a reflection of the intellectual atmosphere within which Schleiermacher moved. As Neander saw the issue, not only did the postulate of determinism conflict with the "ethical consciousness" so prominently displayed by Schleiermacher; it also represented an involuntary mixing of philosophy and religion, the sharp separation of which Schleiermacher had made a hallmark of his work. Only as a result of such an oversight, argued Neander, was Schleiermacher's theological work "able to attach itself to that which we must characterize as the diseased and false in the dominant consciousness of the time."[3]

When in *The Christian Faith* Schleiermacher declared his agreement with the view that "everything is completely determined and grounded in the totality of the nature-system (*Naturzusammenhang*)" and also that the "strictest dogmaticians" had historically considered a robust doctrine of divine preservation as equivalent to the view of "natural causation as the complete determination of everything that occurs by the general *Naturzusammenhang*,"[4] he was doing more than simply aligning himself with a historical orthodoxy. Schleiermacher's embrace of determinism in his dogmatics represents the culmination of his lifelong engagement with the question of the relationship between human existence and the natural order, and in this mature work he once again gave articulation to a conviction that he had first expressed in his mid-twenties: that the best way to understand oneself qua human being, qua ethically responsible agent, and qua resident of a world governed by a provident God is to understand oneself as a being whose every thought, feeling, and action are the necessary product of the operation of chains of natural causes stretching back to the beginning of time.

The topic of determinism in Schleiermacher's writings deserves treatment at the beginning of this essay for two reasons. First, there is quite possibly no other philosophical issue that has a greater potential to affect one's understanding of Schleiermacher's writings on religion than that of determinism. What hangs on the issue is nothing less than the question of whether human activity, and a fortiori human cultural activity, and a fortiori religion stand in a connection to the natural order that is potentially accessible to the sciences dedicated to understanding that order or whether, on the contrary, the *ratio* of human activities such as religion is ultimately cloaked by an ability of human beings to make choices irrespective of prior conditions. Seeing Schleiermacher as committed to the "doctrine of necessity" makes it impossible to assent to the common view that he considered religion to be autonomous in some strong sense from other areas of human life such as the cultural, the political, or the historical in general. Making a case for Schleiermacher's determinism is thus important for my extended argument to the effect that his account of religion fits within the causal-explanatory paradigm to which the tradition of religious naturalism is commonly understood to be devoted. Indeed, as the citations with which this chapter opens suggest, seeing Schleiermacher as a determinist brings him into the company of Durkheim with respect to the question of the relationship between human activity—and in particular the dynamics of culture and society—and the pursuit of knowledge concerning the order of nature.

The second reason determinism is important is that the topic has been an elusive one in the secondary literature on Schleiermacher. This is largely, it seems to me, in virtue of the fact that few of Schleiermacher's theological readers have been familiar with the history of philosophical discussions on the nature of free will and of his relationship to these discussions, and so generally assume that his frequent and fulsome invocation of freedom as a quality of human actions entails that he could not have been an adherent of determinism.[5] However, this assumption is unwarranted on both conceptual and textual grounds. As will become clear below, the notion of *compatibilist freedom*—an understanding of freedom according to which it is compatible with causal determinism—is well represented within the philosophical literature, including the literature with which Schleiermacher was familiar.[6] Moreover, since the appearance of Dilthey's *Leben Schleiermachers* in 1870 it has been clear that as a young man Schleiermacher was a proponent of compatibilism. The first text to be examined in this chapter, the unfinished 1790–1792 essay, "On Human Freedom" (which first appeared in print, in abridged form, as an appendix to

Dilthey's biography), demonstrates his enthusiasm for the view that human beings are both free and determined at the same time.[7] So it cannot be assumed from the outset that Schleiermacher's writings reflect an incompatibilist understanding of human freedom, that is, the view that human choices are free only to the extent that they are not rendered necessary by prior conditions.

Reference to Schleiermacher's youthful writings, however, does not establish that his commitment to causal determinism was a lifelong affair. While clear expressions of determinism and compatibilism are found in texts from his mature period (the lectures on *Dialektik* and *The Christian Faith*), the same cannot be said for his earliest published writings, the *Speeches on Religion* and its companion piece, the *Monologen* ("Soliloquies") of 1800. While those who know where to look within the *Speeches* can, without too much trouble, see deterministic convictions at work within that text,[8] the character of Schleiermacher's writing during his Romantic period makes it possible to discount the deterministic tenor of crucial passages (such as the passage from the *Speeches* cited at the opening of this chapter) as high-flown rhetoric not intended as the expression of philosophical convictions. Furthermore, it is considerably more difficult to read the *Monologen* as a text informed by determinism (although, as we will see, a number of interpreters have done so), for in that text Schleiermacher elevates freedom to the status of "the first and inmost in all things" and also develops a contrast between freedom and necessity redolent of Fichte's absolute idealism. The claim of a lifelong commitment to determinism and a compatibilist understanding of human freedom on Schleiermacher's part thus requires defending.

There is also a sense in which the question of determinism in Schleiermacher's works is of recent vintage. Neander's remarks are representative of a broad strain of nineteenth-century literature that took Schleiermacher's attachment to the doctrine of necessity to be clear on the basis of his writings; indeed, Friedrich Wilhelm Esselborn described determinism as "the most important key to a complete understanding of [Schleiermacher's] much branching system" in his 1897 study, *Die philosophische Voraussetzungen von Schleiermachers Determinismus.*[9] However, the issue largely disappeared from the secondary literature for much of the twentieth century and resurfaced in the early 1980s with the first appearance of the complete text of "On Human Freedom" in the KGA.[10] Readers of English have had access to the contents of the essay since the publication of Albert Blackwell's translation in 1992.[11] Only during the last academic generation, then, has the text that sheds the most light on Schleiermacher's understanding of freedom been widely accessible.

In this chapter I argue that Schleiermacher's commitment to determinism was in fact lifelong and ground my argument in those texts in which this commitment was most clearly expressed. I begin with an examination of "On Human Freedom," in which Schleiermacher sought, with mixed results, to develop a compatibilist alternative to Kant's doctrine of noumenal or transcendental freedom. I call attention not only to the positions with which Schleiermacher aligned himself but also to tensions within his thinking about the relationship between freedom and necessity at this point (as well as to the outright failure, philosophically speaking, of his concluding compatibilist proposal). These tensions achieved formalization in the lectures on *Dialektik*; there freedom and necessity are discussed as forming a "relative antithesis," a phrase that represents a repeating trope within Schleiermacher's mature philosophy. This formulation allows talk of the respects in which freedom and necessity stand in opposition to each other to take place against a background that assumes their identity; it thus allows Schleiermacher to incorporate incompatibilist intuitions and pronouncements regarding freedom as valid within their own sphere but as ultimately trumped by the doctrine that freedom and necessity are "both the same, but viewed from different sides." Taken together, the early essay and the later lectures provide strong evidence for Schleiermacher's ongoing commitment to determinism and a compatibilist understanding of freedom.

In the second half of the chapter I turn from an exposition of the character of Schleiermacher's determinism and compatibilism to the question of how this commitment informs his writings on other topics. I first call attention to the presence of determinism in the *Speeches on Religion*, arguing that in that text Schleiermacher presented the view of the universe as an interconnected whole as the "religious view," and one that contrasted with the narrowly "moral view" of his expected audience; I also explore an issue regarding the origin of particular "positive religions" that is crucial for assessing Schleiermacher's relationship to the causal-explanatory paradigm mentioned in my introduction. The argument of this chapter also requires addressing a recent argument by Jacqueline Mariña that the *Monologen* demonstrate Schleiermacher's embrace of an incompatibilist understanding of freedom by 1800. I take issue with Mariña's argument and offer the outline of a compatibilist reading of the *Monologen* that displays significant continuities with both "On Human Freedom" and the *Dialektik*, and that (in my view) considerably illuminates the basic intentions of the *Monologen*. Finally, I briefly examine the presence of determinism in Schleiermacher's writings on ethics and draw particular attention to the 1825 Academy address "*Über den Unterschied zwischen Naturgesetz und Sittengesetz*" (On the Difference between Natural Law and Ethical Law). What emerges from this examination is a clear demonstration that Schleiermacher understood the goal of the science of ethics, which examines the "activity of reason within history" and in particular those aspects of human behavior that as a whole constitute the course of history, to be the identification of laws that allow for the explanation of human behavior in a sense analogous to the explanations of the behavior of natural objects produced by the science of physics. All together, the material presented in this chapter establishes one important parameter for the reconstruction of Schleiermacher's account of religion to be prosecuted in the following chapters.

1.2 "On Human Freedom"

1.2.1 Background

"On Human Freedom" was composed during the years immediately following Schleiermacher's first set of theological examinations, as part of a series of "philosophical explorations" that occupied his attention during his time as a tutor in the Donha household.[12] Schleiermacher's interest in the relationship of determinism and freedom at this time is not surprising, as this topic had been a prominent locus of philosophical discussion since the early modern period. The Enlightenment view of the natural order as governed by efficient causality, universally understood as a *necessitating* causality, prompted the transposition of scholastic debates about the relationship between human freedom and divine providence into the temporal realm. Enlightenment philosophers concerned with human freedom faced a choice among three primary options: reject determinism in order to defend incompatibilist freedom; accept both determinism and an incompatibilist understanding of freedom, and conclude that human actions are not free; or accept determinism and defend a compatibilist account of freedom.[13] By the end of the seventeenth century a kind of demarcation had become visible in discussions of the topic. The major non-Catholic philosophers of the period—Hobbes, Spinoza, Locke, and Leibniz—chose the third option, offering compatibilist accounts of human freedom (and compatibilism can also be attributed, albeit not as clearly, to Descartes and Malebranche). In contrast, incompatibilist freedom was defended by many Roman Catholic philosophers and within a fairly broad swath of Protestant theology (the positions of Luther and Calvin on the issue notwithstanding), which in part reflected the historical influence of Molinism and Arminianism, respectively.[14] During the first half of the eighteenth century compatibilism was defended as well by Hume and by Christian Wolff, and the dispute between philosophically motivated compatibilism and theologically motivated incompatibilism had been a prominent ingredient in the events at Halle that established the university's reputation as a hotbed of both pietism and atheism. In 1722 Wolff was attacked for the "fatalism and mechanism" of his views by his theological colleagues, which eventually led to his expulsion from Halle and banishment from all Prussian territories by royal decree and under pain of death. The revocation of this decree by Frederick II in 1740 set the stage for Wolff's triumphal return to Halle and the establishment of the Leibniz-Wolffian orthodoxy that formed the background to the philosophical work of both Kant and Schleiermacher.[15]

Two independent events within the Prussian world of letters during the 1780s spurred a revival of interest in the topic of human freedom after a relatively quiet period. The first of these was the appearance of Kant's *Critique of Pure Reason* in 1781, which promised to reconcile a deterministic view of the natural order with an *incompatibilist* doctrine of human freedom. The second was the *Pantheismusstreit* that erupted subsequent to Jacobi's revelation of the recently deceased Gotthold Lessing's inclinations towards the philosophy of Spinoza, which at the time was widely regarded as equivalent to atheism. These episodes presented two independent and conflicting accounts of freedom for consideration: Kant's doctrine of noumenal freedom and Spinoza's resolute compatibilism. Both of these doctrines were possessed of a particular kind of philosophical electricity, Kant's because of its novelty and obscurity and Spinoza's because of its ostensible theological unsoundness. Against the background of a fading Wolffian orthodoxy, these two doctrines opened up a range of possibilities regarding how freedom was to be understood.

In retrospect, it comes naturally to us to regard Kant's proposal as a philosophical juggernaut during this period. In fact, however, the "specialized debate concerning human freedom" that unfolded in the German popular philosophical press in the late 1780s and early 1790s, documented in a recent study by George di Giovanni, was not simply a series of responses to Kant but rather took place roughly within the territory delimited by the proposals of Leibniz, Spinoza, and Kant.[16] In this literature Kant's noumenal freedom was widely suspected of either incoherence, irrelevance, or both: incoherence because the relationship between the undetermined noumenal self and the determined phenomenal self was (and remains) notoriously difficult to understand on the basis of Kant's writings, and irrelevant because absent a satisfactory resolution of this difficulty, it is not clear that incompatibilist freedom can be predicated of *temporal* human activity on Kant's account.[17] Kant's stature notwithstanding, both compatibilism or the outright denial of human freedom were prominently represented in the German popular literature during Schleiermacher's student days. Adam Weishaupt's *Über Materialismus und Idealismus* of 1786 denied freedom and recommended accommodation to fatalism; Herder defended a Spinozistic compatibilism in his *Gott* of 1787; Johann Ulrich's *Eleutheriologie oder über Freiheit und Nothwendigkeit* (1788) argued for Leibnizian compatibilism, and in 1789 Jacobi issued a second edition of his infamous book on Spinoza, supplemented with a discussion that in effect argued that only by means of the *salto mortale* can one believe in incompatibilist freedom.[18] Even some followers of Kant found the postulate of noumenal freedom unsatisfactory: In 1790 Carl Christian Ernst Schmid, while following Kant's distinction between an empirical and an intelligible self, argued that the noumenal self's activities could not be "arbitrary" (i.e., undetermined). Rather, the one who accepts the principle of sufficient reason must see "*necessity everywhere. If we do not want to make room for anything with no reason, then there is nothing left but necessity, for between the two there is absolutely no middle way*" (italics in the original).[19]

Schleiermacher's first exploration of the theme of human freedom thus stood in continuity with both the canonical philosophical tradition and the popular philosophy of the day, and the fact that he opted for compatibilism is not a mark of originality.[20] Indeed, the passage of "On Human Freedom" in which he avowed a willingness for the author of his essay to be classified as a determinist, "provided only that he is promised that no proposition of any other determinist will be attributed to him that is not clearly contained in what he himself has said or will say,"[21] represents a tacit acknowledgment of how crowded the field of discussion was. The ultimate fate of the essay, to lie unfinished among Schleiermacher's *Nachlass*, may also be a product of the popularity of compatibilism at the time. In 1793 Leonhard Creuzer published his *Skeptische Betrachtungen über die Freyheit des Willens*, which, in addition to embracing determinism under protest, executed the same sort of historical survey of the notion of human freedom that Schleiermacher had undertaken.[22] We know from Schleiermacher's correspondence with F. H. C. Schwarz in 1800–1801 (after the *Speeches on Religion* and the *Monologen* had caught the attention of a circle of friends, including Creuzer and Schwarz, prompting the latter to seek Schleiermacher's acquaintance and literary collaboration) that Schleiermacher read Creuzer's book shortly after its appearance,[23] and the similarity between their respective treatments are such that Günter Meckenstock speculates that the appearance of *Skeptische Betrachtungen* may have prompted Schleiermacher to abandon his essay in that "he found the field of his investigations already worked over by another author, such that he must have seen his own efforts already brought to a conclusion from another side."[24]

1.2.2 *"Practical Determinism"*

Although it is likely that Schleiermacher was familiar with Jacobi's book on Lessing, in 1792 his own explorations of the philosophy of Spinoza lay in the near future. "On Human Freedom" moves primarily within the terrain delimited by Kant's critical philosophy, against a background of Halle Wolffianism (represented during Schleiermacher's lifetime by his mentor, Eberhard), with a particular focus on the demands of practical reason. The question that motivates the treatise, particularly in its first two parts, is whether our ordinary moral practices make more sense against the background of a deterministic or an indeterministic understanding of the human self. Schleiermacher's investigation in the treatise's opening pages yield what can be characterized as a doctrine of psychological determinism, the doctrine that human choices are causally necessitated results of the interaction of factors internal to the human psyche (desires, inclinations, beliefs, and apprehensions of objects in the world).

Agreeing with Kant that moral obligation (*moralischer Verbindlichkeit*) is intelligible only to the extent that human beings have the ability to choose between different objects of desire, Schleiermacher considered the fundamental question regarding freedom to be "how must the faculty of desire's mode of action be constituted if it is to be compatible with an acknowledgment of moral obligation?"[25] The following frequently reproduced passage comprises the core of his proposal regarding how human choosing is to be understood: "[T]he preponderance in which every comparison of choice must end in order to pass over into a complete action of the faculty of desire must in every case be grounded in the totality of present representations and in the state and interrelations of all the soul's faculties that have been produced in the progression of representations in our soul."[26]

Translated into a more familiar idiom, this passage describes choice making as determined by two interrelated factors: the way the situation of choice (however broadly this extends) is apprehended by the chooser, and the current state of the chooser's faculties (beliefs, desires, inclinations, etc.), which themselves are a product of a history of prior apprehensions and choices. The passage claims that in order to hold human beings subject to moral obligation, we need to suppose that their choices represent the outcome of a process in which all of an agent's relevant beliefs and desires are taken into consideration in reference to a particular object of desire, in the aspect in which it is apprehended by that agent.

To see how, in Schleiermacher's mind, this understanding of the human faculty for realizing desires secured the validity of moral obligation, we need to understand the contrast he saw between "choosing" in this sense with two other modes of activity: activity "determined by the essence of the soul" and instinctual action. Because "in what is essential to the soul no increase or decrease can occur,"[27] any activities determined by the "essence of the soul" would be such that any creature possessing a particular nature would thereby be determined to perform those actions (with exceptions possible, one imagines, only in cases of physical constraint). In contrast, "instinct" Schleiermacher understood to be an immediate cause-and-effect relationship between an object of desire and some entity's faculty of desire: An action is instinctual when the apprehension of the object of desire leads immediately to activity. So, when we think of an action as instinctual, "we think of the faculty of desire as being determined by a single object of impulse alone, and thus absolutely."[28] So, whereas activities determined by the essence of the soul are determined solely by characteristics of the entity in question, instinctual actions are mere reactions to internal stimuli and are "determined absolutely" by external conditions.

Schleiermacher contrasted choice (*Willkühr*) with both action determined by nature and instinctual action in that choice involves the selection of one object of desire among others that are present to the mind. Choice thus involves *deliberation*, which results in a *judgment* of which object of desire will be adopted as a principle of action. Representing subjects such as human beings, Schleiermacher argued, make such choices on the basis of *maxims*, or "judgments concerning [these objects'] subordination which are considered as rules for future cases."[29] A subject's faculty of desire becomes a *will* when the idea of acting in accordance with maxims can become an object of impulse—that is, when actions can be made to result intentionally in accordance with maxims. Since this process supposes several potential objects of impulse, which maxims bring into relations of super- and subordination, a faculty of desire that is to qualify as a will "must absolutely be a choosing faculty."[30]

Schleiermacher took this understanding of the operation of the faculty of desire to secure the validity of the notion of moral obligation because it entails moral flexibility. Free choices are the result of the interplay of factors that have to do with a particular entity's *character*; they thus have inner determining grounds that are *accidental* in the sense that they do not attach of necessity to the nature of the being in question but can change with time. Moreover, "since impulses are limited by no determined boundary in the essence of the soul, no degree of influence, however great, can be conceived to which an impulse of even higher degree cannot be juxtaposed."[31] It is conceivable, according to this understanding, that all of an agent's choices might be made in accordance with maxims that accord with the moral law. We could summarize Schleiermacher's argument to this point with the claim that in order to intelligibly hold an agent to be subject to moral obligation, we need only suppose that that agent's nature does not by itself determine either how it will act or how it will react to the presence of objects of desire, and thus does not determine whether it will act morally or immorally. In other words, moral obligation makes sense only when we can say that it is possible *for an agent with that nature* to act either morally or immorally.

However, Schleiermacher's proposal allows for the claim that a particular agent "could have done otherwise" only in a qualified sense. One cannot say that an agent has a power for choosing opposites in the sense that "in the moment of a certain act or resolution I could decide in any conceivable way, and nowhere in the preceding course of the world is there a necessitating ground sufficient to have determined this way to the exclusion of every other."[32] This "indifferentist" position was most prominently represented at the time by Kant's definition of freedom as "a causality...through which something happens without its cause being further determined by another previous cause, i.e., an absolute causal spontaneity beginning from itself a series of appearances that runs according to natural laws."[33] Schleiermacher found this postulated "faculty of absolutely beginning a state" both unacceptably mysterious and ethically pernicious.[34] His discussion of indifferentism highlights the fact that because incompatibilists deny that prior conditions determine choices, they must a fortiori deny that any prior facts *about the agent* do so, including facts concerning desires, inclinations, and prior choices.

Against this idea Schleiermacher raised a standard compatibilist objection that had been articulated by Wolff a generation earlier: Because incompatibilism holds that freedom is an ability to act in a way that is not constrained by prior conditions, it must deny a postulate that is indispensable for our ordinary moral practices, the postulate that we can significantly affect our future decisions and those of others through actions we take in the present. "Without this idea [that representations are sufficient grounds for actions] we could in no way justify our efforts to affect wills; producing representations could not be regarded as a means to this end, and there would in fact be no means at all."[35] According to a doctrine of incompatibilist freedom, "we could specify no means by which this scheme [to subordinate other impulses to the moral impulse] could be accomplished.... Neither practical reason nor a striving after conformity with the law—a striving in accordance with an idea and thus more than fortuitous—would be possible. We would be forced to give up our practical conduct as unwarranted."[36] Incompatibilist freedom, that is, would seem to sever the connection between agents and their actions that (according to Schleiermacher) is required to make sense of morality.

In the second part of the treatise Schleiermacher defended his account of human choosing as a matter of "inner determination" against a number of objections. Foremost among these is the objection that moral accountability (*Zurechnung*) seems to require a degree of power for opposites that the doctrine of necessity denies:

> If the grounds of each action are sufficiently and unalterably
> determined antecedently, which as soon as this opinion is adopted
> certainly cannot be denied; if each action thus depends upon
> preceding actions and the first actions always have their grounds
> completely outside ourselves; if persons must therefore act as they
> have in fact acted and could not possibly act otherwise; if this is what
> we are taken to have written, then the thought of such an association
> of notions must stifle at birth the attempt to assign accountability to
> an action.[37]

Unlike moral obligation, which asks about the general nature of human agency, accountability asks after the moral status of particular actions, and according to Schleiermacher's deterministic account of human choosing it cannot be said, *once all of the relevant particulars are in view*, that the agent could have done otherwise. In response to this objection Schleiermacher argued that judgments of accountability by their nature do not take account of many of the circumstantial details pertaining to particular actions. With respect to an action that went wrong, "The moral characteristic that reason required was not only possible in itself but was also possible in the subject; it was simply not possible at the present time and within this train of perceptions. This temporal determination was not what reason was inquiring about, however."[38] In this response the character of Schleiermacher's psychological determinism becomes clear: According to this view, all of an agent's actions take place necessarily, as the result of the interaction of factors internal to the human self; persons "must act as they have in fact acted, and could not possibly act otherwise."

1.2.3 Determination from Within, and from Without

Placed into the context of the Enlightenment understanding of the natural order governed by the necessitating activity of efficient causality, Schleiermacher's psychological determinism yields an understanding of human beings as determined to be who they are, in every respect, ultimately by the operation of forces operating outside the self.[39] Indeed, Schleiermacher described his account of human choosing as "the doctrine of the necessary interconnection of actions with the universal chain of causes and effects."[40] The best-developed expressions of this view of human beings as ultimately determined in their actions by causes operating outside themselves are advanced in the treatise not in Schleiermacher's own voice but in the voices of objectors to the doctrine of necessity:

> [T]his conviction [of the necessity of actions] indicates to us that the actions cannot be otherwise, since such and such external impressions have struck such and such a resonance (*Stimmung*) in the soul. The resonance of the soul is in turn a product of preceding and occasioning impressions, and so, resist as we may, all is at last dissolved in external impressions. So, of all that belongs to the action, what can we then assign to the agent? Do we see the agent act in some way? We can think of the agent only as suffering (*leidend*)! Or where is the power that is active? It dissolves into infinitely many infinitesimally small external forces that leave us with nothing to think of as firmly active in the subject. True, the action remains lofty, noble, beautiful, small or abhorrent, but to whom do we ascribe this?[41]

The proximate ground of this objection is the notion that moral accountability requires a more robust notion of an action's belonging to a person than determinism allows. An understanding of human persons as ultimately determined to be who they are from without would, fairly clearly, deliver the result that the relationship between persons and their moral situation is not, in the final analysis, a matter of their own choosing. Rather, the idea of persons as moral agents seems threatened by the doctrine of necessity:

> The person stands motionless, as it were. The person changes moral situations like garments, clothed by external powers, now with the purple robe of virtue, now with the rags of vice. The purple is ever lustrous, but do you marvel at the person who wears it? ... Thus you

see all mortals as transparent as water their whole life through. They flash all the colors, but merely according to the laws of refraction. Of all that you see in the person's actions, nothing belongs to the person.[42]

Schleiermacher's response to this objection, as to others in a similar vein, was to argue that "all the exceptions taken to the doctrine of necessity from this side rest upon some kind of illusion."[43] In response to this particular objection he deployed an analogy to judgments of artistic merit. "Once we have determined the artistic worth of a piece of work, we are quick to assign the result of our judgment to the artist," he observed. Yet such judgments are not at all in conflict with the idea that "it could not have been any other way, given the situation and capabilities of the artist"; in order to make our judgment "we have simply compared the known characteristics of the artist's capacities with the laws and aims of art and have been affected by their suitability."[44] Judgments of moral accountability, in Schleiermacher's view, have no more need of an account of the ultimate grounds of actions than do judgments of artistic merit.

Rather than arguing that the objections he described placed too stringent an interpretation on the doctrine of necessity, then, Schleiermacher was concerned that his readers reconcile themselves with a view of human persons "flashing all the colors, but merely according to the laws of refraction." Nowhere does this become clearer than at the conclusion of the second part of the essay, where he anticipated the reaction that even if his arguments are correct, "necessity greatly diminishes their feeling of personality (*Personalität*) and self-activity (*Selbstthätigkeit*)."[45] Schleiermacher responded that both of these are actually *enhanced* by a doctrine that allows us to see ourselves and our actions as connected in the most intimate way possible:

[W]e will sense less personality when we do not know how this state interconnects with our preceding states than when we can say: "I have arrived at this way of experiencing things little by little, in this way or that." Here, therefore, our feeling of self-activity and personality is greater the more we are able to see into the mutual interconnection of the various individual workings of the soul in relation to an action, and into the interconnection of an entire state with preceding states according to the rule of necessity, which is thus presupposed; and our feeling of self-activity and personality is smaller the less of this we are able to elucidate in this way—thus, in general, the less necessity seems to be present and the more the soul's workings seem to correspond to freedom.[46]

Finally, Schleiermacher argued that "if we correctly think our way into necessity...so that this conviction gradually passes over into our feeling," this feeling of necessity will then no longer harm our consciousness of personality, not even in relation to ethical actions insofar as they are regarded as such. Rather, even here we shall no longer hesitate to give the name of self-activity to individual conduct graspable in this way. We shall also call our own the actions that occur through us (*durch uns geschehen*), the more so the more particularly they interconnect with our previous actions and with the whole modification of our capacity for action.[47]

This last passage is freighted with significance regarding the possibilities that a deterministic view opens up for understanding the self in relation to the world—a subject that would ultimately form the core of Schleiermacher's account of religion.

1.2.4 Freedom and Necessity

It is fairly clear, then, that the young Schleiermacher held the position that human beings are both free and determined in their actions. However, before we move to his later writings on the subject of freedom, two further aspects of "On Human Freedom" deserve mention. The first is the outright failure, philosophically speaking, of Schleiermacher's attempt to provide a formal definition of "freedom as a predicate of human actions," and the second is a prominent phenomenological tension between freedom and necessity noted by Schleiermacher that the essay does not resolve and which would reappear in his later writings.

In the final, unfinished section of the treatise, Schleiermacher set himself the task of providing a formal compatibilist definition of freedom in three different sorts of usage: freedom with respect to human *actions*, with respect to human *situations*, and with respect to human *faculties*. He began by proposing a "generic concept" of freedom, removing the problematic "*von selbst*" from Kant's definition of transcendental freedom—"the faculty of initiating a series of events from oneself"—thus defining freedom in its most general sense as *the ability to initiate a series of events*.[48]

Using this definition as a starting point, Schleiermacher worked through an argument regarding how "free actions" are to be understood, breaking off the treatise just after the conclusion of this argument. Given the determination of all events by a chain of causes and effects stretching back indefinitely in time, what is needed to make sense of the notion of a "free action" is a way to isolate a series of events related to an action in order to determine which event initiates that series. The mechanism Schleiermacher hit upon was to call a "series" a chain of events *determined by a particular kind of law* and to distinguish the "law of the motion of bodies" on the one hand from "the law of the succession of ideas" on the other.[49] This allowed him to say that a free action is *the first in a series that is determined according to a particular law without itself being determined by that law.* Thus, with respect to a particular human bodily action, if "we go back to the nerves or whatever else is the first ground and seat of motions in the human body, we must hit upon a first that has not arisen from any earlier, according to the law of motion, but that rather relates to a volition determined by the succession of ideas in the soul. The freedom of which we are speaking properly corresponds to this first motion."[50]

This account of what it is for an action to be free both fails to yield the desired result and has absurd consequences. According to this view, when agents decide to perform some action with their bodies, what is free is not the *volition* that results from deliberation but the first event in the *body* caused by the volition; *decisions* are not free, nor are what we ordinarily think of as human actions, involving as these do the movements of arms and legs and so forth, but whatever turns out to be the first mentally caused event in the physical-causal chain leading to bodily movement ("motion in the nerves," for example). But also, as Schleiermacher himself admitted but begged off from discussing in detail, the account entails that any *mental* event with an immediate *physical* cause, which in turn begins a series of *mentally* caused events, qualifies as free, so whatever turns out to be the first mental event in a mental causal chain (say, sensations) would also be free but *not* the mental events—the construal of sensations as experience of the outside world, reasoning, deliberation, or decisions—that follow. The failure of this attempt to define "free actions" in this quasi-Kantian manner is so obvious, in fact, that I suspect that one of Schleiermacher's reasons for breaking off composition has to do with the fact that here he had worked himself into a philosophical dead end (how clearly he saw this is difficult to say).[51]

Schleiermacher's formal definition of freedom as a matter of being able to initiate a series of events vanished after "On Human Freedom," never, so far as I am aware, to appear again (the general strategy that he employed here to make sense of the notion of the first event in a series within a worldview characterized by determinism does, however, recur in his later work, making an appearance in what might seem an unlikely place: Schleiermacher's account of revelation in *The Christian Faith*[52]). As we will see, the notion of freedom that plays a major role in Schleiermacher's later writings is based on his account of human choosing developed in the first part of the treatise: freedom as a matter of inner determination.

The unresolved tension within the account of "On Human Freedom" has to do with one of the courts of opinion to which Schleiermacher stated a willingness to submit his position in the opening pages of the treatise: testimony from "common sentiments" related to our moral self-understanding such as the "feeling of freedom." "Despite their testimony, which often seems contradictory," Schleiermacher remarked, such sentiments "are nonetheless grounded in the nature of the human soul"[53] and thus cannot be dismissed as simple illusions. The detailed examination of the "feeling of freedom" in the second part of the treatise immediately invokes the notion of an opposition between this feeling and determinism:

> This feeling unfailingly awakens in us as often as we become expressly conscious of ourselves as moral beings.... How can we continue to join necessity with it, since this most lively feeling inwardly releases us from everything that appears to resemble necessity's yoke?...we must admit that in our desiring we lie outside the sphere of all sensible necessity, that even an infinite mass of motivating grounds can never be thought sufficient to determine our desiring, and that we can withstand those grounds without any ancillary aid apart from the only other ground that can be mentioned, the existence of our power to will.[54]

Schleiermacher argued for only a partial reconciliation between the feeling of freedom and the doctrine of necessity by drawing a distinction between "that which is true" in this feeling and "that which is false." What the feeling of freedom accurately represents to us, according to him, is the fact that we are not subject to constraint by the objects themselves: that is, our choices are not determined by the objects of desire that we apprehend. Properly construed, the feeling of freedom is "the feeling of exercising choice" and is grounded in "our faculty of desire's characteristic of not being absolutely determinable by one object."[55] It is a reflection of the fact that our characters (that is to say, *we*) play the major role in determining which objects of desire we will pursue. However, since we are ignorant of the precise chains of causes and effects operating within us that lead to our decisions, "the deceptive feeling easily arises that the degree and direction of our power have been determined without there anywhere being a ground for this determination," which results in "a sensation of the complete absence of all necessity in the causal connection."[56] What is false in the feeling of freedom is the sense that we are free from constraint to the point that our decisions are *not determined by prior conditions*.

"That which is true" in the feeling of freedom is thus fully compatible with the doctrine of necessity. Nonetheless, even after Schleiermacher's distinction is taken into account, crucial passages in the essay still speak of a "natural repugnance" between the feeling that one is free and the consciousness that one is determined. Consider again the passage cited earlier:

> [O]ur feeling of self-activity and personality is greater the more we are able to see into the mutual interconnection of the various individual workings of the soul in relation to an action, and into the interconnection of an entire state with preceding states according to the rule of necessity, which is thus presupposed; and our feeling of self-activity and personality is smaller the less of this we are able to elucidate

in this way—thus, in general, the less necessity seems to be present and the more the soul's workings seem to correspond to freedom.[57]

What is noteworthy about this passage is that, in spite of his arguments for the compatibility of necessity and moral obligation and the true feeling of freedom, when Schleiermacher shifted here to discussing our own apprehension of our agency, he reverted to speaking of the two as opposed: One's sense of the "presence of necessity" seems in this passage to diminish precisely in proportion to the extent that "the soul's workings seem to correspond to freedom." This echoes the earlier claim that the feeling of freedom "inwardly releases us from everything that appears to resemble necessity's yoke." Another passage in the same section even suggests that the "consciousness of necessity" is a prima facie obstacle to the consciousness of oneself as a moral agent: "Consider those occasions when we either deliberate concerning impending actions or make preceding actions the objects of sentiment or lay plans for coming actions; if at those times the ethical impulse is to express free effectiveness, the requisite presuppositions exist only in relation to the feeling of freedom, never in relation to the consciousness of necessity."[58]

Schleiermacher further argued that "if a misunderstanding ill humor concerning the yoke of necessity—which we cannot presuppose in a well-instructed adherent of this doctrine—does not infect the soul's natural course," the feeling of necessity is (thus ultima facie) compatible with all of our ordinary deliberative practices. However, fairly clearly, his view was that "thinking ourselves into necessity" requires sustained and disciplined reflection.

It seems to me that in the final sections of "On Human Freedom" Schleiermacher was grasping for an understanding of the relationship between freedom and necessity that would explain the common apprehension of their incompatibility while at the same time arguing for the possibility of seeing through this apprehension.[59] Taken as a whole, this early essay is marked by a tension between the phenomenological awareness of freedom and the reflective apprehension of causal determinism, which the possibility of a formal compatibilist account of freedom does not entirely eliminate. As we will see, this tension reappeared in Schleiermacher's later writings.

1.3 Freedom and Necessity in the *Dialektik*

During his time at the University of Berlin Schleiermacher taught in both the theology and the philosophy faculties. His lectures in the philosophy faculty, offered six times between 1811 and 1831, compose the body of work known as the *Dialektik*.[60] For the purposes of this chapter my discussion of this material focuses narrowly on the question of the relationship between freedom and necessity. Discussion of this relationship recurs in several of the surviving sets

of notes, and in spite of minor variations the basic idea is the same. Freedom
and necessity form the two sides of a "relative antithesis": They stand in opposition to each other only from a limited perspective but, properly understood, are
coextensive. Indeed, Schleiermacher would claim in the 1814–1815 lectures,
"one can say that freedom and necessity are each the measure of the other."[61]

The lectures on *Dialektik* are informed by a central proposal regarding the
structure of human knowledge, a proposal reflected in Schleiermacher's ethics lectures and his dogmatics as well. The proposal is that knowledge is produced by the progressive "division of being" in thought or the imposition of
hierarchically arranged sets of antitheses (*Gegensätze*) upon that which is
known.[62] Each such antithesis delimits a distinct stage of consciousness, in
that taking two concepts to be opposed constrains us to think of concepts connected with them as also opposed. However, to the extent that an antithesis is
only a relative one, it is possible to "rise above" it in thought: to see the concepts that make up the antithesis as in reality compatible with each other and
so to leave behind everything that follows logically from their opposition. This
structure—the validity of an antithesis for a particular area of thought, but
with a yet higher realm opened up by the perception that the terms of the
antithesis are in reality identical—applies to every part of human knowledge.
Only the transcendent ground of knowing—which is constituted by the "identity of concept and object"—stands above all antitheses.[63] Subordinate antitheses that exist within human knowledge are those between the real and the
ideal (which constitutes the "highest antithesis"[64]), between force (*Kraft*) and
appearance (*Erscheinung*); between freedom and necessity; and between physical and ethical knowledge.[65]

The 1814–1815 lectures describe the antithesis between freedom and necessity as follows:

> Everything in the realm of being is just as free as it is necessary.
> Everything is free insofar as it is an identity, posited for itself, of
> unity of force and plurality of appearances. It is necessary insofar as
> it appears intertwined in the system of common being
> (*Zusammensein*) as a succession of states. The more firmly it is
> established as a unity in itself, the more it offers something to the
> external forces which they can approach; and the more something is
> affected by external forces, the more it is urged (*aufgefordert*) in fact
> to realize all of its potentialities. Free and necessary are not set
> against each other as contradictory (*contradictorisch*), but the
> contradictory opposite of both is the accidental. The more accidental
> a thing is, like the transitory productions of vegetables, the less are
> freedom, that is unity grounded in itself, and also necessity, that is
> the persistent mirroring of other things, present in it; it is posited
> only as a point of transmission (*Durchgangspunkt*) for the *Facta* of

general life. Indeed, one can say that freedom and necessity are each
the measure of the other. The freedom of a thing is the whole thing,
and the necessity of a thing is also the whole thing, only viewed
from another side.[66]

In this passage, Schleiermacher's description of what it is for a thing to be
free (that a thing be an "identity, posited for itself, of unity of force and plurality
of appearances") is not terribly accessible; his restatement of the point in the
1818 lectures, which we will encounter momentarily, is far clearer. However,
what should be clear is that, just as in 1792, in 1814 Schleiermacher was describing freedom and necessity as mutually reinforcing terms and contrasting both
with the "accidental," understood (I take it) as that which is only indifferently
related to the nature or constitution of the thing in question. The passage also
expresses the view that while freedom and necessity are coextensive, there is a
difference between regarding a thing as free versus regarding it as necessary,
and this difference is a matter of perspective: Viewed in one way a thing is free,
and viewed in another way it is necessary.

In the 1818 lectures Schleiermacher's statement of the relationship between
freedom and necessity was more straightforward: "What develops its condition
out of itself is free, what is bound by other things in its development is subject
to necessity; and so each thing is simultaneously free and necessary." Here he
also responded specifically to the idea that freedom obtains only when actions
are not ultimately determined by external causes:

We always claim that man is a free being, and now we believe that
we can best prove this to ourselves if we could show how a person's
choice (*Willkühr*) rules in the determination of the sequence of his
states, and that he therefore could choose in two or three different
ways.... But the reason we are so attached to this conception of
choice is because of its negative elements, for insofar as we posit
this, we want to say that the person is not determined by the relation
to the external, but from inside out, and choice, representative of
freedom, can comprehend this negative side within itself only if
there is an absence of external constraint. But choice itself is indeed
already a product of the coexistence of man with everything external.
Freedom, however, is merely the inner unity of that force which
develops a certain system of appearances outwards from within
itself. But each free being is yet again subject to necessity, because
none is isolated.[67]

In other words, Schleiermacher took incompatibilism about freedom to be
grounded in the proper understanding of human choice—as a matter of actions
following from factors internal to an entity—but also incorporating the mistaken assumption that "determination from inside out" can be claimed only in

cases where an agent is cut off from external determining conditions. Here as earlier, he rejected the notion of a power of choosing that is independent of those aspects of an agent's existence that are intertwined with external causes.

The understanding of freedom that informs the *Dialektik*, then, seems to be a generalized version of the conception found in the first half of "On Human Freedom."[68] Whereas in the earlier text Schleiermacher had spoken of freedom as a matter of determination of one's actions by factors internal to the self, in the Berlin lectures freedom is a matter of "developing one's condition out of oneself." In both its earlier, more specific and later, more abstract formulation, there is no conflict between actions being free in this sense and their being determined, ultimately, by factors external to the agent.

In two respects, however, the account of freedom in the *Dialektik* shows development from the position of "On Human Freedom." First, to speak of freedom and necessity as forming a "relative antithesis" implies that the notion that they stand in opposition is not simply an error (as is entailed by a generic compatibilism) but rather that there are ways of thinking, valid within their own sphere, according to which the two are *genuinely* incompatible. To express this opposition between freedom and necessity, Schleiermacher made use of the notion of different ways of viewing the same agent or phenomenon—a theme that returns later in this chapter. As he put it in the 1818 lectures, "Necessity does not restrict freedom at all, but rather both are the same, only viewed from different sides."[69]

Second, while in the early essay Schleiermacher discussed freedom as a property of human actions, in the *Dialektik* the range of the notion has expanded considerably. In a sense this is a logical development of a compatibilist view. If freedom is a matter of "developing from oneself" or of actions being determined by factors internal to an entity rather than by an autonomous and anomalous power for opposites, then freedom is likely to characterize a wider range of entities than merely human beings: It will characterize the activities of any beings whose actions are more than immediate, mechanical reactions to the impingement of external causes. As Schleiermacher wrote in a draft of the 1822 lectures, "Freedom extends as far as life; the question of whether animals are machines is the same as whether they are living, [and] even a plant has its freedom....The stone, which as such is dead, has no freedom, but also no necessity, and so what has little self-development also enters little into the system of causality."[70] A more extended treatment of the same subject is found in the 1818 lecture notes:

> Here we can take up again the antithesis of the free and the
> necessary. [In a previous discussion] each being was subject to
> both, each viewed for itself was free, and subject to necessity
> inasmuch as it was viewed in connection with others. Each living
> being which is posited as power is free. As it is customary to
> connect freedom and willing, so one could say that it is also a

willing being. Only we will not fail to recognize this gradation. Man is the highest willing being, then the animal, and then the vegetable, where willing entirely conceals itself. If we proceed into the inorganic, there life is entirely in the past; if there is to be will therein, then one must return to the whole. So one can see nature as a diminished ethics, because there is always a diminished willing in it.[71]

The idea of nature as composed of an ascending series of developmental stages (inorganic-vegetable-animal-human) returns at the close of this chapter. For the present, suffice it to note that for the mature Schleiermacher freedom is not a possession unique to human beings and applicable only to a subset of their activities but is found wherever life is found, and thus it is not only human beings who are in the position of being both free and determined. "Now this applies throughout all of being, insofar as it is an object of knowledge, that is through the whole of divided being; and freedom and necessity do not hinder each other, and the one is not at its greatest where the other is at its smallest, but the one elevates (*hebt*) the other in the physical *and* the ethical" (emphasis in the original).[72]

Schleiermacher's position in the lectures on *Dialektik*, then, was that human actions are free in the same sense that the actions of animals and even plants are free, but to a greater extent; human actions, even those that are subject to moral evaluation, represent no anomaly but are rather to be understood in continuity with the rest of the natural order.

1.4 The Difference Determinism Makes

The attribution to Schleiermacher of a commitment to determinism of the sort described in the previous sections, if correct, has significant consequences regarding how a number of his texts are to be understood, including but not limited to those that deal with religion. In what remains of this chapter I examine three cases where determinism makes a difference in the interpretation of Schleiermacher. The first of these concerns the *Speeches on Religion*; the second concerns the *Monologen*, a text that has been regarded as the scene of a fundamental change of heart on Schleiermacher's part as regards determinism; and the third, Schleiermacher's understanding of the promise of advancing knowledge in the realm of ethics for understanding human activity.

1.4.1 *Determinism and the* Speeches

Reading the *Speeches on Religion* against the background of determinism illuminates Schleiermacher's argument at a number of points by allowing

important passages to be read in a more straightforward way than would otherwise be required.[73] It provides a fitting framework for Schleiermacher's initial
claim that his religious upbringing rendered him suitable for the office of religious *Mittler* or 'mediator': "That I speak does not originate from a rational
decision or from hope or fear, nor does it happen in accord with some final
purpose or for some arbitrary or accidental reason. It is the inner, irresistible
necessity of my nature; it is a divine office; it is that which determines my place
in the universe and makes me the being I am."[74] Schleiermacher's various
claims about his understanding of human existence in general—not only his
description in the first speech of the human soul as "merely the product of two
opposing drives" but also his extended meditation, cited at the opening of this
chapter, on "the eternal wheels of humanity in their progress...where nothing
movable is moved by itself alone and nothing moving moves only itself"[75]—
also comport naturally with the doctrine of necessity.

Of greater interest is the fact that the idea of a distinction between awareness of the self as a moral agent and awareness of the self as subject to necessity, a distinction we have observed in his earlier and later writings as well,
plays a fundamental role in the argument of the *Speeches*. Schleiermacher
expressed this distinction as follows in the second speech: "Morality (*Moral*)
proceeds from the consciousness of freedom; it wishes to extend freedom's
realm to infinity and to make everything subservient to it. Religion breathes
there where freedom itself has once more become nature; it apprehends man
beyond the play of his particular powers and his personality and views him
from the vantage point where he must be what he is, whether he likes it or
not."[76]

Here Schleiermacher associated the consciousness of freedom with morality or ethics and identified the view of the self as subject to the rule of necessity
both as a *higher* view and as the *religious* view. The continuity between these
passages and both "On Human Freedom" and the *Dialektik* should be apparent. In the early essay Schleiermacher had claimed that the feeling of freedom
"awakens in us as often as we become expressly conscious of ourselves as moral
beings"; in the 1818 lecture on *Dialektik* he remarked that "[n]ecessity does not
restrict freedom at all, but rather both are the same, only viewed from different
sides" and that every living being "viewed for itself [is] free, and subject to
necessity inasmuch as it [is] viewed in connection with others."[77] Thus, two
associations to which Schleiermacher appears to have been committed in both
his early and later writings find expression in the *Speeches* as well: an association of the *consciousness of freedom* with *consciousness of the self as an ethical agent*
and *the view of the self in itself,* and an association of the *consciousness of necessity*
with the *religious view of the self* and the *view of the self in the context of its relationships* to other entities and states of affairs.

Awareness of these associations helps us make sense of Schleiermacher's
criticisms of religion's "cultured despisers," who because they stand merely

"in the first forecourt of morality, and even there [are] still occupied with the basics," "blaspheme" against the harmony of the universe with demands for a "deplorable individualization."[78] Schleiermacher's own view in the *Speeches* was that "everything is a work of the universe, and only thus can religion regard humans";[79] his criticism of the individualism of his audience amounts to the charge that their relatively superficial moral concerns prevented them from taking account of the extent to which all human life is conditioned by the system of nature. "Why do you see everything individually, which surely does not function individually and for itself? The reason of one person and the soul of another affect each other as deeply as could only happen in a single subject."[80] This view of humanity even promises a higher comprehension of history itself, the "highest object of religion," as a unified and continually unfolding causal process: "Here you see the transmigration of human spirits and souls, which otherwise seem like a delicate literary creation, in more than one sense a wondrous event of the universe for comparing, with a sure standard, the different periods of humanity.... Soon a single moment of humanity returns just like its image that a distant bygone time had left behind you, and you shall recognize the path of the universe and the formula of its laws from the various causes through which the moment has now been produced."[81]

However, there is one point on which the question of determinism makes a particularly important difference in interpreting Schleiermacher's claims about religion in the *Speeches* and in particular the relationship between this text and the causal-explanatory paradigm for the investigation of religion discussed in my introduction.[82] Schleiermacher's youthful account of religion is distributed across the final four speeches; the fifth speech presents the final, crucial structural element of this account in that there Schleiermacher discusses the "principle of individuation" of religion, or what makes particular religions distinct from one another. As is well known, what makes for a determinate "positive religion" is the prominence of a single "intuition of the universe" over all others. This single religious intuition comes to constitute the "essence" of a historical religion; other religious intuitions assume subordinate places in relation to this essence or are excluded from that particular religion for reasons of logical inconsistency. The selection of a particular religious intuition to constitute an essence thus represents the moment where a new form of religion comes into existence.

It is a question of considerable significance whether Schleiermacher regarded this, a historical religion's moment of origin, as the fully determined result of prior causes or not. A negative answer would render the essence of religion autonomous from the conditioning effects of history and all it contains; a positive answer, however, would open the door to the doctrine that every aspect of the temporal career of religion, including the view of the universe that makes one religion thematically distinct from every other, is a "product of time and of history."[83] Those who read the *Speeches* in light of a commitment by Schleiermacher to determinism should answer this question in the affirmative and attribute to him the view that (barring supernatural intervention, a subject to be considered in chapter 4), the causal antecedents of particular historical religions are to be found in the environment of their origins.

There are important passages within the *Speeches* that can fairly easily be read in this light, although at first blush they seem in fact to be making the opposite claim. For example, Schleiermacher argued that a positive religion can come about only "through free choice (*aus freier Willkühr*) by making a particular intuition of the universe the center of the whole of religion and relating everything therein to it."[84] This establishment must be a matter of choice because "every single intuition would have similar claims to be established": There is nothing about the content of religious intuitions themselves that makes one more suitable than another as the core of a positive religion. If the *Willkühr* of this passage is understood in an incompatibilist sense, this passage claims that the choice in question is independent of prior causes (i.e., *willkürlich*, 'arbitrary'). However, if the term is interpreted in a compatibilist sense, then Schleiermacher's claim that the origin of a positive religion lies in "free choice" signifies that this event is not determined solely by the content of the intuition of the universe itself but also by the contingent, temporally conditioned character of the agent making the choice. The freedom in question is not a matter of not being determined by prior conditions but of not being "determined absolutely by the objects themselves"—in this case, the religious intuitions that present themselves to an agent as candidates for the essence of a positive religion. This reading is strongly supported by Schleiermacher's 1806 revision of this passage, which reads: "[W]hen viewed only in relation to the idea of religion, this [choice] can appear as pure caprice (*reine Willkühr*); but, when one regards the particularity of the adherent, it rather bears the purest necessity within itself, and is only the natural expression of his own being (*Wesen*)."[85]

Elsewhere, a deterministic reading is somewhat more tendentious but still possible and illuminating. Schleiermacher spoke of the beginning of a particular individual's religious life as "that incomprehensible fact beyond which you are not able to pursue the finite series further, and in which your imagination fails you if you would explain it on the basis of something earlier, whether it be free choice or nature."[86] He also remarked on the fact a religious person's accounts of this incomprehensible fact within his own life are likely to take the form of "a wondrous tale of the origin of his religion, which appears as an immediate influence of the deity and as a movement of its spirit."[87] Prima facie these remarks do not sit comfortably with the idea that even the events that constitute an individual's "spiritual birthday" take place of necessity and are ultimately to be understood as the outcome of the operation of external, natural factors on the religious individual. However, Schleiermacher continued by indicating what a complete understanding of such incomprehensible facts would require: "Each being that arises in this way can be explained only from itself and can never be completely understood, if you do not go back as far as possible to the initial expressions of free choice (*Willkühr*) in earliest times. In the same way each religious personality is also a completed whole, and your understanding of it rests on your seeking to fathom its first revelations."[88] The suggestion, I take it, is that one's understanding of an individual's "spiritual birthday" requires viewing such an event within a broader historical contest, that of the history of a particular religious tradition or perhaps the history of religion as a whole. Such an idea would follow naturally from reflecting on the origins of an individual's religion in a manner informed by commitment to determinism.

1.4.2 *The* Monologen

Immediately following the publication of the *Speeches* Schleiermacher composed a text that eventually came to be regarded as a paradigmatic literary expression of German early romanticism: the *Monologen* or "Soliloquies," which appeared in print in January of 1800.[89] The significance of this text for my reconstructive project lies not in the light it sheds on Schleiermacher's understanding of religion but rather in the fact that its contents have suggested to some scholars that by late 1799 Schleiermacher had performed a complete about-face on the topic of determinism and embraced an incompatibilist understanding of human freedom redolent of the work of Kant and Fichte.[90] The most recent example is contained in Jacqueline Mariña's recent book *Transformation of the Self in the Thought of Friedrich Schleiermacher*.[91]

An important textual basis for Mariña's position is the contrast Schleiermacher drew in the opening pages of his treatise between two viewpoints on the self. Whereas for the "empiricist" who adopts an "outward" view of the self, "[f]reedom seems to him nothing but an illusion, spread like a veil over a hidden and uncomprehended necessity," the narrator, who adopts an "inward" view, enjoys a full and unfettered awareness of his freedom.[92] "Whoever sees and recognizes only the outward spectacle of life," Schleiermacher wrote, "may never set foot within the sacred precincts of freedom.... For in the image he constructs of himself, this very self becomes something external, like all else, and everything in such an image is determined by external circumstances."[93] Mariña takes this contrast between the inward view of the self as free and the outward view of the self as subject to necessity to imply the real autonomy of the inward self from determination by external circumstances.

Her reading also takes account, however, of passages where Schleiermacher speaks of the territory covered by necessity in ways that work against any straightforward contrast between freedom and determination. For example, she cites a crucial passage in which Schleiermacher remarked that "to necessity belong also the rising and falling tides of emotion, the train of images that passes before us, and everything that changes in our soul with time."[94] Mariña takes the point of this passage to be not that necessity governs not only the entire sweep of outward life but also the inward dimensions of human existence but rather a more modest claim: As she puts it, "*That* the world impinges upon us in certain ways, and that our representations must be brought to a unity in accordance with certain laws, is not a matter under our control. Even our emotions may not be fully under our control."[95] Mariña in fact sees in this passage and others room for a narrowly delimited form of incompatibilist freedom. The ground of this freedom, in her view, is the transcendental unity of consciousness, which "is *free* in relation to the world, for it is not a moment in the self's consciousness of the world and cannot be determined by the play of previous impressions."[96] Moreover, Mariña takes her orientation regarding the question of how this freedom is realized within the temporal stream of human existence—the question, that is, of the respects in which human activities are not determined by external circumstances—from Schleiermacher's remark that "[a]ll those feelings that seem to be forced upon me by the material world are in reality my own free doing; nothing is a mere effect of that world upon me."[97] This, then, is the understanding of freedom that Mariña attributes to Schleiermacher in the *Monologen*: "The transcendental self is not compelled to receive or imagine what comes to it from the outside world in any *fully* determinate way (although this does not mean that what the self receives is completely indeterminate, either). The successive series of apprehensions, the fleeting representations and sensations that are the stuff of self-consciousness do not of themselves completely determine *how* these disparate elements of consciousness will be knit together through the imagination."[98] In other words, freedom for Schleiermacher is a matter of *an ability to determine, independently of external factors, how the world is perceived*: "The manner in which the impressions of the world are received...is not determined by what is outside the self. Rather an inner principle is at work."[99]

Three criticisms can be advanced against this reconstruction of Schleiermacher's understanding of freedom in the *Monologen*, and the first two can be set out fairly quickly. First, Mariña consistently assumes that "freedom" must be interpreted in incompatibilist terms, as implying an absence of determination by external circumstances. Thus, in citing Schleiermacher's claim that free actions flow from "an inner determination and from the individual's unique disposition,"[100] she passes over the continuity between this claim and "On Human Freedom" and thus over the possibility that "freedom" in this text might signify "inner determination" *without* implying any claims about determination from without. Second, her treatment does not extend to the discussions of the relationship between freedom and necessity contained in

Schleiermacher's later writings. Elsewhere she has argued for an incompatibilist reading of *The Christian Faith*,[101] but I am not aware of any of her writings where she has taken account of either Schleiermacher's formulation in the *Dialektik* of the relationship between freedom and necessity as a relative antithesis or his remark that "[n]ecessity does not restrict freedom at all, but rather both are the same, only viewed from different sides."[102] If these remarks from the *Dialektik* represent a development of Schleiermacher's position in "On Human Freedom" rather than its abandonment, the postulation of a major reversal in Schleiermacher's thinking about human freedom around 1800 faces a serious textual challenge.

A third criticism that can be advanced against Mariña's reconstruction is that it attributes to Schleiermacher a frankly odd account of what it is for human beings to be free. According to Mariña, Schleiermacher's view was that we choose, incompatiblist freely, how impressions of the world are received and interpreted. It is clear that she understands this freedom to imply some degree of freedom of action or at least of reaction: "To a degree, the self determines how impressions from the outside are received, how they are interpreted through the work of the imagination, and how the self will, as a consequence, react to the world and to other selves."[103] However, she does not argue that on Schleiermacher's view humans are incompatibilist free in *choosing* which courses of action to pursue—in *deciding*, that is, which from among a variety of the various objects of desire that are present to the mind will become principles of action. Rather, human freedom applies at a point prior to decision making proper. This seems to me to locate freedom in the wrong place. Because the *choice* of a course of action in relation to potential objects of desire seems to be logically subsequent to the *construal* of those objects of desire as such, the kind of freedom Mariña describes seems to me to be deficient as a species of incompatibilism.

I do not take these criticisms to amount to a decisive refutation of Mariña's claims, and particularly in view of Schleiermacher's unsuccessful concluding proposal in "On Human Freedom," it is certainly not impossible that he embraced a quixotic and unpromising view of human freedom at this stage in his career. However, I do think that these criticisms raise sufficiently serious questions for her interpretation of Schleiermacher to make the possibility of an alternative construal of the *Monologen* attractive.

It has never been easy to extract clearly delineated philosophical positions from the *Monologen*. This is due not only to the high-flown rhetorical style of Schleiermacher's writing during this period (a characteristic shared with the *Speeches*) but also to the extraordinary rapidity with which the essay was composed (according to Schleiermacher's embarrassed confession to his friend Brinckmann, "not quite four weeks").[104] Nevertheless, a number of readers—Arthur von Ungern-Sternberg, Richard Brandt, Poul Jørgensen, and Paul Siefert—have seen in the *Monologen* signs of the commitment to determinism displayed in "On Human Freedom" or in the *Dialektik*, obviating the necessity of postulating a reversal in Schleiermacher's thinking.[105] If none of their treatments constitute a fully executed interrogation of the *Monologen* on the topic of determinism, taken together they indicate that a compatibilist reading of the essay is at least a prima facie possibility. In what remains of this section I want to accomplish a strategically crucial part of this larger project by offering a rationale for interpreting the *Monologen* through the lens of Schleiermacher's earlier and later writings on the topic of human freedom.

Recall the contrast that Schleiermacher drew in the *Speeches* between the moral and the religious views of the self: The moral view apprehends the self as a chooser—that is, as free—and the religious, as a component of the universe.[106] We saw that this contrast itself echoed the contents of "On Human Freedom," where Schleiermacher had explored what he considered a natural repugnance between awareness of one's moral agency and the postulate of universal determinism. This distinction—whose prominent appearance in the *Speeches*, it should be recalled, only slightly antedated the composition of the *Monologen*—suggests a general rubric for the interpretation of the later text. I suggest that the *Monologen* represent not an attempt by Schleiermacher to set out a revised understanding of the nature of freedom but rather a text written from one of the two viewpoints he had described in the *Speeches*—written, in fact, from the perspective (relatively) antithetical to the one adopted in his treatise on religion. The *Monologen*, in other words, was Schleiermacher's attempt to describe the self and the universe from the perspective of the "consciousness of freedom," the perspective of the one who "wants to extend freedom's realm to infinity and make everything subservient to it."[107]

Two contemporaneous remarks by Schleiermacher indicate the general plausibility of the idea that he understood the *Monologen* to have been written from a specific standpoint and in particular the standpoint of the consciousness of freedom. First, Schleiermacher described the *Monologen* to Brinckmann as "an attempt to transcribe the philosophical standpoint, as the idealists call it, into life, and to portray the character which suits my idea of this philosophy"; second, he opened the dedication of the text with the promise that it would provide the reader with "a clear, unimpeded view into a free being."[108] A later reflection by Schleiermacher directly frames the project of the *Monologen* in terms of the contrast expressed in the *Speeches*. In his preface to the third edition of 1821, responding to an inquiry from an unnamed source regarding the manner of self-presentation intended in the original edition, Schleiermacher noted that it was in accordance with his aims that "here [i.e., in the *Monologen*] a purely ethical view of the self is fashioned, and nowhere therein does the religious, in a narrow sense, emerge."[109]

I am suggesting, then, that the *Monologen* should be interpreted in light of the contrast between the consciousness of freedom and the awareness of determination that Schleiermacher had articulated in several texts prior to 1800 and would continue to explore in his later writings. If it is the case that

Schleiermacher's views on the relationship between freedom and necessity remained largely consistent throughout this period, then at least three themes should be in evidence in the *Monologen*. The first is that freedom should be understood as a matter of inward determination—that is, of the determination of one's choices by one's character. The second is that awareness of the universal extent of the "reign of necessity" over every aspect of human existence should be acknowledged. The third is that there should be a phenomenological conflict between the feeling of freedom and the awareness of universal determination, such that (as Schleiermacher had stated in "On Human Freedom") "this most lively feeling inwardly releases us from everything that appears to resemble necessity's yoke"[110] and such that the consciousness of necessity returns inasmuch as the network of relationships in which the free individual is embedded is brought into view.[111]

The first and third of these themes are clearly in evidence in the text. However, attempts to identify statements of the second principle, concerning the universal reign of necessity, face an interpretive complication, for passages that for a compatibilist signify the "inward release from necessity's yoke," which Schleiermacher had described in his earlier writings, can also be read as outright denials of the "reign of necessity." Thus, while Schleiermacher's observation that "[t]o [necessity] belong the feelings which quickly rise and quickly fall; the images which come and go; and whatever other alterations in the mind time brings and takes away" seems at least at first glance to be a straightforward assertion that necessity governs the inward dimension of human existence, this passage is not easily reconciled with his remark in the same paragraph that "what is necessary is not my doing, it is its reflection, it is the intuition of the world that I help to create in holy community with all."[112]

I think it quite likely that any philosophically coherent reconstruction of the *Monologen* will face recalcitrant passages. Nevertheless, it seems to me that adopting the interpretive framework I have outlined considerably illuminates Schleiermacher's tortured and hurriedly composed claims regarding the relationship between freedom and necessity in this text. At a minimum, this suggestion constitutes a challenge to Mariña's assumption that his initial contrast between the outer and inner views of the self, as well as the association of the first with the awareness of determinism and the second with the consciousness of freedom, constitutes evidence of a new embrace of incompatibilism. A passage from the *Monologen* that to some has suggested Fichtean ecstasies in fact reads quite well as a rhapsodic restatement of Schleiermacher's earlier remarks concerning the phenomenologically liberating character of the feeling of freedom, which at the same time anticipates the expanded sense of freedom that would find expression in the *Dialektik*:

So, freedom, for me you are the original, the first and inmost in all things. When I withdraw into myself to contemplate you (*um dich anzuschaun*), my gaze is turned aside from the realm of time, and free from the limitations of necessity; every oppressive feeling of slavery gives way, the spirit fully realizes its creative nature, the light of divinity arises upon me and pushes back the mist in which those slaves wander in error. The way in which I recognize and intuit myself in contemplation is no longer dependent upon fate or luck....I no longer see myself as one of the slaves for whom the world, iron necessity, indicates what he may become.[113]

If my suggestions are correct, then Schleiermacher did not change his mind about the nature of freedom during his Romantic period, and the frequent and fulsome homage paid to freedom in the *Monologen* does not indicate that he had abandoned determinism. The *Monologen* also represent not a major reversal but a developmental waypoint between Schleiermacher's early essay on freedom and the later view of the *Dialektik*, in which freedom is presented as a possession of everything living and so as a crucial term for the science of ethics—even the "diminished ethics" of the animal and vegetable realms.

1.4.3 Physics and Ethics

In both the lectures on ethics and the *Dialektik*, Schleiermacher's claims concerning the relationship between freedom and necessity occur in the context of a broader discussion about the relationship between physics and ethics. Schleiermacher understood these as the two basic branches of *Wissenschaft*, a division dictated by the fact that human thought generally is unavoidably characterized by a "highest antithesis" between spirit and matter, or the real and the ideal.[114] Schleiermacher's compatibilism feeds directly into his understanding of ethics as a descriptive rather than a prescriptive science, a science aimed at uncovering the laws that govern that sector of human activity that is governed by reason. Ethics in Schleiermacher's sense thus aspires to be the "science of the principles of history."[115]

"Now everywhere in nature necessity is the more evident, as freedom is more evident," Schleiermacher remarked in the *Dialektik*. "Just the same applies to the ethical. Nowhere do we find more freedom and necessity than in the development of peoples."[116] Even in the *Speeches*, as we have seen, Schleiermacher floated the idea that appreciation of the interconnectedness of all things clears the way for grasping "the path of the universe and the formula of its laws" as these apply even to human history, and he incorporated this idea as well in his introductory lectures on ethics. Schleiermacher's mature system of the sciences, as we have seen, observed a distinction between empirical and speculative variants of both physics and ethics. This empirical-speculative distinction amounts to a distinction between sciences dedicated to the collection of data versus those that distill data into explanatory theories; *Sittenlehre*, understood as "speculative ethics," thus seeks a grasp of the general principles that inform the course of history. Thus, "The doctrine of ethics (*Sittenlehre*) and the study of history (*Geschichtskunde*) will always remain divided entities, existing in their own right; taken together, the study of history provides the illustrations to the doctrine of ethics, while the doctrine of ethics provides the formulae for the study of history."[117]

In the ethics lectures Schleiermacher sharply contrasted his understanding of *Sittenlehre* with the view that "ethical knowledge assumes the shape of good counsel which may be followed, but may equally not be followed" (i.e., normative ethics).[118] Fairly clearly, Schleiermacher considered ethics as exemplified by the work of Kant to be an endeavor of a sort that was qualitatively different from anything deserving the name of *Wissenschaft*. Inasmuch as ethics "consists of categorical imperatives" it makes no claim to explain how reason actually operates in the world; as Schleiermacher put it, "in a doctrine of morals of this kind reason is not even posited as a force at all."[119] A science of morals should, according to him, aim higher: "What we are in search of as *Sittenlehre*, namely what stands in the same relation to the study of history in the broadest sense as contemplative natural science does to the knowledge of nature in the broadest sense, is something that can never come about in forms such as these," he argued. "The propositions of any doctrine of morals ought not, therefore, to be commandments, whether conditional or unconditional, but inasmuch as they are laws they must express the true action of reason upon nature."[120]

Schleiermacher expanded upon this point at length in his 1825 Academy lecture, "Über den Unterschied zwischen Naturgesetz und Sittengesetz" ("On the Difference between Natural Law and Ethical Law").[121] Schleiermacher's target in the address was the widely held view that "the concept 'law' in the expression 'natural law' means something different and therefore is not the same as in the expression 'moral law,' and the influence which this has had on the whole formation of *Sittenlehre* since Kant and Fichte."[122] According to the commonplace view, according to Schleiermacher, "natural law is supposed to contain a general expression of something that in and through nature actually occurs; but moral law is not like this, but rather should contain an expression about something which in and through the realm of reason should take place."[123] Schleiermacher's objections to the idea that moral laws do not describe how reason actually functions but merely express an "ought" (*Soll*) echoed and expanded upon his earlier criticisms; what is of greater significance for present purposes is the alternative that he proposed.

In preparation for presenting an account of moral law that in his view stood in the correct relation to natural law, Schleiermacher resisted the restriction of the term *natural law* to the sort of statements "which [refer] to the movements of corporeal bodies, and which expresses the relationships of the elementary forces of nature and fundamental elements (*Urstoffe*)."[124] Because statements of this sort are subject to continual revision as the sciences push further and further into the realm of fundamental substances and powers, prior to the complete success of this endeavor no such statement could be taken for a natural law with confidence—in his words, "we would only have found a law which would be a perfect expression of being when we could reduce the entire universe to a formula."[125] In contrast to this understanding, Schleiermacher argued for a view of natural laws as basically statements that describe the behavior of entities according to their natural kinds:

> That is, all species-concepts of the different forms of individual life are true natural laws. For living beings, vegetation included, arise and persist in activities which always develop themselves in the same way; so true species-concepts should be the complete expression of everything which constitutes a particular life-form in itself and in its difference from other related [life-forms], and indeed so that in their interconnection, which we are always in the process of comprehending more completely, they express the natural law of individual life across our entire world-body.[126]

Natural laws in this sense, then, are statements that describe the characteristic ways in which both inanimate and animate objects, or "a system of functions in their temporal development," behave.[127] Besides enjoying the advantage of a certain amount of independence from the underlying laws—in that descriptions of the characteristic ways in which plants grow and reproduce, for example, will not necessarily be affected by alterations in the statements of the laws that govern their fundamental material constituents—this conception offered Schleiermacher a "natural" analog to the prescriptive force of moral law. The germ of the analogy that Schleiermacher deployed in the address lies in the fact that statements of the ways living organisms *characteristically* behave do not, by themselves, suffice to explain every aspect of their actual behavior:

> Does an "ought" attach to this law? We are obligated to assent to this inasmuch as we establish a law for a particular realm without including in this postulate [the idea] that everything occurs purely and completely according to the law. For the occurrence of deformations (*Mißgeburten*) as a deviation of the process of development, and the occurrence of diseases as a deviation in the process of some life-function, we do not incorporate into the law itself; and these conditions relate to the natural law, in whose realm they occur, just as the unethical and lawless relates to ethical law.[128]

In other words, natural laws of the sort Schleiermacher proposed describe paradigmatic or ideal forms of development and behavior, and statements of this sort enjoy a certain flexibility. The existence of cases that deviate from statements about the characteristic behaviors of vegetable species, for instance, do not force the revision of those statements if these deviations can be accounted for by the admission of external factors. Natural laws in this sense are thus *ceteris paribus* statements: They describe how entities behave not in absolute terms but in the absence of interference from other factors.

Schleiermacher's preference was to diagnose the phenomenon of deviation from expected paths of development as the result of the "insufficient power" of the principles described by higher-level laws over those described by lower-level laws. The clearest expression of this principle is found in the closing pages of the address, where he sketched a view of the natural order premised on this understanding of natural law, which can be extended to intellectual processes as well. This section of the treatise is too lengthy to reproduce in full, but since the basic point is that the laws that describe the vegetable, animal, and intellectual stages of development of the world operate in the same ways, a partial citation will serve:

> Let us assume the elementary forces and processes and the earthly body in its rest (*Ruhe*), contingent upon the separation of the solid and the fluid; and then we can then rightfully say, at least hypothetically (and nothing more is necessary here) that with vegetation a new principle arises, namely the vivification of a species (*specifische Belebung*) in the life of the earth, a principle which, appearing in its multiplicity of forms and gradations, subordinates within its scope the chemical process as well as the formation (*Gestaltung*) given with the development (*Bildung*) of the earth, and fixes both in an individual way. And if we further ask whereupon that is founded which must be regarded within this realm as deformation or disease, which certainly here can almost always be very easily traced back to a lack or surplus, that is to a quantitative disproportion, so we will only be able to answer: not in the new principle in and for itself (for the concept of vegetation is the pure and complete expression of the pure effectiveness of this) but rather in a lack of force (*Gewalt*) of the new principle over the chemical process and the mechanical formation.[129]

Schleiermacher's discussion of "animalization" follows the same pattern: The natural laws covering animal life are statements that describe a particular principle at work within the natural order, which when sufficiently powerful incorporates and subordinates to itself lower forms and powers, and deviations from "paradigms of animality" are to be accounted for by the "weakness" of the animal principle in particular cases in relation to other factors. The final stage of the argument concerns characteristically human activity:

> And now we can finish off this progression by saying that with the intellectual process there emerges again a new principle in the life of

the earth (although we do not need to claim that it is the final one), which however does not appear in a variety of species and kinds, but rather in a variety of individuals of a single species.... And the law which must be established here anew, so that it fully characterizes the entire effectiveness of intelligence, will that be anything other than ethical law? And the new deviations...will they be anything other than that which we call evil (*böse*) and unethical?[130]

Like "counsels of prudence," then, Schleiermacher's moral laws do not by themselves suffice to explain why human beings act as they do in particular cases. However, in sharp contrast to Kantian or Fichtean ethics, Schleiermacher took moral laws to be principles that do in fact explain human behavior when the contributions of lower-level processes are taken into account. To illustrate the sense in which moral laws describe the activity of rational beings, Schleiermacher offered a description of the natural order as governed by an ascending series of developmental stages.[131] According to this hypothesis, reason constitutes one of the forces operating within human existence, and human behavior is ultimately determined by the interplay of reason with lower principles such as the "mechanical" behavior of matter and those forces proper to animal nature. Moral laws, then, describe the activity of reason just as natural laws describe these other domains of existence.[132]

At the beginning of the chapter, we encountered Neander's observation that Schleiermacher's determinism makes evil necessary. We are now in a position to understand Schleiermacher's diagnosis of evil as something that human beings are not free, in an incompatibilist sense, to avoid. An incompatibilism such as Kant's understands evil as possible only in virtue of a human ability to autonomously decide whether to act in accordance with the moral law or otherwise, and Kant famously accounted for the prevalence of evil in observable human behavior by positing a radical "propensity for evil" that, however, did not impinge upon transcendental freedom.[133] In contrast, Schleiermacher understood evil as the spiritual analog of deformation or disease: the failure of an organism to realize a particular paradigm resulting from weakness of the forces that aim at its realization in proportion to lower forces. The remarks on evil in the academy address precisely parallel the discussion in *The Christian Faith* of sin as "a restriction of the determining power of the spirit caused by the independence of the sensuous function."[134] Indeed, Schleiermacher's introduction of the subject of sin in his dogmatics combines theological and philosophical renditions of the notion that evil is a matter of necessity, placing the latter version of the idea within the larger framework of the former: "[T]he turning of men away from God must certainly have been no less ordained by God [than anything else]; for of course man is posited within the natural order even in the state of sin, and it is only in accordance with his place in this order...that sin can develop itself within him."[135] Conjoining the heritages of both the Calvinist theological and the Enlightenment philosophical traditions, Schleiermacher thus understood evil in both its theological and philosophical variants (sin and the "unethical," respectively) as just as much of a result of the interplay of forces within the natural order and thus just as unavoidable a part of that order as any other case of deformation or arrested development.

Schleiermacher's claims regarding the necessity of evil, then, are fully in continuity with the understanding of human activity that he articulated in the Academy address. Furthermore, this understanding in turn displays both his lifelong commitment to the "doctrine of necessity" and his reflections on the consequences of this commitment for understanding the relationship of human activity to the overall natural order. From "On Human Freedom" on, Schleiermacher regarded free human activity as something ultimately determined by the overall "nature-system," and during his mature period he was explicitly committed to an understanding of ethics as a science that aims at uncovering the laws that govern the activity of mind or soul in the same sense in which the laws of physics describe the behavior of matter.

1.5 Conclusion: A Parameter for Understanding "Religion"

If the arguments of this chapter are correct, one statement of considerable import can be advanced with confidence concerning the relationship of religion to the natural order on Schleiermacher's understanding. Absent the impingement upon that order from outside (i.e., supernatural interference, to be discussed in chapter 4), all of the elements that make up the complex phenomenon known as "religion" will be results of the operation of causes within the nature system no less than any other human cultural production and indeed no less than any other temporal phenomenon. This is not a conclusion that we are obligated to impose upon Schleiermacher's writings on religion by virtue of the fact that it is entailed by one of his philosophical commitments; as I argue in succeeding chapters, it is a result that he acknowledged at several crucial points in his discussions of religion and one that he expressed in a particularly clear form in *The Christian Faith*. Indeed, I eventually argue that one of the things Schleiermacher hoped his mature dogmatics would accomplish would be to accustom a broad reading public of Christians to thinking of their own religion in precisely these terms.

2

Religion in Outline

Do not disregard how religion everywhere bears in itself the traces of the culture of every age, of the history of every human type...do not overlook how it has often been stunted in its growth because one did not allow it room to exercise its powers, how it has often lamentably perished in the first days of childhood, owing to bad treatment and apathy.

—Schleiermacher, *On Religion*

My reconstruction begins, properly speaking, with an examination of the *structure* of "religion" as Schleiermacher understood it. As mentioned in the introduction, I intend my reconstruction as a challenge to the "standard interpretation," according to which religion for Schleiermacher can be summarized by phrases such as "a sense and taste for the infinite," "intuition of the universe," and a "feeling of absolute dependence." One of my aims in this chapter is to return these phrases to their proper theoretical context by making it clear that, as Schleiermacher used the term, "religion" is more than simply an "essence," and thus that, rather than sufficing as definitions of religion, these phrases pertain to one component of its definition.

In this chapter I focus on Schleiermacher's canonical texts, the *Speeches on Religion*, and the second edition of *The Christian Faith* (concentrating, as is now standard practice, on the first edition of the former and the second edition of the latter). In restricting myself largely to these texts I make two points. The first is that while a full understanding of Schleiermacher's account of religion requires reference to his lesser-known works at certain points (for example, in connection with the question of determinism), all that is required to reveal the inadequacy of the standard interpretation is careful attention to the very texts to which that interpretation typically refers (bearing in mind the significant change wrought on the interpretive landscape, for readers of English, by the appearance of Crouter's translation of the first edition of the *Speeches* in 1988). The second point is that, while there are significant differences between the discussions of religion in Schleiermacher's early and late work, the general structure of the phenomenon remains unchanged, and thus it is legitimate to speak of "Schleiermacher's account of religion" in the singular in spite of the fact that that account witnessed significant development over the course of his lifetime.

2.1 The "Religion" of the *Speeches on Religion*

2.1.1 *The Varieties and Unity of "Religion"*

The first obstacle any attempt to extract a "theory of religion" from the *Speeches* encounters is the fact that in this text Schleiermacher attached the terms "religion" and "religious" to a bewildering variety of phenomena. As Siefert noted, "religiosity, belief, piety, religious life, religious consciousness, the religious person, the religious precinct of *humanitas* as well as the religious realm of the spiritual world and the appearance of religion in history ('positive religion')—all these the speaker names with one and the same term: Religion. One must keep this unique circumstance in view if one wants to pursue the question of what 'religion' means in the *Speeches*."[1] Adopting the standard interpretation is one strategy for coping with this state of affairs, for this interpretation focuses on that part of the text wherein claims that contain the phrase "religion is" appear with the greatest frequency (the second speech).[2] A remark from Terrence Tice constitutes the most incisive commentary on this practice that I have encountered: In expositing Schleiermacher on the subject of religion "it has usually been thought sufficient to refer to his convincingly carving out a special domain for religion.... [A]n astoundingly large proportion of the extensive literature on his conception of religion virtually ignores the final three chapters" of the *Speeches*.[3]

Schleiermacher's profligate use of the term can, however, be treated not as a problem but as an indication of the territory covered by his broadest conception of religion. My procedure involves imposing an initial measure of order on the text by sorting Schleiermacher's various usages of "religion" and "religious" into a finite number of categories and then discussing the relationships among these. In what follows I identify three broad senses in which the term *religion* and its cognates are used, arranged in order of increasing breadth.[4] I then argue that these three senses stand in well-defined relationships to each other and that the conception that incorporates them in their interconnection deserves to be understood as the account of religion presented in the *Speeches*.

In its *first* sense, "religion" refers to religion's "essence," a term that I leave undefined for the moment. Compare the following passages from the second speech:

> Religion's essence is neither thinking nor acting, but intuition and feeling.

> Thus religion maintains its own sphere and its own character only by completely removing itself from the sphere and character of speculation as well as from that of praxis.

> Intuition is and always remains something individual, set apart, the immediate perception, nothing more.... The same is true of religion: it stops with the immediate experiences of the existence and action of the universe, with the individual intuitions and feelings...it knows nothing about derivation and connection, for among all things religion can encounter, that is what its nature most opposes.[5]

The first of these passages is a straightforward claim about religion's essence: In the first edition of the *Speeches*, this essence is a matter of "intuitions of the universe" and the feelings that accompany them. The other two passages identify as "religion" essentially the same territory: a territory separated from "speculation and praxis" (i.e., metaphysics and morals) and unconcerned with any kind of development (reflective or otherwise) of that which constitutes religion's essence. The first type of usage of "religion" thus restricts its range to the point where it extends no further than the boundaries of religion's essence. As mentioned earlier, the standard interpretation of Schleiermacher is typically grounded in passages of this sort,[6] and indeed, taken at face value, the passages cited earlier state that religion can never extend into the domain of speculation or activity and that, once one goes beyond immediate experience, one has thereby left religion behind.

In its *second* sense "religion" refers to something broader than "intuitions and feelings," and "religious" can be predicated of activities, artifacts, or states of affairs. Consider, for example, the following passages:

> Thus it was religion when the ancients, annihilating the limitations of time and space, regarded every unique type of life throughout the whole world as the work and reign of an omnipotent being. They had intuited a unique mode of acting of the universe in its unity and had designated this intuition accordingly. It was religion when, for every helpful event whereby the eternal laws of the world were illuminatingly revealed through contingency, they gave the god to

whom it belonged his own name and built its own temple to it.... But
when they keep a wondrous chronicle of the descent of these gods or
when a later faith trotted out for us a long series of emanations and
procreations, that is empty mythology.

Once there is religion, it must necessarily also be social. That not
only lies in human nature but also is preeminently in that of religion.

You can imagine, therefore, how much holier still must be the
moment for [religious people] in which this infinite intuition was
first established in the world as foundation and focal point of a
unique religion since the whole development of this religion in all
generations and individuals is just as historically tied to this moment.
Yet this whole of religion and the religious culture of a great mass of
humanity is something infinitely greater than their own religious life
and the small fragment of this religion they personally exhibit.[7]

Each of these passages speaks, in a different way, of religion as something
that extends beyond religion's essence. The first passage, from the second
speech, designates activities such as the association of natural events with super-
human agency, the naming of gods, and the building of temples as part of religion. The second, from the fourth speech, asserts that it is in accordance with
the nature of religion that it be a social affair—indeed, that religion is *necessarily*
social. The third, from the final speech, is part of Schleiermacher's description
of "positive religions" as phenomena that are not simply identical with one or
any number of religious intuitions but are "founded in and focused on" a particular religious intuition and are extended across time and between persons.

The *third* sense of "religion" is the broadest. In this sense religion also
encompasses things like doctrines, activities, and social organizations.
However, unlike religion in the second sense, Schleiermacher does not necessarily consider this type of religion to be praiseworthy. Rather, he tends to portray religion in this sense as an imperfect phenomenon, one in which the pure
and the impure are mixed. The paradigmatic occurrences of this usage are
found, appropriately enough, in the fifth speech, where Schleiermacher turns
to a discussion of positive religion and discusses particular religious traditions.
Here are some examples:

But now I have a new business to carry out and a new opposition to
vanquish.... I want to show you religion as it has divested itself of its
infinity and appeared, often in paltry form, among human beings; in
the religions, you are to discover religion; in what stands before you
as earthly and impure, you are to seek out the individual features of
the same heavenly beauty whose form I have tried to reproduce.

Where have I seen all these forms? In the actual realm of religion (*Gebiet der Religion*), in its particular forms, in the positive religions that you decry as merely negative, among the heroes and martyrs of a specific faith, among the enthusiasts of specific feelings, among the worshipers of a specific light and individual revelations; there I shall show them to you at all times and among all peoples.

Do not disregard how religion everywhere bears in itself the traces of the culture of every age, of the history of every human type...do not overlook how it has often been stunted in its growth because one did not allow it room to exercise its powers, how it has often lamentably perished in the first days of childhood, owing to bad treatment and apathy.[8]

In using "religion" in this third way Schleiermacher appears to be approximating the initial understanding of his audience: This sense encompasses the actually existing complex of beliefs, practices, and artifacts that make up "what is usually called religion." The determinate, historically specific religious traditions discussed in the fifth speech are examples of this type.

Observing a distinction between these three senses of the term "religion" illuminates the structure of Schleiermacher's extended argument with religion's "cultured despisers," which extends across all five of the speeches. After presenting his conception of religion's essence and discussing the way religion develops individually and socially, in the fifth speech Schleiermacher returned to a discussion of religion as it actually exists and can be observed by the religious and the nonreligious alike. In this final speech the notion that religion has multiple senses is put to strategic use: Schleiermacher's intention was to change the way his audience regarded the actual, historical examples of religion with which they were familiar. In writing "in the religions, you are to discover religion," Schleiermacher was not playing games with words. Rather, this passage moves from the third to the second senses of the religion and argues that the critical eye should be able to discern "within" actually existing religion traces of a purer and better form of religion.

Schleiermacher's talk of one type of religion existing within another brings us to the next step of my argument. If there were no robust connection between the three senses of religion described earlier, then much could be said in favor of isolating one of Schleiermacher's categories for examination—say, religion as it applies to religion's essence—and setting the other two aside as peripheral. However, in fact, a pattern extends across the three categories and describes the relationship of each sense of religion to the other. It turns out that Schleiermacher's conception of religion in the *Speeches* has a concentric structure in two distinct senses. The key for understanding both types of concentricity governing the account of religion in the *Speeches* lies with the notion of religion's essence.

2.1.2 Essence

In discussing the notion of an essence as it figures in Schleiermacher's work, we need to distinguish the question of the content or constitution of religion's essence from the functional or structural role it plays within his overall account of religion. It is the second of these topics that is of primary importance at present. For not only has the notion of an essence almost entirely vanished from the literature on the methodology of the study of religion—even from works that acknowledge the importance of a grasp of the field's history—but such mentions of the term that do occur in the literature frequently display a truncated understanding, at best, of the role this term actually played in the nineteenth-century literature.[9] Contemporary criticisms of the project of identifying the essence of religion frequently reflect familiarity with only a very general notion of essentialism and thus miss the specificity of the notion in the historical literature.[10]

There is a respect in which talk of essentialism as a general, undifferentiated phenomenon makes sense. Recent research in cognitive development by Susan Gelman suggests that the common scholarly practice of discussing essentialism as a more or less intuitive notion may be a reflection of the naturalness of essentialist thinking.[11] Gelman argues that an essentialism with three basic components—"a belief that certain categories are natural kinds, a belief that some unobservable property causes observable similarities shared by members of a category, and a belief that everyday words reflect the real-world structure of categories"[12]—represents an early cognitive bias among human beings in the sense that these beliefs come to inform the noetic activities of young children as a result of normal patterns of development. Essentialism in Gelman's view is not a result of enculturation and thus is not a historical accident; rather, the convergence of several distinct cognitive capacities yields the habit of mind that treats natural kinds and social kinds (but not artifacts) as categories defined by essences.[13] Gelman's hypothesis makes sense of the frequent association found in the literature between essentialism and the commonsense view of natural and social kinds; if she is correct, essentialism in this generic sense is a human universal, if a defeasible one.[14] If this is indeed the case, then it seems reasonable to me to regard this generic essentialism as the operative notion in literature that uses the term without elaboration.

However, where essentialism has been taken seriously as a strategy for picking out the identities of things, more specific claims about the natures of essences and their role in the determination of identity have emerged. Discussions of essentialism in analytic philosophy, for example (where this notion is often considered viable or at least interesting), observe several different kinds of distinctions among essentialist positions. Historically, the essentialism of Aristotle constitutes a tradition distinct from that of Locke, with the former describing essences as complex properties of things that serve both an explanatory and a classificatory role and the latter distinguishing *real* essences, understood as "the very being of any thing, whereby it is, what it is" from *nominal* essences, understood as sortal ideas (ideas, that is, by virtue of which we sort things into groups).[15] Contemporary literature adds to these historical descriptions the proposals that essences be understood as the collection of those properties that a thing of a particular kind cannot possibly exist without, as well as homeostatic cluster theories, which regard natural kinds as defined by properties that the members of a kind possess in a statistically high proportion but which need not be exemplified by every member of that kind.

If it is initially coherent to speak of essentialism as a monolithic phenomenon, then, in practice there is not one essentialism but many. It follows from this, I suggest, that no serious engagement with a specific essentialist proposal can take place entirely at the highest level of generality.

To understand the role that the notion of an essence plays in Schleiermacher's account of religion, we must distinguish his use of this idea from both the generic essentialism described by Gelman and the essentialisms of analytic philosophy. What unifies these various ways of talking about essences is the fact that all of them are concerned with *objects*—whether these be material objects in general, living material objects in their natural kinds, or human beings in their socially constructed kinds (race, gender, class, and so on). These forms of essentialism thus speak most naturally about essences as *properties* or collections of properties and understand the question of whether an individual thing belongs to a natural or social kind as settled by the properties that thing exemplifies or possesses.[16] It is for this reason that a statement of the components of the essence of a kind can be considered equivalent to a *definition* of that kind.

Schleiermacher's talk of essences is best understood, I suggest, as the transposition of the basic habit of mind that characterizes essentialism from the domain of objects to the domain of history. His investigations concerned not a collection of objects but a temporally extended and historically variable phenomenon containing not only objects but also practices, beliefs, attitudes, and artifacts. The most important ramification of this difference has to do with understanding the role that the notion of an essence plays in identifying the extension of the term "religion." It cannot be said that for Schleiermacher religion's essence consists of one or more properties the possession of which determines, even only probabilistically, the membership of particular cases within the category "religion"; for where the question concerns not objects but practices or attitudes, the model of property possession is inapposite. In effect, the notion that a phenomenon like religion might have an essence required a novel account of the notion of essence itself and also of the mode of its presence within the phenomenon whose identity it secures, and it is this aspect of Schleiermacher's writings on religion that in my judgment is of greatest interest for understanding his account in historical perspective.

The question of how an essence could play a role in relation to a phenomenon like religion analogous to the role that notion plays in relation to natural and social phenomena was one of the issues that animated critical reflection on the methodology of the study of religion during the early decades of its development.[17] A crucial treatise on the topic from the first decades of the twentieth century—Ernst Troeltsch's "What Does the 'Essence of Christianity' Mean?"—focused on precisely this problem and pointed to a central feature that distinguishes the notion of essence as Schleiermacher used it from essentialism about objects.[18]

After a century of mixed fortunes, the notion of an essence of religion had recently been prominently on display in Adolf von Harnack's wildly popular *Das Wesen des Christentums*, and while Harnack represented Troeltsch's proximate partner in conversation, it is clear from the essay that he regarded the prominence of the notion in the study of religion to be a component of Schleiermacher's legacy. Troeltsch classified the search for the essence of a religion as a component of the historical study of religion, and a fundamental problem of the essay has to do with the method by which claims about the essence of a religion are to be derived. Troeltsch described the essence of a religion as in the first instance an *abstraction* from the observed particulars of religion: To identify the essence of a religion is "[t]o grasp the decisive and driving religious idea and power out of this complex whole,"[19] to distill out of a mass of historical data that which accounts for the unity of the phenomenon in question:

> The "essence" of such a complex is the abstract idea, the abstraction peculiar to history, by means of which the whole known and precisely researched context of related formations is understood in terms of the basic driving and developing idea. The essence can be found in *a broad view over the totality of all the manifestations which are related to this idea,* and its discovery demands the exercise of historical abstraction, *the art of seeing the whole, both the details and the fullness of the various methodically studied materials, with a synoptic vision.*[20]

The problem, in short, is that identifying the essence, the idea that represents the driving force, of a phenomenon as massively multiform as Christianity depends on an ability to see "within" the variety of the observed instances a principle of unity that at the same time is responsive to the entire sweep of the phenomenon. That there is more art than science to this endeavor was one of Troeltsch's first points. The sheer mass of the relevant data is one difficulty. However, more important—indeed, crucially important for my purposes—is

Troeltsch's observation that it cannot be assumed that this essence is in fact represented in all instances of the religion in question:

> Reality nowhere displays the essence as the absolutely clear, complete and convincing result of the process. It displays instead great, divided churches, in none of which the essence can be perceived to be realized, and which do not even realize the essence all together. It displays moreover all kinds of sects and groups and also completely individual conceptions of Christianity. In all these is to be found not merely the imperfection of an essence which is not yet fully clear about itself, but at the same time, sometimes more and sometimes less, a variety of positive perversions and distortions of the essence.[21]

Troeltsch here attributed to the nineteenth-century tradition the position that the essence of Christianity may not in fact be in evidence in all instances of the Christian religion: There may be instances where in place of this essence there is only a "perversion or distortion" of it. It might seem paradoxical to claim as the essence of a phenomenon something that, in the end, not all instances of that phenomenon possess, but I take Troeltsch to be entirely correct in this attribution. What distinguishes nineteenth-century essentialism about religion from a generic essentialism about objects—and thus a point that is crucial for my reconstruction—flows directly from this observation. "With respect to all of these the conception of the essence is at the same time a criticism. It is *not merely an abstraction from the manifestations, but at the same time a criticism of the manifestations*, and this criticism is *not merely an evaluation of that which is not yet complete in terms of the driving ideal, but a discrimination between that which corresponds to the essence and that which is contrary to it.*"[22]

The essence of a religion, in other words, is not simply a description of those characteristics that all and only examples of the phenomenon possess. It is from the first a principle of criticism, a criterion relative to which claims can be advanced about what the religion in question *should* be. As Troeltsch puts it, "a comprehensive view of the essence is only sought at all in order to make possible an evaluation of what is essential, on the basis of which the inessential can be ignored and that which is contrary to the essence can be condemned."[23]

2.1.2.1 ESSENCE AND THE IDENTIFICATION OF RELIGION. Troeltsch's observation that the essence of religion is not merely a descriptive principle but also a critical one provides the key for understanding the relationship among the three senses of religion outlined earlier and so for deriving a unified sketch of an account of religion from Schleiermacher's *Speeches*.

In brief, "religion" in both the second and third senses of the term is defined by a relationship to "religion" in the first sense—by a relationship, in other words, to religion's essence. However, the relationship in question is not a matter of the exemplification of properties; rather, the relationship that examples of religion bear to the essence of religion is a matter of *location along a developmental path*. "Religion" in its second sense is defined by what falls along an *appropriate developmental path* out of this essence and thus stands in a *fitting* relationship to religion's essence. The third sense of "religion" extends to elements that stand in what can be described as a *distorted* or *degenerate* relationship to religion's essence in the sense that they represent a *departure* from the appropriate developmental path that defines "religion" in its second sense.

In what follows, I use the terms *essence of religion, ideal religion*, and *actual religion* as labels for the three senses of "religion" I have distinguished within the *Speeches*. Thus, if the essence of religion is a matter of intuitions and feelings of the universe, "ideal religion" refers to that collection of activities and artifacts that are related in a fitting way to this essence, and "actual religion" refers to the forms of religion observable within history, which for Schleiermacher represented a mixture of elements that have resulted from an appropriate developmental path out of religion's essence with elements that represent a departure from that path. I take Schleiermacher's occasional references to "the realm of religion" (*die Gebiet der Religion*) to be coextensive with what I call "actual religion": The "realm of religion" is thus not restricted to an ideal conception but contains "diseased" or degenerate conditions of religion as well.

The unity of the category of "religion," then, lies in the fact that for each of the senses enumerated above, religion's essence is the criterion on the basis of which religion is identified—not in the sense that all examples of religion possess some or all of those properties that constitute religion's essence but in the sense that in order to qualify as part of religion, a phenomenon must be *connected to* religion's essence as either an appropriate development or a degeneration.[24] It is in virtue of the twofold relationship in which religion's essence stands to ideal and actual religion that a description of a religion's essence represents not a definition but only the beginnings of one. Schleiermacher grounded his discussion of religion on the conviction that it should be possible, once one understands what the essence of religion is, to discern what flows appropriately or naturally from this essence and also to identify cases where this natural path of development has been curtailed or corrupted. What defines religion, in other words, is ultimately not a list of properties but a "formula" or principle according to which particular phenomena can be classified as part of religion: "I entreat you to become familiar with this concept: intuition of the universe. It is the hinge of my whole speech; it is the highest and most universal formula on the basis of which you should be able to find every place in religion, from which you may determine its essence and its limits (*Gränzen*)."[25]

I understand the formula to which this passage refers roughly as follows: Whatever is related to "intuition of the universe" (that is, to religion's essence) in the proper way is part of "ideal religion"; whatever constitutes a deformation or distortion of this essence still belongs to the "realm of religion"; whatever is not at all related to this essence is not at all part of religion.

As we move to a closer examination of "religion" in the second and third senses, the terms I use to characterize the various kinds of relationship to its essence are in some cases deliberately vague. Some clarity can be drawn from specific examples that Schleiermacher used to illustrate the distinction between healthy and degenerate forms of religion. However, for the most part he seems to have thought that he could count on his readers to discern more or less intuitively what follows appropriately from or corresponds appropriately to religion's essence.

2.1.3 Ideal Religion

A central concern of the *Speeches* is to describe what religion *should* be or, to put it differently, what religion *would* be if it were to faithfully reflect the character of its essence. By using the term "ideal religion" to indicate this material, I mean to signal the fact that while in some places Schleiermacher appeared to have historical examples (or at least historical types) in mind, for the most part his examples of ideal religion are something like thought experiments or counterfactual constructions whose characteristics are deduced from his claims about religion's essence rather than from instances of actual religion.

How, then, are these examples of ideal religion constructed? I have suggested that the formula for ideal religion is "whatever stands in the right sort of relationship to or follows the appropriate developmental path from religion's essence," but what sorts of relationships are the right ones, and what is the appropriate developmental path? Here, as was the case with Schleiermacher's various uses of "religion," the best way to proceed is to try to identify patterns among the examples Schleiermacher offered of what religion looks like when it is related to its essence in the correct way.

The broadest division we can mark in these examples is between *interior* and *exterior* religion. Some of the things that are related appropriately to religion's essence are, for lack of a better term, mental activities or states; others are interpersonal relationships, activities, or artifacts. Discerning what makes for *interior* ideal religion involves a fair amount of reconstructive guesswork, and it is difficult in the end to advance a single principle that accounts for all of the examples Schleiermacher offered. However, the principle that explains what makes for *exterior* ideal religion is one of the most clearly delineated in the whole of the *Speeches* and in fact is probably the most important structural feature of Schleiermacher's understanding of religion across all of his texts.

2.1.3.1 INTERIOR IDEAL RELIGION.   Consider the following passages:

> [T]o accept everything individual as part of the whole and everything limited as a representation of the infinite is religion. But whatever would go beyond that and penetrate deeper into the nature and

substance of the whole is no longer religion, and will, if it still wants to be regarded as such, inevitably sink back into empty mythology.

To love the world spirit and joyfully observe its work is the goal of our religion, and in love there is no fear.

It is irreligious to hold that humanity's genius prepares vessels of honor and vessels of dishonor; you must consider nothing individually, but rejoice over each in the place where it stands.

Humanity is only a middle term between the individual and the One, a resting place on the way to the infinite.... All religion strives after such an intimation (*Ahndung*) of something outside and above humanity in order to be seized by the common and higher elements in both.[26]

Here Schleiermacher described some interior, mental activities as part of religion: activities such as *viewing* the world in particular ways, *loving* certain aspects of the world, or *striving* after certain experiences. How these activities flow naturally from religion's essence is not stated explicitly, but in some cases context makes the connection fairly clear.

In the first edition of the *Speeches* Schleiermacher's description of the content of religion's essence is grounded in the notion of an "intuition of the universe." This is a view or an impression of some overarching, structural feature of the world as a whole or of all that exists; to have an intuition of the universe is to have a sense of its overall character.[27] The activities described in the passages just cited are related in a variety of more or less intuitive ways to this notion. The idea of "accepting everything individual as part of the whole and everything limited as a representation of the infinite" suggests either a kind of apperceptive *habitus* that provides fertile ground for the having of intuitions of the universe or an awareness of the relatedness of all things that is stimulated by the impact of one or more such intuitions. Either way, there is a kind of natural fit between the notion of an intuition of the universe and a general disposition to see all individual things as part of a larger whole, which disposition comes to expression repeatedly throughout the second speech. The person who has "intuitions of the universe" (and, plausibly, who is reflectively aware of these) will see everything as "holy and valuable" by virtue of its connection to the greater whole; will welcome the discovery of the laws governing the workings of the universe, as this contributes to the sense that the universe is ultimately an ordered totality; and will particularly value interpersonal relationships and knowledge of humanity as resources for understanding the overall character of the universe.[28] Such a person will also come to take a dim view of valorizations of human individuality and autonomy and may even feel an affinity for the doctrine of necessity. "See how attraction and repulsion determine everything and are uninterruptedly active everywhere, how all diversity and all opposition are only apparent and relative, and all individuality is merely an empty name," Schleiermacher admonished his readers, advocating an attitude that extends even to the self: "[S]trive here already to annihilate your individuality and to live in the one and all."[29] What it is to be religious in this ideal and interior sense, then, is a matter of allowing one's view of the world and its contents to be informed by a sense of the interrelatedness of all things and colored by the particular intuitions of the universe with which one is familiar.

In the first edition of the *Speeches* Schleiermacher linked intuition with feeling (*Gefühl*) in such a way that the feelings that attach to particular religious intuitions are also plausibly part of religion's essence.[30] However, some of the feelings that he described have a different character: They seem to represent the results of the interaction of religion's essence with a person's particular circumstances. If this is the case, then interior ideal religion will also encompass feelings that are not properly speaking part of religion's essence but rather represent a development of that essence within the life of the individual.

The most prominent examples of feelings that fall into this category are attitudes toward one's fellow human beings. For example, because intuitions of the universe are susceptible of an infinite variety of juxtapositions and subordinations, those who understand religion properly will feel a marked tolerance for someone who entertains different intuitions and arranges them differently; these people will naturally feel "reverence in the face of the eternal and invisible" and will embrace their fellow human beings "with heartfelt love and affection without any distinction of disposition and spiritual power."[31] They will also feel a profound compassion for the sufferings of others and "remorse over everything in us that is hostile to the genius of humanity."[32] The first edition's definition of *piety*, a crucial term in later editions and in *The Christian Faith*, follows on these remarks. "All these feelings are religion," Schleiermacher stated, "and likewise all others in which the universe is one pole and your own self is somehow the other pole between which consciousness hovers. The ancients knew this. They called all these feelings 'piety' and referred them immediately to religion, considering them its noblest part."[33]

There are also suggestions in the second speech that interior ideal religion is not a purely passive affair but that "religious intuitions and feelings" properly motivate activities. Early on in his discussion of religious feeling, Schleiermacher remarked, "This is how far the realm of religion concerns us in this respect: its feelings are supposed to possess us, and we should *express, maintain,* and *portray* them" (emphasis added).[34] Each of these three terms refers not simply to the possessing of pious feelings but also to an action that the person who possesses them is supposed to perform. While "expressing" and "portraying" (*aussprechen* and *darstellen*) belong to the realm of exterior activity and so will be discussed in the next section, "maintaining" (*festhalten*) pious feelings can plausibly be thought of as an interior affair.

All in all, then, interior ideal religion seems to involve, at its core, the possession of religious intuitions and feelings and, surrounding this, a penumbra of other mental states and activities that stem in certain appropriate sorts of ways from this essence and in which its content is involved.

2.1.3.2 EXTERIOR IDEAL RELIGION. In contrast to the ambiguity of what constitutes interior ideal religion, the principle that accounts for Schleiermacher's understanding of exterior ideal religion is readily identifiable. What makes certain kinds of activities and states of affairs outside the realm of the human mind religious is that they are part of the process whereby *religion's essence and the "interior religion" that develops out of this is transmitted between persons.* As Rendtorff noted, the idea of "religious communication" is central to Schleiermacher's thinking concerning what it is to be religious in a concrete sense; it forms the basis of his claim in the fourth speech that religion is "necessarily social" and also grounds the continuity of particular religious traditions (a theme emphasized more in Schleiermacher's later writings). The double-sided nature of communication in general (for example, of speaking and hearing) is reflected in the two needs that Schleiermacher described in his discussions of distinctively religious communication: The person who has interior religion needs to *express* it and also needs to receive the *impression* of the religion of others.

In unpacking his claim that religion is necessarily social at the beginning of the fourth speech, Schleiermacher offered the following:

> You must admit that it is highly unnatural for a person to want to
> lock up in himself what he has created and worked out. In the
> continuous reciprocity, which is not only practical but intellectual, in
> which he stands with the rest of his species, he is supposed to
> express and communicate all that is within him. The more
> passionately something moves him, and the more intimately it
> penetrates his being, the stronger is the urge also to glimpse its
> power outside himself in others, in order to prove to himself that he
> has encountered nothing other than what is human.... Therefore, we
> see that even from childhood on, man is primarily concerned to
> communicate these intuitions and feelings.[35]

Here Schleiermacher advanced a general claim about the sociable nature of human beings: that we naturally desire to reflect upon those experiences that move us strongly by comparing our experiences with those of others. We come to understand ourselves and our humanity, in other words, not only through pure introspection but also through communication. Interior religion's need to find expression is grounded in this claim: In the realm of religion, the sharing of intuitions and feelings is aimed at saving ourselves from submission to "alien and unworthy powers."[36] Religious communication, then, is a natural result of the possession of interior religion.

However, on the other side, "[i]f, therefore, urged by his nature, religious man necessarily speaks, it is this very nature that also finds hearers for him."[37] It is also natural for individuals to be on the receiving end of religious communication. Such communication has the potential to accomplish two things, both of which can fairly obviously be classified as appropriately related to religion's essence. Proximately, such communication can accomplish the *transmission* of religious intuitions and feelings from one person to another, and ultimately such communication can "awaken" within the hearer the capacity to produce new religious intuitions and feelings.

Late in the second speech Schleiermacher offered a reinterpretation of the notion of religious *inspiration* as "merely the religious name for freedom....[E]very expression of a religious feeling that really communicates itself so that the intuition of the universe is transferred to others (*so daß auch auf andre das Anschauung des Universums übergeht*) took place upon inspiration."[38] The basic function of religious communication, then, is to make religious intuitions and feelings the object of interpersonal awareness in the interest of transmitting them from person to person. In his imaginative portrayal of the "city of God" (a notion to be explored further in the next chapter), Schleiermacher described how religious communication is supposed to proceed. The individual who is moved to speak "steps forth to present his own intuition as an object for the rest, to lead them into the region of religion where he is at home and to implant his holy feelings in them; he expresses the universe, and the community follows his inspired speech in holy silence.... Then the audible confession of the accord of his view with what is in them answers him."[39]

In other words, the constituent elements of the essence of religion—religious intuitions and feelings—are, if not a common *possession* (because, for the young Schleiermacher, the ideal religious community does not necessarily contain only one form of religion), at least commonly *available* for reflection and appropriation through the common discourse.

In this early text, an important goal of religious communication is the "awakening" of the ability to produce one's own religious intuitions and feelings. In the *Speeches* Schleiermacher distinguished sharply between those who have such an ability and those who do not. Recall that he had claimed that religion "arises of itself in every better soul": The paradigmatic example of the religious person is the "virtuoso of religion," who needs no interpersonal stimulation in order to come into possession of religious intuitions and feelings. In fact, it was his position that religious virtuosity is a rare trait and that the majority of persons come to religion through participation in religious communication. "Except for a few chosen ones," he argued in the second speech, "every person surely needs a mediator, a leader who awakens his sense for religion from its first slumber and gives him an initial direction."⁴⁰ In the third speech this principle develops into the relationship of "master and disciple" within the realm of religion, which ideally is a provisional arrangement. "He who, by expressing his own religion, has aroused it in others, no longer has it in his power to keep them for himself; their religion is also free as soon as it lives and goes its own way."⁴¹ Part of the claim that religion is necessarily social, then, stems from the fact that for all but a "chosen few," religion (even as regards its essence) is acquired socially, and this in a double sense: Religious communication not only awakens the ability to produce religious intuitions but also transmits the content of specific religious intuitions between one person and the next. Schleiermacher's understanding of religious tradition, to be explored more fully in the next chapter, is predicated on this second dynamic.

Thus far, the characteristic elements of ideal exterior religion have been presented in a fairly abstract manner as *acts of communication* and *religious community*. It is possible to say a bit more about the particular *material vehicles* of religious communication and particular *social forms* that conduce to this activity, although in the *Speeches* Schleiermacher's remarks on the second of these are more fully developed than those on the first.

The *Speeches* discuss the material vehicles of religious communication in considerably less detail than his later writings. In the second speech Schleiermacher characterized *religious concepts* as expressions of religion's essence—sometimes "free" expressions and sometimes more reflectively derived "abstract" expressions—and included under this heading a number of familiar terms from Christian theology (miracle, revelation, inspiration, divinity, and immortality). Fairly clearly, the point of this identification is that the distinctive stock of phrases and ideas of a particular religious tradition are to be understood as elements of the process of religious communication: They are vehicles by means of which religious intuitions and feelings are transmitted between persons. Schleiermacher also presented a few examples of nondiscursive religious activity as part of the process whereby religious intuitions are expressed. One is music, which he described as "speech without words" or a means of communicating "that which definite speech cannot comprehend";⁴² he also mentioned baptism, confirmation, and marriage together with some remarks on their religious significance.⁴³ It also seems to me that it would be reasonable to include the activities of the construction of temples and their dedication to particular gods, which we encountered above, as activities whose religious character lies in their functions as vehicles for the communication of religious intuitions or interior religion more generally.

In general, then, the *Speeches* explains the traditional stock of religious activities and artifacts as the material elements of the communicative process that constitutes exterior religion. What makes these distinctively religious is a relationship to the essence of religion—specifically, the fact that they represent faithful or appropriate developments of this essence, in the sense that they serve as vehicles for the transmission of interior religion between persons. I think it is also reasonable to attribute to Schleiermacher the position that *whatever* materials are used to express and thus transmit interior religion in this way would thereby be made religious—that *any* activity or artifact that serves to transmit and develop interior religion thereby becomes part of exterior religion.

Finally, in the fourth speech Schleiermacher offered a set of reflections about the way an ideal religious community is structured. Although I examine these reflections in greater detail in the next chapter, for the present a few points are directly relevant. Not all forms of community are equally conducive to religious communication. The form of religious community that corresponds most faithfully to a proper understanding of the essence of religion, Schleiermacher thought, is radically *egalitarian*. In the ideal religious community there is no distinction between clergy and laity; all are equal contributors to the process of religious communication and formation.[44] Such a community is also religiously *diverse* and religiously *tolerant*: Membership in the community is not predicated on a similarity of religious sensibility, and in fact a diversity of religious intuitions is to be welcomed as enriching the communal pool of religious resources.[45]

I suggest, then, that ideal religion in both its interior and exterior forms is a category constructed by the application of a rough formula: Whatever results appropriately or "naturally" from the essence of religion, whether in the realm of the spirit or in the interpersonal realm, is included under this heading. Two major points should be made clear at the end of this discussion. First, it is not the case that exterior religion is only an expression of interior religion: It is also the means by which interior religion is formed.[46] The relationship of exterior to interior religion is thus not one of "husk and kernel," to cite a metaphor that is sometimes taken to represent the basic thrust of religious essentialism; exterior religion is not an occlusion of interior religion but rather the means of its perpetuation and development. Second, it should be clear that there are definite limits to this category: Elements that do not flow naturally from religion's essence or that stand in some kind of distorted relationship to it will not be part of ideal religion. Consideration of this characteristic leads to our next topic.

2.1.4 Actual Religion

As stated earlier, I understand Schleiermacher's phrase "the realm of religion" to cover the entire range of that which is observable respecting religion and thus to point to a sense of "religion" distinct from the ideal forms we have examined up to this point. This category thus includes all of "what is usually thought of as religion"—and, crucially, everything on the basis of which Schleiermacher takes his "cultured despisers" to have formed their opinions about religion. In what follows I use the phrase "actual religion" to describe the contents of the "realm of religion" as Schleiermacher understood it. As my discussion in the introduction should have made clear, it is toward understanding Schleiermacher's account of actual religion that a contemporary reconstruction of his account of religion should work.

In expositing the category of ideal religion, I argue that Schleiermacher believed it was possible to imagine how certain phenomena could flow naturally or appropriately from the essence of religion. Not everything in the realm of religion has this character: Religion as it actually exists contains not only ideal religion but also what might be called *degenerate religion*, the result of the natural or ideal developmental process of religion going astray. In the *Speeches* Schleiermacher discussed two ways in which religion's natural development could be diverted or perverted: *contamination* and *dissolution*.

When an "alien element" enters and influences the religious developmental process, religion is "contaminated." Schleiermacher introduced the possibility of the contamination of religion at the beginning of the second speech in distinguishing religion's essence from metaphysics and morals; the idea recurs in the fourth speech, where the relation of religion and politics is discussed. We can see both of these cases as variations on the theme of the contamination of religion: contamination "from within" and "from without" respectively.

Recall Schleiermacher's distinction between religion and mythology in the second speech, which he based on the distinctness of religion's essence from metaphysics. "To present all events in the world as the actions of a god is religion; it expresses its connection to an infinite totality, but while brooding over the existence of this god before the world and outside the world may be good and necessary in metaphysics, in religion even that becomes only empty mythology, a further development of that which is only the means of portrayal as if it were the essential itself, a complete departure from its characteristic ground."[47]

"Empty mythology" represents a contamination of ideal religion by a "metaphysical interest"—an interest, that is, in knowledge about the world and about what lies behind the world.[48] What makes this a contamination "from within" is that metaphysics distorts religion's natural path of development: Intuitions of the universe are taken to be resources for drawing conclusions about the natures of things, which contributes a new trajectory to the developmental process that these elements motivate. The result is a state of affairs in which that which is religious in the ideal sense and what is recognizably a distortion of religion are intertwined. Schleiermacher diagnosed the development of religious dogmas into fixed and unchangeable forms, which is one focus of the ire of the "cultured despisers," as a result of a "contamination" of this sort by metaphysics.[49]

This can be contrasted with contamination of religion "from without," a primary example of which is the entry of broadly political factors into religion. The narrative that Schleiermacher presented in the fourth speech portrays agents of the state taking an interest in already established religious communities and convincing them to take on responsibility for civic functions in exchange for granting them privileged status. The problem this poses for religion is that "as recompense for the services it demands, the state now robs the church of its freedom":[50] The state begins exerting a determining influence on the activities of the religious community, such that these are no longer purely religious (i.e., no longer oriented solely toward the communication of interior religion). The ecclesiastical circumstance that Schleiermacher intended this story to explain was state control of religious offices: As a result of this political contamination the state acquires a civic interest in the affairs of religion and eventually comes to install as religious leaders state functionaries who cannot express their own religious intuitions and feelings (since they possess none) but can only repeat the expressions of others. This is contamination from without in the sense that it takes the form of interference in the *social dynamics* or *social form* of religion, which obstructs the natural processes of religious communication. The consequences of this interference subsequently extend into the interior dimension both by choking off the religious development of those within the community and by alienating the potentially religious. "Now there is nothing in all its manifestations that would be directed to religion alone or in which religion by itself would be the main affair; in sacred speech and teachings as well as in secret and symbolic actions, everything is full of moral and political references, everything is diverted from its original purpose and concept."[51]

If *contamination* represents the intrusion into the natural process of religious development of alien factors, *dissolution* represents an attenuation of the connection between religious phenomena and the essence of religion. Like cases of contamination, cases of dissolution result in recognizably distorted or degenerate forms of religion, but unlike cases of contamination, the primary factor in this distortion appears to be not the strength of a principle at odds with ideal religion but the weakness of the religious elements that are already ingredients in the developmental and communicative process.

Some of Schleiermacher's passing references to religions that have simply lost their vitality over time can be included in this category. A primary symptom of such a loss of vitality is a kind of discursive sclerosis: Expressions of religious intuitions and feelings harden into inflexible formulas that are repeated out of little more than historical habit, and new forms of expression cease to arise. The understanding of Judaism presented in the *Speeches* is predicated on this notion. Schleiermacher, who borrowed this understanding from his assimilated Jewish friends in Berlin, believed that the discerning eye could still see the traces of Judaism's original sources of vitality within its texts but little more than this. Judaism, he claimed, "died when its holy books were closed; then the conversation of Jehovah with his people was viewed as ended."[52]

It should be possible at this point to appreciate the importance of the category of degenerate religion for the apologetic aims of the *Speeches*. The account of religion presented in the *Speeches* was intended to convince a skeptical audience that religion as it actually exists is not religion as it should and could be, and the method by which Schleiermacher attempted to accomplish this involved describing actual religion as the result of a developmental process unfolding under less than ideal conditions. His ultimate goal was to enlist his readers for the cause of religious reform by convincing them that traces of ideal religion remain within actual religion and that it might be possible for actual religion to come to resemble ideal religion more closely.[53] Schleiermacher's apologetic aims, then, required him to sketch an explanation of the actual condition of religion.

With this survey of the *Speeches* in mind, we turn now to Schleiermacher's mature work of dogmatics, *The Christian Faith*.

2.2 *The Christian Faith*

The task of exegeting *The Christian Faith* on the topic of "religion" is made considerably easier by the fact that the term has almost no presence in this text. In fact, Schleiermacher discusses religion most substantively in the section of the prolegomena where he lays out his reasons for *avoiding* the term.

A principal failing of the extant English translation of *The Christian Faith* is the fact that it does not respect Schleiermacher's distinction between *religion* (*Religion*) and *piety* (*Frömmigkeit*), treating the terms as synonymous. The rationale that the translators offered is that Schleiermacher himself remarked that his preference was to speak exclusively of piety and to use the term *religion* "only for the sake of variety."[54] However, this is beside the point, as in the same section in which he advanced this remark Schleiermacher offered a comprehensive overview of the sense of the term *religion* in relation to his project, one that allows for a clear understanding of the difference between religion and piety. The conflation of religion and piety in many commentaries on Schleiermacher in English is due in large part, it seems to me, to this single decision on the part of the translators of *The Christian Faith*; and it should be obvious that this conflation offers support to the standard interpretation of Schleiermacher, as it suggests that for him the term "religion" refers to a mental or spiritual condition, a form of consciousness, or even just a feeling.[55]

Schleiermacher introduced the term "religion" at a decisive point in the opening sections of the *Glaubenslehre*. After the purpose of the introduction is laid out in §1, §2 is concerned with the notion of the Christian church as the proper locus of the dogmatic enterprise. Section 3 introduces the term "piety" as that which forms "the basis for all ecclesiastical communions"; §§4–5 describe the "feeling of absolute dependence" as the essence of piety and introduce the terms "pious self-consciousness" and "God-consciousness"; and in §6 Schleiermacher claimed that the development of the pious self-consciousness leads naturally to communication and community. It is at the conclusion of §6 that the term "religion" is introduced; Schleiermacher's reason for discussing religion at this point, I suggest, is that it is only once the topic of religious community had been introduced that the entire extent of the territory that the term covers is finally in view.

Schleiermacher's remarks at the end of §6 took the form of spelling out how his talk of "pious self-consciousness" and of Christianity as a "community related to piety" might be recast in terms of "religion." A *particular religion* (*eine bestimmte Religion*), for example, would be the collection of pious states of mind (*Gemütszustände*) around which a "determinate church" is formed (thus corresponding to the "positive religion" of the *Speeches*). The term *religiosity* (*Religiosität*) would refer to "the individual's susceptibility...to the influence of fellowship or communion, as also his influence upon the latter, and thus his participation in the circulation and propagation of the pious emotions," and *religion in general* (*Religion schlechthin,* or in the first edition, *Religion überhaupt*), a term that Schleiermacher disparages in accordance with his preference for positive religion, can for him mean only "the movement of the human spirit in general toward the production of pious emotions, though always understood together with their expressions and therefore with the drive towards community" (here I understand the point to be that when the contingent features of "particular religion" are stripped away, all that is left is a general set of human propensities toward religion).[56]

Of particular interest for the present purposes are Schleiermacher's definitions of the final two pairs of terms:

> Now insofar as the constitution of pious states of mind of the individual is not entirely coextensive with that which is recognized as uniform in the community, one usually calls this purely personal element, in regard to its content, *subjective religion*, but that which is common [is called] the *objective*.... Finally, in the pious emotions (*Erregungen*) themselves, although they properly belong together, the inner determination of self-consciousness and the manner of its expression can indeed be distinguished: so one usually calls the structuring of the communicative expressions of piety within a community *outward religion*, while the total content of the pious emotions, as they actually occur in the individuals, is called *inward religion*.[57]

The similarity between this description and the structure of religion in the *Speeches* should be evident. Religion as Schleiermacher presents it here comprises both inward and outward elements, with the defining element of the outward being that it serves the purpose of communicating the inward. Here, religion's inward elements can be divided into two classes: those that are peculiar to discrete individuals, on the one hand, and those that are the common possession of all of the members of a particular community (*subjective* and *objective* respectively). As in the *Speeches*, it is a relationship to the more inward or central elements of religion that makes particular outward acts distinctively religious, and as in the *Speeches*, religious communication fosters the "transmission" of inward religion from person to person, with the end result that multiple individuals come to possess *the same* inward religion (i.e., the same structure of "pious states of mind").

Thus, in both the *Speeches* and *The Christian Faith*, "religion" has a structure in which inward elements stand in a closer relationship to the core of religion than outward elements. There are two primary differences between the early and the late accounts of religion, one structural and one stylistic. The structural difference has to do with Schleiermacher's claims about what comprises the core of religion, and the stylistic has to do with the fact that in the *Glaubenslehre* the bulk of attention rests on one particular sector of the overall phenomenon of religion, "piety."

2.2.1 *Essence in the* Glaubenslehre

Schleiermacher introduced the central terms of his discussion of piety in §4: "That which is common to all expressions of piety, however diverse...[and] therefore the self-identical essence of piety is this, that we are conscious of ourselves as absolutely dependent, or as in relation to God, which amounts to the same thing (*was dasselbe sagen will*)."[58]

The "feeling of absolute dependence" has been more or less thoroughly digested in the secondary literature, and I have little new to say about it. Briefly, this feeling is a matter of having an immediate (i.e., nonreflective) consciousness of not merely oneself but also the entire world as absolutely dependent.[59] Schleiermacher unpacked the notion of absolute dependence using the language of causality: Absolute dependence is a matter of being incapable of exercising an influence upon a thing that influences one. The feeling of absolute dependence thus represents us to ourselves—indeed, represents all "finite being" to us—as *neither self-creating nor self-sustaining beings* but rather as such that "our entire self-activity comes from elsewhere."[60] Konrad Cramer's description concerning the content of the feeling of absolute dependence seems to me to be broadly correct: This feeling is "the feeling of my irreducible finitude and therewith the feeling of the contingency of the world in which I find myself, of such a kind that the 'whence' of myself and the world is capable of no objective (*gegenständlich*) interpretation."[61]

In both editions of the *Glaubenslehre* Schleiermacher claimed an intimate link between the feeling of absolute dependence and the feeling of being dependent on God. However, he was also careful to state that at this point in the text

"God" is given a purely formal definition as the "other party" in the relation of absolute dependence: "[T]his is to be understood so that the *whence* (*Woher*) of our receptive and self-active existence co-posited (*mitgesetzt*) in this self-consciousness should be characterized by the expression 'God,' and this is for us the truly original meaning of the term."[62] The identification of "God" as the other party in the relationship to which the feeling of absolute dependence testifies, then, is a stipulative one, and what Schleiermacher calls "God-consciousness" is not identical with the feeling of absolute dependence but (as we will see shortly) represents a first step in the development of "piety" out of this feeling.[63]

2.2.2 *Piety*

As in the *Speeches*, in the *Glaubenslehre* Schleiermacher presented religion as something that develops out of its central core or essence. The term "piety" in this text refers to the innermost circle of religion's development. "Pious states of mind" are in his understanding states of "immediate self-consciousness" strongly influenced by the feeling of absolute dependence. Pious states of mind thus have a composite structure: They result from the combination of the feeling of absolute dependence with moments of "sensibly determined self-consciousness."[64]

As Schleiermacher used the term, *sensible self-consciousness* refers to awareness of the condition of the self as the self exists at a particular time and within particular circumstances. This self-consciousness comprises "all determinations of self-consciousness which develop out of our relations to nature and to human beings...we understand the expression 'sensible' to include social and ethical no less than selfish feelings."[65] The sensible self-consciousness, in other words, contains everything that the individual's circumstances contribute to self-understanding. Piety is a matter of the combination or integration of states of consciousness whose content is drawn from a person's contingent circumstances with the feeling of absolute dependence. This combination Schleiermacher describes as the "consummating point (*Vollendungspunkt*) of self-consciousness,"[66] and the measure of a person's piety is the extent to which this "consummation" occurs: "[T]he more the subject, with his partial freedom and partial dependence, posits himself in each moment of sensible self-consciousness as at the same time absolutely dependent, the more pious he is."[67]

It is important at this point to note how substantive the contribution of the "sensible self-consciousness" to piety is. Schleiermacher took pains to state explicitly that the feeling of absolute dependence, although it can be named and reflected upon in isolation from other feelings, in fact occurs only as a concomitant of people's awareness of their particular circumstances: Only "as already determined, within the realm of the antithesis, for this moment and in a particular way is [a person] conscious of his absolute dependence."[68]

One corollary of this arrangement is that, without exception, the source of all *variations* of pious feeling are the circumstances of the individual. Schleiermacher made this point most clearly in the first edition: "The feeling of absolute dependence regarded in itself is entirely simple, and even the concept of the same provides no ground for heterogeneity. But since pious emotion is always a real self-consciousness only in the unification of that feeling with a sensible feeling, and the sensible must be regarded as infinitely diverse, so the latter provides the ground for the heterogeneity in which pious feelings form themselves."[69]

The implication is that all of the features that distinguish religions from each other—in fact, everything about piety other than the bare feeling of absolute dependence—will be contingent, a product of the environment within which religion develops.

This point applies even to "God-consciousness," which "as nothing other than the expression of the feeling of absolute dependence, is the most immediate reflection upon the same."[70] Because God-consciousness is a product of reflection, and thus always arises within historically and culturally specific circumstances, Schleiermacher argued that the sensible self-consciousness is always implicated in its development. In fact, only the involvement of the sensible self-consciousness makes it possible for the God-consciousness to contain a richer content than that yielded by the stipulative identification of the unknown "whence" as God. The contribution of the sensible self-consciousness is thus "the source of all anthropomorphism which in this realm is unavoidable in expressions concerning God, and which forms so great a point of dispute in the ever recurring strife between those who accept this fundamental presupposition and those who deny it."[71]

So God-consciousness as Schleiermacher understood it is never a "pure" reflection of the feeling of absolute dependence but always incorporates elements drawn from the life of the individual in question. The contribution of the sensible self-consciousness accounted, in his view, for the diversity of conceptions of the nature of the divine, from "fetishism" to polytheism to monotheism and pantheism.[72] Thus, piety is marked by a contingency that extends to its most inward component, conceptions of the nature of the "whence" of absolute dependence. These generic characteristics of piety as described by Schleiermacher thus represent a skeleton to be fleshed out by history: What actually constitutes the inward dimension of particular religions is not a set of abstract reflections on absolute dependence but particular, historically determined forms of piety.

2.2.3 *Religion beyond Piety*

As we have seen, Schleiermacher identified "outward religion" by means of a familiar criterion: Acts become part of religion in virtue of being related to religion's center in the appropriate manner (specifically, by being expressions of the pious self-consciousness). Having called attention to this device, we can see that Schleiermacher used it elsewhere and not only in connection with outward religion. In particular, early on Schleiermacher used this idea to structure his presentation of the relationship of piety to *knowing* and *doing*. Although considered in itself, piety is a matter of feeling or immediate self-consciousness,[73] Schleiermacher was careful to state that there is a religiously significant connection between piety and both knowledge and action:

> If, in general, immediate self-consciousness mediates the transition between moments wherein knowing and moments when doing predominate, such that for example out of the same knowing a different doing proceeds in one [person] than in another inasmuch as a different determination of self-consciousness enters it: so it will befit piety to stimulate knowing and doing, and every moment in which piety emerges as preponderant will contain both, or one of the two, within itself in germ.... For were it otherwise, the pious moments could not combine with others into a single life, but rather piety would be something existing only for itself, without all influence on other spiritual life-processes.[74]

Thus, "there is knowing and doing which belong to piety (*zur Frömmigkeit gehörig*), but neither of the two constitutes its essence."[75] Schleiermacher did not say that knowing and doing that are suitably informed by pious feeling are thereby part of religion; these passages occur prior to his introduction of that term. However, certainly, the relationship between piety and these forms of knowing and doing would seem to be precisely that which is required, if my arguments are correct, for the latter to be "religious."

The final topic to be discussed here concerns religious doctrines or "faith statements" (*Glaubenssätze*), which Schleiermacher described as "conceptions (*Auffassungen*) of Christian pious states of mind presented in speech."[76] Schleiermacher's account of religious doctrines is grounded in his understanding of religious communication, which had undergone significant development since 1799. For the present, what needs to be established is that this area of outward religion is identified by the same device that (I have been arguing) structures Schleiermacher's understanding of religion in general.

As in the *Speeches*, here Schleiermacher argued that the communication of pious feelings is grounded in a natural tendency for states of mind that attain a certain degree of affective power to seek outward expression—"by means of facial expression, gesture, tones, and mediately through the word"—and ultimately to stimulate the formation of dedicated social circles as loci of religious communication.[77] Although he considered direct expression (i.e., expression unmediated by thought) to be a bare possibility, this was not how religion ordinarily develops in his view:

[W]e can hardly imagine so low a point of development of the
human spirit…that each person, according to the stage of reflection
at which he stands, should not at the same time become an object to
himself in his various circumstances, in order to grasp these as
representations and retain them in the form of thought. Now this
endeavor has from time immemorial been oriented in particular
towards pious emotions, and this, regarded in and for itself in its
inwardness, is what the phrase "conception of pious states of mind"
comprehends.[78]

In other words, the expression of inward religion in language presupposes (in
all but "defective" cultures) significant reflective development and is mediated
by the structures of thought: "Only a development of this procedure which has
continued so far that it can present itself outwardly in definite speech produces
a genuine faith-statement."[79] Religious doctrines, then, are acts of communication that are related to pious self-consciousness in that they express its content
in a manner mediated by reflection. The purpose of such communication is "to
promote the living circulation of the religious consciousness": In other words,
just as in the Speeches, inward religion is transmitted from person to person
and developed communally through specific forms of discourse.[80]

Schleiermacher's discussion of the contamination of the developmental
processes that produce religious doctrines constitutes another element of continuity between the Speeches and The Christian Faith. In the later text
Schleiermacher argued that religion becomes contaminated when elements
whose aim is other than to "promote the living circulation of the religious consciousness" enter the process of reflection and communication of pious feeling, and the primary agent of contamination in his discussion of the development
of religious doctrines is "speculation." Although he does not define the term
precisely, I think we can understand by this term an autonomous interest in
truth: that is, an interest in the truth, for its own sake, about either mundane or
transcendent realities.[81] To resist "speculation" is to resist mining expressions
of piety for their truth content (i.e., using them as premises from which conclusions about the world or God can be drawn). Schleiermacher described such
resistance as a defining feature of the Protestant theological tradition:

The Evangelical church in particular contains in itself the
unanimous consciousness that the distinctive form of its dogmatic
propositions does not depend on any form or school of philosophy,
nor has it proceeded at all from a speculative interest, but simply
from that of satisfying the immediate self-consciousness solely
through the means ordained by Christ, in their genuine and
uncorrupted form; thus it can consistently recognize only such
propositions which can display this same lineage as dogmatic
propositions belonging to it.[82]

In speaking of the satisfaction (*Befriedigung*) of pious self-consciousness, I take Schleiermacher to have been indicating that the character of that self-consciousness motivates certain forms of behavior (i.e., behavior that aims at the communication of piety). Here this notion is used as a critical principle: Only claims that can plausibly be understood as motivated solely by this communicative drive can be admitted as "uncorrupted" dogmatic propositions.[83] As received, the Christian doctrinal tradition combines elements that have developed in this manner with elements stemming from an "alien origin", and Schleiermacher's ambition was to "purify" these doctrines by stripping them down to their functional core, that part of their content that serves to express pious feelings and thereby communicate piety.

2.3 Summary and Conclusions

From this all-too-brief investigation I conclude that the descriptions of "religion" in both the *Speeches on Religion* and in *The Christian Faith* follow the same basic pattern. In both texts religion is composed of a "core" out of which further phenomena develop along lines determined partly by the content of the core and partly by circumstances, and within the resulting collection of states of affairs and activities a distinction can be drawn between elements that correspond in the appropriate manner to the character of religion's core and elements that do not. The elements that constitute religion can be inward or outward; it is difficult to isolate a single principle that renders particular inward states religious, but outward phenomena become part of religion to the extent that they serve to *express* or *communicate* inward religion or, more generally, to promote its circulation.

We are now in a position to appreciate the fact that religion as Schleiermacher understood it has a concentric structure in a double sense. One sense has to do with the distinction between religion's inward and outward components: the essence of religion represents the center or core of the phenomenon, and around this exists an "inner ring" of mental states and activities and an "outer ring" of discourses, practices, and material productions. The other sense has to do with the relationship between ideal and actual religion: If ideal religion represents the imagined result of an optimal developmental trajectory and actual religion the product of various deformations and diversions of such a trajectory, then we can understand Schleiermacher's claim that one should be able to see "within" actually existing religion traces of something higher as equivalent to the claim that one can evaluate actually existing religion against an image of how the same *could have* and *should have* developed. So far as I can see, it is not possible to reduce these two types of concentricity to one; inward religion can become contaminated, in Schleiermacher's view, in precisely the same sense as outward religion, and outward religion is not, in virtue of being outward, less ideal than inward. The twofold concentricity of religion thus entails that there be two distinct scales according to which the distance, so to speak, of a particular example of religion from religion's essence can be assessed.

There is, however, one significant difference between the accounts of religion in the early and late texts in relation to ideal religion. In the *Speeches* Schleiermacher took pains to describe what religion would look like if it were free to develop without outside interference; the circumstances of actual religion were for the most part presented as at best a dilution of this ideal and at worst a positive corruption. In contrast, the *Glaubenslehre* presents religion as incorporating elements drawn from history from its very beginnings, in the emergence of God-consciousness. Furthermore, the involvement of these elements is regarded not as a contamination but rather as simply one of the factors that bear on the development of actual, historical religion. The critical function of the notion of religion's essence is the same in *The Christian Faith* as in the *Speeches*, but in the later text Schleiermacher did not devote space to sketching a counterfactual developmental history of an ideal Christianity. This difference between the earlier and later texts is also reflected in the disappearance of Schleiermacher's occasional charge in the *Speeches* that what are recognizable examples of "degenerate" religion are in fact not religion at all, as represented, for instance, in his claim that "whatever would go beyond [accepting everything individual as part of the whole] and penetrate deeper into the nature and substance of the whole is no longer religion, and will, if it still wants to be regarded as such, inevitably sink into empty mythology."[84] This is a recognizable example of the contamination of religion by a speculative interest, and any suggestion that such contamination destroys altogether the religious character of the activities that it affects is missing from *The Christian Faith*.

It does not seem to me that these differences reflect an alteration in the way Schleiermacher understood either the general structure of religion or the processes whereby it develops historically. The basic idea of a distinction between appropriate and wayward development is clearly present in both texts, and the differences between the claims produced by the application of this idea in his early and late writings seem to me to be primarily rhetorical. There is, however, at least one salient difference in the methods Schleiermacher followed in pursuing the immanent criticism of actual religion in the two texts. In the *Speeches* the criticism proceeds as it were wholesale, by way of a vivid portrayal of a sharply delineated and yet historically abstract ideal religion and then the comparison of actually existing religion taken as a whole with this imaginative construction. *The Christian Faith*, in contrast, proceeds piecemeal, through the evaluation of individual examples of religion (specifically, of particular religious doctrines) in light not of a overarching depiction of ideal Christianity but rather of an understanding of the relationship to religion's essence which would be required for the example in question to be truly ideal.

I conclude this chapter with consideration of the utility of my reconstruction of the structure of religion as Schleiermacher understood it for identifying that which is uniquely religious. Briefly put, if "religion" in these texts by Schleiermacher is as I have described it, then what is its extent? Where do the boundaries between the religious and the nonreligious lie?

The question is of significance partly because, according to the standard interpretation, religion has fixed and stringent boundaries. On this view Schleiermacher's writings on religion amount to a "limitation of religion to feeling"; that is, one leaves religion behind as soon as one moves away from the stage of feeling to that of knowledge or action or into the realm of the interpersonal. I have been arguing that religion as Schleiermacher understood it does not come to an end either at the boundary between the inward and the outward or at the boundary between the ideal and the degenerate, but if these claims are correct, what are its limits? If the realm of religion contains a host of phenomena whose religious character grows increasingly attenuated the greater their remove from religion's essence, at what point does one exit this realm and enter that of the nonreligious?

I do not think it is possible to locate a clear outward boundary of the phenomenon of religion on Schleiermacher's understanding. Rather, if religion is defined by a relation to its core or center, then it is something that "trails off" rather than ending abruptly. While there will be paradigmatic examples of religion and paradigmatic examples of nonreligion, there will also be substantial gray areas.[85] If we restrict ourselves for a moment to outward religion, paradigmatic examples of religion will be activities or artifacts that constitute the process whereby a particular form of pious self-consciousness circulates within a particular community. Certain speech acts will fit this description, but so will artifacts like church buildings or religious works of art when these are utilized for the purpose of religious communication. Paradigmatic examples of "not-religion" would be any activities or artifacts that lack any significant connection to religion's essence—affairs of a secular state and purely economic activities are possible examples.

But how firm does the connection to religion's essence have to be in order for a phenomenon to stand within the realm of religion? How much contamination can the activities of an ostensibly religious community—say, by the affairs of state—stand before religion ceases? How directly must activities relate to the communication of piety in order to be truly religious—would activities geared toward the maintenance of religious buildings or the performance of the musical works of a "dead religion" count? What about activities that are intended to communicate piety but in fact fail to do so?

So far as I can see, Schleiermacher's account provides no answers to questions of this sort; it does not tell us at what point in the twofold drift away from religion's essence the designation "religious" no longer applies. But it is not clear to me that such vagueness should count as a defect of his account, and on the interpretation I have been presenting not terribly much hangs on the question of religion's boundaries. It is possible to say something about the extent to which each of these cases presents religion by discussing how each is related to the process of the communication of religion's essence; to ask, in addition to this, for a summary judgment on whether the case *is or is not* "religion" is to demand more precision, I think, than this form of religious essentialism can provide.

3

Religion and "the Social"

The dominant position in the field today is based on a tradition that goes back at least to the late-eighteenth-century German romantic Friedrich Schleiermacher; responding to the Enlightenment's commitment to rationality and objectivity...Schleiermacher defended religion against its so-called cultured despisers by re-conceiving of it as a nonquantifiable individual experience, a deep feeling, or an immediate consciousness.

> —McCutcheon, *Critics Not Caretakers*

Once there is religion, it must also necessarily be social. That not only lies in human nature but also is preeminently in the nature of religion.

> —Schleiermacher, *On Religion*

3.1 Introduction

In this chapter I aim to fill in a significant area of the general outline presented in the previous chapter by examining religion's "social dimension" as Schleiermacher understood it. This topic is of importance for at least two reasons. The first is that the idea that Schleiermacher was a social thinker in any significant respect has until recently been foreign to English scholarship. Sentiments such as that of Bernd Oberdorfer, who has characterized Schleiermacher as "one of the first and at the same time one of the most subtle theorists of modern society,"[1] have no parallel in the English literature. The second reason is that any exploration of the relationship between religion and the *natural* order in Schleiermacher's thought would be incomplete without an investigation of the relationship between religion and the *social* order. For it is above all within the social order that religion as Schleiermacher understood it has its concrete historical life, and it was from his general account of human socialization that he derived the theoretical resources to explain religion's particular modes of historical existence and persistence.

The argument of this chapter unfolds in three phases. I open with an overview of Schleiermacher's ethical writings and a brief discussion of his understanding of ethics as a science. The point of this discussion is twofold: to provide support for the notion that a substantive interest in religion's social existence is fully in line with the broader concerns of the "science of the principles of history," and to make it clear that Schleiermacher's explorations of the themes that would inform his university lectures on ethics began early and informed his writings on religion from the beginning. In the second part of the chapter I offer a reading of the fourth of the *Speeches on Religion*, which in my estimation is at least the equal of the second in its importance to the young Schleiermacher's overall conception of religion. The fourth speech describes three different forms of religious association; the content of each form and the relationship between each and the others can be understood in terms of the doubly concentric structure of religion laid out in the previous chapter, and reading the speech in these terms illuminates the account of actual religion presented in the text as a whole.

The third part of the chapter is dedicated to an examination of the account of religion found in Schleiermacher's lectures on ethics. In these lectures religion appears as a specific version of what Schleiermacher termed the *ethical process*: the process, found in every type of human association, whereby individuals establish a collective identity through their discursive activity and receive the "stamp" of that identity upon their own persons. These lectures provide a crucial piece of theoretical context for understanding Schleiermacher's reliance on feeling (*Gefühl*) to characterize "inward religion" after 1806 (in contrast to the "intuition and feeling," which had been the focus of the 1799 *Speeches*), for they portray religion as the process of the *socialization of feeling*. In this section I also explore a number of themes in the ethics lectures that flesh out Schleiermacher's claim of religion's "necessary sociability" through reference to specific ways in which religion intersects with the more general dynamics of human sociality to produce the formations of religion observable within history. What emerges from these lectures can be thought of as a theory of tradition: a theory, that is, that explains how a set of semiformalized collective activities, themselves changing with time and existing within a wide variety of cultural and social environments, could be the vehicles of a particular form of *consciousness* or collective self-understanding and thus the means of its historical persistence and development.

3.2 Schleiermacher's Ethical Writings in Overview

The corpus of Schleiermacher's writings on ethics spans his productive career and falls into two clearly distinguished phases separated by a brief middle period. From the first decade of Schleiermacher's literary activities dates a series of essays on related topics: Aristotle's ethics, the nature of human freedom, the highest good, "free sociability," and others.[2] The later phase comprises Schleiermacher's systematic ethical writings: principally the lectures on philosophical ethics offered at Berlin,[3] but also six Academy lectures based on these[4] and the lectures on *christliche Sittenlehre* (Christian theological ethics).[5] From the period in between these phases date three texts that both summarize Schleiermacher's earlier explorations and take the first steps toward his later system: the *Monologen* of 1800; the *Grundlinien einer Kritik der bisherigen Sittenlehre* of 1803, which in the end was Schleiermacher's only published monograph on the subject of ethics;[6] and the *Brouillon zur Ethik*, which comprise Schleiermacher's notes for his 1805–1806 course in ethics at Halle.[7]

The relationship between this chronology and that of Schleiermacher's canonical texts on the topic of religion is instructive. Schleiermacher had reflected substantively on ethical topics prior to publishing the *Speeches on Religion* in 1799, and in fact his drafting of that text coincided with the composition of his essay on sociable conduct, a circumstance to which we return later. His 1806 revisions to the *Speeches* took place on the heels of Schleiermacher's first course in ethics, during the period when his mature terminology was taking shape. In addition, the understanding of religion presented in *The Christian Faith* benefited considerably from the development of Schleiermacher's ethical thought evinced by the surviving notes from the Berlin lectures. I expand on each of these remarks later.

As we have seen, for Schleiermacher, ethics is the *geistlich* correlate of physics: Where physics is dedicated to isolating the laws governing the behavior of bodies in the material realm, ethics is dedicated to the identification of the laws that govern the "activity of reason." In examining Schleiermacher's 1825 Academy lecture we also observed the distinction Schleiermacher drew between his approach to ethics and that of Kant and Fichte: Where these were reduced, in his view, by their understanding of human freedom as an unconstrained power of choice to offering "counsels of prudence" in the place of genuine moral laws, Schleiermacher's aim was to identify principles actually in operation within human activity, which when conjoined to natural laws would generate unified, lawful explanations of historical events.[8] General characterizations of ethics across a variety of Schleiermacher's texts cohere with its status as a robustly descriptive rather than prescriptive science. In the *Brouillon* he characterized ethics as "the science of history, that is, of intelligence as appearance";[9] in the *Brief Outline of the Study of Theology* of 1811, as "the science of the principles of history";[10] and in the 1812–1813 lectures as "the depiction of finite being under the potency of reason" and thus as the converse of physics, which describes "finite being under the potency of nature."[11] Ethics for Schleiermacher was thus not restricted to the exploration of morality (*Moralität*) but rather assumed the form of *Sittenlehre*, an inquiry into the concrete ethical life of human populations (*Sittlichkeit*).[12] The ambitious nature of ethics for Schleiermacher is registered as well in characterizations by recent scholars. Gunter Scholtz has described Schleiermacher's ethics as a "general theory of human culture"; Brent Sockness, as "a comprehensive theory of the distinctively human-historical world," and Peter Grove, as "a philosophy of culture, or as a theory of history or of the social."[13]

As the citation from Grove suggests, given that ethics according to Schleiermacher encompasses the entire field of human activity, it also includes the territory claimed by the social sciences.[14] One strand of Schleiermacher's "science of the principles of history" was a body of reflections concerned with the domain of regularized interpersonal activity: concerned, that is, with both the formation and dynamics of social groups considered as independent units of analysis and the effects of group dynamics on the members of social groups.[15] As Schleiermacher himself put the point in the 1812–1813 lectures, "Just as natural science renders both the fixed forms and the transitory functions of nature comprehensible, and reduces each to an aspect of the other, in the same way ethics explains both the fixed forms of ethical existence, family, state, etc., and the transitory functions, or their various ethical capacities, and reduces each to an aspect of the other."[16]

The sociological strands of Schleiermacher's ethical thought are strongly marked by application of the classical distinction between *form* and *content* to the domain of human sociability. A primary interest of Schleiermacher's within the ambit of sociology was the idea of fundamental *patterns* or *types* of human interrelationship, not only between single individuals but also among the members of larger groups. A significant proportion of his reflections on the social dynamics of human life took the form of identifying and exploring these fundamental types of relationality—a tendency displayed early on in his fascination with Aristotle's conception of friendship, as Oberdorfer has documented.[17] Schleiermacher's signature concept of "free sociability," which is explored in the next section, relies heavily on this distinction, and the "fixed ethical forms" that figure prominently in the Berlin lectures are also outgrowths of the form-content distinction.

Within the history of sociological theory, Schleiermacher is not alone in diagnosing actually existing social relations in terms of a distinction between form and content. The thought that this distinction can be made to do substantial theoretical work is commonly acknowledged as a hallmark of the work of Georg Simmel, who flourished a century after Schleiermacher and drew substantially on both his social-theoretical and theological writings[18] (and more recently, a number of German scholars have pointed to important respects in which Schleiermacher's work anticipates themes in that of the contemporary German sociologist Niklas Luhmann[19]). Schleiermacher, so far as I can see, subscribed to the position expressed later by Simmel, that "society exists wherever a number of individuals enter into interaction."[20] Actually existing social phenomena (societies) are thus understood by Schleiermacher as a product of the infusion of social *forms*—which may overlap or combine in various ways—with *content* drawn from the circumstances of the individuals involved. Understanding the dynamics of a particular society, then, is a matter of correctly identifying fundamental patterns of relationality, however complex and interrelated, and correctly discerning the presence and effects of particular kinds of social content. The distinction that we observed in the previous chapter between ideal constructions and actual conditions also has a place within Schleiermacher's ethics; ethical reflection in his sense assumes the form of describing ideal forms of social interaction and ideal types of social organization, with the understanding (not always clearly expressed) that actually existing social arrangements represent manifestations of these ideal types, which are compromised by actuality and thus reflect the types only imperfectly.

With the contents of this brief overview in mind, we turn to Schleiermacher's "precocious treatise in the sociology of religion,"[21] the fourth of the *Speeches on Religion*.

3.3 The Fourth Speech

The fourth of the *Speeches* contains Schleiermacher's first articulation of the accounts of religious sociability and religious socialization that would reappear in a more sophisticated form in the ethics lectures and *The Christian Faith*. Understanding the argument of the speech will require both an appreciation of the twofold concentricity of religion discussed in the previous chapter and the importance for Schleiermacher of the distinction between the form and the content of social arrangements and activities.

As mentioned in the previous chapter, in the *Speeches* Schleiermacher was attempting to influence the view of religion held by its "cultured despisers" for the better. His description of religion's essence was a component of his apologetic strategy. However, it was not until the fourth speech that Schleiermacher pulled the threads of his argument together into a program of action in relation to the present state of religion, and the specific kind of action he advocated had to do with the reform of actually existing religious communities. Schleiermacher, in other words, was concerned to offer his readers not simply a description of religion's essence but also a description of a form of social existence or religious community appropriate to that essence, and his hope was that his "cultured despisers" would find this vision sufficiently compelling to engage in the project of moving actually existing religious communities toward this ideal.

The argument of the fourth speech proceeds by offering three distinct visions of religious community in such a way that the relationships among them are clearly delineated and intelligible. The first of these is referred to in the text as the "city of God" and corresponds to what I have been calling "ideal religion." The third is not given an explicit label by Schleiermacher, but we can understand it as referring to the condition of actual religious communities; for reasons that I make clear below I use the term *state religion* to refer to this description. In between these two stands Schleiermacher's vision of the church as a "mediating institution," a complex arrangement that is recognizably degenerate in relation to the "city of God" but still capable of serving as a locus of religious discourse. Schleiermacher presented these three visions of religious community within a narrative describing a movement from ideal to actual religion as a process of progressive degeneration or contamination. The reformist program articulated in the speech involves "rolling back" the most objectionable form of contamination of religion, the entanglement of the church with the affairs of state in order to realize the vision of the church as a mediating institution.[22] It is the widespread attainment of this mediating type of religious community rather than that of the city of God that Schleiermacher hailed as the arrival of a "golden age of religion."

3.3.1 Ideal Religious Community: Religiously Inflected "Free Sociability"

In the previous chapter I described "ideal religion" in general terms as what religion *should* be and *would* be if it were to faithfully reflect the character of its essence. If this is correct, a truly ideal religious community will be one whose character corresponds most adequately to the essence of religion. When the discussion takes place (as does the fourth speech) in abstraction from the specific content of any historical religious tradition, this adequacy will itself be understood in the abstract: An ideal religious community will be one characterized by patterns of social interaction that represent optimal collective activity in relation to the *sort of thing* an essence of religion is. Schleiermacher's conception of ideal religious community in the *Speeches* was in fact predicated on the idea that there is *one* particular social pattern or social form that most adequately corresponds to religion's essence. We can understand this social form as *religiously inflected free sociability.*

Schleiermacher had explored the notion of "free sociability," a social form realized most perfectly in settings like the salon,[23] in "Toward a Theory of Sociable Conduct," whose composition was contemporaneous with that of the *Speeches*.[24] In this essay he had described free sociability as social interaction "that is neither tied to nor determined by any external purpose,"[25] in contrast with that predicated on preexisting social content such as political, professional, or family identities. The defining character of free sociability is precisely the insulation of social interaction from the influence of such content, so that "[l]eft to the free play of one's powers, one can further develop these powers harmoniously and be ruled by no law except that which one issues to oneself. It all depends on whether one is able to expel for a time all limitations of domestic and public (*bürgerliche*) relationships as far as one wants."[26] What is supposed to determine the character of social activities under the condition of free sociability is nothing other than the characters, interests, and desires of the participants, and the overarching goal of such activity is mutual enrichment. "The purpose of society is not at all to be conceived as lying outside it. The action of each individual should be aimed at the activity of the others, and the activity of individuals should be their influence on the others...[the object of this activity] can, therefore, be conceived as nothing other than the free play of thoughts and feelings whereby all members mutually stimulate and enliven each other."[27]

Schleiermacher took free sociability to combine two contrasting social directives. On the one hand, unconstrained expressive activity is a desideratum of social interaction; Schleiermacher associated this desire with "the youth who enter the confines of society, often right from the halls of the muses with pretensions of intellect and aspirations to freedom."[28] On the other hand, each individual's discourse is not to be so idiosyncratic that it is inaccessible to some participants. Taken in isolation, this desire leads the members of a group to aim for "the mean average of the totality"; Schleiermacher takes this policy to represent "the language of the courtiers" and assigns it responsibility for creating "that void that one has cause to lament most frequently in the highest and finest circles."[29] Free sociability harmonizes these two by integrating the individual and the collective: "I am to offer my individuality, my character, and I am to assume the character of the society. Both should take place at the same moment, both should be one and be united in a single operation."[30] That is to say, communication under the conditions of free sociability involves both the expression of individual particularity and the assumption by the individual of the group's character. This notion of "reciprocal formation" as the result of group-directed individual activity anticipates what Schleiermacher would later describe as the "ethical process."[31]

The idea of free sociability was of sufficiently enduring importance for Schleiermacher's ethical thought that in the later lectures it constitutes one of the four primary forms of human sociality (alongside the state, the academy, and the church) and thereby as distinct from religious sociability.[32] However, it is fairly clear that Schleiermacher's understanding of ideal religious association in 1799 was constructed on the model of free sociability. Consider the description of the "city of God" in the fourth of the *Speeches*:

I wish I could draw you a picture of the rich, luxuriant life in this city of God when its citizens assemble, all of whom are full of their own power, which wants to stream forth into the open, all full of holy passion to apprehend and appropriate everything the others might offer them. When a person steps forth before others, it is not an office or an appointment that empowers him to do so, not pride or ignorance that fills him with presumption. It is the free stirring of the spirit, the feeling of most cordial unanimity of each with all and of the most perfect equality, a mutual annihilation of every first and last and of all earthly order. He steps forth to present his own intuition [of the universe] as the object for the rest...he expresses the universe, and the community follows his inspired speech in holy silence. If he should now disclose a hidden miracle or, in prophetic confidence, link the future to the present...a practiced sense of the community accompanies him everywhere; and when he returns to himself from his wanderings from the universe, his heart and the heart of each are but the common stage for the same feeling.[33]

In this early text there are two specific points of commonality between an ideal religious community and a society characterized by free sociability. First, both kinds of society are sheltered from outside influences, so that the content of that society's discourse is informed by the participants' characters and desires rather than by factors having to do with the external social relations in which they stand. Second and more important, in both kinds of society communication is supposed to be reciprocal, so as to promote the formation of a common discourse out of the contributions of a diverse membership and facilitate the formation of each by all and all by each. However, religion and free sociability are distinct from one another in a crucial respect. Free sociability begins, so to speak, with a fairly disparate initial group, and its discourse proceeds on the basis of whatever content, flowing from the characters of the individuals involved, can serve as a suitable basis for reciprocal formation.[34] Ideal religious community, on the other hand, is devoted to a particular genre of "social content"—religious intuitions and feelings, which all participants are assumed to already possess—and thus to a particular mode of reciprocal communication. Thus, free sociability as Schleiermacher understood it is possible under a wider range of conditions than is ideal religious community:

This communication with the innermost part of humanity also cannot be carried on in common conversation.... Where joy and laughter also dwell and seriousness is supposed to be compliantly joined to jest and wit, there can be no place for what must forever be encompassed by holy reserve and awe. People cannot toss religious views, pious feelings, and serious reflections upon them to each other in small snatches, like the ingredients of a light conversation.... The communication of religion must occur in a grander style, and another type of society, which is especially dedicated to religion, must arise from it.[35]

In other words, religious communication most effectively takes place within a social context in which all parties are aware of the nature of religious discursive content and agree to focus their activities on the communication of that content, and the nature of this content imposes constraints on the form of social interaction of which the participants can make profitable use. While "jest and wit" are the lifeblood of free sociability, these are out of step with the requirements of ideal religious communication.[36]

This imaginative construction of a religious community that would most adequately reflect the general character of religion's essence lacks two characteristics of observable religion: one the one hand, a distinction between clergy and laity, and on the other, any formalization or standardization of religious discourse. These characteristics put in their first appearance within the second type of religious community presented in the speech, as Schleiermacher's argument moves away from the realm of pure ideality and in the direction of actuality.

3.3.2 The "Mediating Institution"

Schleiermacher's description of the church as a "mediating institution" is the midpoint of the argument of the fourth speech in the sense that this institution represents a contamination of "ideal religion" by extrareligious factors but is nevertheless a purer form of religious community than "state religion." Whereas the city of God was defined as a religious community in which all parties are religiously "awake" and dedicated to the process of reciprocal religious communication, in the actual world such "virtuosi of religion" are rare. In the actual world religious communities are populated in large measure by individuals who neither understand religion correctly nor possess the ability to produce their own religious intuitions and feelings. The second form of religious community, then, is defined by its inclusion of those who are not religiously "awake," and its social dynamics are predicated in large measure on this circumstance.

In the *Speeches* Schleiermacher painted an unflattering picture of religiously "unawakened" persons, attributing to them the mistaken belief that religion is something that can be *learned* in the form of concrete expressions such as creeds and formulas. These bring a "wholly different form of sociability" to the enterprise of religion: Instead of reciprocal formation, "here in the common church you find a thoroughly different form: all people want to receive, and there is only one who is supposed to give. Completely passive, they allow themselves to be influenced in one and the same way through all their senses."[37] Such people Schleiermacher refers to as "negatively religious" (*negativ religiös*), who merely "seek religion" and "press in great crowds towards the few points where they surmise the positive principle of religion." However, in reality "no religion dwells within them": "not religion but merely a little taste for it…is all that one can grant even to the best among them."[38]

Both the distinction between clergy and laity and the formalization of religious discourse are, on the account of the *Speeches*, concessions to the negatively religious. Such people form, in Schleiermacher's terms, "an external religious society," or more pejoratively, "a false and depraved church."[39] The structure of the "mediating institution" is thus complex: It comprises central and peripheral patterns of social interaction, an *internal* and an *external* religious fellowship. Within the inner circle stand leaders and priests whose communication among themselves most closely resembles ideal religion; these also address themselves to the "seekers after religion" within the outer circle, communicating their own religious intuitions and feelings and attempting to awaken these others. According to Schleiermacher, the sort of pedagogy that these seekers demand, however, contributes to the codification and thus the ossification of "living" religion. Because "they would first like to get their religion from outside," they "need the symbolic actions, which are actually last in religious communication, as stimulants to arouse what properly ought to precede them,"[40] and in societies of this type a "ruinous sectarian spirit" develops of necessity since "where religion is something that can be given only from outside, being accepted on the authority of the giver, then those who think differently must be viewed as disturbers of calm and sure progress."[41]

In spite of the strength of his language, Schleiermacher ultimately described this form of religious community in a positive light. For one thing, the creation of the "common church" is in itself a natural development for religion: The entry of the negatively religious into religious communities "has happened at all times, among all peoples, and in every particular religion."[42] For another, in the actual, imperfect world, the institutional church's proper function is to be a point of contact between the city of God and the common run of humanity. In spite of its recognizable "degeneracy," the mediating institution serves as the "binding agent" between the realms of the ideal and the actual.[43] The twin purposes of religious communication, after all, are to transmit religious intuitions and feelings between persons and to awaken the ability to produce such; the proper function of the church as a mediating institution is thus to make religion's essence available through religious communication to precisely these *negatively* religious in the hopes of making them *positively* religious. The "golden age of religion" for which Schleiermacher hoped involves numerous churches, "smaller and less definite" than those presently existing, which have precisely this religiously mixed character: "preparatory for those in whom some sense of religion had arisen and decisive for those who had found themselves incapable of being stirred by religion in any way."[44]

For this golden age of religion to be realized, however, the most serious form of contamination of religion by "alien factors" needs to be acknowledged and remedied.

3.3.3 State Religion

The sort of interference in the social dynamics of religion that Schleiermacher identified as particularly destructive arises when the state takes an interest in the religious community as an institution capable of serving civic functions.[45] What results from this interest is the imposition of political significance and political functions upon religious activities, such that the affairs of church and state become intermixed. The most religiously problematic outcome of this combination occurs when the contamination of religion by politics extends to the point where genuine religious formation, even the unidirectional formation characteristic of the church as a mediating institution, can no longer effectively take place.

In line with his presentation of the three forms of religious community as a matter of progressive degeneration, Schleiermacher described the interaction of church and state as a matter of creeping contamination. This process begins with the state assigning responsibility to the church for education in general, for "inducement to moral sentiments" that cover cases not strictly governed by law, and for the instillation of loyalty to the state, "that its citizens be made truthful to it in their utterances."[46] Once the church has assumed these functions, however, it becomes important to the state that they be executed in accordance with its needs and designs, and from this flows ever-tightening control of the church by the state: "As a recompense for the services it demands, the state now robs the church of its freedom, as is the case in almost all parts of the civilized world where there is a state and a church; it treats it as an institution it has established and invented, and indeed the church's defects and abuses are almost all the state's invention."[47]

Schleiermacher's most vociferous objection was to state control of clerical positions. According to his description, when the leadership of a religious community becomes a matter of state sanction, the equation, essential for the mediating function of the church, between "religious virtuosity" and clerical office is disrupted, and the possibility opens up that churches will end up with leaders suited for carrying out state functions but devoid of religious intuitions and feelings. Thereby the dynamic whereby the religious sensibilities of the "external religious fellowship" can be nurtured and stimulated by those at the community's center is disrupted, and the natural reason for the community to exist at all are overridden. Most lamentable is the fact that the tolerance of difference and social fluidity, which flow naturally from the essence of religion, already challenged by the requirements of religious mediation, lose their natural defenders when the clergy are no longer religiously "awake." The institutional hierarchy becomes the more rigid as the leadership is given responsibility for ensuring that the church performs its civic functions, and the most an "uninspired" church leadership can do by way of promulgating religion is to repeat the doctrinal and liturgical formulations of the past, now modified in order to serve a new and foreign set of purposes:

> Now there is nothing in all its manifestations that would be directed to religion alone or in which religion by itself would be the main affair; in sacred speech and teachings as well as in secret and symbolic actions, everything is full of moral and political references, everything is diverted from its original purpose and concept. Hence, there are many among its leaders who understand nothing of religion and many among its members to whom it does not occur to want to seek it.[48]

This diversion of religious activity extends to the ritual life of the church as well. Schleiermacher laments, for example, the fact that baptism, which should be the occasion when the church "consecrates newborns to the deity and to striving for the highest" becomes instead the occasion when the state "wants to receive them at the same time from the church's hands into the list of its own charges," and that the confirmation of a young adult, rather than being "the first kiss of brotherhood as one who has now taken a first look into the sanctuaries of religion," "is also supposed to be the sign for the state of the first stage of his civil independence."[49]

For the "golden age" of religious mediating institutions to be realized, this state of affairs must be reversed: "Away, therefore, with every such union of church and state! That remains my Cato's counsel to the end, or until I experience seeing every such union actually destroyed."[50] The "purification" Schleiermacher envisioned would require changes to the social structures of religious communities, one component of which would be the relaxation of confessional boundaries: "The external society of religion will be brought closer to the universal freedom and the majestic unity of the true church only by becoming a flowing mass where there are no outlines, where each part is found, now here and now there, while all mingle peacefully with one another."[51] However, he also anticipated that religious reform would involve a substantial amount of social experimentation:

> But if there is supposed to be a mediating institution through which the true church comes into a certain contact with the profane world with which it has nothing to do directly, an atmosphere, as it were, through which it simultaneously purifies itself and also draws to itself and shapes new material, what form shall this society then take, and how might it be freed from the corruption it has absorbed? Let the last question be left for time to answer. For everything that must happen sometime there are a thousand different ways, and for all

diseases of humanity there are manifold methods of healing; each
will be tried in its place and will lead you to the goal.[52]

In Schleiermacher's view, in other words, a significant proportion of the
ills affecting actually existing religion were ills of social form—the decoupling
of clerical office from functional religious roles, for example, or the rigidly
drawn and enforced boundaries of religious fellowships. Understanding the
essence of religion correctly was thus no more than a first step toward religious
reform. Genuine reform as Schleiermacher understood it required a willingness to imagine forms of religious association that would be more conducive to
religiously inflected reciprocal formation than actually existing institutions and
thus would require a willingness to intervene in and even experiment with the
social forms of religion.[53]

3.3.4 Summary: The Early Vision of Social Religion

The fourth of the *Speeches* adds considerable detail to Schleiermacher's claim
that religion is "necessarily social": Even in its most ideal form, religion requires
not just interpersonal communication but also a particular kind of social structure for its development, and even the virtuosi of religion desire and require the
kind of discourse that defines the city of God. Beyond this, however, two principles of particular importance for understanding Schleiermacher's early vision
of religion's social dimension are on display in the fourth speech.

First, it is clear that for members of the "common church," religion is
something that is socially acquired: Those who are not religiously "awake"
develop religiously, first, by passive participation in religious discourse, and
second (if all goes well), by becoming capable of producing their own intuitions
and feelings. In the *Speeches* Schleiermacher clearly prefers the religion of the
"virtuosi of religion" to that of the negatively religious, but it cannot be denied
that he offers an account of religious socialization that locates the origin of
inward religion (for all but an exceptional few) in *outward* religion. Religion is
necessarily social, then, not simply in the sense that religious intuitions and
feelings stimulate their own expression but also in the sense that it is only
through religious practice that ordinary individuals come to possess piety.

Second, in the fourth speech Schleiermacher describes the conditions of
actual religion as a combination of elements that are in accord with the nature
of religion and alien elements. Religious rituals, under the conditions of actual
religion, not only serve as expressions of religious intuitions and feelings and
thus not only serve the purpose of religious socialization but also perform
broader social and political functions such as induction into public citizenship,
education in social roles and expectations, and public recognitions of changes
in social status such as maturation and marriage. Schleiermacher even went so
far as to suggest that under particularly degenerate conditions religious rituals

might perform *only* these nonreligious functions, their original purpose being more or less thoroughly forgotten or obfuscated. Actual religion, in other words, is a social affair not merely in the sense that it necessarily involves interpersonal communication and collective activity but also in the sense that it reflects the broader network of social forces within which religious community is embedded. Again, Schleiermacher considered this state of affairs to be problematic to a certain extent, and the *Speeches* mark the first episode in his lifelong efforts to "purify" actual religion by separating it from "alien influences" and bring it to more closely resemble ideal religion. However, to repeat a theme from the introduction to this book, scholars of religion need not share Schleiermacher's view on this point and should not be distracted from the project of reconstructing Schleiermacher's understanding of *actual* religion by his negative evaluation of this in comparison to his ideal.[54]

3.4 Religion in the Ethics Lectures

Schleiermacher's developing thought on religion during the first two decades of the nineteenth century are documented most fully in the notes from his Halle and Berlin lectures on ethics. The significance of this material for understanding his account of religion cannot be overstated, for these lectures contain the only sustained discussions of the nature of religion that Schleiermacher conducted in a nontheological context. Had Schleiermacher succeeded in publishing a "system of ethics" characterized by the same clarity of organization and expression as his mature dogmatics, the history of his reception among scholars of religion would, in my estimation, have been significantly different. As it is, however, the account of religion contained in the ethics material must be reconstructed by way of extraction from a mass of surrounding material. In this section I attempt such an extraction, which involves following a fairly narrow discursive thread through the massive and fiercely abstract discussions contained in the surviving lecture notes.

The fifty-eighth instructional hour of the *Brouillon zur Ethik* presents a characterization of religion that in my view represents the core of Schleiermacher's understanding of the phenomenon in the ethics lectures generally.[55] The context of the relevant remark is a discussion of "good" and "bad" as these terms refer to ethical activity—that is, individual activity within the ambit of a social group. The general idea expressed in the passage is that the fundamental metric of ethical activity is the degree to which it is oriented not toward the individual but toward the group.[56] "Bad" (*böse*) activity is that which leads to the persistence of "isolated existence" or a failure to seek or acknowledge a connection to that which is common to the group; "the good," in contrast, is "to refer the subjective side of the community to the identity of reason and of the organization, that is, to posit it as the relationship of isolated existence to the rest as a whole, as World in the proper sense." "Now through this," Schleiermacher remarked, "feeling is raised to the potency of *Sittlichkeit*, and this procedure is nothing other than that which we name religion."[57]

The fact that English lacks a term suitable for rendering *Sittlichkeit* makes it difficult to see just what Schleiermacher was proposing in this brief passage. To say simply that religion according to him is a matter of feeling's becoming *moral* will not do; rather, to speak of the "*Sittlichkeit* of feeling" refers to two respects in which religious feeling is related to the domain of collective human existence. On the one hand, religious feelings are "referred to the identity of reason"—referred, that is, to the "universal" pole of human existence—in that religious individuals feel their own isolated existence to be integrated into a larger whole: proximately that of their religious community and ultimately that of "the world in a proper sense." On the other hand, religious feeling is *sittlich* in the sense of being *customary*: Within particular religious communities a "common store of feeling" develops as a result of communal participation in activities characterized by reciprocal exchange, to the character of which the feelings of each individual, ideally, conform themselves. It is this last idea that is central for understanding the social dimension of Schleiermacher's thought on religion as this unfolded in his writings on ethics. Religion in the ethics lectures, it turns out, is that form of ethical activity whereby individuals become socialized with respect to the most radically individual and private dimension of experience—feeling or "immediate self-consciousness."

3.4.1 *Ethical Activity*

"All ethical knowledge," Schleiermacher wrote in the 1816–1817 lectures, "is the expression of reason becoming nature, a process which has already always begun but is never complete."[58] The subject matter of ethical investigation is the activity of reason (i.e., reasonable human activity), and this Schleiermacher understood as a matter of reason's seeking unity with nature or seeking to make nature "reasonable." The notion that is central to his understanding of how this unification takes place is that of the formation by reason of organisms or "organs": "To the extent that reason has only acted when nature has been united with it, and the nature which has become one with active reason must also be active and productive alongside it, the action of reason upon nature is the formation of an organism from the mass."[59]

In order to understand the idea of reason "organizing" nature and the significance of this notion for religion, we need a grasp of a pair of distinctions that give structure to the ethics lectures. The first of these distinctions is drawn within the area of ethical *activity*; the second, between forms of ethical *existence*.

In the *Brouillon*, Schleiermacher distinguished between organ formation (*Organbildung*) and organ use (*Organgebrauch*) as two fundamental forms of ethical activity;[60] in the later lectures he would term these *organizing* and *symbolizing* activity, respectively.[61] Roughly, *organ formation* or *organizing activity* is a matter of reason taking up raw natural materials and shaping them into entities that can then be used for reason's ends. *Organ use* is that activity whereby reason makes its presence within nature known through those aspects of nature previously organized or formed into organs of reason; Schleiermacher's choice of the term *symbolizing* to describe this activity in the later lectures indicates that he understood this activity to be primarily a matter of reason causing elements of nature to signify its presence therein, and all forms of expression by individuals and communities are subsumed under this heading.[62]

The two forms of ethical existence are described in the various lectures by a panoply of different terms. In general the distinction amounts to that between the particular and the general or between the individual and the universal. Schleiermacher's clearest expression of the distinction in the *Brouillon* uses the terms *abgeschlossenes Dasein* (which I render as "isolated existence") and *Gemeinschaft mit dem Ganzen* (community with the whole),[63] but the "general" pole is also described by the terms *identity*, *universality*, and *communality* (*Gemeinschaftlichkeit*), and the "particularity" pole by *individuality*, *personhood* (*Persönlichkeit*) and *nontransferability* (*Unübertragbarkeit*).[64] The idea of nontransferability in particular will be important for Schleiermacher's discussion of religious feeling.

Ethical life for Schleiermacher involves the two types of ethical *activity* working to mediate between the two forms of ethical *existence*. That is, ethical life comprises the continual alternation between reason *organizing* nature into organs or organisms and reason *using* these organs to express or symbolize itself. Moreover, what it is for a natural "mass" to be organized in this way is for a stable and productive relationship to come to exist between the poles of particularity and generality which exist within it.[65] What the science of ethics studies, then, is the always advancing but never completed organization of nature by reason, the result of which is that the natural order displays the marks of reason's activity to an ever-increasing extent. Schleiermacher in places referred to the general pattern whereby the organizing and symbolizing activity of reason continually alternate within the natural order as "the ethical process."[66]

Expressed more concretely, what "ethical process" describes is the continual formation, re-formation, and development of *social entities* at several levels. The organizing effects of ethical activity extend not only to social groups but also to the individuals that compose them: As Schleiermacher understood the matter, not only collective identity but also individual identity are products of the ethical process and thus of social interaction.[67] The mechanism by which the ethical process unfolds within the context of social groups is a familiar one: The expression of particularity leads to the formation of common character and its appropriation by individuals.[68] Thus, understanding the basic character of the ethical process, in Schleiermacher's view, constituted a first step toward understanding the behavior not only of individuals but also of families, nations, and peoples.[69]

Schleiermacher employed the distinctions between two forms of ethical existence and two forms of ethical activity to produce a fourfold scheme for distinguishing between "fundamental ethical forms." This scheme understands the state as *universal organizing* activity; the academy, or the sciences in general, as *universal, symbolizing* activity; free sociability as *individual organizing* activity; and religion (in the form of "church") as *individual symbolizing* activity.[70] This designation provides an initial orientation to the general place Schleiermacher assigned religion within the life of human society generally. As an *individual* rather than *universal* activity, religion contrasts with the state on the one hand and science on the other. Religion is rooted in the most radically particular aspect of human existence, feeling, and it is of the nature of religion to assume cultural and historical specificity and thus to assume a variety of concrete forms. In addition, as a form of *symbolizing* rather than *organizing* activity, religion contrasts with the state and free sociability in that, unlike these, religion is not in the first instance a matter of the production and maintenance of social order or organization out of a relatively unstructured human "mass." Rather, religious activity is predicated on the existence of something already organized by reason (in fact, as we will see below, Schleiermacher described the social form "church" as constituted by the unification of individuals of the same religious "type"), which in turn becomes a symbol of reason's effectiveness within the natural order.[71] It will become clear from what follows that this architectonic cannot be interpreted rigidly as implying a restriction of religion to the pole of individuality and the activity of symbolizing. Rather, his view was that everywhere in the realm of ethical activity forms of existence and activity interpenetrate, and both the pole of communality and formative activity are well represented within religion.[72] Furthermore, while his initial classification discusses religion under the heading of a particular kind of social organization (church), it was not his position that religion is to be found only within this particular social form. Rather, as we will see, religion can historically be found in a variety of social settings from the family to the state.

As both Schleiermacher's architectonic and the citation above from the *Brouillon* suggest, religion figures in the ethics lectures as a specific form of the general ethical process. In the next section I defend the claim that in the context of the lectures religion is understood as *the ethical process operating upon "feeling."*

3.4.2 Feeling

Schleiermacher's revised understanding of feeling and its relation to intuition appear in the forty-fifth instructional hour of the *Brouillon*. Here Schleiermacher described both intuitions and feelings as developments of perceptions

(*Wahrnehmungen*). However, whereas intuitions represent an "objective" development, feeling represents a "subjective" one: "What we posit as intuition, that we posit as a uniform relation to the communal subjectivity, to the nature of human beings. What we posit as feeling, that we posit on the contrary as personal, individual, local, temporal subjectivity. The former we consider everywhere and unconditionally to be the same in everyone; concerning the latter we are satisfied that it is in no-one entirely the same as in us."[73]

In other words, both intuition and feeling are principles of human subjectivity. But whereas intuitions are produced in all human beings in the same way, feeling represents a principle of particularity in that it occurs differently in all individuals. Inasmuch as the members of a particular group share the same experiences, their intuitions will also be shared, but the same is not true with respect to feeling. "My feeling is absolutely my own, and so can belong to no other," Schleiermacher claimed later. "Indeed, we say that even under entirely similar circumstances, a different feeling would have to arise in each one."[74]

Schleiermacher's practice in the *Brouillon* of referring to intuition as "objective cognition" and to feeling as "subjective cognition" indicates that both have cognitive content, but the type of content each contains differs. In the fifty-eighth instructional hour Schleiermacher (much like Kant in the first *Critique*) postulates in human beings a faculty of bringing fleeting mental events into some kind of determinate relationship as a condition of the possibility of coherent experience (which he refers to as "the higher faculty"). Where the relationship between self and world is the source of experience, either the world or the self can emerge as the content of experience:

> Just as the objective side, in the community between isolated
> existence and the world, depicts the world in relationship as
> determinate intuition, so the subjective side depicts isolated
> existence in the determined relationship, that is as a fixed moment,
> as a changeable condition in determinate feelings. But just as
> perception is merely something changeable without the influence of
> the higher faculty and only through this influence attains to ordered
> intuition, [or] world, so also sensation (*Empfindung*) without this
> influence is something changeable, in which no unity of
> consciousness is to be fixed in succession. No I without the higher
> faculty, but only through it.[75]

Both intuition and feeling are thus products of a process that brings the initially disordered elements of experience into a determinate order under the influence of the "higher faculty," a process that is necessary for the existence of the unified and perceiving self. Intuitions will have as their representational content something external to the self and will be produced the same way in each person. Feelings, on the other hand, have the self as their content and will occur differently in each person. Intuitions will thus represent the pole of generality within the ethical process, while feelings will be manifestations of "personal, individual and local subjectivity" and thus will represent the pole of particularity.[76] In the later lectures this understanding of feeling develops into the claim that would inform Schleiermacher's dogmatics, that feeling is equivalent to *self-consciousness*.[77]

The discussion up to this point should have made it clear that Schleiermacher's characterization of feeling as "nontransferable," as a radically individual and particular affair, does not imply that it is isolated from the sphere of the public and the interpersonal. In spite of its nontransferability feeling intersects with that realm in two respects. First, feeling is not an autonomous creation of individual persons but is itself a product of the ethical process: Generically considered, it is a human universal, as much an "expression of reason in nature" as thought.[78] Second, it is of the nature of feeling to enter once again into the ethical process, to find expression and seek its own development through reciprocal communication.

In the *Brouillon* the drive for the "externalization" of feeling is presented as a matter of natural necessity, for "the unity of life and the identity of reason distributed among individuals would be entirely nullified (*aufgehoben*) if that which is nontransferable could not again become something communal and communicative."[79] Thus "each influence on the inside which becomes a feeling also drives, through organic necessity, again towards the outside,"[80] and indeed, as Schleiermacher would state the point in the Berlin lectures, the desire for genuine reciprocity between persons "would always remain empty if feeling could not become known (*kund*) between one and the other."[81] More completely expressed,

> My feeling is absolutely my own, and so can belong to no other.
> Indeed, we say that even under entirely similar circumstances, a
> different feeling would have to arise in each one. Now if this
> characteristic [of nontransferability] were exclusive (*ausschließend*),
> then feeling would be absolutely isolated and thereby would lose
> entirely the characteristic of reasonableness, by virtue of which that
> which takes place only in the person [also] happens for reason in
> general in its identity. For this reason a tendency to communicate
> itself is given in feeling. In that feeling which in itself comes to
> clarity, there is also a striving to arouse the same in others.[82]

In at least one significant respect, the *Brouillon*'s account of the "communication of feeling" differs from the corresponding material in the *Speeches on Religion*. In the *Speeches*, it will be recalled, Schleiermacher had spoken of the "transmission" of intuitions of the universe from one person to the next. In the *Brouillon*, the simple "transmission" of feeling between persons is ruled out by the nontransferability of feeling. Here Schleiermacher contrasted the communication of feeling with that of thought:

Feeling is posited as absolutely inexpressible (*unaussprechlich*) and is usually described in speech only through its reaction as an object of reflection; and only in generality, not in individuality. That which is communicated also cannot be the same. Through speech, the same activity is re-created (*nachgebildet*) in the other (at least this is the intent, even if one never entirely accomplishes this on account of the intertwined character of nontransferability). This cannot occur with feeling, and it also cannot emerge in this way. Rather, it can only be made out (*hingestellt*) as the object of the relationship, so that thereby the other's feelings are aroused.[83]

The public expression of feeling does not lead directly to the simple reduplication of the feelings of one individual within another; thus, the passive "copying" of religious intuitions that characterizes religious activity within the church conceived as a mediating institution, is not possible within the terms of Schleiermacher's revised account of religious communication. Rather, religious feelings, even as they find expression in discourse and ritual activity and so become publicly "known," remain tethered to the pole of particularity. As he would state this point in 1816,

> no-one feels because of the feeling of another become known to him, much less that he should feel just so. Rather, only because and insofar as each knows that a certain emotion in him would be externalized in a similar way does he conclude that the other is gripped by a similar emotion, which however in its particularity remains hidden to him. So here there is no articulating and reproducing (*Aussprechen und Nachbilden*), but only intimating and surmising (*Andeuten und Ahnden*), no making intelligible (*Verständigung*), but revelation (*Offenbarung*).[84]

However, if the expression of feeling cannot yield the simple reproduction of the feelings of one individual within another, nevertheless, through this process "nontransferable feeling at the same time necessarily becomes something external again and takes on the character of the community."[85] What makes this possible is the fact that feeling, although a principle of particularity and technically nontransferable, is nevertheless a product of reason; thus, those who apperceive the expressive activities of others not only become aware of the state of their own feelings but also have their own feelings "stirred in response" and will tend by natural necessity to experience feelings that are analogous to those expressed by the others. The communication of feeling, even if only in an approximate form, is thus possible in virtue of the ultimate unity of human nature:

> All communication, the answering recognition of a feeling, takes place here only through the medium of an analogical process; just as the movement to depiction is similar to one that appears in my self,

so the feeling producing the movement is similar to one that forms the basis of my self. This process must rest on an identity which, in this case, can only be that of the formation of the human organism, so that here, too, what is individual rests on the foundations of what is universal.[86]

The "mysterious nature" of this process is indicated by the fact that, to describe the communication of feeling through such channels, Schleiermacher used the same term, *revelation* (*Offenbarung*), as was used in the *Speeches* to describe the transmission of religious intuitions between persons, although "it is not something supernatural that is meant by the word here...but only something generically human, to which we can also trace back the supernatural meaning of these words."[87]

The product of the ethical process as this applies to feeling, then, is a *rough equivalence* or *common character* among the feelings of the members of a particular discursive circle. As in the *Speeches*, the theme of religious community proper emerges in the *Brouillon* as a product of religious discourse: "[T]he communication of [feeling] individualizes itself, and even develops a particular circle of intelligibility (*Verständlichkeit*) in accordance with the identity of great organic conditions; and this individual unity of feeling itself and its depiction is the idea of a church."[88] "Church," then, is defined as a social form grounded in and dedicated to the idea of common feeling—thus as a social manifestation of a particular species of the ethical process.

A basic continuity between the first edition of the *Speeches* and the ethics lectures thus survives Schleiermacher's replacement of the notion of "intuitions of the universe" with "religious feeling." Whereas in the *Speeches* religion was a matter of the communication of intuitions from one person to the next, in the *Brouillon* religion is the process whereby feeling is made communal and "customary." In the *Brouillon*, however, Schleiermacher's early account of religion is radicalized in at least one sense: Here that which is made into both the common possession of a group of individuals and a publicly acknowledged principle of common identity is the most individual and private aspect of human experience. From the *Brouillon* on, then, "religion" describes a process whereby the most intimately particular aspects of personhood become principles of social formation. It is through religion that the most profound "individuality and particularity" that characterizes human existence is brought into the stream of social life.

In what remains of this section I draw attention to three topics that Schleiermacher explored in the Berlin lectures. The theme that is common to these topics is the intersection between human sociality and history: Each concerns a specific respect in which the dynamics of human sociality provide an avenue for religion to assume concrete form. The first topic is that of "preformations of feeling," Schleiermacher's claim that specific human populations are predisposed toward particular types of religious feeling in virtue of the "large organic conditions" that bear upon them. The second has to do with his further exploration of the idea that religious communication requires and produces a set of material vehicles, which he refers to in the ethics lectures as a "body of art." The third has to do with Schleiermacher's discussion of the social forms that religion assumes in various stages of the development of human society, both prior and subsequent to the development of the social form "church" proper. Each of these topics eventually found expression in those sections of *The Christian Faith* that rely on "propositions borrowed from ethics," albeit in compressed form; in reviewing this material we are thus witnessing the development of Schleiermacher's mature view of religion and its relationship to the natural order.

3.4.3 Religious "Types"

Schleiermacher's remarks in the Berlin lectures about the respects in which different groups of human beings are "preformed" with respect to feeling are both suggestive and underdeveloped. They are suggestive in that they point to an intimate connection between large-scale contingent characteristics of human beings such as race and nationality on the one hand and religion on the other, such that the development of the latter owes much to the specifics of the former. Yet the surviving notes from Schleiermacher's lectures do not contain enough detail to discern just how Schleiermacher understood this connection, if indeed his position on the matter extended beyond the content of the notes.

Ethical activity in general presupposes "a twofold original given: 1) by which the originally identical is nevertheless originally separated, and 2) whereby the originally different is nevertheless originally linked."[89] What originally links the individual members of any given mass is, however, always something more specific than bare human nature: Even considered as an original "mass," the human species is internally diverse and yet roughly divided into distinct groups by "large organic conditions." "Particularity, taken as what is quite simply separate, is originally unified in human nature by means of biological descent brought about by procreation; identity, taken as what is quite simply bound up, is originally divided by climatic variations between peoples, i.e., by variations in race and folk tradition. Both, then, are fixed elements of measure, which have always been given."[90] Among the "large organic traditions" Schleiermacher in various places listed race, language, nationality, gender, and "folk tradition" (*Volksthümlichkeit*); by the term *climatic variations*, which seems to encompass these others, I take his intent to be to describe those respects in which human existence is so fundamentally marked by both natural and broadly cultural contingency that no examples of the ethical process are exempt from such conditions.[91] "It is within these natural boundaries that ethical relationships are determined," he remarked in 1816, "and everything indeterminate can be traced back to them and measured accordingly."[92]

This initial division of the human species also extends to feeling: To account for the historical development of a finite number of discrete religious traditions and the particularity of the "body of art" of each, Schleiermacher argued that "we must therefore posit, as something given by nature, several schematisms of feeling which are particular to great masses."[93] The postulation of these "schematisms of feeling" follows on the observation that religion tends toward a cultural specificity whose boundaries are not entirely clear: "[E]ven if individual churches have an urge to spread [their message] indefinitely, it is nevertheless clear that they lose their own particular character in many respects and can only enjoy a productive and reproductive life if they remain within a certain mass; this mass, however, certainly cannot be determined by unity of race."[94] These schematisms of feeling explain the local nature of the religious traditions observable within history in that they result in the original existence of distinct religious characters or "types."

A religious "type" represents, in the ethics lectures, a predisposition toward certain kinds of religious formation and conversely an inaptitude toward others; the naturally given distinction between religious types thus represents a basic constraint on the historical development of religions. As described earlier, the successful "revelation" of feeling requires the achievement of a kind of resonance between two persons, whereby one person correctly surmises the feelings of the other on the basis of the expressions of those feelings. As Schleiermacher understood it, a similarity of religious type is required for this communicative process to succeed: the rise of a particular religion within a particular population by way of revelation "presupposes that the type is already present in the mass—since otherwise revelation would find no answering faith."[95]

In significant (but only vaguely explored) respects, then, the "feeling character" of a particular religion is constrained in advance by the religious types present within that sector of the population within which it arises. As Schleiermacher stated the point in a later marginal addition to his notes for 1812–1813, "A revelation cannot be accepted unless it truly expresses the religious consciousness of a mass. Thus every revelation which has entered history is also true, if imperfect."[96] Moreover, Schleiermacher's definition of the ethical form "church" in the 1812–1813 lectures incorporates this idea of religious types directly: "The essence of the church lies in the organic unification of a mass of people *of the same type* for the purposes of subjective activity of the cognitive function under the opposition of clergy and laity"[97] (emphasis added).

The idea that the human population is divided in advance, so to speak, into groups within which the "feeling character" of religion is to some extent predetermined suggests an intimate connection between religion and contingent characteristics of human beings that varies by sociogeographical location. However, the precise extent to which religious types constrain religious development in Schleiermacher's thought is not clear. It is not clear, for example,

whether an individual's "preformation" with respect to feeling could be overridden by sufficiently powerful religious socialization or whether such preformation renders certain kinds of religion forever unthinkable for particular
persons (a passage from the *Glaubenslehre* suggests the former view but not
decisively[98]). A note appended to the discussion of religious character in the
1812–1813 lectures indicates that Schleiermacher may have understood these
feeling types as at least coterminous with cultural distinctions and possibly
as supervenient upon them: "Indian=phlegmatic; Greek=sanguine; Jewish=
choleric; Christian=melancholic?"[99] In the end the notion of religious types
remains an underdeveloped idea whose purpose is to explain the geographical and broadly cultural specificity of religious traditions even under the
condition of substantial cross-cultural interchange,[100] and it is possible that
Schleiermacher's view of the subject was no more developed than his remarks
in the Berlin lectures reveal. It can nevertheless be concluded from these
remarks that according to Schleiermacher the human race is not by nature a
"blank slate" with respect to religious formation but that the character of actual
religion, even at the level of feeling, is determined to a certain extent by the pre-
or extrareligious aspects of human existence. This doctrine of "schematisms of
feeling" suggests that the observable religions of the world are in effect articula-
tions of the "feeling character" of particular segments of the human populations—developments of characteristics that existed in latent form prior to the
development of religious particularity.

Although the notion of schematisms of feeling does not appear in *The
Christian Faith*, the idea of religious "types" does put in an appearance in §9 of
the second edition, in the context of Schleiermacher's discussion of the distinction between "aesthetic" and "teleological" religions that (in his view) could be
observed within history. As he explained the matter, what accounts for the existence of distinct "species" of religion is a differential predisposition within the
human population toward the formations of certain kinds of religious feelings,
a diversity that distinguishes not only individuals but also great masses of people from each other, "so that either among some people a certain class of sensible feelings develops into pious emotions easily and surely, but another,
opposed to this, with difficulty or not at all, while with others just the reverse is
the case; or that the same sensible states of self-consciousness develop into
moments of piety for one person under one condition, but for another under
the opposite."[101]

3.4.4 Material Religion: Art and the Cult

The ethics lectures contain a significantly expanded treatment, in comparison
to the *Speeches*, of the subject of nonlinguistic modes of religious expression.
The term *art* (*Kunst*) in the ethics lectures refers to material artifacts and routinized behaviors that serve as the material vehicles of the communication of

feeling. Schleiermacher grounded his discussion of the relationship between religion and art in an analogy: "[A]rt stands in the same relation to religion as language does to knowledge."[102]

In the ethics lectures (as generally throughout Schleiermacher's mature corpus) the relationship between knowledge or thought and language is described as one of dependence, in that thought must assume linguistic form in order to become determinate; in the terminology of the *Glaubenslehre*, "thought does not take place, even inwardly, without the use of speech."[103] It follows from this view that the thoughts of any given individuals will depend in large measure upon the condition and uses of language within their environment, a point to which Schleiermacher drew attention in his 1816 lectures: "[T]he individual develops his consciousness only by means of language and must therefore consider his thoughts to be modeled [on those of others], and the thoughts of those whose signifying terms constitute language, so to speak, as the archetype of his own."[104]

The position expressed in the ethics lectures is that while feeling is "absolutely inexpressible" (i.e., not in itself linguistically structured), it nevertheless stands in a relationship to its own proper forms of expression that is analogous to the relationship between thought and language. In 1816 Schleiermacher advanced the term *gesture* (*Geberde*) as the correlate to language in the realm of feeling: "[G]esture, taken in the broadest sense of the word, stands in the same direct and original relation to feeling as language does to thought; and just as no thought is mature and complete until it has simultaneously been made word, so no feeling is a complete and perfected act until it has been made gesture."[105] "Gesture" as a general phenomenon would seem to incorporate the entire range of nonlinguistic modes of expression; in places within the ethics lectures Schleiermacher also assigns a capacity to serve as a vehicle for the communication of feeling to "tone," facial expression, and music.[106] If these various kinds of phenomena constitute ways of depicting feeling, "the various kinds of depiction (*Darstellung?*) thus form a system (in the place of the single system of language on the objective side) which includes everything that can be an element of one of the arts."[107]

Within the ethics lectures, the arts represent the material vehicles of the communication of feeling. Besides making it possible for feelings to attain determinate form within the individual, the concreteness of the arts also makes it possible for the expression of feelings to assume a form that can persist over time. Art makes possible the "raising of feeling to the potency of *Sittlichkeit*" beyond the boundaries of a circle of immediate, face-to-face interaction, for in art, "feeling is meant to compose itself and momentary expression is to become fixed and objectivized, so that art becomes the repository of all feelings and each person receives from it his communicating and communicated existence."[108] So understood, art represents the natural embodiment of religion:

Just as all knowledge can be reduced to language, so all actions of
subjective cognition can be reduced to art. The highest tendency of
the church is the development of a treasury of art (*Kunstschaz*), on
the basis of which the feeling of each one develops, and in which
each lays down his most exemplary feelings and the free
presentations of his way of feeling, just as each one whose depictive
production might not keep pace with his feeling can also appropriate
[his] presentations.[109]

Art makes possible the regular, if always approximate, reproduction of specific forms of feeling within members of a discursive community. A religious community's "treasury of art" both represents and embodies the progressive development of its common character on the level of feeling. Such a treasury also makes possible the development of criteria of appropriateness in relation to feeling, the development of particular forms of feeling that come to be regarded as normative for members of the community. The activity whereby individuals interact with a particular "treasury of art" both by contributing to it and by forming their own feeling in response to it, Schleiermacher refers to as the cult (*Cultus*): "Insofar as the treasury of art develops a real mass, each person has access to it at any time. But for presentation under transitory forms, in order to articulate and nourish the common life, there must be a common participation (*Zusammentreten*), for which reason a cult develops in each church."[110]

Although the notes do not go into great detail on the subject of the cult, I take the following to be more or less what Schleiermacher has in mind. Each generation of church members encounters a repository of artistic productions within the church—hymns, liturgical and ritual practices, and so on—which constitute a formalized "system of depictions" of religious feeling. It is through exposure to and participation in such practices that the capacity of the new generation to respond in feeling to the world in a common way is formed. What is more, each of these new members, if they participate fully in the life of the church, will contribute something to the church's repository of art from the depths of their own particularity. In this way a dynamic, always-developing performative and formative tradition develops along with the material artistic productions of the church.[111] Indeed, the cult itself can be seen as a work of art, although a "living" one: In the *Brouillon*, Schleiermacher describes the cult "as an institution for formation (*Bildungsanstalt*), as the self-developing self-activity of the whole, but also as the immediate creation of a communal work of art."[112]

Cultic activity as Schleiermacher understood it is thus ethical activity par excellence; it involves the reciprocally formative interplay between the individual persons and the common feeling character of the group. Religious ritual, then, is understood within the ethics lectures as a routinized means of forming up individual subjectivity in accordance with a common standard, which standard is on the one hand embodied (with some degree of permanence and authority) by a received "treasury of art," and on the other hand is subject to development (and revision) as successive generations make their own contributions to it.

Schleiermacher's discussion of religious art and cultic activity in the ethics lectures has much in common with both the *Speeches on Religion* and *The Christian Faith*. For the most part the differences among the three texts can be characterized as one of continuous development, with the *Speeches* presenting the idea of religious expression in embryonic form, the ethics lectures developing the notion more completely, and *The Christian Faith* applying the developed idea to a particular theological topic (the critical evaluation of religious doctrines).[113] One difference between the *Speeches* and the later texts, however, strikes me as more of a genuine shift of position than a matter of simple development. The ethics lectures mark the disappearance of the idea, prominent in the *Speeches*, that the routinization of religious expression is a necessary evil, a concession to the "negatively religious," who populate a "false and depraved church." Instead, from 1805 on, the formation of a body of art and of regularized cultic practice is described impartially as the way religion naturally develops within a population.

3.4.5 *The Historical Social Forms of Religion*

Earlier in the chapter we saw that in the *Speeches*, Schleiermacher's description of the stages of religion's social development was one of progressive degeneration, from the pristine city of God to a thoroughly compromised state religion. I argued in the last section that this developmental narrative is a thought experiment aimed at presenting a vision of what religion *could* and *should* be; Schleiermacher did not, in other words, intend the fourth speech as in any sense a historical narrative of religious development. It is in the ethics lectures that Schleiermacher offered an account of the social-developmental stages through which religion passes in the course of its historical development.

As we have seen, in the ethics lectures "church" appears as one of four "completed ethical forms," alongside the state, the academy, and free sociability.[114] The specific ethical form "church" covers the same territory as that indicated by the mediating institution of the fourth of the *Speeches*; the term designates a social organization dedicated to religion and characterized by a differentiation between active and passive religious roles (i.e., an antithesis [*Gegensaz*] between clergy and laity). "Inasmuch as in the church each has his religious feeling not only as something personal but at the same time as something common, he also strives to transplant (*fortpflanzen*) his affections in the other persons and in return present their affections as well. All gradations of the churchly antithesis [between clergy and laity] are only different spheres and forms in which this occurs."[115]

While "church" names a social arrangement specifically dedicated to the purpose of religion, it was not Schleiermacher's position that "church" is the only social form within which religion can take place. His view of societal development was one of progressive functional differentiation: The more a society's different ethical functions secure for themselves relatively autonomous spheres of activity, the more advanced the society is.[116] "Church" as a specific social form arises only at a relatively high level of societal development, and the emergence of "church" as a relatively autonomous social arrangement does not mark the first societal appearance of religion. Rather, religion, considered as an example of the ethical process, first appears as a dimension of life within a more original social form, that of the family.

"In every family, taken as a unity, we may posit an adequacy for the ethical process," Schleiermacher remarked in the 1812–1813 lectures.[117] We can understand his conception of "household religion" as follows: Inasmuch as the ethical process as it occurs between members of a family extends to feeling, within a particular household there will develop a common "family character" of feeling. Thus, one strand of discourse among the members of a household will qualify as religious. On Schleiermacher's account the difference between the sexes counts as one of the factors informing the dynamics of household religion: "Religion becomes rooted and individualized in the family, because the relative antithesis between masculine and feminine relates particularly to feeling. In men in general cognition is predominant, in women feeling. And on the other hand in feeling the external side of depiction [is predominant] in men, the inner in women."[118] "Household religion" thus has a "patriarchal" character as a result of the fact that Schleiermacher saw the drive toward the externalization of feeling to be primarily a masculine affair: "[I]n the household cult the father performs the priestly function."[119]

The first historical appearance of religion is thus not characterized by the egalitarianism of the city of God but partakes of the natural hierarchies of gender and generation that mark family relations. In assigning to the father the original priestly function, Schleiermacher suggests that religion within the family is primarily a matter of the father producing "expressions of feeling" that have some degree of authority or normativity within the circle of the family and then of the wife and children receiving "formation" at the level of feeling in response. The extent to which family religion involves *reciprocal* formation, with wife and children contributing their own particularity to the common store of feeling within the family, is not clear, but it seems reasonable to me to think that on Schleiermacher's account the degree of reciprocity in family religion is generally lower than within the social form "church" proper and also that reciprocality within the family increases as children grow to maturity.[120]

Religion retains this patriarchal character in the forms of social organization that represent natural outgrowths of the family: "horde," tribe, and nation or people (*Volk*). As Schleiermacher used the term, a "horde" is a simple assemblage of families whose common character and internal organization have not yet been produced by ethical activity;[121] tribes and peoples/nations are such assemblages in which there is such a common character, one based on kinship (in the tribe) or on a broader similarity of type (in the nation).[122] That the religion of these organizations is patriarchal indicates that the authority structure of the tribe or clan also dictates the division of religious labor. The necessary condition for the development of "church" proper is the separation of religious from kinship roles: "The horde condition (*Hordenzustand*) of religion, usually known as the patriarchal state, only ever passes over into the organized state, that of the church, once an antithesis has been awakened, namely between clergy and laity."[123] The social organization "church" thus emerges historically only when religious leadership is decoupled from the authority structure of the family or clan.

In both the *Brouillon* and the 1812–1813 lectures, Schleiermacher indicated a close relationship between the development of "church" proper and that of the state. If the condition for the development of "church" is the emergence of a relatively autonomous clergy-lay distinction, the emergence of a similarly autonomous distinction between leaders and subjects is the condition of the development of the state.[124] However, both church and state emerge within social environments already marked by some form of collective identity (i.e., horde, tribe, or nation); thus, it is possible for the processes whereby each develops to overlap and interpenetrate. "If each individual inner unity must also have a body," Schleiermacher remarked in the *Brouillon*, "how does the church obtain its body, and how is [this body] to be determined? Particularly by the relation to the state, which lies closest to it. Since the church also grows out of heterogeneous family relations, its outer sphere naturally coincides with that of the state."[125] The *Brouillon*'s account of the development of church as a distinct social organization is close to that of the *Speeches on Religion*: Church emerges only when the social form of *friendship* combines with that of family to create social circles in which contrasting family characteristics are brought together.[126] The poles of the ethical process within the social form "church" are the "family element" (particularity), contributed by "the laity as congregation," and the "art element" (generality), contributed by the priests;[127] this echoes Schleiermacher's later claim that the development of a treasury of art is characteristic of the social form "church." Because church develops out of family relations in this way, presupposing only commonality of language and of "organic conditions," church and state are in principle distinct, and "conflict and interference can arise only from misunderstanding."[128]

In the 1812–1813 lectures, Schleiermacher described two ways in which both church and state emerge out of the "horde condition." The first way in which the state develops is through a gradual increase of common consciousness within all of the members of a mass: "The state can be coterminous with the horde, in which case the transition is rooted in the gradual development of consciousness." The other possibility is that common consciousness emerges suddenly and locally at a certain place within the mass: "[The state] can also arise if several hordes are fused together, when consciousness develops out of the larger living unity which is the same in all of them and then emerges energetically at some point."[129] Such a local emergence of the idea of the state is a recipe for conflict between those who are in alignment with the new form of collective identity and those who are not: "[G]enesis of the state in this form will always be revolutionary."[130]

Transposed to the realm of religion, the second of these models of ethical formation fairly obviously echoes Schleiermacher's description of the development of religious community in the *Speeches*. In general terms the development of "church" is only possible inasmuch as a particular mass is strongly marked by a particular religious type: "[S]imilarity of type is originally posited in the homogeneous mass, even if in an undeveloped form. People who are in spatial contact with one another are attracted to one another as homogeneous beings, and their community comes entirely under the [general] character and extent of the horde."[131] In this context Schleiermacher observed that it is possible for the development of a church to be "analogous to the genesis of the state from an idea holding sway within an individual, which is actually the concept of revelation":[132] As in the *Speeches*, the idea here is that religious community is the result of the local emergence of the kernel of a new form of collective identity and its subsequent spread through a population through the channels of ethical activity (i.e., religious communication).

Here, however, Schleiermacher presented this local mode of the development of church subsequent to an alternative path of development: "[T]he emergence of the church can just as well be an analogue to the emergence of the state as a simple democracy."[133] The suggestion is that religious community develops in some cases through a gradual development of a common character of feeling distributed evenly across the members of a particular mass. In such a case Schleiermacher anticipated that church and state will be in close alignment; absent decisive and intentional activity aimed at establishing a social organization dedicated to "raising feeling to the potency of *Sittlichkeit*," awareness of the particularity of the emerging religion sufficient to prompt differentiation from the *political* identity of a people will be lacking. In cases where church develops in this way "it has a less powerful life force, which is revealed partly by the incomplete way in which it breaks free of the state and partly by a greater readiness to merge with similar systems so that its own pure particularity is not disclosed."[134]

The 1812–1813 lectures, then, offer an alternative account of state religion as a result of the gradual development of a common character of feeling within the members of a particular mass of people in close relationship with the development of their structures of governance. As in the *Speeches*, in the ethics lectures Schleiermacher clearly indicated that the progressive development of religion is in part a matter of its working its way clear of entanglement with the state. In the *Speeches*, however, Schleiermacher was primarily interested in offering an ideal and possibly realizable vision of a church independent of state control; the ethics lectures, in contrast, represent an attempt to account for the relationships between religion and both particular states and also for the national character of religions observable within history. The first edition of the *Brief Outline of the Study of Theology* makes the point in a form that I think could be attributed to the *Speeches*, as well as to Schleiermacher's later writings: "[T]he development of the common Christian life is affected primarily by political circumstances and by the general social situation."[135]

In the *Brouillon* Schleiermacher provided support for the claim that religious social unity is distinct in principle from political unity by observing that "all cases can be found in history: equivalence [*Gleichheit*], the assemblage of several churches within one state and several states under one church."[136] Although it is possible for religious and political unity to diverge, historically the development of a collective religious consciousness is often coterminous with that of a collective political consciousness. In 1812–1813 he suggested that the close relationship between church and state is to be understood in the same way as that between the state and the academy, understood as the "national community of knowledge": "The historically given dependence of [educational] institutions on the state can be explained as an as-yet-incomplete separation of the domains of the [cognitive and formative] functions, originating with the family, where the two are as one, or else as a favoring of the state, which secures the basis of the scientific organization in order to be sure of its own influence on the formative function."[137]

The suggestion, then, is that there are reasons, rooted in the laws of ethical formation, for church and state to develop in close connection but that the progressive development of both requires their eventual separation. Thus, "if individual churches do not go beyond the limits of national unity, that is partly because they have not properly detached themselves from the state (the Jews, who made a naturalized citizen of everyone who professed their faith, represent an extreme here), partly because the force with which they spread their message was weak from the beginning."[138]

To summarize, in the ethics lectures Schleiermacher retained his early view that the development of religion requires a social circle for the communication of inward religion, but he also explored the idea that religion can inhabit social structures not specifically dedicated to this particular kind of ethical formation. In historical perspective religion first arises as a concomitant of relationships within the family and develops through a "tribal" condition as families themselves merge into larger social wholes. What might be called "state religion" in the ethics lectures is a natural condition within societies at relatively advanced stages of ethical development; independence of church and state is described not as an original and vanished condition but as a goal of ethical (i.e., social) development. The development of religion's social form thus follows the development of society generally, with the separation of the various spheres growing with time and tending toward a state of relative autonomy from one another.

3.5 Conclusion: Religious Tradition

During the twenty years between the publication of the *Speeches on Religion* and that of the first edition of *The Christian Faith*, Schleiermacher developed and regularly presented to his students what can be understood as a theory of *religious tradition*. In his hands this project assumed the form of explaining how a form of collective activity predicated upon a particular constellation of "subjective cognition" could persist and maintain that particular form of "feeling" in living circulation. What makes it possible for forms of feeling to become the common possession of a historically extended collection of individuals is, first, the way feeling is related to its natural vehicles of expression and, second, the fundamental similarity between individuals with respect to feeling, particularly within specific religious types:

> Cognition, in the form of the tradition, rests upon the possibility of transferring something from one consciousness to the other. This is conditional upon the fact that the act, as something internal in origin, becomes external: something which appears to the person bringing it forth to be an expression, but exists for everyone else as a sign by means of which—by virtue of the identity of the schematism—he is able to recognize what is internal, or the original act.[139]

Since, as I argue in the previous chapter, what defines religion according to Schleiermacher is a relationship to an inward core, the development of religion as a historical reality requires that the inward dimensions of human life be both transparent and plastic: transparent so that the inward aspects of a particular religion can become public, and plastic so that that which is publicly available can exert a formative effect upon the inward.[140] Schleiermacher's ethics lectures present humanity as a species formed through a wide range of social interactions—with living persons and the material productions of previous generations, with the dynamics of family and state, as well as those of religious community proper—down to the level of that which is most personal and particular. Thus, religion, as had already been emphasized in the *Speeches*, is an outgrowth of rather than an exception to the fundamentally social nature of the human animal.[141]

A passage from the 1812–1813 lectures expresses something of the range of socially produced factors operative within religious activity as Schleiermacher understood it:

In high religious style the particularity of the person engaged in depiction diminishes in importance; in depicting he is merely the organ and representative of the church; for his depiction must be as objective as possible for the whole domain of the particular religious type. In private religious depictions, representing the church in the family, particularity comes to the fore somewhat more, since here the intention is for the ecclesiastical type to appear modified specifically by the character of the family. In the profane style personal particularity ought to come right to the fore while the part played by the ecclesiastical type is almost purely passive—that of a boundary which may not be exceeded. This is also the reason why in the great modern forms of religion, in the high ecclesiastical style, nationality hardly comes to the fore, if at all, compared to the profane style, where it is dominant.[142]

This passage describes religious communication as involving a fluctuating relationship between particularity and generality, as is the case with any species of ethical activity. But there are two features of this discussion that are particularly noteworthy. The first is that here Schleiermacher explicitly made the point that extrareligious forms of identity formation find their way into the life of religion; specifically, in the "profane style" of religious practice, the national character of the participants, their character as a distinct people, is strongly in evidence. This point is far from incidental in light of Schleiermacher's own public career, which was strongly marked by the intermingling of the religious and the political. By 1812 he had applied the idea of a link between the religious and the national identities of particular populations in his own activities as a preacher. As is commonly known, during the French occupation of Prussia Schleiermacher preached a number of high-profile sermons aimed at awakening the "spirit of the Prussian people"—at times invoking the notion that Napoleon's ultimate aim was the destruction of Protestantism itself—with the goal of fomenting a popular uprising against the occupation and the institution of a Prussian state more responsive to the aspirations of its citizens.[143] This observation of the political character of much of Schleiermacher's religious activity is an example of the fact that, as Heino Falcke has put it, "his social doctrine [Gesellschaftslehre] was not developed in solitary reflection at his desk but in close contact with political events, from an intensive consciousness of history and from a social responsibility which wanted not only to satisfy a scientific need but also to contribute to shaping the future of political reality."[144]

The second feature of this passage is more interesting on religion-theoretical grounds. In 1802 Hegel famously criticized Schleiermacher for predicating religious community so directly and intimately on the characteristics of its individual members that any sort of stable and continuing sense of collective identity seemed ruled out: "[T]he little congregations and peculiarities assert themselves and multiply ad infinitum; they float apart and gather together by happenstance; every moment the groupings alter like the patterns in a sea of sand given over to the play of the winds."[145] Hegel's comments are an accurate reflection of Schleiermacher's call in the *Speeches* for experimentation with the social form of religion as an avenue to religious reform (a call echoed in Schleiermacher's approving remarks concerning the separation of church and state in the United States[146]). They do not, however, reflect Schleiermacher's understanding of the historical life of actual religious communities, either in the *Speeches* or in the ethics lectures. As Schleiermacher's remarks on styles of worship suggest, there is more in play within the dynamics of religious community than the expression of individual particularity.

In fact, this passage from the 1812–1813 lectures suggests that to think of religion as a dialectical relationship between *individual particularity* and *communal generality*—between, that is, the diverse religious states of mind of the individual members of a religious community and the subset of these that all members share in common, even if only in approximation—is too simple, for there is a third factor in play. This third factor, described in terms Schleiermacher might use, is exemplified for members of the religious community by its particular "repository of feelings"—that is, by its "treasury of art." This "treasury" represents for the members of a religious tradition a form of feeling that is distinct in principle from the actual religious states of mind of currently existing persons; it represents a standard to which these are expected to conform and exerts a formative influence upon them, but its ability to serve these functions does not depend on its being exemplified within the currently existing religious community. Rather, this form of feeling is itself a historical artifact.

This observation has significant consequences for a topic to be explored more fully in my concluding chapters. Considered as a species of ethical activity, religion involves more than the reciprocal formation of individual and collective forms of self-understanding by each other. It also involves a dynamic interplay of both individual and collective subjectivity with the material productions of previous iterations of this same process, and within the context of a "living" religious tradition, these productions will collectively constitute a source of religious normativity that constrains and informs the ongoing activity of the current generation of religious adherents even as these make their own contribution to it. The moral to be drawn from this observation is that understanding the historical life of religious traditions will not be a matter of identifying, sharing, or empathetically "resonating" with the most inward and private sentiments of religious individuals. Such a resonance, if it were to be achieved, would provide firsthand acquaintance with one component of religion but would not by itself inform the scholar about the ways in which religious feeling, thought, and practice are shaped by the historical inheritance of a tradition, or indeed by the entire range of extrareligious circumstances that bear on religious life. Ultimately I will apply reflections of this sort to the question of whether Schleiermacher is best categorized as a theorist of "autonomous religious experience." For the present, suffice it to say that if the arguments of the present chapter are on track, directing attention to the nature and content of the religious feelings of currently existing religious persons constitutes at best a beginning to the process of exploring religion as Schleiermacher understood it.

4

Religion, Christianity, and the "Eternal Covenant"

There are times and places where religiosity perishes and the entire life of a people is led out of its old, ancestral beds of religion and into other channels, such that it becomes difficult for the individual even to sense that religion is that which can satisfy the one who desires more than to eat, to drink and to wash himself.... The German who has raised himself above common sensuality and has not found his life in religion places science and art in its place.

> —Ernst Wilhelm Hensgtenberg, "Der Kunst- und
> Wissenschafts-Enthusiasmus in Deutschland
> als Surrogat für Religion"

The intolerant lovelessness of our newly pious, which is not content with drawing back from that which is opposed to it but uses every social connection for vilification, which may soon render all free spiritual life hazardous; the anxious listening for particular expressions according to which they characterize one person as white and another as black... and the general fear of all science, these are no signs of an open sense, but rather of a deeply rooted diseased condition which must be treated with love but also with strict firmness, if the detriment to the whole of society which grows out of this is not to be greater than the spiritual profit which the awakened religious life brings to individuals.

> —From Schleiermacher's "explanations" appended
> to the *Speeches on Religion* in 1821

4.1 Introduction

An assessment of the place of the natural order in Schleiermacher's account of religion can claim a measure of completeness only, it seems to me, on the strength of an examination of the respects in which the treatment of Christianity in Schleiermacher's theological work respects or transcends the boundaries of that order. The aim of this chapter is to explore in some detail the place of the account of religion whose development we have been tracking within *The Christian Faith*. I argue that Schleiermacher incorporated this account into his dogmatics in a manner calculated to respect and preserve the integrity of the project of investigating religion from a *naturalistic* standpoint while enabling the theologian to go beyond this project by *adding to* or in some cases *redescribing* its deliverances. Thus, the overall description of Christianity in *The Christian Faith* can be thought of as composed of a "base" and a "superstructure," with the former comprising an account of Christianity as a natural phenomenon and the latter provided by theological reflection. As a whole this description can be characterized as an example of a "supplemented naturalism": as a naturalistic account of religion supplemented by additions generated by theological reflection.

It is important for me to argue that the relationship between religion-theoretical and theological material that Schleiermacher envisioned required that the latter not conflict with the former: that theologians, while they may incorporate claims in their work that *go beyond* what might be established by the investigation of religion as a part of the natural order, do not introduce claims that *conflict* with its deliverances. It is also important for me to argue that it is possible to distinguish fairly cleanly between these two types of material within the text of the *Glaubenslehre*. I eventually claim that (in part by way of the application of the notion of multiple standpoints, which we encountered in the introduction) the point of transition between these can be identified with a fair degree of precision.

In what follows I focus on the second edition of *The Christian Faith*. The first and more obvious reason for this choice is the fact that, in contrast to the case of the *Speeches on Religion*, it is the final edition of *The Christian Faith* that has been the standard point of reference for investigations of Schleiermacher's theology in both German and English (a circumstance abetted for Anglophone scholars by the fact that the first edition has not been translated).[1] More important for my purposes, however, are two specific aspects of Schleiermacher's editorial activity surrounding the production of the revised edition. The first of these involved his explanation in the *Sendschreiben an Lücke* of the aims of his dogmatics in relation to current events unfolding within Prussian religious and intellectual culture, as well as his famous call in these letters for an "eternal covenant between the living Christian faith and completely free, independent scientific inquiry, such that faith does not hinder science and science does not exclude faith."[2] The second was his addition to the introduction of his dogmatics of material intended to make clear the relationship between theological inquiry and several other branches of scientific investigation, most notably ethics and what he referred to as philosophy of religion.[3] These two sources of information are crucial resources for reconstructing Schleiermacher's understanding of the place of the "naturalistic paradigm" of religious investigation within his theological treatment of Christianity.

I begin my exposition not with textual analysis but with discussion of Schleiermacher's call for an "eternal covenant"—and most important, discussion of the historical circumstances that prompted him to issue this call.

4.2 Interpreting the "Eternal Covenant"

That Schleiermacher described his dogmatics as an attempt to establish an "eternal covenant" between Christian faith and scientific inquiry is well known, as is the fact that the nineteenth-century project of theological mediation found its canonical articulation in this project. Brent Sockness's recent book *Against False Apologetics* has, however, highlighted the fact that by the end of the nineteenth century the terms of this covenant had become a matter of dispute among those who claimed Schleiermacher as an intellectual progenitor.[4] Sockness finds the work of Wilhelm Herrmann and Ernst Troeltsch to represent two competing interpretations of theological mediation and thus reads the disagreement between the two of them as the historical outworking of the ambiguity of Schleiermacher's basic project:

> The ambiguity of the covenant lies in the fact that there are logically at least two ways to avoid a clash between a religious doctrine and the current state of scientific knowledge—be it natural, historical or philosophical. The first way is to locate Christian piety or faith in a domain of the human spirit so distinct from intellectual knowing that Christian doctrines, understood as the interpretations of that piety, by virtue of their peculiar source and object possess a cognitive status of an entirely different order than the knowledge of "objective consciousness" or reason. The second way to avoid the conflict of religious belief with science is continually to adjust the doctrinal content of Christian faith to the current state of science. I think it could be demonstrated that in practice Schleiermacher's theology employed both means of keeping the covenant.[5]

Sockness's presentation of the disjunction between the driving assumptions of the work of Herrmann and Troeltsch is invaluable.[6] Nonetheless, I take exception to the even-handedness with which he suggests that the approaches of both men stand at the same distance, metaphorically speaking, from that of Schleiermacher. It seems to me that close study of Schleiermacher's dogmatics, particularly when this work is read in the context of his entire corpus, renders practically unavoidable the conclusion that Troeltsch's historicism represents the continuation of the basic thrust of Schleiermacher's work, while Herrmann's appeal to an irreducible, inexplicable religious experience as the ground of religion constitutes (as Troeltsch himself argued) a retreat from genuine mediation into a posture of simple protectionism.[7] This is not to deny that Troeltsch's historicism is more thoroughgoing than Schleiermacher's or to claim that there is nothing in Schleiermacher's writings that can be appropriated by protective theories of religious experience. But particularly in view of Schleiermacher's relationship to those of his contemporaries who were primarily interested in shielding religion from the advancing *Wissenschaften*—a topic that is explored further below—it is difficult to imagine that he would have acknowledged Herrmann's work as the successor to his own.

4.2.1 *Segregation and the Question of "Protection"*

Bracketing for the moment my disagreement with Sockness's even-handedness, it is certainly the case that the eternal covenant has been presented in the English secondary literature in terms that comport more with Herrmann's approach than Troeltsch's. Here, for example, is how Richard Brandt described the covenant in 1941:

> Schleiermacher believed that religion requires protection from the
> intellectuals, both from scientific enemies and professed
> philosophical friends. The particular protection he was prepared to
> offer was in the form of a reconciliation of religion with intellectual
> claims by segregation. That is, the entire realm of knowledge about
> the objects in which traditional theology had been interested, whether
> philosophical or scientific, is to become the province of secular
> thinkers, and secured from theological or religious interference. On
> the other hand, the realm of religious experience is to be given to the
> theologian as a datum for the formulation of doctrine, clear of all
> dependence on this philosophical knowledge, and theology is to be a
> scientific expression of this religious experience.[8]

Call this the "segregation model" of the eternal covenant: Science and religion are to be kept in harmony by virtue of a separation of the "territories" over which each holds sway. The sciences can claim authority over their rightful domain but acknowledge that religious experience is the exclusive province of the science of theology and thus off limits. Likewise, theology is to evacuate altogether the territory of the sciences and confine itself to the exegesis of religious experience.

There are at least two reasons for skepticism about the cogency of this model as an interpretation of Schleiermacher's project. The first of these can be set out briefly: Schleiermacher's general understanding of the natural order does not at any point in its development support the notion that there is some area of human experience that is naturally off limits to scientific investigation. Schleiermacher's determinism entails the notion that every element of human experience—as he stated the point in the *Monologen*, "whatever alterations in the mind time brings and takes away"[9]—is the product of the operation of chains of cause and effect that extend throughout the whole of the natural order; and this extends even to immediate self-consciousness or "feeling," the locus of inward religion, and thus of whatever in the end could constitute "religious experience." Thus, the only kind of boundary that could demarcate a science-free zone within the natural order would be entirely ad hoc.

The second reason for skepticism concerning the segregation model is historical. Both the notion that Schleiermacher was interested in "protecting" religion from scientific investigation and the idea that he was primarily interested in establishing a "nonaggression pact" between religion and science misrepresent the political context of his call for an eternal covenant.[10] The years of Schleiermacher's academic career at Berlin coincided with the resurgence of a deeply conservative neopietist "awakening" within Prussia, which quickly became closely aligned with opposition by the state to demands for political liberalization that dated from the period of French occupation—demands that Schleiermacher had prominently supported.[11] After 1817 this movement was centered at the revived seminary at Wittenberg under the leadership of H. L. Huebner and Baron H. E. von Kottwitz. Aligned with and supported by the powerful Junker land-owning aristocrats, the neopietists embarked on a campaign to expunge the toxic (to their minds) combination of theological rationalism and political liberalism from Prussia's universities and seminaries. Pressure from this movement, in concert with the consequences of an increasingly paranoid and repressive central government, soon bore down on the faculty at Berlin. In 1817 Schleiermacher was forbidden to offer his lectures on political theory (*Staatslehre*) on the grounds that, in the opinion of state chancellor Hardenberg, they "served a political tendency, namely to worry and divide souls without providing any real benefit," a prohibition that endured for twelve years.[12]

In 1819 the biblical scholar Wilhelm de Wette, Schleiermacher's Berlin colleague and sometime political ally who had publicly opposed the establishment of Wittenburg as a pietist stronghold, was ensnared in the *Demagogenverfolgung* that followed the assassination of the poet Kotzebue and dismissed from his post.[13] Calls for his removal had come from Kottwitz and Bishop R. F. Eylert, who voiced suspicion that de Wette's liberal views threatened to further estrange the minds of the young from "throne and altar." Schleiermacher, too, who had become known as a critic of state power and of the "caste spirit" of

Prussian society, was caught up in the reaction to Kotzebue's murder, and it is likely that he was saved from the fate of de Wette only in virtue of his personal popularity.[14] As it was, after 1819, when the Karlsbad decrees established a regime of close surveillance of university professors to prevent them from spreading "harmful ideas that would subvert public peace and order and undermine the foundations of existing states," Schleiermacher's lectures and sermons were frequently attended by members of the undercover police.[15]

If in 1806 Schleiermacher's revisions to the *Speeches on Religion* constituted in part a capitulation to conservative anxieties, the tone of his preface to the third edition of 1821 was sharply different. Where speaking to the religious situation of 1799 had for the unknown hospital chaplain required addressing the "cultured despisers" of religion, twenty years later and by this point notorious for his liberal activism, Schleiermacher remarked that the one who wanted to write on the topic of religion "might rather find it necessary to write speeches to the sanctimonious (*Frömmelnde*) and to the slaves of the letter, to those unknowing and unloving superstitious and hyper-believing persons (*Aber- und Übergläubige*)" than to the original audience of the *Speeches*, "who seem no longer to be there at all."[16] The scathing remarks in the second passage cited at the opening of this chapter concerning the "intolerant lovelessness" of the neopietists and the danger to the general social condition presented by their movement are of a similar character.

The same year Schleiermacher's political notoriety came to something of a head, when a royal investigative commission issued a report noting that he "stands acquainted with many individuals who are now known for and absorbed by the revolutionary tendency, and the better part of these regard his writing as an excellent source of support (*Stützpunkt*)" and concluding ultimately that "whoever speaks, writes and behaves as Professor Schleiermacher has written, spoken and behaved...should no longer be tolerated as a pastor, preacher and academic lecturer on religion and morals."[17] The recommendation of this report, that Schleiermacher be dismissed from his post at Berlin and transferred to Königsberg, was never acted upon, although his conflicts with the crown continued through much of the 1820s.

Schleiermacher issued the call for a covenant between faith and science in preparation for the publication of the second edition of his dogmatics, in the second of his open letters to Lücke. By this time Berlin had itself become the center of gravity for the neopietist movement. In 1824 Ernst Wilhelm Hengstenberg, whose own religious "awakening" had been more or less engineered by Eylert, was appointed as a lecturer at Berlin and despite a lack of relevant academic training was rapidly elevated to de Wette's still-vacant chair.[18] As Wolfes has noted, for Schleiermacher this development represented "not only a scandalous encroachment by the government on the freedom of research and teaching, but also a serious impairment of the quality of the biblical studies faculty at the University of Berlin."[19] Hengstenberg's publicly stated position as a professor of theology and biblical studies was that matters of religion could not be penetrated by "philology, philosophy and human reason,"[20] and as the first citation at the opening of this chapter indicates, he regarded the high profile of the sciences as a sign that the religious fiber of the German *Volk* was weakening. Partly in virtue of Hengstenberg's position as editor of the tremendously influential *Evangelische Kirchenzeitung* after 1827, the attempt to impose theological conformity on the Prussian educational establishment became largely identified with his name.

This, then, was the context within which Schleiermacher called for an "eternal covenant" between faith and science. In his letters to Lücke Schleiermacher spoke of the eventual attainment through scientific advances of "comprehensive knowledge of the world," knowledge that would make it impossible for the educated person to adhere to historically important Christian doctrines, as a state of affairs with which the religious would one way or another be obliged to reckon, and "in times such as these our primary concern should be to take into account what appears to me to be the inevitable and immediate future."[21] His proposed covenant was an attempt to avert the looming cultural disaster that he believed would result from attempts by religious conservatives, already well under way, to construct a shelter for religion from such advances—the "detriment to the whole of society" of which he had written eight years earlier. Schleiermacher anticipated that those of Lücke's generation would be the ones to face the onrushing crisis in its sharpest form:

> Do you nevertheless intend to barricade yourself behind such fortifications and cut yourself off from science? The barrage of ridicule to which you will be subject from time to time causes me no concern, for it will do you little harm once you are resigned to it. But the blockade! The complete starvation from all science, which will follow when, because you have repudiated it, science will be forced to display the flag of unbelief! Shall the tangle of history so unravel that Christianity becomes identified with barbarism and science with unbelief? To be sure, many will make it so. Preparations are already well under way, and already the ground heaves under our feet, as those gloomy creatures who regard as satanic all research beyond the confines of ancient literalism seek to creep forth from their religious enclaves.[22]

Thus, what was in question for Schleiermacher when he addressed his reflections to Lücke was not whether religion or Christianity would wither away under the assaults of science. On the contrary, what was in question was the form Christianity would assume and the role it would play within a culture characterized by a high level of scientific development: whether the waxing power of a reactionary orthodoxy unafraid to call upon the power of the state would curtail the advance of knowledge concerning matters of religious import and whether the Christianity of the future would consist only of "those who can hack away at science with a sword, fence themselves in with weapons at hand to withstand the assaults of sound research and behind this fence establish as binding a church doctrine that appears to everyone outside as an unreal ghost."[23] What Schleiermacher feared was an explosion of theological conservatism from its historic enclaves, one that would result in the polarization of Prussian culture into a religious wing ignorant of and hostile to the life of the mind and a learned wing consequently forced into a position of antagonism toward things religious.

The segregation model misses this fact that Schleiermacher's call for an eternal covenant was directly addressed to an intensifying conflict between the liberalism of which he had become a well-known proponent and an explicitly protectivist and anti-intellectual neopietism. In point of fact, the sort of demarcation of territories that the segregation model describes would not represent much of an improvement over the outcome that Schleiermacher feared. A mere "nonaggression pact" between theologians and scientists might well solve the problem of theologians "hacking away at science with a sword," but the complete separation of the spheres of science and religion would also seem to be a recipe for the kind of intellectual starvation and societal fragmentation that Schleiermacher decried. The segregation model comes perilously close to presenting Schleiermacher as recommending that theologians lay claim to the territory known as "religious experience" and declare it off limits to scientific research by means of a line drawn, as it were, in the sand—in so many words, that they "fence themselves in with weapons to hand to withstand the assaults of sound research." To recall the work of Sockness once more, the fact that Troeltsch's critique of Herrmann's appeal to religious experience echoes so closely Schleiermacher's critique of his neopietist contemporaries is, it seems to me, a powerful reason to regard the segregation model of the eternal covenant with suspicion.

4.2.2 Accommodation

Let us call the alternative (which I favor) to the segregation model the *accommodation model*. According to this model Schleiermacher was not aiming at a parallelism between theology and the sciences, such that each one restricts itself to a territory over which it holds exclusive sway. Rather, the accommodation model sees Schleiermacher, first, refusing to place any limitations on scientific investigation and, second, imposing upon the religious an obligation to understand themselves and their religion in terms compatible with the sciences—in a word, accommodating to the past and future deliverances of natural-scientific research.

The accommodation model makes better sense than the segregation model, it seems to me, of the fact that Schleiermacher imposed upon his religious readers the duty of not hindering the sciences (indeed, with Troeltsch

I cannot see how the "line in the sand" required by the segregation model could constitute anything other than a hindrance to science). The most natural way to interpret "not hindering," it seems to me, is to say that the question of what sectors of the natural order the sciences can and cannot examine is for scientists—and not for the religious or for theologians—to answer. It is impossible to read Schleiermacher as one who claimed that *religion in general* is off limits to scientific investigation if one acknowledges that his view was that religion is not a purely "inward" phenomenon but extends from the innermost depths of the human soul through the realm of human social structures to the realm of material artifacts. Moreover, as argued above, it is difficult to see how any nonarbitrary line could be drawn around "piety" or religion's inward dimension that could render it immune to investigation. The accommodation model refrains from positing such a line and instead takes Schleiermacher's position to be that religion *in its entire range* is an object for investigation by whatever scientific approaches are appropriate.

This idea finds support in the opening pages of *The Christian Faith*, where Schleiermacher strongly and publicly registered his opposition to the neopietist position on both the propriety of state control over religious affairs and on religion's immunity to scientific scrutiny. Protestants, Schleiermacher argued, "regard it as equivalent to the deterioration of a church" when it takes it upon itself to pronounce on the business of the sciences or of external orders, "just as we always resist when the leaders of State or those of science as such, want to order the affairs of piety." However, he continued: "But on the other hand we do not want to prevent the latter [i.e., the leaders of science] from treating and evaluating both piety itself and the community which pertains to it from their standpoint, and determining their proper place in the whole realm of human life, inasmuch as piety and church are raw material for knowledge (*ein Stoff für das Wissen*); moreover we ourselves are entering upon such an investigation here."[24]

If, however, one side of Schleiermacher's eternal covenant involved acknowledging the right of the sciences to investigate religion itself in whatever manner these see fit, the question arises as to how the other side, which stipulates that "science not hinder faith," is to be understood. In his letters to Lücke Schleiermacher described the point of his reinterpretations of traditional religious doctrines: "I thought I should show as best I could that every dogma that truly represents an element of our Christian consciousness can be so formulated that it remains free from entanglements with science."[25] If "freedom from entanglements with science" is not to be achieved by means of the confinement of "religion" to a zone off limits to scientific investigation, then how is it to be achieved?

The segregation model correctly acknowledges the fact that avoiding such entanglements involves the surrender of doctrines that conflict with the deliverances of the sciences or, in Schleiermacher's words, that "[w]e must learn to do without what many are still accustomed to regard as inseparably bound to the essence of Christianity."[26] However, it is overreaching to say that Schleiermacher was determined that theology should separate itself entirely from the territory of the sciences. On the accommodation model, theology takes the deliverances of the sciences to constitute not a territory to be avoided but a source of positive information for its own labors. The eternal covenant necessitates an understanding of Christianity that is based in and consonant with, although not restricted to, what the natural sciences have to say *about religion*—based, in other words, in an understanding of religion as a natural phenomenon. Indeed, both *The Christian Faith* and the *Brief Outline of the Study of Theology* emphasized theology's dependence on the deliverances of the "science of the principles of history" or ethics in particular, which, as we have seen, is the general domain within which the account of religion we have been surveying was articulated. In the *Brief Outline* Schleiermacher had noted that "without constant reference to ethical propositions, even historical theology can be only a disorganized preliminary exercise, and must degenerate into a spiritless custom."[27] The account of religion with which the *Glaubenslehre* opens is presented by way of "propositions borrowed from ethics," and Schleiermacher noted later in the introduction that "insofar as [questions such as] how feeling diversifies itself and to what it refers encroach upon the psychological, the ethical and the metaphysical [realms]," dogmatic theology is obligated to make use of the terminology of the corresponding fields of inquiry.[28]

In my view Schleiermacher aimed at avoiding "freedom from entanglements with science" by means of a presentation of Christianity with two principal moments. The first moment concerns those areas where the interests of theology fall within the domain of the extratheological sciences. Here, Schleiermacher's intent was to encourage his Christian readers to accept a view of themselves and their religion that was consistent with and would continue to be fleshed out by the advances of natural scientific knowledge, and for this purpose he positioned his account of religion as a natural phenomenon as the basis for his presentation of Christianity.[29] The second moment then comprises a series of claims *over and above* but not in conflict with either the actual or the anticipated deliverances of natural-scientific investigation. Thus, the contents of the first moment stand entirely under the authority of the extratheological sciences, and those of the second moment are bound merely by the requirement that nothing be claimed that these have contradicted or are likely to contradict. Altogether, the account of Christianity that Schleiermacher's dogmatics presents consists of the combination of these two types of material and thus can be thought of as a "supplemented naturalism."

The point of a composite account such as this should not be difficult to discern. Schleiermacher's intent, as reflected in his remarks to Lücke, was neither to produce a body of theology based solely on the deliverances of scientific research nor to "take faith on loan from speculation," translating

Christian doctrines entirely into metaphysical terms (which, he noted, might indeed "safeguard" faith from natural science[30]). Rather, his intent was to provide a dogmatics that would minimize the opportunities for the religious and the scientifically minded to separate into camps either opposed or irrelevant to each other. In pursuit of this aim he superimposed on an account of Christianity as a natural, historical phenomenon an "overlay" of claims intended to secure those doctrinal ideas that he considered essential to the tradition. By means of this device Schleiermacher intended to account for and ensure the historical continuity of Christianity while at the same time providing space for advancing scientific knowledge to inform the tradition itself.

It serves the purpose of forestalling a separation between the spheres of religion and science both that the theological "overlay" be a minimalist one and that the presentation of Christianity as a historical phenomenon—that is to say, a natural phenomenon—be maximized. The parsimonious treatment given in Schleiermacher's dogmatics to propositions directly concerned with the transcendent testifies to the first of these desiderata.[31] What is more, the extent to which he pursued the latter goal can be appreciated from the fact that he ruled out two obvious ways in which the events that constitute religion might elude even complete knowledge of the natural order: Besides explicitly rejecting miracles (understood as events with supernatural rather than natural causes), Schleiermacher also refrained, on the grounds that will by now be familiar, from appealing to freedom as a principle that exempts human actions from the fate of being understood as the product of prior causes.

4.3 Christianity in *The Christian Faith*

My exposition of the presentation of Christianity in *The Christian Faith* has four parts and is intended to flesh out my claim that this presentation has the composite structure I have described. In the first part of the section I discuss Schleiermacher's invocation of determinism as a point of contact between the Christian and the scientific views of the natural order. The second sketches the components of the first moment of Schleiermacher's presentation of Christianity—his discussion of Christianity as a natural phenomenon. The third part explores the theological "overlay" that is then superimposed upon this understanding. Finally, the fourth part discusses his treatment of the "appearance of the Redeemer" or the Incarnation as an example of the mode of presentation I have described.

4.3.1 *The* Naturzusammenhang *in Theological Perspective*

We have already encountered Schleiermacher's remark in the *Glaubenslehre* that "divine preservation as the absolute dependence of all events and changes upon God, and natural causality as the complete determination of everything which occurs by the general *Naturzusammenhang* are not distinct from each other, nor is there a boundary between them, but rather both are the same thing merely regarded from different viewpoints: this has always been acknowledged by the most strict dogmaticians."[32] This passage asserts a functional equivalence between the correct understanding of God's relationship to the world and a natural determinism, which is the view that all temporal things are "conditioned and determined by the *Naturzusammenhang*."[33] Both ideas present events occurring within the natural order as determined in advance, indeed as far in advance as one cares to look (in theological terms, "from eternity"). A comprehensive determinism governing the natural order, then, is a basic premise of Schleiermacher's dogmatics.

As there have been those who have argued against the presence of determinism in the *Glaubenslehre*, a review of the textual evidence is in order.[34] Schleiermacher's discussion of the doctrine of divine preservation in particular leaves little room, it seems to me, for doubt about his attachment to the "doctrine of necessity" in this text. One of his objections to the notion of miracles, traditionally understood, was that the idea that God might intervene in the natural order invites the thought that events in that order might unfold otherwise than God had originally ordained. However, Schleiermacher found this thought to imply a less than absolute dependence of all things upon God: "[I]t is difficult to grasp how omnipotence should be shown to be greater in the interruptions of the *Naturzusammenhang* than in its original, immutable, and indeed also divinely ordained course....[I]f one wanted to postulate such an encroachment by the highest being as a virtue of the same, one would first have to assume that there was something which was not ordained by this being, which could oppose him and thus impinge upon him and his work, whereby our fundamental feeling would be entirely overturned."[35]

In this discussion Schleiermacher distinguished free causes from those operating within the "nature mechanism"—but not for the purpose of arguing for incompatibilist freedom. Freedom is understood in the *Glaubenslehre*, in continuity with Schleiermacher's earlier writings, as a matter of "inward determination" and contrasted with activities that are simply the "blind" transmission of causal impulses. Thus, although in places Schleiermacher distinguished free activity from "mechanical" causality, in §49 he noted that this thought does not support the idea of a sharp contrast between the "nature mechanism" and the realm of human freedom. Rather, he argued (after the manner of the *Dialektik*) that "there is a complete absence of freedom only where without moving itself, a thing moves others only insofar as it is moved; so we will be able to regard the causality of living things only as a diminished freedom, and will have to say that true causality exists only where there is life."[36] In other words, "the activities of free beings are determined from within,"[37] and thus "in reference to absolute dependence within finite existence, we can accept no strict antithesis between freedom and natural necessity, since that which really exists for itself, even if it has no part in spiritual life, nevertheless moves itself in some sense."[38]

The correct understanding of divine preservation, then, takes the course of all events within the world, including the activities of free beings, to have been determined in advance as a matter of divine decree.[39] Schleiermacher's arguments to the effect that this doctrine is equivalent to natural-causal determinism mostly make use of the same device that (as we will see) accounts for much of the logic of the doctrinal sections of his dogmatics, asserting that any other view conflicts with the content of the feeling of absolute dependence and thus is incompatible with piety. However, throughout the discussion Schleiermacher also presented the compatibility of his account of divine preservation with the "scientific" view of the world, as he understood this, as an independent consideration in its favor. Indeed, one of the first arguments he presents for this equivalence echoes his remarks to Lücke. "It is said," he remarked, "that the more clearly we conceive of something in its complete determination (*seiner volkommenen Bedingtheit*) by the *Naturzusammenhang*, the less we are able to arrive at the feeling of its absolute dependence upon God." However, if there were in fact a conflict between the feeling of absolute dependence and the thought of complete determination by natural causes, then "the persons most knowledgeable about nature (*jeder Naturkundigste*) would always be the least pious, and vice versa," for "with the completion of our knowledge of the world, since this always presents everything to us within the *Naturzusammenhang*, the development of the pious consciousness in ordinary life would entirely cease.... And on the other hand, conversely, the love of piety would oppose all efforts towards research (*Forschungstrieb*) and all expansion of our knowledge of nature."[40] Thus, Schleiermacher offered a *reductio ad absurdum* in defense of the ultimate compatibility of natural determinism and Christian piety.

At the beginning of this chapter I argue that one of Schleiermacher's intentions in crafting his dogmatics was to safeguard the integrity of the scientific investigation of religion itself. Beyond his affirmation of scientific treatments of piety and pious community in §3, this intention is most clearly in evidence in those sections of the *Glaubenslehre* where Schleiermacher touches on the question of how events that "stimulate the pious self-consciousness" are to be understood. Attention has rarely been called in the literature to the fact that Schleiermacher's denial of "absolutely supernatural" events, combined with his determinism, has an important consequence regarding what sorts of explanation of religion are possible within the context of his writings. In particular, it cannot be said within this context that any discrete moment of pious self-consciousness is the result of the operation of discrete causes outside the natural order. Rather, as with any event within the natural order, moments of pious self-consciousness will be the result of the operation of natural causes within the overall "nature system."

It should not be controversial, in this context, for me to claim that in discussing the "stimulation of the pious self-consciousness" Schleiermacher was in effect discussing the question of how the events that constitute religion are to be accounted for. Since, according to him, the feeling of absolute dependence accompanies every moment of human consciousness, it cannot be invoked to explain the occurrence of any particular moment of pious self-consciousness; rather, such moments arise only as a result of the "stimulation" of the sensible self-consciousness by natural events.[41] When it is also recalled that it was his understanding that piety motivates the various activities that constitute (ideal) religion, it should be clear that understanding which events stimulate the pious self-consciousness will be crucial for any attempts to provide an overall account of religion.

Schleiermacher's recommendation to his readers in connection with this subject is clear: The idea that events that stimulate piety have natural causes that the sciences will eventually understand constitutes no threat to piety and should be embraced. "[I]t is obviously incorrect," he stated, "to claim, as if on the basis of a general experience, that that which is uncomprehended as such always stimulates pious feeling more than that which is understood . . . even the greatest confidence with which we accept any particular hypothetical explanation of these phenomena does not overturn that feeling."[42] Schleiermacher advanced this recommendation both as a counsel of piety and in the interest of compatibility with the sciences. One ground, for example, of his objection to the idea that human evil is to be understood as ultimately the product of the activity of malevolent supernatural beings is that such a view "restricts, at every difficult step, the attempt to understand all phenomena within an individual soul on the basis of its own particularity and the influences of common life, which in the interest of blessedness (*Gottseligkeit*) certainly cannot be encouraged enough."[43] Piety, in other words—and specifically, fidelity to the feeling of absolute dependence—positively requires the ideas that every event that stimulates it is a natural one and that everything that occurs within the human soul is a product of the overall *Naturzusammenhang*.

A passage from §45 summarizes this discussion and indicates in compact form Schleiermacher's view of the relationship between piety and the scientific interest:

> Thus even in reference to the miraculous, the general interest of science, particularly that of the natural sciences (*Naturforschung*), and the interest of piety seem to meet at the same point, namely that we abandon the conception of the absolutely supernatural, since there is not a single case in which we would be able to identify something as such, and no such acknowledgment is demanded of us. . . . In this way everything, even the most wondrous thing that happens or has happened, remains a task (*Aufgabe*) for scientific research, but at the

same time where it arouses pious feeling in virtue of its purpose or otherwise, this is in no way affected by envisioning the possibility of a future understanding.[44]

It should be sufficiently clear, then, that Schleiermacher's view in the *Glaubenslehre* was that all events within the natural order, including the "innermost" events within the human soul, are appropriate objects of scientific research and that the ideal "completion" of scientific knowledge would entail the knowledge of the causes of all temporal events, including those that constitute piety. This, then, is the general understanding by which Schleiermacher intended his account of Christianity to be informed and with which he intended it to be compatible. Nothing about this position should be surprising, for it is nothing more than a straightforward entailment of the understanding of the natural order that Schleiermacher understood to be a premise of natural-scientific research.

4.3.2 *Christianity as a Natural Phenomenon*

As he had promised in his letters to Lücke, Schleiermacher opened the introduction to the second edition of *The Christian Faith* with remarks about the dependence of dogmatics on other forms of scientific investigation. According to him, dogmatics requires knowledge of what sort of thing the Christian church is, and "this itself is to be properly attained through the general concept of 'church,' together with a proper comprehension of the peculiarity of the Christian church." Understanding of "church" in general is drawn from the science of ethics, for "in every case 'the church' is a community which originates only through free human action and which can only through such continue to exist."[45] What follows in the introduction is a compressed version of the account of religion as a natural phenomenon whose development I have traced in previous chapters, presented by way of "propositions borrowed" (*Lehnsätze*) from ethics and the philosophy of religion, to which is conjoined a discussion of the particularity of Christianity in relation to other religions.[46]

For present purposes no more than an outline of this material is needed. In the most general terms a church is "a community relating to piety" or a historically extended social endeavor whereby piety is passed from one individual to another and hence from generation to generation.[47] This "piety" is a constellation of states of mind centered around states of immediate self-consciousness or feeling. What makes certain states of mind rather than others part of piety has to do with their relationship to the feeling of absolute dependence, the sense that "our entire self-activity comes from elsewhere": The measure of the piety of a person is the extent to which this feeling combines with and thus influences the content of that person's mental states.[48]

What makes particular religions distinct from each other is a matter of both the "outward" and the "inward" unity that each enjoys.[49] With respect to

outward unity, religions are historically particular: Their identity is established
in the first instance by their historical origins and developed by their historical
careers. In some cases the origins of a religion will be a matter of historical
record; in others this will not be the case. In some cases a religion will have a
single moment of origin; other religions will be "a whole, gradually woven
together from diverse starting-points or even growing together of itself."[50] In
addition, a religion's inward unity is a matter of the distinctness of the form of
piety that it exhibits, with lesser or greater degrees of distinctiveness and historical continuity possible. In every case there will be an intimate relationship
between a religion's inward and outward unity, and in the case of Christianity
the former is explicitly derived from and directed toward the latter.

The distinctiveness of Christianity is a function of its relationship to the
event that constitutes its historical point of origin, the life and work of Jesus of
Nazareth. Christian piety is defined by this relationship in two distinct respects.
First, Christian piety is the *historical descendant* of the pious self-consciousness
of Jesus, and the various Christian churches are the historical descendants of
the circle of association formed by the disciples of Jesus. Beginning with the
preaching of Jesus, Christian religious practice has consisted of a variety of acts
of communication that are intended to express the form of piety that Jesus
exemplified and that have resulted in the formation of social groups and institutions as embodiments of this process, as well as formalized rituals, statements, and artifacts as means of communication. Second, as regards *content*, it
is definitive of Christian piety that "redemption is posited as something generally and completely accomplished through Jesus of Nazareth." Thus, this conviction counts for Schleiermacher as the specific essence of Christianity—the
principle that distinguishes it from other similar forms of piety.[51]

Schleiermacher's presentation of Christianity throughout *The Christian
Faith* makes it clear that, as in the case of any religion, it was from the beginning marked by exposure to historical contingency. Schleiermacher denied, for
example, the traditional ascription of omniscience to Jesus and argued that not
only Jesus's preaching but also his self-understanding were informed by the
language and prevalent ideas of his day (to believe anything else, he argued,
would be to deny true humanity to Jesus).[52] Because the communication of
Christian piety has always made use of the available conceptual and linguistic
vehicles, particular forms of expression (doctrinal formulations) that adequately
serve the purpose of the communication of piety at one time may not do so at
another; the "ecclesiastical value" of religious doctrines is, in other words, historically specific.[53] Part of the development of the tradition has involved the
diversification and refinement of the linguistic vehicles of Christian piety,
resulting in the interaction and oftentimes the confusion of poetic, rhetorical,
and "descriptively didactic" (*darstellend belehrende*) modes of expression.[54]
Christianity's course of development has also not been an ideal one but has
been marked by both contamination by "speculation" and other alien factors

and fragmentation into different subtraditions. The doctrinal tradition and the enterprise of dogmatic theology are both outgrowths of this nonideal historical process, with the former purporting to formalize those expressions that are most essential to the tradition or subtradition and the latter dedicated to subjecting received doctrines to critical evaluation.

Thus, the initial understanding of Christianity on which *The Christian Faith* is premised takes it to be an ongoing historical process of the transmission of a particular form of piety from one person to the next and one generation to the next, a process beset by all of the vagaries of history and vulnerable to corruption and decay, as well as development and diversification. That Schleiermacher understood this description to have been derived from a standpoint "above" Christianity is clear from his remarks in §11, where he identified his initial presentation as an anticipation of what might be produced by a fully developed philosophy of religion. Should this discipline reach maturity, "the inner character of Christianity in and for itself might perhaps be presented in such a way that its particular territory in the religious world would be secured for Christianity." In spite of the fact that he understood himself to be writing for a Christian audience, Schleiermacher emphasized that both such a "complete systematization" of the contents of piety as could be produced by the philosophy of religion and his own abbreviated presentation leave aside the question of whether or not Christian piety is veridical: "It is clear in and for itself that someone who adheres to another faith can perhaps be completely convinced, by the above presentation, that what has been set out here is the particular essence of Christianity without this itself becoming truth for him, such that he might find himself compelled to accept it."[55]

4.3.3 The "Overlay" of Christian Piety

In this section I discuss what I take to be a representative sample of the claims that make up what I have described as the "overlay" that Schleiermacher superimposed upon the basal understanding of Christianity as a religion presented in the introduction to *The Christian Faith*. My argument, it will be recalled, is that Schleiermacher's complete account of the contents of Christianity amounts to a "supplemented naturalism": an understanding of Christianity as a natural phenomenon combined with claims that go beyond what the sciences have or can establish. Schleiermacher's intent, it seems to me, was that the contents of this overlay should be scientifically unobjectionable in that nothing should be claimed that the past or likely future deliverances of the natural sciences would contradict.

For the most part, the interpretive work that Schleiermacher performed on traditional Christian doctrines follows a regular pattern. As we have seen, his account of Christianity holds that its *generic* essence, so to speak, is the feeling of absolute dependence and its *specific* essence is the conviction that in Jesus redemption has been accomplished once and for all. Christian doctrines originated as expressions of Christian piety—acts of communication intended to make the contents of that piety publicly accessible—and developed historically as formalized versions of such expressions. Schleiermacher's method of doctrinal criticism consists, in the main, of surveying received versions of Christian doctrines and looking for places where particular formulations conflict with what can be transcendentally deduced from either the generic or the specific essence of Christianity—which is to say, conflict with what must be the case if the feeling of absolute dependence and the defining claim of Christian piety are veridical.[56] Anything claimed in a received doctrinal formulation that is incompatible with what can be transcendentally deduced in this way cannot count as a genuine expression of Christian piety and thus cannot be relied upon to serve the communicative purpose of doctrines generally, and so is discarded. Anything that is compatible with what can be transcendentally deduced in this way—which can, so to speak, be transcendentally corroborated—is a candidate for inclusion in what is finally presented as the real content of the doctrine in question. Schleiermacher's opposition, however, to "speculation" within Christian theology and to "entanglements with science" motivated him to be extremely conservative in his doctrinal pronouncements. We can understand him as consistently following a minimalist policy: He consistently refrained from including as the contents of Christian faith any claims (and any expositions of claims) beyond what he estimated was necessary for the successful transmission of Christian piety.[57] The contents of the theological overlay that constitutes the second moment of Schleiermacher's presentation of Christianity, then, are derived by the immanent criticism of the received doctrinal tradition—by the subjection, that is, of Christian doctrines to critical examination in light of the generic and specific essences of Christianity—constrained by a policy of epistemic parsimony.

The contents of this overlay can be sorted into three categories, each of which represents a different sort of "blind spot" for natural-scientific investigation: metaphysical claims, claims about singular events in the past, and claims about repeating processes within the natural order. In what follows I offer examples that fall under each of these headings.

By metaphysical claims, I have in mind claims about states of affairs beyond the boundaries of the *Naturzusammenhang* and thus out of reach of natural-scientific investigation. Here I offer three familiar examples of such claims.

The divine causality. As we saw earlier, Schleiermacher considered the doctrine of divine preservation equivalent, in a sense, to the doctrine of the "determination of all things by the *Naturzusammenhang*." What the doctrine of divine preservation implies over and above natural determinism, however, is the claim that God exercises toward the natural order an activity that undergirds all discrete events and sustains the cosmos in existence.[58] This absolute or divine causality is "posited as equivalent in extent" to the *Naturzusammenhang* and the finite causality that this contains but is not to be confused with it.[59] Where finite causality is temporal, the divine causality is eternal; where finite causality is local, the divine causality is omnipresent; where finite causality is multifarious, the divine causality is simple. The entirety of God's activity in relation to the world is in fact encapsulated in this notion of the divine causality: God's single, eternal act constitutes the causal impulse that undergirds every finite event, even those that constitute sinful human activities.

The doctrine of creation. Schleiermacher did not accept the creation accounts of Genesis as Christian doctrine and for the most part counseled agnosticism regarding questions about the origins of the cosmos. He did, however, argue that "it is quite clear that our feeling of absolute dependence could not be referred to the general createdness of all finite being if anything in this were independent of God or had ever been so. But it is just as certain that if in all finite being as such there were anything that entered into its existence independently of God, then, since this would have to exist even within us, the feeling of absolute dependence could have no truth in reference to ourselves."[60] This is perhaps the clearest example of the "transcendental corroboration" of a received doctrine in the *Glaubenslehre*: A condition of the possibility of the veridicality of the feeling of absolute dependence is that nothing came into existence and nothing is sustained in existence otherwise than through God's activity.

The divine teleology. As Robert Adams in particular has noted, Schleiermacher did not restrict himself to the language of efficient causality with reference to God's activity but was also willing to speak of God's "will," "good pleasure," and "ordination" with respect to the natural order. Claims about the divine teleology emerge in various places throughout *The Christian Faith*, although Schleiermacher's worries about anthropomorphism imposed severe limits on the extent to which such claims could be advanced (as did the notion that the divine causality refers to a single, simple, and eternal act on God's part). Such restrictions notwithstanding, Schleiermacher argued that "when we trace our consciousness of fellowship with God, restored through the efficacy of redemption, back to the divine causality, we posit the establishment and broadening of the Christian church as the object of the divine government of the world," implying as this does that "the whole arrangement of nature from the beginning would have been different, if redemption through Christ had not been determined for the human race after sin."[61] The logical extension of this idea is a claim about the purpose of the natural order itself: that is, that "the world is the scene (*Schauplatz*) of redemption."[62]

A second category of claims concerns singular events in the past. Here are two examples.

The perfect God-consciousness of Jesus. Schleiermacher attributed to Christians the conviction that "no more perfect form of the God-consciousness stands before the human race" than that possessed by Jesus of Nazareth "but rather that any new one would be a step backwards."[63] What Schleiermacher meant by "perfection" here was that in the person of Jesus "the power of the God-consciousness to give the impulse to all moments of life and to determine them" was perfectly realized—which is to say that in every waking moment the consciousness of Jesus was maximally aware of his—and the world's—absolute dependence.[64] This perfection is a condition of the possibility for the state of affairs of redemption having been universally and once and for all accomplished in the person of Jesus—a transcendental deduction, in other words, from the assumption of the veridicality of the essence of Christianity. Put somewhat differently, the postulate of Christ's "sinless perfection," understood in this manner, represents an answer to the question of "how in virtue of [Christian] consciousness the Redeemer is posited."[65] Denying the perfection of the God-consciousness of Jesus opens the possibility of a form of God-consciousness more perfect and thereby better suited to serve as a religious exemplar than Jesus, the thought of which for Schleiermacher "marks the boundary of the Christian faith."[66]

Scripture kept relatively free from errors. For the most part Schleiermacher's discussion of Scripture in *The Christian Faith* represents an attempt to safeguard and incorporate the emerging discipline of higher biblical criticism. In Schleiermacher's view not only the composition of the individual books of the New Testament but also their collection into a canon was the work of fallible human beings, and for this reason an objective, historical study of Scripture is required that makes use of the same "hermeneutical and critical treatments" that apply to textual studies in general.[67] Nevertheless, in the final analysis Schleiermacher found it appropriate for Christians to believe not only that "nothing essential to the preservation and well-being of the church"[68] has been lost through the various alterations to the canon that the historical study of Scripture brings to light but also that the process of the formation of the New Testament resulted in the production of the "most error-free" document: "[E]ven in the pious thoughts of the Apostles the general possibility of error became a reality in individual cases without thereby impinging upon Scripture, which was assembled under the guidance of the holy spirit as the compilation of that which was most free from error (*als Zusammenstellung des irrthumsfreiesten*)."[69]

The final category to be illustrated consists of claims about persistent states of affairs or processes located within the natural order. Once again, here are two examples.

The persistence of Christ's sinless perfection. So far forth, our survey of Schleiermacher's account of Christianity has noted that he looked to the pious self-consciousness of Jesus of Nazareth as the historical point of origin of Christian piety. It would be consonant with what we have encountered thus far for Schleiermacher to claim that the piety that informs the various Christian communities is connected with that of Jesus only by way of this process of historical transmission and that since his day it has undergone its own process of development, with the result that its content is by now significantly different from its historical original. However, in fact Schleiermacher advanced a stronger claim than this. The "consciousness of grace" entails, according to him, that although the piety of any given individual constitutes at best an imperfect approximation of the piety of Jesus, nonetheless the very form of piety that Jesus exemplified—his "sinless perfection"—continues to exist within the Christian tradition considered as a whole and to act as a force within that tradition. Schleiermacher makes it clear that the conviction that even in the present "in the community established by him there is a communication of [this perfection]" is not an empirical observation and in fact is at odds with the manifest imperfections within and divisions among the observable Christian churches.[70] That the sinless perfection of Jesus continues to circulate within Christianity and that it is in virtue of its continued communication and appropriation that redemption is possible are claims derived from the analysis of the contents of Christian piety. This consciousness requires, according to Schleiermacher, the presupposition that in Christian community, in spite of the presence of sin, "there is nevertheless that communication of the absolutely powerful God-consciousness in Christ as something inward, but indeed, since faith rests only on a received impression, something capable of being experienced."[71] This process takes place entirely within history—to postulate "an efficacy of Christ without mediation by space and time," according to Schleiermacher, "destroys the essence of Christianity"[72]—and thus involves no recourse to causes outside the natural order. However, here a claim is added to the general account of Christianity presented in the introductory sections of the *Glaubenslehre*: that the form of piety that the Christian tradition embodies has, in spite of the vicissitudes of history, remained self-identical in a crucial (if elusive) respect since its origin.

The Lord's Supper. Finally, Schleiermacher was similarly not content with a merely symbolic understanding of the sacrament of the Lord's supper. His discussion of the sacrament is premised on the notion that "Christians experience a particular strengthening of the spiritual life in taking communion,"[73] but in fact he was also willing to support the view that unworthy participation in the sacrament "is suited to produce a condition of unreceptivity and stubbornness, which we have every cause to regard as an element of damnation."[74] His summary of the two sides of the sacrament holds that it "appears to be a means of discrimination, in that appropriate and worthy participation promotes living fellowship with Christ, but unworthy participation always makes less effective the most powerful means of strengthening the same, and therefore always increases the force of all impediments."[75]

The forgoing examples should make it sufficiently clear that Schleiermacher's strategy for avoiding "entanglement with science" was not a matter of staking claims only within a purportedly inscrutable realm of human subjectivity. Before I draw my final conclusions regarding this strategy it will be useful to examine one example of the critical interpretation of doctrines more closely. Schleiermacher's interpretation of the doctrine of the Incarnation is particularly instructive regarding the lengths to which he was willing to go for the cause of mediation; it is also illustrative of the limitations of his proposal for an "eternal covenant," for here his pursuit of this project yields results unlikely to satisfy either the scientific or the pious mindset.

4.3.4 Christian Revelation: The Appearance of the Redeemer

Schleiermacher indicated to Lücke that he had paid particular attention to the "appearance of the Redeemer" in his attempt to strike a mediating position between religion and science: "I hope that even this teaching has been elaborated in such a way that it will not endanger the faith and that science need not declare war on us."[76] In dealing with the doctrine of the Incarnation Schleiermacher faced a formidable problem. The position I have attributed to him would constrain him to deny that any discrete supernatural causes were operative in the historical career of Jesus of Nazareth—that Jesus was, in other words, no less "natural" than any other human being. This would seem to flatly rule out talk of Jesus as a divine revelation, as this term is traditionally understood.

Schleiermacher's strategy for validating talk of Jesus as a divine revelation turned on his reinterpretation of the terms *revelation* and *supernatural*, which renders them compatible with the view of the world as a relatively self-enclosed *Naturzusammenhang*. On his reinterpretation both of these terms ascribe an exceptionality or noteworthiness to particular events without implying that these events have discrete supernatural causes. The most formidable challenge this strategy faced was in identifying a kind of exceptionality that was compatible with a deterministic view of the natural order but would also plausibly support the high status traditionally ascribed to Jesus by Christian theology. On Schleiermacher's reconstruction what was unique about Jesus was the fact that he possessed perfect God-consciousness, and so the question surrounding the "appearance of the Redeemer" was the question of how a human being could come to possess perfect God-consciousness absent the possibility of supernatural intervention in the course of history.

Schleiermacher first discussed the term *revelation* in the context of his treatment of the inward and outward unities of different religions, noting that it is commonplace for the members of a religious tradition to claim the status of revelation for the facts or events within history that mark their point of origin (to the extent that this can be ascertained). His preliminary definition of revelation is as "the originality of the fact which lies at the ground of a religious community, insofar as it, as conditioning the individual content of the pious emotions which are found within the community, is not itself to be understood (*zu begreifen ist*) once again from the earlier *Zusammenhang*."[77]

One problem with this understanding of revelation, Schleiermacher noted, is that it would seem to apply too broadly. There is an argument for applying the term to anything that we lack the ability to explain: to the appearance of any "archetype (*Urbild*) within the soul," for example, "whether it be a deed or a work of art, which can neither be understood as an imitation nor be satisfactorily explained by means of external stimulations and preceding circumstances," particularly where these ideas and their originators figure in the self-understandings of religious traditions.[78] On the other hand (and more decisively), there is the question of whether there are any *ultima facie* revelatory events, or whether on the contrary the conviction that all events are the result of preceding circumstances simply rules out the notion altogether:

> But [these reflections] may again have the result that no individual thing, inasmuch as it always belongs to the world, may in itself be viewed as a divine revelation. For just as the arising of an archetype in an individual soul, even if it is not to be understood from the earlier conditions of that same individual, must certainly be capable of being understood from the general condition of the society to which that individual belongs: so also the persons to whom divine descent is attributed certainly always appear to be determined by their peoples, and are thus to be understood in their existence from the people's common force.... Thus we will naturally have to find that that the application of the concept to the fact which lies at the ground of a particular pious community will be contested by all others, while they themselves will claim it for their own foundational fact.[79]

This initial discussion makes it clear that claims of revelation face a formidable challenge from a scientific understanding of the natural order, for the more comprehensible a particular revelatory figure appears in the light of information regarding that person's historical background, the more grounds there are for skepticism about the claim. Absent further discussion, it would seem that Schleiermacher has accomplished little more here than to set the stage for a confrontation between Christian claims to the revelatory status of Jesus and advancing historical knowledge that could only result in the abandonment of the doctrinal claim. Indeed, the path of least resistance to avoiding "entanglements with science" would seem to be the surrender, even in advance of historical investigation, of the claim that the historical appearance of Jesus constitutes a revelation.[80]

In brief, Schleiermacher's bid to rescue the notion of "revelation" repeats a tactical move that we encountered in his early essay "On Human Freedom." In chapter 1 we saw that in the last section of that essay Schleiermacher attempted to defend a Kant-style formal definition of freedom by identifying a sense in which a series of events could be said to have a first or initiating member. His proposal, it will be recalled, was to distinguish chains of events according to the particular law (or kind of law) that operated within them and to identify the first in a series of such events (i.e., the one that is not itself determined by that law but from which subsequent events follow in accordance with that law) as the initiating event; an event thus determined by the "law of succession of ideas" that initiates a series of events determined by the "law of the motion of bodies" can thus be thought of as a *free* event. This strategy, as we saw, led to unhappy results in the early treatise. What appears at this crucial juncture in *The Christian Faith*, nevertheless, is clearly a variant on this idea, for in the final analysis Schleiermacher's account of revelation turns on the identification of a specifically delimited series of events within the natural order as that on the basis of which a "revelatory" event cannot be explained. Schleiermacher relied on this strategy to account for both the revelatory character of the appearance of Jesus within history and also the sense in which this event deserves to be termed "supernatural." Both of these terms rely on what I call *context-specific inexplicability*: the idea that a phenomenon cannot be explained solely on the basis of some delimited set of prior conditions. What makes this notion strategically useful for Schleiermacher lies in the fact that context-specific inexplicability is not inexplicability *tout court*.

Making a case for these claims requires a careful account of just what Schleiermacher claims can and cannot be explained as a consequence or development of what. An initial framework for this account can be extracted from the *Brief Outline*. At the beginning of section II, dedicated to a description of historical theology, Schleiermacher remarked that any prominent historical event can be regarded as either a development of preexisting circumstances or as something that "arises suddenly."[81] The same applies to "historical wholes," considered as epochs with particular historical starting points: They, too, can be seen as either discrete, self-contained epochs or as phases of larger historical developments. The option between these two principles applies as well to Christianity, the course of which "can also be treated, on the one hand, as a single period of a branch of religious development, but also as a particular historical whole, which arose as something new, and has progressed as an independent entity in a series of periods separated by epochs."[82] According to Schleiermacher, historical theology, of which dogmatics is a division, adopts the second of these views, taking the originating fact of Christianity to mark its own starting point as well; and in doing so it reflects the structure of the faith toward which it is oriented, which "could not be what it is if its originating fact were not posited exclusively as something original."[83]

If Schleiermacher's procedure in *The Christian Faith* follows the structure presented in the *Brief Outline*, then his discussion of the "original fact" of Christianity should respect the assumption, required by Christian piety, that the appearance of the Redeemer was something original within history, while being at the same time compatible with (i.e., standing only in "relative antithesis" to) a view of Christianity as one phase in the religious history of humankind in general. As we will see, he tried to accommodate both views of Christianity by speaking carefully about just what parts of preceding history could and could not be regarded as sufficient to explain the appearance of Jesus in history.

The proposition defended in §13 of *The Christian Faith* reads, "The appearance of the Redeemer in history is, as a divine revelation, neither something absolutely supernatural nor something absolutely supra-rational,"[84] and it was here that Schleiermacher advanced the claim that the perfect God-consciousness of Jesus, which represented the "veritable existence of God" in him, was the realization of "a power of development inherent within our nature as a species."[85] In commenting on the sense in which the historical emergence of perfect God-consciousness represents a revelation, Schleiermacher referred to the discussion of §10, but his summary of the earlier argument is disingenuous. For in contrast to the formal definition of revelation provided earlier, here the inexplicability of revelatory events is explicitly presented as context-specific: "Regarding revelation, it has already been conceded above that no starting-point of any uniquely formed being, and still more of a community and especially a pious one, is to be explained by the condition of *the circle within which it emerges and operates*, in that otherwise it would be no starting-point, but itself the result of a spiritual cycle (*Umlauf*)."[86] This context-specificity is emphasized in what follows:

> But although its existence extends beyond the nature of that circle, nothing prevents us from supposing that the emergence of such a life is an effect of a power of development inherent within our nature as a species, which expresses itself in individual men at individual points according to laws which are indeed divinely ordained, even if hidden from us.... That such [revelatory individuals] appear from time to time we must regard as something lawful (*Gesetzmäßig*), if in general we want to adhere to the higher significance of human nature.[87]

What is being suggested here is that the appearance of "revelatory individuals" within history represents the realization of capacities within human nature, according to the operation of laws that are immanent within the natural order, and that knowledge of these capacities and these laws would make possible the explanation of phenomena that otherwise we lack the ability to explain. Only if this is granted can it be said that the appearance of a revelatory individual represents neither a break in the general interconnectedness of all things nor any superaddition to human nature. The discussion comes to a head when the point is applied to the case of Jesus:

> [E]ven the most rigorous view of the difference between [Jesus] and all other men does not hinder us from saying that his appearance,

even regarded as the Incarnation (*Menschwerden*) of the son of God, is something natural.... So that the notion that the divine revelation in Christ should in this respect be something absolutely supernatural does not at all stand the test.... Even if only the possibility of this lies within human nature and the actual implanting of this divinity in the same must be only a divine and therefore an eternal act, in the second place the temporal emergence of this act in a particular individual person must at the same time be regarded as an act of the same, grounded in the original constitution of human nature, and prepared for by everything earlier, and thus as the highest development of its spiritual power, even supposing that we could never penetrate so deeply into these innermost secrets of the general spiritual life that we could develop this general conviction into a determinate perception (*Anschauung*).[88]

This, then, is what it is for the appearance of the Redeemer to be a "natural fact." Perfect God-consciousness was always possible for any member of the human species, and as an event within the flow of time its emergence was "prepared for by everything earlier" and required no intervention by God in the natural order. Christian piety holds that this historical event was something intended from eternity and accomplished in accordance with the divine plan, but this does not permit the Christian to think of the appearance of Jesus as a "miraculous" event in the traditional sense of the word (i.e., as an event directly caused by a discrete and contemporaneous act of God).[89]

Schleiermacher's discussion of the person of Jesus in the doctrinal sections of the *Glaubenslehre* follows the same pattern, offering a more detailed account that also depends on the assertion of context-specific inexplicability. The final formulation, as it were, of his claim that Jesus represents a supernatural, revelatory event adopts the traditional ascription of sinlessness (glossed by Schleiermacher as the maximal and uninterrupted influence of God-consciousness upon his self-consciousness) to Jesus as the central "wonder" of his existence and advances a claim of context-specific inexplicability on this basis:

An unlimited potency of the God-consciousness in Jesus cannot be understood on the basis of the common life of sinfulness, because in this sin naturally reproduces itself; rather, it can only have come to be such as it shows itself in this potency outside the sinful common life. And since this encompasses the whole human race, so it is to be believed that this [God-consciousness] came about as something supernatural, albeit only in the sense of this expression accepted above [§13.1].[90]

The reference to §13 makes it clear that what is at stake in this later section is the relationship between Jesus's special status for Christian faith and the integrity of the natural order that (according to Schleiermacher) is required by the feeling of absolute dependence. In this passage and throughout the discussion of the "sinless perfection" of Jesus, the phrase "common life of sinfulness" and its equivalents specify the context in relation to which the perfect God-consciousness of Jesus is inexplicable. Schleiermacher reiterated the point in a later section, along with a hint as to what sorts of factors might suffice to explain the sinless perfection of Jesus:

> But now if sin is posited as a common act of the human race, how then does a possibility remain that an archetypal (*urbildlich*) individual being could have developed out of this common life?...Thus if the man Jesus is supposed to have been an archetype, or if the archetype in him is supposed to have become historical and actual...then he must certainly have entered into the common life of sinfulness, but he cannot have come out of it, but must rather be acknowledged as a miraculous (*wunderbar*) appearance within the same, but certainly, in accord with the analogies asserted above (§13.1), only in the meaning of the word fixed once and for all here. That is, his particular spiritual content cannot be explained on the basis of the content of the circles of human life to which he belonged, but rather only on the basis of the general source of spiritual life through a creative divine act, in which, as an absolute maximum, the concept of the human being as a subject of the God-consciousness is completed.[91]

The view expressed here, as I understand it, is the following. Jesus of Nazareth represents a "divine revelation" inasmuch as his possession of perfect God-consciousness cannot be explained solely as a development out of the "common life of sinfulness" preceding him. Viewed solely in relation to that common life he represents a historical novelty, a new beginning, and Christian piety looks to his life as the point where its ideal or archetype (*Urbild*) appeared within history. This perfect God-consciousness could never have come about apart from the introduction of a new element into the common life of sinfulness—that is, into the historical career of the human species. However, this does not require thinking that the appearance of perfect God-consciousness in the person of Jesus was anything other than a natural fact when considered in a broader context—a fact determined by the operation of causes and effects within the natural order. In fact, the appearance of the Redeemer, when viewed within this broader context, is *not* a supernatural fact:

> Now if we take all of this together, then everywhere we posit, on the one side, an initiating divine activity as something supernatural, but at the same time posit a living human receptivity, in virtue of which the supernatural can become something historically natural.... [S]o for

this total area (*Gesamtumfang*) even the appearance of the Redeemer in the midst of this natural process is the emergence of a new stage of development which is no longer a supernatural emergence of a new developmental stage, but rather one which is conditioned by what preceded it, whose cohesion (*Zusammenhang*) with that which preceded admittedly lies only within the unity of the divine thought.[92]

This passage contains the clearest expression, I believe, of the claim that the appearance of the Redeemer was a result of the operations of chains of causality operating within the natural order rather than something inexplicable in an absolute sense. The appearance of a perfect God-consciousness in the person of Jesus of Nazareth is a supernatural event relative to the common life of sinfulness. However, relative to a wider context, it is a natural fact in every sense of the term, a (divinely ordained) development of factors immanent within the natural order. Schleiermacher, then, made no exception for the God-consciousness of Jesus of Nazareth from the general fate of being a product of history, even in light of the fact that this claim cannot be validated by scientific inquiry—even, in fact, if the only one who understands the connection between the God-consciousness of Jesus and the preceding circumstances is the one who knows everything that there is to know about the natural order (i.e., God).

The thinking behind Schleiermacher's remark to Lücke that it was his hope that his account of the appearance of the Redeemer "will not endanger the faith and that science need not declare war on us" should by now be fairly clear, as should the import of Karl Barth's remark that "*mutatis mutandis* the coming of Christ is similar to the formation of a new nebula."[93] Schleiermacher's intent was to propose an account of the appearance of Jesus that, on the one hand, would require believing nothing that conflicts with a scientific view of the world and, on the other, incorporate additional claims that would represent a plausible replacement for the traditional understanding of his supernatural status.

I find it difficult to regard this proposal of Schleiermacher's as successful or even promising as a moment of mediation between faith and science. A major problem with the proposal is the fact that it is simply not clear just what is being claimed about events in the world in the statement that the sinless perfection of Jesus cannot be explained on the basis of the common life of sin. Formally, this amounts to a claim that one particular fact cannot be explained solely on the basis of another set of facts. However, to know whether this claim of inexplicability sits comfortably with what the natural or historical sciences have established or are likely to establish, we would need to know more than we do about just what collection of facts constitutes this common life of sin. It is possible that the claim of inexplicability is nothing more than a platitude, if Schleiermacher's view was that any adequate understanding or explanation would require taking into account the entirety of the natural order. However, if the claim is not platitudinous—if, that is, Schleiermacher's view was that the piety of Jesus represents a natural event that was, in an intuitive sense, truly remarkable—then it is simply not clear whether the possibility of "entanglements with science" has been entirely precluded.

It is also not clear whether Schleiermacher's mention of laws hidden from our view that account for events of a "miraculous" character provides grounds for the charge of entanglement with science; on one interpretation it clearly does.[94] The general thought is that even *wunderbar* events take place according to laws that are immanent within the natural order rather than being the result of supernatural interference. However, it makes a difference whether such laws are "hidden" from us merely in fact or in principle. If the ignorance of the *Wissenschaften* of such laws is simply an index of their incompleteness, then here Schleiermacher should be understood as issuing a promissory note on behalf of the sciences: promising, that is, that one day even such *wunderbar* events will be comprehensible in scientific terms. However, it is possible that Schleiermacher had in mind laws that God has decreed will remain *forever* hidden from human view, and in this case, the fact that miraculous and revelatory events are law-governed is small comfort to the scientist, for the implication would be that no matter how advanced the sciences become, these events will always remain scientifically inexplicable. It should be pointed out that the very claim that accounting for the piety of Jesus of Nazareth would require knowledge of laws of which the sciences are currently ignorant can itself hardly be said to be scientifically innocent, and while the in-fact interpretation of the hiddenness of these laws comports better with the general intent of Schleiermacher's "eternal covenant," Schleiermacher's brief remarks do not clearly rule out the in-principle option.

On the basis of this survey of the "overlay" of Christian piety, the overall character of the view of Christianity presented in *The Christian Faith* as a "supplemented naturalism" should now be clear. What should also be clear is that the relationship between what Schleiermacher was willing to advance as the content of Christian doctrine and what he understood to be the actual and potential deliverances of the natural and historical sciences is more complex than the segregation model allows. While some of the claims that result from the critical examination of Christian doctrines are straightforwardly metaphysical, others fall within the territory of the natural sciences.

Indeed, in one place Schleiermacher even hinted that the doctrinal account of redemption that he had presented might find confirmation of a sort from the empirical investigation of human psychology. In discussing the relationship between dogmatics and the philosophy of religion in §11, he suggested that the philosophy of religion might some day succeed in "systematizing" all of the characteristic moments of pious consciousness:

> If it should become evident (*zeigte sich*) that that which we describe
> by the term *redemption* becomes such [a moment] as soon as a fact

which liberates God-consciousness enters into a region where God-consciousness is constrained: then Christianity would be made secure as a particular form of faith and in a certain sense understood (*construiert*). However, this itself could not be called a proof of Christianity since even the philosophy of religion could establish no necessity either to acknowledge a particular fact as redemptive (*erlösend*) or even to really grant a central place within one's own consciousness to a moment which can be such.[95]

The suggestion here is that the basic dynamics, or formal characteristics, of the psychological process that Schleiermacher named "redemption" (i.e., the increase in the "potency" of God-consciousness through participation in Christian ritual and communal activity) might be corroborated in some objective fashion, and I take this thought to be illustrative of his remark later in the introduction that questions about the internal workings of piety "encroach upon the psychological."[96]

Here, it seems to me, Schleiermacher was performing exactly the opposite of what the segregation model claims: Rather than restricting theology to the exposition of a domain of human existence off limits to scientific investigation, he in fact proposed as an interpretation of Christian doctrine a description of processes operating within the mind that he anticipated the natural sciences might someday be able to observe independently. To be sure, Schleiermacher did advance claims that can be understood as immune to falsification: for example, the claim that the redemption that comes by way of Christian socialization is *a work of Christ* not in a supernatural sense but in the sense that the original "impartation" of Jesus is still at work within history. However, it is emphatically not the case that nonfalsifiability is the only mechanism through which he hoped to avoid "entanglements with science."

Schleiermacher's "eternal covenant," then, should be interpreted not as a call for theology and science to go their separate ways, with each in command of its own territory, but for theology to accommodate its work to the deliverances of the natural and historical sciences.

4.4 Naturalism and the Question of Absolute Dependence

I have to this point been defending the claim that the presentation of Christianity in *The Christian Faith* should be understood as a "supplemented naturalism": as the combination of a naturalistic theory of religion with various kinds of additions presented by the theologian. In what remains of this chapter I focus on the issue of naturalism, for there is a question much discussed in the secondary literature on Schleiermacher that is crucial to the question of whether his account of religion deserves to be thought of as an example of religious naturalism in any meaningful sense.

We saw in the introduction that in the earliest phases of his public career Schleiermacher was suspected of atheism on the grounds of his claim (which appeared in the first edition of the *Speeches on Religion*) that the idea of God is a product of *Fantasie*, and that he effectively obfuscated his position on the issue in the revised edition of 1806.[97] His position on what is basically the same topic in *The Christian Faith* has occasioned much commentary and no little confusion since his death. In the dogmatics the issue centers on the relationship between the claim that a feeling of absolute dependence is a universal feature of human subjectivity and the idea that the universe and all it contains is absolutely dependent upon God. Schleiermacher claimed that recognizing the existence of this feeling "entirely replaces (*ersetzt*), for the *Glaubenslehre*, all so-called proofs of the existence of God";[98] the question that has animated the literature is whether or not this language of "replacement" indicates that his postulation of a feeling of absolute dependence itself amounts (or was intended to amount) to a "proof" of God's existence.[99]

What has been at stake for Schleiermacher's theological readers regarding this question has been whether his dogmatics provides a metaphysical grounding for Christian doctrine. The criticism of "subjectivism" that was a mainstay of nineteenth-century interpretations of Schleiermacher is premised on the idea that his dogmatics provides no such grounding and that the "replacement" at issue amounts to basing religion only in a fact of human psychology, and thus reduces it to a merely human affair whose legitimacy can all too easily be called into question.[100] The most famous early articulation of this criticism was that voiced by Hegel in his preface to Hermann Hinrichs's 1822 book *Die Religion im inneren Verhältnisse zur Wissenschaft*: "If religion in man is based only on a feeling, then such a feeling rightly has no further determination than to be the feeling of his dependence, and the dog would then be the best Christian. . . . The dog also has feelings of redemption, whenever his hunger is satisfied by a bone."[101] Translated out of Hegel's acerbic language, the charge against Schleiermacher is that his account of religion requires nothing more to be true than that human beings have feelings, feelings that in fact bear a family resemblance to those of the lower animals; the account fails to ground religion in or connect it meaningfully to the transcendent. Troeltsch's later description of Schleiermacher's theology as premised on a "dogmatic agnosticism" is a more moderate expression of what is recognizably the same understanding.[102]

It should be readily apparent that there is a close relationship between religious "subjectivism" in this sense and religious naturalism, between Hegel's hostile characterization and the position I have been defending in this chapter. If Schleiermacher's account grounds religion in a feature of human subjectivity and not in a set of claims about transcendent states of affairs, then the characterization of his account as an example of religious naturalism is apposite, but if the "subjectivism" criticism is inaccurate and Schleiermacher's invocation of a feeling of absolute dependence is equivalent to claiming that a "divine whence" really exists, then his account presupposes the existence of God and so is not an example of religious naturalism. My view is that an understanding of the role that Schleiermacher's claims about the feeling of absolute dependence plays within the overall argument of *The Christian Faith* is crucial for understanding the relationship he sought to establish between religious faith and scientific inquiry and thus for understanding his relationship to religious naturalism.

Two initial questions can be asked about relationship between the feeling of absolute dependence and the existence of God. The first of these is whether the former is equivalent to or entails the latter, such that one who acknowledges the existence of the feeling of absolute dependence is thereby constrained to acknowledge God's existence. The second is whether Schleiermacher thought that there was such a relationship between the two claims, such that in invoking a feeling of absolute dependence as the essence of religion he understood himself to be basing his account of religion on the claim that God exists. If the correct answer to both of these is a negative one, then the most significant challenge to my characterization of Schleiermacher's account of religion as an example of religious naturalism is obviated. If both are answered in the affirmative, then that account cannot be claimed for religious naturalism; and if the answer to the first is negative but the second positive, then describing Schleiermacher as a religious naturalist would be, if accurate, somewhat awkward.

In a penetrating 1977 essay Robert C. Roberts offered a concise and clearly articulated answer to the first question. It is worth noting that Roberts was skeptical of Schleiermacher's claim that there is such a thing as a feeling of absolute dependence, a skepticism I believe is warranted.[103] However, the issue that matters for naturalism concerns the relationship between that feeling, if it exists, and the existence of God. "[M]uch of the apologetic force of [Schleiermacher's] theology," Roberts noted, "would seem to hang on the propriety of inferring from the fact that a man feels absolutely dependent to the proposition that there is a One on whom he is absolutely dependent."[104] Roberts found this inference difficult to defend, observing that only certain kinds of states of the self can be testified to with certainty by feelings: It follows from the fact that I feel grumpy that I am grumpy, for example, but not from the fact that I feel triumphant that I am triumphant.[105] The state of the self to which the feeling of absolute dependence testifies is clearly of the latter sort, for it is certainly conceivable that I might feel absolutely dependent and not be so. Thus, Roberts concluded flatly that "from the fact that I feel dependent upon God it does not follow either with certainty or with probability that I am dependent upon him."[106] This answer seems to me to be the correct one.

If it does not follow from the fact that one feels absolutely dependent that one actually is so, the question remains whether Schleiermacher took this to be the case. Roberts adopted an agnostic position on this question, making it clear that this position leads to agnosticism on the further question of whether appeal to the feeling of absolute dependence constitutes an apologetic move in the first place. During the following decade, however, Ronald Thiemann made a positive answer to this question central to his criticism of Schleiermacher's theological foundationalism. In *Revelation and Theology* Thiemann took Schleiermacher to be engaged in an attempt to "justify the Christian claim to revelation" by positing an experiential ground for this claim, which was, in his terms, "self-authenticating." Like Roberts, however, Thiemann found the idea that a feeling of dependence could testify with certainty to the existence of a "divine whence" suspect, concluding that appeals to self-authentication "only establish the indubitability of the report of my own feelings...but hardly suffice to justify a claim to *revelation*."[107] Like Roberts, Thiemann answered the first of our two initial questions in the negative, but unlike Roberts, he took a firm position on the second, arguing that Schleiermacher mistakenly believed that the existence of a feeling of absolute dependence somehow demonstrated the existence of God.

Thiemann's charge that Schleiermacher was a "foundationalist" is, in historical perspective, an oddity. It is diametrically opposed to both the hostile charge of "subjectivism" and the more moderate characterization of Schleiermacher's dogmatics as a species of agnosticism, which taken together constitute the majority report of the interpretive tradition. It is worth noting that in expressing a view that ran counter to much of the existing literature Thiemann provided little in the way of support for his position, offering only the vaguest kind of textual justification for the crucial claim that Schleiermacher took the feeling of absolute dependence to be "self-authenticating."[108] It has been standard practice to take at face value Schleiermacher's explicit refusal to offer proofs of the "truth or necessity of Christianity" in both editions of *The Christian Faith*[109] and to understand this refusal as based on his view that the project of metaphysically grounding theology would be an example of the commingling of religious reflection and "speculation"—in my terms, as a recipe for the contamination of religion by an "alien" interest in truth for its own sake. In a response to Thiemann, Brian Gerrish spoke for the majority report in observing simply that "the quest for a 'full-scale justification for Christian belief in God's prevenience' was not Schleiermacher's." If anything, Schleiermacher was engaged in something more akin to Thiemann's own "descriptive" theological project, "an interpretive activity which seeks to illuminate the structures embedded in beliefs and practices," avoiding altogether the project of offering theoretical justifications for Christian belief.[110]

I take Gerrish, along with the bulk of Schleiermacher's theological readership, to be correct and Thiemann to be mistaken in claiming that Schleiermacher took the feeling of absolute dependence to be "self-authenticating." The correct answer to our second initial question in my view is also a negative one: Schleiermacher did not hold the view that the claim that human beings feel absolutely dependent either is equivalent to or entails the claim that God exists.

If, then, Schleiermacher's account of religion is premised on a feature of human subjectivity the existence of which does not entail the existence of God, and if while recognizing this he refused to provide any other epistemological "foundation" for religion, then it would seem that his account should be regarded as an example of religious naturalism. However, providing a negative answer to our two initial questions does not entirely clarify the relationship between the claim of the existence of a feeling of absolute dependence and the claim of the existence of God in *The Christian Faith*. For neither Schleiermacher himself nor *The Christian Faith* was ultimately agnostic regarding the question of whether the state of affairs to which the feeling of absolute dependence testifies obtains. Rather, as we have seen, Schleiermacher's critical analysis of Christian doctrines proceeded on the assumption that the feeling of absolute dependence is veridical, that God exists, and that human beings and the universe that contains them are absolutely dependent upon God. Schleiermacher's considered position, as he described it to Lücke, was that the feeling of absolute dependence is "the original expression of an immediate existential relationship" and thus not merely a free-floating fact of human psychology.[111] My characterization of the account of religion presented in *The Christian Faith* as an example of religious naturalism and thus the characterization of its presentation of Christianity as a "supplemented naturalism" will not be on firm ground until the place of Schleiermacher's assumption of the veridicality of the feeling of absolute dependence is discussed.

I propose to address the subject through attention to Schleiermacher's distinction between different species of *Wissenschaft* and his understanding of the specific tasks and presuppositions of each of these. As we have already seen, in the second edition Schleiermacher presented the science of dogmatics as coordinated with and dependent upon a number of other sciences. Three forms of *Wissenschaft* in particular are relevant to understanding the positions Schleiermacher articulated in *The Christian Faith* on the relationship between the feeling of absolute dependence and the question of God's existence. In a nutshell, in his understanding the science of *dogmatics* proper takes place entirely "within" Christian faith, which in practical terms means that it assumes the truth of the essences of both religion in general and Christianity in particular as fundamental postulates (as Schleiermacher put it, dogmatics "must everywhere presuppose immediate certainty, [or] faith (*Glaube*), and thus regarding God-consciousness in general its task is not initially to bring about its acknowledgment but rather only to develop its content").[112] Consideration of whether God's existence can be inferred from what can be observed about the natural order or the structure of human subjectivity—the traditional task of natural theology—falls for Schleiermacher not to dogmatics or to any branch of theological science but to philosophy or *metaphysics*.[113] And

if God's existence is simply presupposed by dogmatics and considered a problem by metaphysics, it is a matter of indifference for the *philosophy of religion*,
which takes its standpoint "above" the phenomenon under investigation and
is concerned with "a critical presentation of the different given forms of pious
communities."[114]

The structure of the *Glaubenslehre* can be analyzed with reference to this
distinction between three forms of inquiry. We have seen that in the second
edition Schleiermacher labeled the material concerned with the general structure of religious communities and the piety that defines them as propositions
"borrowed" from the philosophy of religion; and in the second of his letters to
Lücke Schleiermacher specifically placed the introduction as a whole within
the philosophy of religion as part of a denial that his initial description of religion could "provide anyone with a foundation (*Begründung*)" for Christian dogmatics.[115] If the introduction is to be identified with the philosophy of religion
and thus understood as a "propadeutic and exoteric" treatment of Christianity,[116]
then dogmatics proper comprises the subsequent doctrinal sections of the text,
where the critical analysis of Christian doctrines is executed (in the second edition, from §32 on). Finally, what is perhaps most noteworthy is that the contribution of the remaining science, philosophy or metaphysics, is simply absent
from *The Christian Faith*: Arguments for the existence of God as the "transcendent ground" of thinking and being that Schleiermacher had developed in the
Dialektik find no place in his dogmatics.[117]

What this suggests, in terms directly relevant to the question at hand, is
that the notion that the feeling of absolute dependence is veridical and thus that
there exists a God on whom the universe is absolutely dependent (1) is *not*
assumed within the introduction to *The Christian Faith*, (2) *is* assumed as a
fundamental postulate in the doctrinal sections, and (3) is *argued for* nowhere
in the text. This result supports my description of the account of religion on
which Schleiermacher's presentation of Christianity is based as an example of
religious naturalism: for as indicated above, the primary threat to this description was the thought that Schleiermacher's account of religion presupposes the
existence of God. However, if this presupposition is confined to the doctrinal or
properly theological sections of the text, then it plays a role not in Schleiermacher's
initial description of religion but in the arguments that generate the claims that
constitute his "supplement" to this account.

The suggestion that the assumption of the veridicality of the feeling of
absolute dependence is absent from the introduction to *The Christian Faith* will
be contentious. In fact, what I want to defend is a more modest claim, that the
general account of religion contained in the introduction—the material that is
rightly to be regarded as falling under the heading of philosophy of religion—
does not depend on this assumption. Since a substantial portion of the introduction is given over to discussion of the nature and task of dogmatics, there
are ways in which the assumption does appear within Schleiermacher's

argument prior to the doctrinal sections.[118] However, it is the more modest claim that my argument requires.

A crucial section of *The Christian Faith* presents a prima facie obstacle to my position, the section wherein Schleiermacher considered and rejected the possibility of "nonpious" explanations of the feeling of absolute dependence—explanations, that is, that deny the veridicality of that feeling. Properly understood, however, Schleiermacher's rejection of this possibility supports rather than challenges my claims regarding the naturalistic tenor of his initial description of Christianity.

Schleiermacher's treatment of the "system of doctrines" opens in §32 with a consideration of the possibility that the feeling of absolute dependence might be illusory, marking the only place in *The Christian Faith* where the question of the veridicality of this feeling is explicitly raised (a placement retained from the first edition).[119] Specifically, Schleiermacher noted the existence of a "nonpious explanation" (*unfrömme Erklärung*) of the feeling of absolute dependence, according to which the other party in the relationship that it indicates is not God but the world, and signaled his disagreement with this explanation. However, his treatment of this subject must be followed with care. Contra Thiemann, he did not argue that this nonpious explanation is obviously false because the feeling of absolute dependence is "self-authenticating" or self-evidently true. In fact, he did not say that this explanation is false. Rather, he simply observed that "we can do nothing other than regard this explanation as a misunderstanding" because "we" recognize a consciousness of dependence upon the world that is phenomenally distinct from the feeling of absolute dependence.[120] This response amounts to claiming that this explanation in fact confuses the feeling of absolute dependence with a qualitatively different feeling, and Schleiermacher's elaboration on this line of argument observes that one could posit absolute dependence *upon the world* only if one denied the veridicality of the feeling of freedom (i.e., the feeling of being able to exercise a causal influence upon the world).[121]

It is important to note that this initial form of *unfrömme Erklärung* does not declare the feeling of absolute dependence to be illusory: It accepts the idea that this feeling testifies truthfully to a relationship in which human beings stand but disputes the claim, produced by reflection on this feeling, that the other party in this relationship exists outside the natural order. However, Schleiermacher also considered a second type of explanation that denies the relationship of absolute dependence itself. This explanation comes "from those who dismiss all distinction between the ideas of God and of the world, in that they maintain that there is nothing upon which we could feel ourselves to be absolutely dependent."[122] Thus, where the first type of *unfrömme Erklärung* admits absolute dependence but entails that the *feeling of freedom* is an illusion, the second directly claims that the *feeling of absolute dependence* is itself illusory, on the grounds that there is no being on which we could in fact be absolutely dependent.

Two aspects of this rejection of different types of nonpious explanation of the feeling of absolute dependence are important for my purposes. The first is that Schleiermacher did not claim that such explanations are false; rather, he observed that in order to accept such an explanation one would have to deny either the veridicality of the feeling of freedom or that of the feeling of absolute dependence itself. But he provided no *defense* of the veridicality of either of these feelings and was content instead to note that the project in which he would be engaged would, in effect, proceed on the assumption that they are not illusory. The second important aspect is the textual location of the discussion: Schleiermacher first raised the question of the veridicality of the feeling of absolute dependence and took a position on the subject *not in the introduction but at the start of the doctrinal sections* of The Christian Faith, wherein (as he noted in the same paragraph) "we no longer set foot outside (*hinausgehn*) the realm of Christian piety."[123] Taken together, these observations support my claim that the veridicality of the feeling of absolute dependence is a presupposition of the science of dogmatics specifically rather than of Schleiermacher's account of religion generally: It is assumed rather than argued for and is operative within Schleiermacher's analysis of Christian doctrines rather than in his initial description of Christianity as a religion. In fact, it seems to me that a stronger claim is in order: Schleiermacher chose the discussion of the question of the veridicality of the feeling of absolute dependence and his statement of a position on the topic to mark *the point* in the text where the standpoint of his treatment of Christianity shifted from "exoteric" to "esoteric", from philosophy of religion to dogmatics. In my terms, it is with the introduction of the veridicality of the feeling of absolute dependence as a postulate that The Christian Faith moves beyond a naturalistic treatment of Christianity and into the production of the claims that constitute Schleiermacher's theological "supplement."[124]

4.5 Conclusion: *The Christian Faith* and Religious Naturalism

A passage from the conclusion of Byrne's *Natural Religion and the Nature of Religion* crystallizes the issues at play in the discussion of this chapter and so is useful as a preface to my conclusions.

> A Humean picture of religion as an illusion using categories derived
> from modern psychological and sociological theory may be argued
> for on a variety of grounds. The point maintained here is that such a
> picture needs independent argument and does not simply follow
> from the anthropocentrism implicit in the concept of religion which
> structures the modern scientific study of religion. The question of

how naturalism should proceed, once the anthropocentric bias in the science of religion is accepted, turns out to be a matter of the final philosophical judgment to be made of the status of human religiousness.... Some may argue that its character shows it to be a reflection of a universal awareness of a real, sacred reality; others that it can be reduced without remainder to the simple effect of non-religious factors in human life (for example, neurotically based fantasies or the ideological expressions of class consciousness); yet others may be content to leave the status of human religiousness undecided and undecidable.[125]

In my view Schleiermacher's treatment of Christianity in *The Christian Faith* is informed by a position very much like Byrne's. The crucial point of agreement between Schleiermacher and Byrne is that the question of whether there are or not transcendent realities to which religions may refer is ultimately a philosophical question and not one that the adoption of a naturalistic approach to the investigation of religion resolves.[126] It is this conviction, it seems to me, that lies at the heart of Schleiermacher's vision of an eternal covenant between religious faith and scientific inquiry, for this principle, if true, entails that while natural-scientific investigation may challenge and even falsify particular religiously important claims, it will never yield results that reveal all religion as such to be illusory or otherwise illegitimate. The project of *The Christian Faith*, then, is a critical reconstruction of Christianity that not only is intended to cohere with what Schleiermacher understood to be a properly "scientific" view of the natural order but also contains a chastened set of claims to truth regarding both immanent and transcendent realities licensed by theological reflection upon the historical doctrinal tradition.

Early in the present chapter I called attention to the cultural situation to which Schleiermacher addressed his proposal for an "eternal covenant": the rising power of a reactionary pietism whose cultural and political influence threatened to polarize the existing social order, with dire consequences for both religion and intellectual freedom. There my aim in invoking this context was to counter the common tendency to interpret Schleiermacher's eternal covenant as a call for a withdrawal of religion and science into self-enclosed and autonomous spheres of influence. However, in concluding the chapter I want to recall his anxieties about the condition of Prussian society to make a different and more ambitious point, one on which I expand in the following chapter. His remarks to Lücke indicate that Schleiermacher did not understand himself to be writing exclusively for theologians and did not intend that the effect of his dogmatics should remain confined to the academy. Rather, what he intended was an intervention in the religious self-understanding of those of his contemporaries (and their descendants) whose commitment to received versions of Christianity rendered them vulnerable to the sort of defensive anti-intellectualism, "loveless intolerance," and hermeneutical partisanship currently on display in the work of Hengstenberg and his allies. Schleiermacher hoped that his dogmatics would demonstrate to such as these that viewing religion as the scientific mindset requires—as a phenomenon unfolding within the natural order and hence subject to an increasingly sophisticated causal-explanatory accounting with the advance of time—could by nature neither destroy Christian faith nor pronounce the final word concerning its content, even if such a posture would require an unaccustomed degree of doctrinal flexibility and epistemic humility. Briefly put, then, one of Schleiermacher's central aims in his magnum opus of dogmatics was *the public dissemination of religious naturalism* through the medium of academic theology as a strategy for heading off societal polarization.

5

Conclusion

Religion and the Natural Order

Since God said, let there be light, and there was light, theories
have made no difference in the recurrence of night and morning;
and so it will be with the inward light which Jesus has kindled.
Faith clings to this light, rejoices in it, seeks by it; but science
explores its nature and laws. We may argue the sun out of the
heavens, but it will keep on shining still.
> —K. R. Hagenbach, *German Rationalism in Its Rise,*
> *Progress, and Decline*

I do not say that the Science of Religion is all gain. No; it entails
losses, and losses of many things which we hold dear. But this
I will say, that, as far as my humble judgment goes, it does not
entail the loss of anything that is essential to true religion, and
that if we strike the balance honestly, the gain is immeasurably
greater than the loss.
> —F. Max Müller, *Lectures on the Science*
> *of Religion*

When [scientific theology] asks for the friendly participation
and support of such theologians as agree with its stated
fundamental principles, it hopes as well for the interest of
cultured non-theologians, for whom in light of recent experiences it can hardly be a matter of indifference whether a
scientific or an unscientific spirit (*Wissenschaftlichkeit oder
Unwissenschaftlichkeit*) reigns in theology, and whether the
German people are to have a clergy of zealots (*Schwärmerei*)

hostile to spiritual enculturation (*geistigen Bildung*) or rather a clergy thoroughly educated in the sciences.

—Adolf Hilgenfeld, "Die wissenschaftliche
Theologie und ihre gegenwärtige Aufgabe"

In previous chapters I have explored what seem to me to be the themes of greatest significance for understanding Schleiermacher's account of religion and its relationship to religious naturalism: his determinism, the structure of his essentialist account of religion, his understanding of religion's social dimension, and the constructive relationship that he sought to establish between religious adherence and scientific inquiry. This chapter is dedicated to summarizing the explorations of the previous chapters and drawing conclusions regarding Schleiermacher's historical and contemporary significance.

I first offer a set of answers to the question "what is religion according to Schleiermacher?" The three answers I present differ with respect to length and, consequently, both nuance and fidelity to Schleiermacher's texts. My intention in presenting not one but three summaries is to acknowledge the practice in the secondary literature of compressing the works of historically important figures into single paragraphs, sentences, or even catchphrases and to suggest how one might responsibly reduce (in the culinary sense) my reconstruction of Schleiermacher's account of religion. Following these summaries I turn to three themes that tend to recur in discussions of Schleiermacher and that are relevant to any interesting assessment of his significance as a theorist of religion: the questions of how religion is affected by historical contingency, of how religion and politics are related, and of how religion, as Schleiermacher understood it, might figure as the object of scholarly investigation. I conclude with reflections on Schleiermacher's place within the history of the academic study of religion and on his relevance for contemporary scholars of religion.

5.1 What Is Religion?

I offer, first, a rather lengthy answer to this question, which touches on the most important aspects of Schleiermacher's account.

One approach to the question of what religion is involves asking after the range of phenomena the term encompasses. Religion for Schleiermacher incorporates mental states such as emotions, attitudes, beliefs, and desires; human activities, including but not limited to acts of discourse and nonlinguistic communication; social organizations, in some cases dedicated specifically to the business of religion (churches) and in others oriented toward other social purposes (family, tribe, and state); and a variety of symbolic and material artifacts such as the various media of cultic practice and works of art and architecture. The identity of both religion in general and particular religions is rooted in a particular way in the first category in this list—in the "inward" dimension of human existence—but is not restricted to it. Whether or not some members of this first category can be described as "intrinsically religious,"[1] the religious identity of members of the other categories is a contingent affair: a belief, an act of discourse, a routinized practice, or an artifact can be religious or nonreligious depending on the circumstances.

A second part of the answer to the question of what religion is—and the part that makes clear the conditions under which contingently religious phenomena are part of religion—has to do with its structure. As described by Schleiermacher, religion has a concentric structure, and this in a double sense. One of the senses has to do with the relationship of religion's "essence" to the phenomena whose development it motivates under the proper conditions; the other has to do with the relationship between the constituents of actual religion and that ideal of religion that the first line of thought represents.

The category of *ideal religion* represents Schleiermacher's imaginative construction of religion as it would take shape if religion's essence were allowed to stimulate and inform human activity in the absence of any contaminating or deforming factors. Bracketing for the moment the question of the referent of the term *essence*, his view was that if the elements that constitute the essence of a particular religion were to be found existing within a particular individual or population, and in the absence of "alien" factors (that is, under ideal circumstances), these elements would catalyze the development of further phenomena, both inward and outward. Among the innermost of these fall what Schleiermacher after 1805 labeled *Gefühl* or "immediate self-consciousness."[2] This important category has three salient characteristics. First, *Gefühl* is "subjective cognition": It consists, properly speaking, of states of awareness of the condition of the self. Second, *Gefühl* is "immediate" in the sense of being prereflective: It is not the product of the intentional operations of consciousness but rather contributes the material with which such operations (i.e., reflective thinking) work. Third, *Gefühl* is both conceptually vague and affectively charged: The contents of *Gefühl* cannot be exhaustively and definitively restated in linguistic form, although they can be described with enough precision that the feelings of one person can become known to others. Considered under ideal circumstances, reflection upon the contents of *Gefühl* produces a further layer of "inward" religious phenomena: linguistically structured representations of one's feelings, notions or beliefs concerning their causes or implications, and so on. Taken as a whole, these constitute "inward religion," which Schleiermacher sometimes describes as piety (*Frömmigkeit*) and sometimes as a form or kind of faith (*Glaubensart, Glaubensweise*). The relative prominence of the term *Frömmigkeit* in Schleiermacher's writings on religion indicates the explanatory priority, in general, of the inward over the outward in his understanding of "ideal religion." In describing *Gefühl* as the "seat (*Siz*) of piety" and piety as a "modification (*Bestimmtheit*) of feeling,"[3] Schleiermacher did not simply equate feeling and piety but indicated that piety is more closely associated with feeling than with representations or beliefs. I take his point to have been that religious beliefs, for example, are relatively superficial components of inward religion in comparison to feelings, such that religious identity is not in the main predicated on commitment to a particular set of religious beliefs.[4]

Paradigmatic "outward" components of ideal religion are *expressions* of inward religion to others (described most often by Schleiermacher as "expressions of piety"), coupled with the reception of the expressive activities of others similarly stimulated. The formation in turn of social circles, communities, and institutions dedicated to this discursive activity represents a further stage of the same developmental process. Writing in 1799, Schleiermacher explicitly distanced ideal religious community from any notion of standardization with respect to inward religion: It was his youthful view that the ideal realization of the religious impulse would result in the embrace and encouragement of religious individualism, and that development toward commonality represented a concession to the circumstances of actuality. However, by the time of his lectures on ethics, Schleiermacher had come to regard the reciprocal "inward formation" of the members of any community of discourse toward a common standard as a natural consequence of the "ethical process" rather than a contamination of it. Thus, for the mature Schleiermacher, religion as a fully formed and yet still ideal phenomenon took the form of determinate and yet intimate communities of discourse centered around particular forms of piety. He envisioned such communities as self-perpetuating since, as a result of their participation in cultic practice, the younger members of the community come to be "stamped" at the deepest level—the level of feeling or immediate self-consciousness—by the form of piety particular to the community as a whole, which they would in their turn impress upon the following generation of participants. As a result, particular forms of piety or ways of believing have careers that extend beyond the lifetimes of religious individuals and thus constitute the "inward unity," or internal principle of identity, of particular religious traditions. Thus "ideal religion" displays the first of two types of concentricity that characterize Schleiermacher's account of religion, with an "essence" at the center, an inner ring of piety or faith (subdivided in turn into a prereflective and a reflective band), and an outward periphery of acts, institutions, and artifacts dedicated to the transmission and development of inward religion.

Ideal religion, considered in its entire extent, can be thought of in turn as the core of the second sense of concentricity that informs Schleiermacher's account. The idea that dominates his various pronouncements about actually existing religion seems to me to be one of a *genealogical connection* to ideal religion. That is, what makes religion as it actually exists religion is its status as a *not-necessarily-appropriate development* or *historical descendant* of ideal religion (more accurately, of some stage of its partial realization). Actual religion is the result of the developmental process described earlier (i.e., the process that, if operating in isolation, would produce ideal religion) unfolding within history and thus reflects the influence of the various nonreligious influences and tendencies that are the stuff of historical life. Not all of these will be distorting or otherwise negative influences: Indeed, for Schleiermacher the essences of particular religions are historically contingent phenomena, and in general as a champion of religious "positivity" he was committed to the view that it is history that provides religion with its specific content. However, besides contributing formally contingent but materially necessary elements to the process of religion's development, history also presents obstructions and diversions to this process, resulting in phenomena that display not only historical concreteness but also a recognizable degree of degeneration relative to ideal religion. Schleiermacher's various observations about the distance between ideal and actual religion generally fit, so far as I can see, within this scheme. Actual religion can display *underdevelopment* in some areas in comparison to ideal religion, as when religious communities have "not yet separated" from either family structures or from the state; the historical development of religion can be *diverted* by "alien interests" both inwardly (by "speculation") and outwardly (by state interference); or a religious tradition can "die inwardly" in that its characteristic form of piety can *atrophy*, leaving only the empty shell of routinized discourse and cultic practice (which is roughly the view of Judaism expressed in the *Speeches*).[5] Thus, ideal religion constitutes not the *historical* but the *conceptual* core of actual religion: Schleiermacher's view, if I understand it correctly, was that actual religion constitutes a recognizable "penumbra" around ideal religion in that specific cases will be comprehensible as products of a historically informed (for better and for worse) iteration of the religious developmental process.

I have left discussion of the nature of religion's "essence" for the end of this summary, largely as part of my attempt to counter the tendency of the standard interpretation to focus on that notion to the expense of all else. Formally speaking, the essence of a religion is the principle of final appeal with respect to the identity of a religious tradition. One and the same religion can display both synchronic and diachronic diversity with respect not only to ritual practice or doctrine but also to the forms of *Frömmigkeit* and the *Glaubensweisen* that inform these. The piety of one and the same religion can both change over time and differ across sectarian divisions; it is only by virtue of standing in some intelligible relationship (within the broad parameters described above) to its essence that any internal or external phenomenon constitutes part of a particular religion.

On the question of the *content* of the notion of essence, it is important to note, first, that without reference to historical particulars no more can be done than to identify the general features of this notion, and second, that the later Schleiermacher distinguished in a way the younger did not between the essence of religion as such and the essences of particular religions. In the most general terms, for the young Schleiermacher the essence of an actually existing religion can be described roughly as an idea or impression regarding the overall character of the universe. It is worth noting that in spite of the relatively technical manner in which the notion of essence was presented in the second of the *Speeches*, Schleiermacher made use of a variety of locutions to refer to the particular essences of both Judaism and Christianity in the fifth. While consistently describing the essence of Christianity as its "original intuition" (*ursprüngliche Anschauung*) even after largely excising this term from the second speech in 1806, when discussing Judaism Schleiermacher moved from "idea of the universe" in 1799 to "view (*Ansicht*) of the universe and of the being of humanity therein" in 1806, finally settling on the phrase "the consciousness of human beings of their place within the whole and their relationship to the eternal" in the final edition.[6] Hallmarks of an essence are, first, that it implies something of significance about the ultimate standing or status of the individual who apprehends it; second, that it carries a significant affective charge, in that a powerful emotional response to this idea is natural; and third, that it is a relatively abstract notion that admits of a wide range of more precise restatements (i.e., philosophical or doctrinal elaborations).

Schleiermacher's early and late writings provide a different answer to the question of whether the essences of actually existing religions share any common elements. For the young Schleiermacher the essence of an actual religion was simply *some position* on the relationship of every finite being to the totality of that which exists. For the later Schleiermacher, however, one such relationship—absolute dependence—constituted the defining feature of the religious. In spite of this difference, in both of Schleiermacher's canonical discussions the essences of positive religions are more or less variations on the theme of the place of finite beings within the grand scheme of things.

Schleiermacher attempted to identify the essences of only two positive religions, Judaism and Christianity. The essence of Judaism he described in the *Speeches* as "a universal and immediate retribution, of the infinite's own reaction against every individual finite being that proceeds from free choice by acting through another finite element that is not viewed as proceeding from free choice."[7] In the same text Schleiermacher described the essence of Christianity as "the intuition of the universal straining of everything finite against the unity of the whole and of the way in which the deity handles this striving...by scattering over the whole individual points that are at once finite and infinite, at once human and divine."[8] As we have seen, in *The Christian Faith* Schleiermacher advanced a slightly different proposal, identifying "the consciousness of redemption through the person of Jesus of Nazareth" as the essential principle of Christian piety.[9] Thus, for Schleiermacher actually existing religions were centered around relatively determinate ideas—even, as in the case of Christianity, ideas that make reference to particular historical persons and events. It should also be apparent that contrary to what a reading like Proudfoot's suggests, the particular essences of "positive religions" are in no sense independent of language, concepts, or thought. The idea of "redemption through Jesus of Nazareth" is as Schleiermacher understands it a somewhat protean notion since its constituent elements can be parsed in a multitude of ways, but it is not the case that for Schleiermacher the specific core of Christianity or indeed of any actual religion is "preconceptual."

So religion as a whole—actual, historical religion—is an ongoing social and historical process that is produced and sustained by a complex set of forces and displays a complex set of dynamics. What might be called the "religious developmental dynamic" is represented by Schleiermacher's understanding of how religion would take shape under ideal circumstances. However, actual religion is not the result of this religious dynamic alone; within actual religion this is intertwined with nonreligious dynamics contributed by, for example, politics and "speculation." Thus, the way religion is constructed as a historical phenomenon in Schleiermacher's writings stands in continuity with his understanding of the historical careers of organisms, including human beings, as the product of multiple and competing drives operating with different degrees of vitality and hence effectiveness. The characteristics of an actually existing religion at any particular time will be comprehensible, in Schleiermacher's terms, only as the outcome of the confluence of the religious developmental dynamic, informed by the historical content particular to the religion in question, and the various extrareligious dynamics that operate within and upon religion. In my view a statement from the theological encyclopedia of Schleiermacher's student Karl Rudolf Hagenbach that "we can only really know something, when we know how it has developed" can be attributed to Schleiermacher as well: In order to understand religion one needs to understand the forces that have brought it into being.[10]

I offer the preceding as a fairly comprehensive summary of what religion amounts to for Schleiermacher. In the interest of the usability of this chapter I also want to provide a digest of this summary that presents the most important points in condensed form. The following paragraph is recommended to the scholar who lacks sufficient time or space to digest or utilize the preceding material.

Religion, for Schleiermacher, is a form of activity that ideally involves the reciprocal formation of individuals at the level of "immediate self-consciousness" through discourse and other modes of communication. Particular religions are collections of attitudes, practices, and artifacts defined by characteristic forms of religious self-consciousness—roughly, characteristic ways in which the adherents of a religion understand themselves and their relationship to the whole of what exists—which center in turn on "essences," ideas that constitute the central principle or theme of the forms of self-consciousness in question. Religion involves the communication among the members of a group of a particular form of religious self-consciousness, an activity that comprises both the expression of religious self-understanding (in a broad range of ways that include both ritual and discourse) and the reception and appropriation of this expression. As a result of participation in the activities of a religious community, individuals receive "inward formation" by the piety proper to the community, in effect becoming socialized into understanding themselves and the world—indeed, *feeling* themselves and the world—in a specific way. Religion as it actually exists is the result of this process taking place within history, and as a result particular religions are marked not only by historically specific forms of piety but also by the intertwining of the dynamics of ideal religion with a variety of extrareligious factors, such as contingent features of language and culture, as well as political or "speculative" interests. Thus, besides historical specificity, actual religion can differ from ideal religion in being "diseased": The influence of forces other than that which would produce "ideal religion" can be so strong—or the force of the "religious dynamic" within a particular religion so weak—that the communicative and formative activity that defines religion as such is hindered, diverted, perverted, or even extinguished. So actually existing religion is the product of a central "religious dynamic" that operates at times in cooperation with and at times in competition with extrareligious dynamics.

Finally, it often seems as though the conviction is widespread in the contemporary secondary literature that one has not really answered the question "what is religion?" unless one has done so in a sentence or less. Although I am not fond of the practice of reducing theories of religion to slogans or catchphrases, for those who simply must have their theories in this form I suggest the following: Religion, for Schleiermacher, is *the social life of piety*. Although this slogan rides roughshod over a great deal of the content of Schleiermacher's understanding of religion—in particular it elides the crucial distinction between ideal and actual religion—at least it has the virtues of observing his distinction between religion and piety and of noting religion's "necessary sociality." While I take this way of boiling down Schleiermacher to be less of a caricature than statements of similar length derived from the standard interpretation, I frankly do not endorse the citation of this slogan alone as the net result of my efforts at reconstruction.

5.2 Three Themes in Schleiermacher Interpretation

Church history in a broader sense should first of all, as a theological discipline, distinguish that which has resulted from the particular power of Christianity from that which has its ground partly in the constitution of the organs which are set in motion and partly in the influence of alien principles, and should seek to measure both in their dominance and recession.

The development of church life is co-determined primarily by political circumstances and by the overall social condition; the development of doctrine (*Lehre*), on the other hand, is co-determined by the overall condition of science and primarily by prevailing philosophical views (*Philosopheme*). Being co-determined in this way (*dieses Mittbestimmtwerden*) is natural and unavoidable and does not produce diseased conditions in and of itself, but it does certainly contain the ground of their possibility.[11]

These passages are drawn from Schleiermacher's *Brief Outline of the Study of Theology* and encapsulate his understanding of religion's engagement with historical contingency. They are relevant to each of the three topics of discussion in this section.

5.2.1 The Question of Origins

An initial issue with respect to religion's historical nature has to do with the question of how it arises. Since Proudfoot, it has been common to attribute to Schleiermacher the position that "religious experience" constitutes not only the *conceptual core* of religion but also its *temporal point of origin*. The process whereby individuals express religious experience runs in one direction only, producing phenomena such as doctrines and rituals without these exerting any subsequent conditioning effects on religious experience itself. According to Proudfoot, Schleiermacher was concerned to deny the possibility that religious experience could be a result of participation in religious activities such as communication; thus it was as an intended corrective that he observed, "Religious language is not only the expressive, receptive medium Schleiermacher takes it to be. It also plays a very active and formative role in religious experience."[12] This position has since been echoed by Grace Jantzen, who stated in *Becoming Divine* that "[f]or Schleiermacher the individual subject of the Enlightenment has private intense feelings which are seen as the core of religion. Cultural or material positioning would not at bottom affect the experiences or even the subjects who have them; only the way they would later describe the experiences would be affected."[13] And for Russell McCutcheon, Schleiermacher epitomizes the "private affair" tradition in the study of religion, which insists that "religion cannot be explained as a result of various cultural or historical factors and processes" and that "religious feelings can be considered a cause, but never simply an effect."[14]

The suggestion is that religion originates with feelings whose causes, whatever they may be, do not lie within the natural, observable realm. Religious experience is not the result of the religious individual's immersion in history, and whatever (if anything) religion contains beyond this experience is subsequent not only in the order of explanation but also chronologically. As should be clear by now, this understanding is inadequate as a reconstruction of Schleiermacher's description of the ongoing historical life of positive religions. His view in the *Speeches*, as well as the later writings, was that in the ordinary course of events individuals are socialized into the life of piety through participation in cultic and discursive activities.[15] However, this observation leaves open the question of how this process ever gets going in the first place.

On this point Schleiermacher's earlier and later texts differ. In brief, in the *Speeches* Schleiermacher's only discussions of the historical beginnings of religion take the form of his claim that particular religions have arisen historically in the activities of "revelatory individuals" or "virtuosi of religion." It is these individuals who first conceive the "central intuitions" or ideas that come to constitute the essences of positive religions, and it is their expression of these ideas that inaugurate the historical life of particular forms of religion. It is this claim that is reflected in the characterizations of Proudfoot, Jantzen, and McCutcheon. However, as I have argued, it is incorrect to suppose that the particular ideas that constitute the essence of a religion are, even at their first origin, untouched by historical contingency. Schleiermacher's commitment to determinism rules out any robust notion of the autonomy of religion, historically speaking, from the circumstances in which it arises and persists; indeed, as we have seen, in the revised *Speeches* he claimed that the "choice" of a particular religious intuition as the core of a positive religion, "viewed in relationship to the adherent...bears the purest necessity within itself, and is only the natural expression of his being itself."[16] Thus, the arising of an original religious idea within the soul of a "revelatory individual" will be no more or less of a historical phenomenon than any other event.

By the time of *The Christian Faith*, however, the idea of "revelatory individuals" had receded considerably in importance, and in fact Schleiermacher's later writings are noteworthy for their refusal to offer a story about the first origins of religion. The position expressed in the ethics lectures is that in its chronologically original form religion is a dimension of family life that naturally "scales up," as it were, into a clan, a tribe, and ultimately a national or state phenomenon as these social forms develop, attaining social independence from these only at a relatively late stage of development. Thus, Schleiermacher's mature view seems to have been that religion as such has no particular moment of historical origin but rather emerges gradually out of the general matrix of human sociality.

Schleiermacher did retain the idea that particular religious traditions (as opposed to "religion itself") may have discrete historical origins in the "revelatory" activities of their founders—Christianity and Islam in particular. But two points need to be emphasized about the presence of this idea in the later texts. First, the activity of revelatory individuals represents one among a number of ways in which particular religious traditions can arise. It is also possible, as we have seen, for a religious tradition to assume definite form as the result of the combination of previously existing traditions or to coalesce over time out of the collective life of a particular "mass" of people.[17] Second, whether or not a religious tradition's historical origins can be located with precision, Schleiermacher's determinism entails that the events that constitute these origins are, so to speak, thoroughly historical: That is, they are events within the *Naturzusammenhang* and as such have natural causes that are possibly knowable. It is precisely this commitment that explains Schleiermacher's insistence, in *The Christian Faith*, on a principle that poses significant problems for any robust understanding of (special) revelation and results in his tortured account of the "appearance of the Redeemer": the principle that the activities of even revelatory individuals are to be understood as products of their socio-historical background. Thus, Schleiermacher's account rules out appeals to theophanies or revelation in the traditional Christian sense as explanations of the origins of a religious tradition. For him such appeals were frankly at odds with the *wissenschaftlich* view of religion and thus constituted not a theoretical resource but a problem for his project.[18]

5.2.2 Religion and Politics

The purported "inwardness" and "autonomy" of religion as Schleiermacher described it have served for some recent scholars as grounds for claiming that religion for him is in principle untouched by politics. For McCutcheon, the discourse of sui generis religion purportedly fathered by Schleiermacher has made possible "a series of related practices that together constitute a regnant discourse that is intimately connected with disguising all issues of sociopolitics" in connection with religion.[19] This charge loses much of its force as one moves away from the standard interpretation of Schleiermacher. The epigraphs that open this section should make it sufficiently clear that it was not his position that *actual* religion is divorced from politics as he understood it. On the contrary, his view was that political states of affairs figure among the environmental conditions that affect religion's concrete historical life. However, a distinction between the religious and the political does inform his writings on religion, and I think it important that he be correctly understood on this topic. Schleiermacher associated the political dimensions of human existence largely with the affairs of nation or state, and my later remarks are initially concerned with this narrow sense of the political. However, his account can also be interrogated regarding its position on religion's relationships to questions of power in the broader sense, and I offer reflections on this subject as well.

It is in the *Speeches* that Schleiermacher distinguished religion most radically from politics in the narrow sense. As we have seen, in the fourth speech he presented involvement with politics as the paradigmatic example of the "contamination" of outward religion by alien interests. Overall, the argument of the *Speeches* suggests that the historical life of religion both *could* and *should* take place in the absence of any entanglement with the business either of the state or of civil society. However, this condemnation of the politically mixed character of contemporary Prussian Protestantism should not obscure the fact that that even in 1799 the political constituted an important resource for Schleiermacher in accounting for the actual condition of Prussian Protestantism, in explaining the character and function of its mores and practices. The point of describing "ideal religion" as an apolitical phenomenon was to provide a theoretical basis for the project of criticizing, reenvisioning, and reforming the social and political conditions of actually existing Christianity.[20]

The view expressed in the *Brief Outline* is, however, more nuanced than that of the *Speeches*. Schleiermacher remarked in the 1811 edition that "the development of the common Christian life is affected primarily by political circumstances and by the general social situation"[21] without the tone of condemnation evident in the *Speeches*, although it is clear that to some degree the resulting political dimensions of religion count as part of "everything which is indeed in the church but did not originate from within it, and from which it ought to purify itself."[22] Schleiermacher's addition to this passage for the 1831 edition, however, notes explicitly that the impact of political circumstances on the development of religion, while it provides the "ground" of diseased conditions, does not in and of itself constitute such conditions. It seems to me that here the ground has shifted since 1799; whereas the early text seems to have envisioned an idealized Christianity entirely purified of political elements, the mature Schleiermacher drew a distinction between those political aspects of religion that do and do not count as corruptions of religion. If I understand him correctly, the resulting position is that Christianity ought to be freed only from those entanglements with politics that result in "diseased conditions"; some degree of mixing between the political and the religious is in keeping with religion's, or Christianity's, character. Moreover, the understanding of the ideal developmental process of religion that I have presented in previous chapters, if it is correct, suggests a hypothesis regarding the criterion that establishes the difference between corrupting and noncorrupting forms of political involvement. *Corrupting* political interference is that which either obstructs the social transmission and development of piety or diverts this process into alien channels by introducing an alien interest into the life of a religious community; the examples in the *Speeches*, of the state selecting religious leaders or rituals taking on civic functions, provide illustrations of these dynamics. However, if it is possible to imagine the religious and the political mixing in ways that *inform* the religious developmental process without *compromising* it in these ways, then it is possible to envision a historical form of religion that has a political cast or dimension and yet is not, on that account, "diseased." So the mature Schleiermacher seems to have held open the possibility for actual religion to appropriate political circumstances in just the same way as it does any dimension of culture, without (necessarily) compromising its integrity.

This interpretation makes it possible to respond to criticisms advanced by Talal Asad in *Genealogies of Religion* of attempts to distinguish the religious from the political, which for him seems to figure as an essential feature of religious essentialism:

> [T]he insistence that religion has an autonomous essence—not to be confused with the essence of science, or of politics, or of common sense—invites us to define religion (like any essence) as a transcultural and transhistorical phenomenon. It may be a happy accident that this effort of defining religion converges with the liberal demand in our times that it be kept quite separate from politics, law and science—spaces in which varieties of power and reason articulate our distinctively modern life.... Yet this separation from power is a modern Western norm, the product of a unique post-Reformation history. The attempt to understand Muslim traditions by insisting that in them religion and politics (two essences modern society tries to keep conceptually and practically apart) are coupled must, in my view, lead to failure. At its most dubious, such attempts lead us to take up an a priori position in which religious discourse in the political arena is seen as a disguise for political power.[23]

Asad uses these reflections to preface his critique of Clifford Geertz's "Religion as a Cultural System," an exercise that represents an examination of "the ways in which the theoretical search for an essence of religion invites us to separate it conceptually from the domain of power."[24] The passage presents two substantive criticisms of essentialist distinctions between the religious and the political. If the wording of the first criticism is straightforward, its force is elusive. Asad says that any attempt to impose such a distinction upon Muslim traditions is "doomed to failure" but does not say why or in what respects this must be the case.[25] The second criticism is subtler and more germane to the present discussion. Asad argues that viewing the world through the lens of an "essential" difference between the religious and the political encourages us to discount the possibility of "authentic" religious discourse in the political sphere and to regard any admixture of the two as at bottom political rather than religious.[26] While Asad intended these remarks as a criticism of essentialism generally and specifically of Geertz, it is worthwhile to see whether the charge can be applied to Schleiermacher's essentialist account of religion.

It is clearly the case that Schleiermacher's account "invites us to separate [religion] conceptually" from affairs of state (bracketing for a moment Asad's reference to "the domain of power").[27] However, it is a different question whether Schleiermacher's account encourages the view that any example of religious discourse in the political sphere must be regarded as only "inauthentically" religious. My earlier remarks suggest a formula, internal to that account, for "authentic" religious discourse in the political sphere: Authentic

political-religious discourse is that which represents an appropriate development of the essence of a particular religion and serves the interests of the
upbuilding of religious consciousness within a particular *polis* without divert-
ing the energies of religion into "alien" channels. So long, that is, as political
aims mesh with what flows naturally from the essence of a particular religion, there are no grounds for considering political activity oriented toward
the realization of these aims as only "inauthentically" religious. Indeed, this
formula provides a rationale for understanding Schleiermacher's political
sermons during the French occupation of Prussia, which were aimed not
only at the preservation of Protestantism in the face of purported Catholic
aggression but also at facilitating the general development of the collective
self-awareness of the Prussian citizenry, goals with both religious and political dimensions.[28]

The reservation voiced by Asad can be pressed further, however. Thus far
the position I have attributed to Schleiermacher allows for "authentic" political
activity in the realm of religion, but only as an accidental feature of that realm:
only, that is, insofar as the political enters the realm of religion "from without,"
as a reflection of the circumstances within which a particular positive religion
is embedded. However, fairly clearly, Asad's reservation is grounded in the
idea that in relation to some religious traditions (and in particular Muslim traditions) the very attempt to specify the identity of the religion in question in a
manner that brackets all questions of politics is, in some sense, to misconstrue
the tradition. I think the right way to press this issue against Schleiermacher is
to ask whether on his account *the essences of all actually existing religious traditions,
considered purely in themselves, have no substantive political implications.* If this
question is to be answered in the positive, then all religion for Schleiermacher
is "essentially apolitical"; but if not, then the possibility is open that some forms
of religion may not be susceptible to identification even in essentialist terms
without political implications.

Since Schleiermacher offered different accounts of the essences of positive
religions in his early and late texts, this question must be answered twice. In
neither case is a positive answer clearly indicated. In the first edition of the
Speeches, the essences of particular religions are "intuitions of the universe,"
vague but significant ideas of how the finite and the infinite are related. The
examples that Schleiermacher offered of actual essences abstracted from all
historical particulars, as we have seen. However, it is not difficult to imagine an
idea that would qualify as an "intuition of the universe" and be abstract in this
sense but at the same time have significant political ramifications. Imagine, for
example, an intuition of the universe as an organized whole containing a number of organized subtotalities, each of which is similarly structured, such that
in the end every individual finite being is related to the infinite through harmonious membership in an expanding series of ordered wholes. It would be very
much in character for a religion that adopted this intuition as its essence to

place a premium on the stability of an individual's membership in larger exist-ing organizations and to prize ordered and persistent relationships among these, regarding the disruption of such organizations as tantamount to a dis-turbance in the appropriate structure of the universe. It is thus possible to imagine an essence of a positive religion, after the manner of the *Speeches*, which cannot be as cleanly divorced from the political as Schleiermacher thought was the case with Christianity.

Schleiermacher's discussion of the essences of particular religions in *The Christian Faith* differs from that of the *Speeches* in two important respects. First, an essence is not limited a priori to a particular conceptual territory. It is no longer just intuitions of the universe, located fairly precisely as these are in relation to thoughts and feelings, which are candidates for the role of essence. Rather, essences are merely the "common element" among historically and geographically distinct forms of piety, without significant initial restrictions as to the content such essences can contain beyond the fact that they must relate in some appropriate way to the feeling of absolute dependence. Second, Schleiermacher's revised description of the essence of Christianity in *The Christian Faith* makes it clear that by 1821 he accepted the possibility that an essence might make reference to one or more concrete historical reference points (in the case of Christianity, the person of Jesus of Nazareth). So far as I can see there is no reason to think that the essence of a religion could make reference to a particular historical *person* but not, say, a particular historical *nation* (for example, the nation of Israel) or a particular transnational sociopo-litical identity (say, membership in the *umma* established by the prophet Mohammed). Fairly clearly, either of these kinds of historical referencing would make some degree of political engagement an essential feature of the religion in question.[29]

Thus, the question of whether the essences of any actual religions have substantive political implications is left open by both Schleiermacher's early and late texts. However, it is also important to remember that he considered the determination of the essences of particular religions to be predicated in large part on historical research. Essences, the principles whereby healthy and diseased conditions of religion are to be distinguished, are derived neither by a purely empirical procedure nor by speculative theorizing but "only critically, through comparison of the general differences set out [by ethics] with that which is historically given."[30] Asad's first criticism suggests that familiarity with the actual conditions of Muslim traditions counts decisively against any attempt to claim an explicitly apolitical essence for Islam; but this type of obser-vation is actually internal to Schleiermacher's religious essentialism, in that it was his view that the project of identifying essences is responsible to the results of the historical investigation of the traditions in question.

Finally, when "the political" is not construed narrowly as referring to the affairs of state or civil society but also to any and all power relations, the case for the claim that Schleiermacher's account of religion obscures or denies religion's political dimensions is different but not appreciably stronger. Trivially, it can be observed that in the *Speeches* Schleiermacher described the "city of God" as a community to which any form of religious intolerance or coercion is alien, but this can be presented as a denial of any connection between religion and power only when the point is overlooked that Schleiermacher presented this description of ideal religion as a way of calling attention to the deficits of actually existing Christianity in these precise areas. In fact, something stronger can be said than that religion, according to Schleiermacher, is enmeshed in power relations precisely to the extent to which extrareligious factors impinge upon its natural process of development. In at least one area, as we have seen, Schleiermacher called attention to a respect in which differential power relations are themselves part of this natural process: Both within the context of the family and the tribe, Schleiermacher understood religion to be patriarchal since in his view the activity of "expression" was primarily a masculine affair and "reception" primarily feminine.[31]

I conclude, then, that even if Schleiermacher's account of religion invites us to separate religion conceptually from the domain of the political, it also provides a framework for discussing the relationship between the two, one that allows the possibilities of "authentically religious" political activity and "essentially political" religion, and one that in no substantive sense implies the removal of religion—at least, *actual* religion—from the domain of power.

5.2.3 Religion as an Object of Study

In *Religious Experience*, Proudfoot offers the following set of reflections:

> [Schleiermacher's] conception of the nature of religion has definite implications for how it ought to be studied. Religious language should not be regarded either as an instance of ordinary language or as a vehicle for scientific or philosophical assertions. It functions in a special way as an expression of the various forms of the religious consciousness. In order, then, to study that language as religious language, one must adopt a distinctive approach. One might, of course, investigate the same language and practices for other purposes. A social scientist might study anchorites or monastic communities in order to see what light they shed on the dominant social order and why individuals sometimes leave family or other institutions for the desert or the cloister.... The language of worship in a Reformed parish in Berlin might be studied as an example of early nineteenth-century German, or as the language of a particular social class. But each of these requires an understanding of the particular form of the religious consciousness that has shaped the

relevant intentions, symbols, attitudes, and language. To study
religion is to seek to grasp these varied data as expressions of diverse
modifications of religious consciousness. To view them in some
other way is to engage in a reductive approach and to lose the
distinctive character of the religious.[32]

In Proudfoot's view, Schleiermacher's account of religion entails that there
is a certain infelicity in seeking after the nonreligious factors that cause or condition observable religious phenomena (paradigmatically, religious discourse).[33]
The "right" way to study religion is to regard such phenomena *only* as expressions of religious consciousness. In characterizing the treatment of religious
language in some way other than this as "reductive," I take it that Proudfoot
was attributing an either-or position to Schleiermacher, the position that if one
regards religious language as a reflection of environmental conditions, one
cannot at the same time regard it as an expression of religious consciousness.
Thus, the conditioning of observable religious phenomena by factors other
than religious consciousness is simply of no interest to the scholar of *religion*.

Proudfoot's remarks are, so far as I can see, the result of reflection in the
abstract on Schleiermacher's conception of religion as he understood it, premised on the notion that the project of studying religion is above all a matter of
recapturing or sharing "religious experience" and is to be carried out within the
theoretical framework of Schleiermacher's hermeneutics. A better way, I think,
to address the question of how religion, as Schleiermacher understood it, could
be studied would be to turn to those of his writings that address the subject.[34]
Although Schleiermacher did not propose a unified academic discipline dedicated to the study of religion, a fairly comprehensive sense of what such an
endeavor would look like can be extracted from the *Brief Outline on the Study of
Theology*, particularly when the second edition of 1831 is viewed against the
background of the revised edition of *The Christian Faith*.[35]

Schleiermacher described academic theology as a "positive science," thus
ascribing to it a practical *telos*: The ultimate aim of theology is not the accumulation of knowledge about religion (even about Christianity) but rather church
governance. However, he also took pains to make it clear that theology, like any
positive science, required accurate and reliable information about its object,
which if not produced internally would have to derive from other branches of
inquiry.[36] Academic theology, as Schleiermacher described it, is "the embodiment of that scientific knowledge and rules of art, without the application of
which Christian church governance (*Kirchenregiment*) is not possible," and
"this same knowledge, without this connection [to church governance], ceases
to be theological, and each component returns to a different science."[37] In his
1831 additions to this passage Schleiermacher offered a list of the sciences in
question: "the knowledge of linguistics and history (*Sprachkunde und
Geschichtskunde*), the study of mind and ethics (*Seelenlehre und Sittenlehre*), and

also the disciplines which proceed from them, the general study of the arts (*Kunstlehre*) and philosophy of religion."[38]

An outline for the "study of religion," then, understood as the project of pursuing objective and reliable knowledge of religion, can be extracted from the *Brief Outline* by bracketing those components of Schleiermacher's discussion that are oriented specifically toward church governance and attending to his discussion of the methods by which theology obtains the information concerning religion that this practical task requires. Schleiermacher divided the overall field of academic theology into three components: philosophical, historical, and practical theology.[39] The first two of these are, in different ways and to differing extents, concerned with the production or appropriation of knowledge of religion. Thus, an exclusively *theoretical* study of religion would incorporate some projects that fall under these headings in addition to drawing upon the nontheological sciences which count as resources for theology, and would have little to do with *practical* theology, which within Schleiermacher's proposal is concerned with the application of knowledge of religion and Christianity to the task of church governance.

For Schleiermacher the term *historical theology* referred to that part of the study of Christianity predicated on the notion that the present condition of Christianity "can only be understood as a product of the past."[40] This project, as he understood it, is "a part of the modern study of history" and in particular the modern history of ethics and culture; thus, it makes use of the methods of the general historical sciences.[41] Schleiermacher further subdivided historical theology diachronically (into the study of early Christianity, the history of Christianity generally, and the present condition of Christianity) and thematically (into the study of the "social condition of the church" or church history, and the study of the "religious ideas of the community" or history of dogma). Thus, two subdisciplines within historical theology focus on the study of present-day Christianity: the study of the "social condition of the church" or *church statistics*, and the "systematic representation of doctrine" or *dogmatics*.[42] Finally, *exegetical theology*, understood as the study of the Christian scriptures, also falls under the heading of historical theology. This subdiscipline combines the philological and linguistic sciences with the science of interpretation or hermeneutics and also requires historical "knowledge of older and newer Judaism, and also knowledge of the spiritual and civic condition of those regions in which and for which the New Testament writings were composed."[43] Just as historical theology generally is bound to the standards and methods of extratheological historical disciplines, so too does the critical study of the Christian scriptures require the use of the same methods of historical and textual investigation that are employed in other fields.[44]

Philosophical theology is the project of identifying the normative core of Christianity on the basis of the data provided by historical theology and of utilizing this conception for the critical understanding of both the history of Christianity and contemporary Christianity. The practical dimension of philosophical theology is thus more pronounced than in the case of historical theology. In particular, Schleiermacher identified as components of philosophical theology the projects of *apologetics* and *polemics*. As he used these terms, *apologetics* is the defense of Christianity or of a particular form of Christianity (e.g., Protestantism or even of more specific subdivisions) by way of an account of its history that highlights the positive relationship between the actual course of church history and the essence of the form of religion in question, and *polemics* the immanent criticism of "diseased conditions" of religion on the basis of this same conception.[45] As practiced within historical theology, apologetics and polemics are driven by a confessional interest—an interest, that is, in either defending or purifying a particular form of religion. However, Schleiermacher made it clear that the basic pattern of inquiry followed by each—the distinction between those elements of the actual history or condition of religion that do and do not correspond to an essence—is an integral part of church history as well, since on his conception the actual history of Christianity is the result of the interaction of the "distinctive force of Christianity" (in the terms I have been using, the ideal religious developmental process informed by the particular essence of Christianity) and the historical environment.[46]

A final and highly important "scientific" resource for academic theology is *philosophy of religion (Religionsphilosophie)*. As he described it (more adequately in the revised edition of *The Christian Faith* than in the *Brief Outline*), philosophy of religion represents not a component of theology but a nontheological branch of ethics. The task of philosophy of religion is "a critical presentation of the different given forms of religious community, inasmuch as in their totality they are the complete appearance of piety in human nature."[47] *Religionsphilosophie* is a critical discipline in that it applies the results of "speculation" to the data on existing religious communities gathered by historical investigations and categorizes their distinctive and distinguishing features in accordance with principles drawn from ethics generally. Its interest extends not only to forms of communal piety (as expressed in the typology fetishism-polytheism-monotheism, together with their nontheistic counterparts, as well as the distinction between aesthetic and teleological religions) but also to the social forms of religion (e.g., family, horde, clan, state, church); and indeed, in *The Christian Faith* Schleiermacher addressed the material borrowed from philosophy of religion to the topic of "diversities of pious communities in general."[48] So *Religionsphilosophie* as Schleiermacher understood it is an enterprise dedicated to organizing the historical data concerning religions under a theoretical apparatus generated by the "science of the principles of history" generally. As such it provides a "foundation" (*Grundlage*) for philosophical theology.[49]

An outline of the "study of religion" extracted from this material would look something like the following. Such an endeavor would have both an empirical and a speculative side. The empirical side of the study of religion would consist in the gathering of information about both the history and the present circumstances of religion. Religious communities or forms of religious organization would constitute the principal objects of this sort of investigation, with the various ideational and material components of religion (e.g., piety and belief on the one hand, discourse and ritual on the other) regarded as elements of these specific historical entities and viewed within the context of their particular dynamics. The speculative side of the study of religion would consist, first, in the organization of the historical data by way of the development of categories and typologies, an endeavor predicated on theoretical materials drawn from ethics, and subsequently, the attempt to comprehend the particular history and character of discrete "positive religions" by way of the critical identification of "essences" and the evaluation of the historical record in light of these. The ultimate promise or goal of such a field of study would be the attainment of a comprehensive body of knowledge about religion containing two sorts of components. The first would comprise the historical understanding of particular religions (i.e., narratives of the temporal careers of particular religious traditions that would track the interaction between the "distinctive force" of the religion in question and a variety of environmental factors). The second would consist of a theoretical distillation of historical knowledge: a set of theories, drawn from and tested against the historical data, concerning the "elements of human nature" operative within religion and the various developmental trajectories that religion typically follows within history.

So understood, the study of religion would be both narrower and broader than Schleiermacher's academic theology. It would be narrower in that the practical concerns that drive apologetics, polemics, and practical theology would not constitute part of the study of religion. It would be broader, however, in that, while theology's interest in those phenomena it identifies as "diseased conditions" of religion is, in Schleiermacher's conception, both minimal and parasitic upon its apologetic or polemical aims, the study of religion would have no grounds for downplaying the significance of such conditions within the historical career of the religion in question and in fact would likely consider them interesting in their own right. Thus, theology and the "study of religion" might find themselves in agreement regarding the extent to which particular historical episodes count as faithful expressions of a religion's "distinctive force." However, where the interests of the study of religion would come to an end once the episodes in question have been explained as the results of the differential operation of the religious developmental dynamic and a range of external factors, academic theology would go further, making use of this explanation as a resource for bringing the current state of the tradition more fully into alignment with the essence of the religion in question.

5.3 Schleiermacher and the History of the Study of Religion

How, on the basis of the reconstruction presented in this volume, should Schleiermacher's place within the history of the academic study of religion be assessed?

I begin with reflections on Schleiermacher's relationship to the currently dominant master narrative of the development of the field of religious studies, which maintains that this endeavor emerged, properly speaking, in the late nineteenth century with calls by Max Müller and others for the establishment of an explicitly nontheological "science of religion." Schleiermacher neither proposed nor envisioned a unified and autonomous academic discipline dedicated to the study of religion. However, what he did do was to position a variety of thematically and methodologically specific *wissenschaftlich* investigations of religion as indispensable resources for, or components of, academic theology. In so doing he imparted to academic theology a trajectory that remained strongly in evidence through the remainder of the nineteenth century, one that understood theology to be intimately bound up with the *wissenschaftlich* investigation of religion.

The clearest manifestation of this trajectory was the rise to prominence, following Schleiermacher's death, of the notion of "scientific theology" itself, as articulated and defended, for example, in the pages of the *Zeitschrift für wissenschaftliche Theologie*. The inaugural essay of this journal in 1858 by Adolf Hilgenfeld was an apology for the notion of a scientific theology set against the backdrop of an epochal struggle within German Protestantism between the forces of criticism and the forces of reaction. The former Hilgenfeld associated with an insistence on "freedom of research and science" in relation to religion and located within the historical trajectory of German rationalism; the latter he described as a "theology of regression" (*Rückschritts-Theologie*), exemplified paradigmatically in the work of Hengstenberg and his followers, which with its "half-Catholic essence" represented a degeneration of Protestantism (recalling Schleiermacher's remarks in his letters to Lücke about "the ground heaving under our feet," Hilgenfeld noted ruefully that "what Schleiermacher said at the end of his life about the preparations for this retrogressive tendency in its first beginnings was entirely fulfilled").[50] Schleiermacher figured for Hilgenfeld among the defenders of the rights of the *Wissenschaften* within the domain of religion and in particular of the rights of historical and text-critical scholarship; since his lifetime, Schleiermacher's influence, "along with rationalistic scripture studies, contributed essentially to the result that the ever-increasing darkening of the theological atmosphere through hollow phraseology, empty sophistry and learned nonsense was confronted by the illuminating torch of criticism."[51] A journal for "scientific theology" was necessary at the present time, Hilgenfeld noted, particularly in view of the rise to prominence within German theology of a "new scholasticism," whose origins lay in the "anathematizing of all true science" embodied by the *Evangelische Kirchenzeitung*.[52]

That Schleiermacher's program had profound consequences for the self-understanding and academic standing of theology has been commonly acknowledged. In Schleiermacher's work and as a result of his activities at Berlin, academic theology was demoted from the position of "queen of the sciences" to that of a supplicant in the temple of science, seeking *wissenschaftlich* knowledge that could be applied to the life of the church; as Thomas Albert Howard has put it, "Schleiermacher invested science with a predominantly active role and the church with a passive one: the church was presented as the needy recipient of scientific tutelage, whereas science appears as autonomous and self-justifying."[53] However, more significant for my purposes is that Schleiermacher premised academic theology on what in historical retrospect amounts to a prototype of the "science of religion." So, for example, Troeltsch saw the matter in 1908, in reflecting on the half century following Hilgenfeld's call for "scientific theology." Troeltsch considered "a general science of religion or philosophy of religion," whose goal is not the production of knowledge of God but rather the discovery of the "general laws and gradations of value" within religion, to be an essential propaedeutic to academic theology, and "[i]f we look closer, this demand for such a discipline was already made by Schleiermacher, the man who separated scientific historical work from the practical mediating disciplines and so created and recognized the whole situation."[54]

It would be too strong a claim to assign to Schleiermacher primary credit for the later appearance of the idea of a unified, autonomous "science of religion." However, it can clearly be said that his program for academic theology prefigured the development of such a science, diverging from conceptions such as that of Müller primarily by stipulating a practical aim for the sake of which knowledge of religion was to be gathered and to which it was to be applied.[55] The trivial point to be gleaned from this observation is that the case of Schleiermacher provides corroboration for a claim recently advanced by Ivan Strenski: that "the historical record shows that *religion itself* has been a powerful factor in the origins and growth of the study of religion.... The scientific study of religion came about because of devoted *religious* concerns to uncover ultimate truth about the world—not in spite of them."[56] However, a less obvious and more concrete point is that in describing the research projects that would later figure in the "science of religion" as indispensable for theology, Schleiermacher extended *religious legitimation* to these discrete "sciences" and positioned theology, still a powerful wing of the Prussian academy, as their patron. The importance of such legitimation and patronage within a context in which the growing prominence and critical potential of historical and critical researches appeared to be mirrored by the growth of religiously motivated resistance should not be underestimated. The potential for academic theology to assume a position of indifference or hostility toward the nontheological investigation of religion was no less high in Schleiermacher's day than in our own; in the early nineteenth century the consequences of such indifference or hostility for the prospects of the study of religion were, however, considerably higher than is currently the case.

However, if one side of Schleiermacher's historical significance is manifested in the determination of later theologians to advance the *wissenschaftlich* investigation of religion (as represented by Hagenbach's "mediating theology," Hilgenfeld's "scientific theology," and Troeltsch's historicism), there is another side to the story as well. In chapter 4 I allude briefly to the influence of Hegel and his followers over the history of Schleiermacher reception, a topic I have explored more extensively elsewhere.[57] A primary result of this influence was a drastic truncation of Schleiermacher's understanding of religion in late nineteenth-century descriptions of the "progression of thought" within German theology, to the point where mention of his having made religion "a matter of feeling" was taken to exhaust the significance of his work. Although the firsthand investigation of Schleiermacher's texts more than once prompted reservations about this judgment among Hegel's followers,[58] it is fair to say that by the latter part of the nineteenth century Schleiermacher's proposal concerning religion's core or essence had come to be remembered as his signal contribution to scholarly reflection on religion across a broad swath of the literature, standing in tension with and in some cases displacing memory of his work on religious sociality or on the scientific character of academic theology.

The most interesting and historically significant reflection of this selective scholarly memory, to my mind, is found not within the Hegelian tradition but rather within the work of those who continued to invoke Schleiermacher as an intellectual progenitor. To illustrate this point I return to the work of Brent Sockness on Troeltsch and Herrmann mentioned at the opening of chapter 4. Sockness has observed that in a sense, the seeds of the programs of both Troeltsch and Herrmann—Troeltsch's insistence on a strict adherence to historical method and Herrmann's postulation of a sui generis and scientifically inexplicable "experience of redemption" as the core of the Christian religion— lay in the work of Schleiermacher. I have already registered my reservations with the suggestion that Schleiermacher's work is equally amenable to both kinds of appropriation, but there is more to be said about the significance of this historical episode. While this volume is not a treatise on Christian theology, there is one general movement within the history of that field that seems to me to be of relevance for understanding Schleiermacher's legacy within the broader history of the academic study of religion.

In addition to noting that Herrmann and Troeltsch were regarded as the proponents of antithetical theological positions even during their own lifetimes, Sockness calls attention to the fact that "readers wishing to understand better the genesis of dialectical theology will find in Herrmann's polemics against Troeltsch most of the argumentative patterns and even many of the specific indictments which would later punctuate the broad assault on liberal theology in Germany between the wars."[59] This resonance between the work of Herrmann and the antiliberalism of later neoorthodox theologians is no coincidence. Sockness cites Robert Morgan in arguing that Herrmann's suspicion of the approach to religion represented by Troeltsch exerted a formative influence on those of his students who dominated the following generation of theological scholarship; according to Morgan, Herrmann's influence had the effect of "immunizing" theologians such as Barth and Bultmann against a "Troeltschian appreciation for real history."[60] The resolute opposition voiced by Karl Barth to the idea, epitomized for him by Schleiermacher, that theology is to draw its understanding of Christianity from a "general science of religion" and thus concern itself with one member of a general category of human cultural productions thus represents a recognizable development of Herrmann's worries about the corrosive effects of extratheological scholarship. Moreover, if Herrmann claimed the mantle of Schleiermacher in appealing to a distinctly Christian "experience of redemption" as the primary datum of the theologian, for Barth such an appeal effectively grounded theology in a fact about human beings rather than in God and thus represented another episode in theology's epochal drift away from an authentic concern with God and God's act of self-revelation.

However, it should also be recalled that Herrmann's worries and his influence extended along another historical trajectory as well. His successor at Marburg was Rudolf Otto, who in 1932 dedicated to Herrmann's memory an essay on "The New Awakening of the *Sensus Numinis* in Schleiermacher." In this essay Otto attributed to Herrmann a crucial realization regarding what Schleiermacher really meant in the second of the *Speeches on Religion*: the realization that "with his 'feeling of the universe' Schleiermacher in fact means the 'feeling of the otherwordly' (*Überweltlich*)."[61] This clarification of Schleiermacher's intent made it possible to name his "most significant accomplishment": "[F]or a time which had forgotten the concept of *revelation*, he opened in his own manner a way to understand revelation, real revelation: that is, something which no understanding can fathom (*erklügeln*), which no evidence can cobble together, but which gives *itself* and makes *itself* known to the experiencer."[62] Thus viewed through the lens of Herrmann's appropriation, Schleiermacher figured for Otto as a pivotal figure in the recovery, from beneath the "intellectualism and moralism" of the Enlightenment, of the "old religious idea" of direct experience of the transcendent—in his terminology "numinous experience," the suprarational and scientifically inexplicable experiential core of religion.

Bracketing the sharp divergence between Barth's and Otto's estimations of Schleiermacher's relationship to the concept of revelation, I call attention to a point on which they, along with Herrmann, appear to have been in broad agreement. Each of them pointed to a principle that eludes scientific investigation or explanation as the basic datum on which the theologian must insist in order to secure the distinctiveness of religion, or Christianity, among the other dimensions of human activity. Thus, each of them in his own way, it seems to me, refused the terms of Schleiermacher's "eternal covenant," in that to varying degrees they seem to have regarded the pursuit of scientific knowledge of the natural order as a threat to religion rather than as a resource. Taken together, they bear witness to the facts that Schleiermacher's covenant imposed duties and restrictions on academic theology—the duty, above all, to look to the extratheological sciences for their basal understanding of religion as a human phenomenon—which not all of its practitioners were willing to bear, and that Schleiermacher's efforts did not ultimately succeed in dislodging the defensive and protective mentality represented during his lifetime by his neopietist colleagues from its positions within the academy.

The stream of Schleiermacher's historical influence that runs not through von Harnack and Troeltsch but through Herrmann and Otto can thus be characterized as a selective appropriation in the service of an aim that ran contrary to his own hopes for the future of academic theology. The selectivity of this appropriation, which ran parallel to the selective memory concerning Schleiermacher's understanding of religion among the Hegelians, cannot to my mind be emphasized too strongly. Schleiermacher's work can be seen as a favorable precursor to Herrmann's "experience of redemption" or Otto's "numinous experience" only when the context, both theoretical and practical, within which Schleiermacher advanced his claims regarding religion's essence has been forgotten or ignored. Schleiermacher, too, spoke of the "consciousness of redemption" among Christians and indeed spoke of this as the essential (in his sense) feature of Christian piety. However, in his work this consciousness was anything but inexplicable or sui generis. As we have seen, not only did he postulate this consciousness within the context of a comprehensive determinism according to which not only the motions of material bodies but also "the feelings which quickly rise and quickly fall, the images which come and go, and whatever other alterations in the mind time brings and takes away" are governed by necessity;[63] it is also a clear implication of his account of religion that analogues to this state of consciousness, referring to other historical figures and episodes and other types of relationship, are to be found in other religions as well. The "consciousness of redemption" figured for Schleiermacher as a principle that marked the distinctiveness of Christianity within the overall "realm of religion." However, for him this consciousness was not a locus of resistance to the advance of scientific knowledge of religion but rather one of the features of Christianity to which the sciences might address themselves. And as we have seen, he seems to have envisioned the possibility that this very consciousness, understood theologically as a historical result of the influence of the God-consciousness of Jesus of Nazareth, might in fact be amenable to redescription and investigation as a datum for the science of psychology.[64]

In concluding this section, I call attention to the first two quotations with which this chapter opens. These passages, from Karl Hagenbach and Max Müller, date from roughly thirty years after Schleiermacher's death. Both articulate a positive view of the relationship between the "science of religion" and religion itself, but they differ in one important respect. The passage by Hagenbach promises, in effect, that the scientific investigation of religion would have no negative impact upon religious faith: "We may argue the sun out of the heavens, but it will keep on shining still." Müller, in contrast, was less sanguine about the impact on religious faith of the "science of religion," noting that in his view it will indeed result in the loss of "many things which we hold dear," but it remained his view that even the most perspicacious scientific investigation would not lead to the loss of anything "essential to true religion." It should come as no surprise at this point for me to claim that Schleiermacher's position anticipates that of Müller more closely than it does that of Hagenbach. Schleiermacher, too, anticipated that the advance of scientific knowledge would not leave the religious self-understandings of his contemporaries untouched. Like Müller, he argued that only a revised and purified religion might ultimately be able to coexist comfortably with scientific knowledge. However, Schleiermacher was intimately concerned with the possibility that attempts at accommodation might fail and that Christianity might come to be identified with barbarism and science with unbelief. Schleiermacher's aim, like Müller's, was with "striking the balance honestly" between religion and the advance of knowledge; and if Müller's concern that the science of religion relate itself "honestly" to religion is to be reckoned as among his contributions to the history of the academic study of religion, then Schleiermacher should be credited with attempting to bring about the religious correlate of this honesty by way of his account of religion. Schleiermacher, that is, should be regarded as having advanced an understanding of religion that, in part by requiring from its adherents the "loss of many things held dear," would allow for the advance of scientific knowledge of religion precisely *within* the "realm of religion." If the passage by Hagenbach, a self-described practitioner of "mediating theology" and an avowed follower of Schleiermacher, does not mention the possibility of such loss, then his remarks reflect an occlusion of the realism with which Schleiermacher viewed the religious landscape; they also foreshadow, it seems to me, the future possibility of disillusionment with the terms of the eternal covenant among theologians with a lower tolerance than Schleiermacher's for the at times painful process of religious accommodation.

5.4 Schleiermacher's Contemporary Relevance

If Schleiermacher's work on the topic of religion is of more than merely historical interest, it seems to me that this is not primarily in virtue of the content of his account, at least not in virtue of his claims regarding the essence of religion or the broader claim that religion is the sort of thing that has an essence. There are aspects of his account of religion, viewed as a whole, that are closer in spirit to contemporary positions among scholars of religion than the dominant ste-reotypes acknowledge (in particular, his seldom-appreciated understanding of religion as a process of the social formation of individual subjectivity and, I would also argue, his view of the relation between religion—*actual* religion— and politics). However, to my mind the greatest point of Schleiermacher's rel-evance for contemporary scholars of religion lies elsewhere. If, as I have argued, a program for the purely *theoretical* study of religion can be extracted from Schleiermacher's description of the nature and task of academic theology by bracketing the practical aspects of his proposal, there is also a substantial con-tinuity between the way he pursued the *practical* goals of academic theology and a longstanding and still vital trajectory within the field of religious studies.

In 1986, shortly before welcoming Proudfoot's *Religious Experience* as a bulwark against the threat of a "militant, politically motivated theosophism" within religious studies,[65] Carl Raschke accused his fellow scholars of a gener-alized failure of intellectual and moral discernment in relation to the forms of religion active and observable on the historical stage. In "Religious Studies and the Default of Critical Intelligence," Raschke described an uncritically positive attitude toward anything resembling religion as a pervasive feature of scholarly discourse.[66] Such an attitude, Raschke argued, had served the field well for the previous two decades, when its constituency was strongly informed by "the privatized, syncretistic, psycho-spiritual experimentalism of middle-class con-sumer society, which was seeded within the drug culture of youth, watered by the rise of 'alternative' religious groups that followed, and harvested in the so-called human potential movement of the late 1970s."[67] However, the "end of the mandate of the 1960s" and the rise of religious cults revealed this wide-spread "academic neopaganism" as "not the grand, liberal rebuke of dogma-tism and methodological monarchy it often purports to be. It is actually a deliberate *default* of our critical intelligence."[68]

Raschke appropriated the term *critical intelligence* from Ernst Cassirer, who had described it as the "heritage of the enlightenment." Critical intelligence, according to Raschke, is "the ability and drive to penetrate beneath the mere surface of things and to apperceive their essential makeup. It is a capacity to winnow the relevant from the strictly episodic, the valuable and enduring from the pernicious and inconsequential, the veracious from the merely specious."[69] "Academic neopaganism" counted, for Raschke, as precisely a refusal of this kind of discernment: "To enforce the now familiar regiment of deference and respect for anything that appears to have the faint signature of 'religious' life is to perform a lobotomy on one's critical intelligence, which the tutored profes-sional is supposed to possess. Moreover, it is to bare an inexcusable blind side to the potential aberrations of religious thinking and behavior."[70] In the face of an increasingly visible series of such aberrations (Jonestown, the neo-Nazi group known as the Order, Sun Myung Moon, "violent, conspiratorial, and black occultist fashions," "the appeal of Khomeini [and] Satanist murders in Los Angeles"[71]), Raschke argued that scholars of religion should regard themselves as under obligation not simply to study religion but also to provide "normative guidance"—"the willingness of recognized authorities or luminaries to exert sharp judgment or vigorous intellectual leadership, other than to simply entertain us with the facts at hand, when ambiguous and perplexing sorts of public circumstances arise"—within the public sphere.[72]

It should be readily apparent that Raschke was in effect assigning to the academic field of religious studies responsibility for a practical aim in addition to the purely theoretical one of "studying religion." That practical aim, broadly stated, involved exercising judgment regarding the desirability or undesirability of actually existing forms of religion in a manner calculated to escape the confines of the academy and inform a broad public audience and also involved "vigorous intellectual leadership" regarding religion—a notion susceptible to a wide range of interpretations but implying some measure of willingness to intervene in the course of religious events. It is also worth noting that while Raschke did not understand his call for "normative guidance" to be equivalent to a call for the field to return to its theological roots ("I am not plumping, directly or indirectly, for a return to the era of Christian theological hegemony"[73]), he was willing to acknowledge a continuity between theologians and scholars of religion with respect to "critical intelligence": "The 'theological' observer can no more commend the phenomenon of the *Schwärmerei* within his sector of research than the clinical psychologist can glorify the pathological."[74]

In view of this last remark in particular, it should not be controversial for me to point to similarities between the kind of application of critical intelligence advocated by Raschke and the practical project to which Schleiermacher dedicated *The Christian Faith*. Both Schleiermacher and Raschke espied "aberrations of religion" within current events, for Schleiermacher neopietism and for Raschke the cult movement. Furthermore, if Raschke's argument for the claim that scholars of religion should exercise "vigorous intellectual leadership" was ultimately a prudential one (i.e., in an era of cults only the public relevance of religious studies could ensure its survival as a field[75]), it seems reasonable to me to attribute to him the view that confronting the cult phenomenon would also serve something like the overall good of society. Schleiermacher explicitly embraced a similar view: In chapter 4 we encountered his statement in 1821 that the sensibilities on display within "awakened" pietism "must be treated with love but also with strict firmness, if the detriment to the whole of society which grows out of this is not to be greater than the spiritual profit which the awakened religious life brings to individuals."[76] I suggest, then, that the practical project embraced by both Schleiermacher the theologian and Raschke the scholar of religion is this: the application of reflectively obtained knowledge concerning religion to the public sphere, in the interest of the good of society as a whole.[77]

Hilgenfeld's 1858 apology for "scientific theology" concludes with the third passage cited at the opening of this chapter, a passage that I will use to illustrate this notion. The "recent events" to which Hilgenfeld referred were the aftershocks of the uprisings of 1848, which in Prussia had provided the crucial occasion for the neopietists, after more than two decades of the cultivation and placement of scholars, administrators, and clergy, to seize effective control of the apparatus of the state church and mobilize its resources against political and intellectual liberalism and their "blasphemous violation of temporal and divine authority."[78] In assessing the role that the academy might play in the wake of this episode, Hilgenfeld identified the education of the clergy as a crucial fulcrum for attempts to apply the benefits of the *Wissenschaften* to the social condition of religion. Moreover, he identified this education as a matter of broad public interest: For "cultured non-theologians" as well, "it can hardly be a matter of indifference whether a scientific or an unscientific spirit reigns in theology, and whether the German people are to have a clergy of zealots hostile to spiritual enculturation or rather a clergy thoroughly educated in the sciences." For recent history had demonstrated how easily a clergy socialized— that is, educated—into a posture of zealous anti-intellectualism could be made into the junior officers of a militant, reactionary orthodoxy whose activities could not be counted on to remain confined to the boundaries of the church.

This claim by Hilgenfeld seems to me to be entirely reasonable, and so does its extension by analogy to present circumstances. That is, it seems to me that both recent events and in fact much of the history of the past several hundred years offer compelling grounds for regarding the attitudes and activities of religious persons (including religious leaders) as potential objects of general concern, and to regard religion as a field not only for scholarly investigation but also at times for scholarly criticism and engagement. Even in light of the fact that the work of Schleiermacher and Hilgenfeld took place within the context of a state church and state-supported positions in academic theology—thus providing them with both an obvious public field of activity and a relatively uncontroversial public responsibility—it is not difficult to appreciate the extent to which Raschke's concerns and his proposal both echoed those of his nineteenth-century theological predecessors.

The thought that the responsibilities of the scholar of religion extend beyond *studying* religion and into some form of public *engagement* with or *intervention* in religion is controversial, not least because of the suspicion among some scholars that meaningful engagement with religion exposes the scholar to the risk of "doing" religion rather than studying it (i.e., the risk of "committing theology"). One response to Raschke's proposal strongly informed by such an anxiety is Russell McCutcheon's essay "A Default of Critical Intelligence? The Scholar of Religion as Public Intellectual."[79] McCutcheon initially embraces the idea that scholars of religion should be public intellectuals in some meaningful sense (and in fact laments the fact that liberal Protestant theologians have generally been more successful at this task than nontheological scholars of religion) but refuses Raschke's call to exercise "critical intelligence" on the grounds that he rejects both the idea that scholars of religion have access to "the essential make-up of things" and the idea that any religion could be "healthy." "For the scholar of religion as public intellectual," he writes, "what is most intriguing is that many of our colleagues think there is such a thing as good and healthy religion, as opposed to aberrations of religious thinking and behavior"; his preference is for a Durkheimian view according to which "religious discourses, which are neither good nor bad, are simply a brute fact of social ideologies and rhetorics."[80] For McCutcheon, the scholar of religion is to serve as a "critical rhetor" within the public sphere—one dedicated to the project of "uncloaking and laying bare the conditions and strategies by which their fellow citizens authorize the local as universal and the contingent as necessary" and to "uncovering, and teaching others to uncover, rhetorical and ideological window dressings—wherever and whenever we may find them."[81] However, this activity differs from Raschke's call to provide normative guidance in important respects: Scholars of religion are not to employ any distinction between "healthy and unhealthy" religion, are not to engage in any degree of "ideology management" (the scholar "comes not to inform the world of how it *ought* to work, but explains how and why it *happens* to work as it does"[82]), and are not to accommodate their work to the sensibilities of a religious readership ("Our scholarship is not constrained by whether or not devotees recognize its value; it is not intended to celebrate or enhance normative, dehistoricized discourses but, rather, to contextualize and redescribe them as human constructs."[83])

To be sure, there are also defenders of an understanding of the study of religion as a purely theoretical enterprise for whom any degree of practical interest constitutes a source of theoretical contamination and a drift backward toward theology. Donald Wiebe, in reviewing McCutcheon's more recent essay collection, *The Discipline of Religion*, finds McCutcheon's position virtually indistinguishable from "the religio-theological approaches that pre-date the establishment of the field of Religious Studies as a secular enterprise and that still finds itself ensconced in most modern departments of Religious Studies and in organizations like that of the American Academy of Religion."[84] In Wiebe's view, McCutcheon's "wish to replace the religio-theological students of religion and their ideological agendas with the engaged, public intellectual is, so far as I can see, simply to pit a new ideological agenda over against the old. Calling this 'redescriptive scholarship' simply does not differentiate McCutcheon's 'redescriptive scholars' from the currently dominant religio-theological scholars in the field since neither group of scholars is primarily concerned with gaining objective knowledge about the (religious) world."[85] Thus, for Wiebe, McCutcheon's stance represents not a reinvention but "a degradation of Religious Studies as a modern academic undertaking."[86]

There are also scholars, however, for whom theoretical and practical interests in religion are inseparable and for whom the thought of seeking societal application for the results of scholarship concerning religion carries no particular theological overtones.[87] Consider, for example, recent remarks by the urban sociologist Omar M. McRoberts, advanced in the context of a presidential address to the Society for the Scientific Study of Religion (SSSR):

> As we think about moments of internal scholarly cross-pollination,
> and as we acknowledge the impact of current political events and
> trends on what we study, we might also consider how to position
> ourselves, with the institutional support of SSSR, to bring our
> research to bear on current events. We would do so not with the aim
> of becoming "hot" in a public way, or of making religion "hotter."
> Religion cannot get any hotter. Rather we would foreground the
> purpose that motivates so many of us to study these matters with
> scientific discipline and tenacity—that purpose is to improve
> societies through right understanding.[88]

The question of whether religious studies as an academic discipline is a purely theoretical enterprise or whether the activities of the scholar can legitimately extend into the public sphere seems to me to be an open one, and one distinct in principle from questions regarding the place of theology within the academic study of religion.

At the close of chapter 4 I argue that one of Schleiermacher's aims in offering his dogmatics to the public was the dissemination of religious naturalism through the medium of academic theology, and I return now to this claim.[89] To recapitulate briefly, Schleiermacher's ambition, as I have described it, was to encourage Protestant Christians to embrace rather than resist the advance of the sciences toward "comprehensive knowledge of the world" and specifically to embrace rather than resist the view that among the phenomena that the sciences would soon come to comprehend would be those aspects of human nature and the dynamics of human sociality from which flow the phenomenon known as religion. Schleiermacher presented his account of religion as a natural phenomenon within a broader context: *The Christian Faith* incorporates this understanding of religion (and indeed Christianity) as its first "moment" but then proceeds to superimpose upon this a theological interpretation of not only Christianity but indeed the entire natural order, one that does not conflict with but *frames*, *contextualizes*, and *legitimates* the scientific investigation of that order and of Christianity. His vision for the future of Prussian Protestantism was that Protestants might come to regard the doctrinal tradition as the result of a historically extended, collective enterprise of reflection on the various forms of piety that constitute the most basic content of the Christian religion, rather than as divinely delivered; might look to the advance of scientific knowledge as a resource for understanding not only the material world but also themselves and their religion; and might exercise critical discernment regarding religion's historically given and unavoidable entanglement with external affairs, whether these be expressly political or more broadly cultural. His activities on behalf of this vision were targeted at the specific political and cultural circumstances of Protestant Christianity during his day, for the alternative to his vision—one whose outlines were already clearly in evidence—was a Christianity violently afraid of challenges to its current self-understanding, prone to claiming the sanction of eternal revelation for its identity and ambitions, and more than willing to take up and use political power to curtail both religious and intellectual freedom for the sake of its own preservation and extension.

The enduring relevance of Schleiermacher's writings on religion, I suggest, lies in the fact that they constitute a core element of a historically prominent episode in the history of the project described by McRoberts—the project of scholars of religion seeking to "improve societies through right understanding" of religion itself. If this is correct, then there is one class of contemporary scholars who should regard Schleiermacher's practical, theological work as not only a historical prototype of their own but also a resource for reflection on their project in historical perspective. This class consists of scholars of religion who think it possible, desirable, and maybe even important that work informed by a naturalistic perspective on religion not remain confined to academic circles but also have an effect within the broader public sphere.

In the years since Raschke's defense of the notion of "critical intelligence" in relation to religion, any number of events (including, of course, not only the terrorist attacks of September 11, 2001, but also every American presidential election) have served as reminders, in case any were needed, of the fact that the social effects of religion are not always and perhaps not ever limited to its adherents. Scholars of religion are, it seems to me, perfectly at liberty to regard the religious condition of their society—indeed of all societies—as a matter of common concern. They are also at liberty to bring critical intelligence to bear on the question of whether all formations of religion are equally conducive to the common good, whether or not they state the point in terms of the "essential natures of things" or of a difference between "good" and "bad," "healthy" or "unhealthy" religion.[90] They may find themselves believing that broad acceptance of the idea that religion is a natural phenomenon would improve the overall condition of their society. For some of these, religious naturalism will be "the whole story" about religion, and broad acceptance of religious naturalism will serve the common good by hastening religion's disappearance from the stage of history or perhaps by weakening its hold on a particular population. For others, religious naturalism will not answer questions concerning religion's final status and value but will increase religious understanding and religious self-understanding; it may also provide resources to be applied to the alteration of religion, perhaps by way of the amelioration of all-too-evident tensions between the life of religion and the life of the mind and the populations and institutions that embody these.[91] There are many good reasons, as well as many bad ones, for scholars of religion to refrain from proceeding down any such "practical" path and to remain content with the posture of the pure "research scholar," conversing with and concerned only with their peers in the academy. However, those who do so proceed and who set for themselves the goal of improving society through the dissemination of religious naturalism will be working within the broad stream of scholarly work of which Schleiermacher's is a paradigmatic example, whether or not they are willing to acknowledge him or any theologian as a fellow traveler.

My closing suggestion has to do with the way in which the line of thought I have been pursuing bears on the currently dominant master narrative concerning the historical development of the academic study of religion. It seems to me that the portrayal of this history as the progressive emergence, in the face of concerted opposition, of the study of religion as an exclusively *secular* endeavor (with the thought that only as a *secular* affair could the study of religion be properly *scientific*) obscures a second and equally important development: the emergence of the idea of the academic study of religion as the collective project of subjecting religion to intentional guidance, of directing its historical course, and of imposing some measure of control over its societal impact by means of the application of knowledge obtained through *Wissenschaft* rather than from religious tradition. I think the history of the academic study of religion could be told in terms of the differential development and relationship—sometimes tensive, sometimes collaborative—between these two imperatives, the theoretical and the practical. Both of these imperatives were in evidence long before the late nineteenth century, and a historical narrative attentive to both would not regard the rise to prominence of the idea of the study of religion as a purely secular affair as an unambiguously positive development. For while a secular posture serves the theoretical imperative by obviating one potential source of scholarly bias (if by no means every such source), it also threatens to diminish the ability of the scholar of religion to communicate meaningfully with a religious public and hence to pursue the practical imperative (particularly, one imagines, in cultural contexts in which religious communities have come to prize an intentional segregation from "corrupting" secular influences). In such a narrative Schleiermacher's proposal for combining the accumulation of knowledge concerning religion with its application to actually existing religion would figure not as simply a foreshadowing of the emergence of the academic study of religion proper, depreciated of course by its theological provenance, but also as a prominent episode in the history of the self-understanding of this field, and one whose significance is far from exhausted.

Notes

INTRODUCTION

1. *Schleiermachers Briefwechsel mit Johann Christian Gaß*, 44f. Cited in the Schleiermacher *Kritische Gesamtausgabe* (KGA) I.12, xiii.

2. Ibid.

3. KGA I.12, 7.

4. *On Religion: Speeches to Its Cultured Despisers* (1996, 24, 53); cf. KGA I.2, 245. In what follows I refer to Crouter's translation of the first edition of the *Speeches* simply as *On Religion* and to John Oman's older translation of the third edition as *On Religion* (Oman). My citations from the first edition use Crouter's translation unless otherwise noted. I take the characterization of God in the *Speeches* as a "product of religion" from Pannenberg, *Systematic Theology*, vol. 1, 126.

5. Schleiermacher to Herz, Feb. 22, 1799; KGA V.3, 15.

6. See KGA I.2, LVf.

7. Blackwell, "Antagonistic Correspondence," 113.

8. The phrase is from Schröder, *Die kritische Identität*, 34.

9. A useful discussion of the "pantheism controversy" is Gerrish, "The Secret Religion of Germany: Christian Piety and the Pantheism Controversy," in *Continuing the Reformation*, chapter 5, 109–26. On the "atheism controversy" see Martin, "Transcendental Philosophy and Atheism." Ulrich Barth discusses Schleiermacher's allusions to the atheism controversy in the *Speeches*; see *Aufgeklärter Protestantismus*, 273ff.

10. "Über die Religion," 49. This review appeared anonymously; its author is identified as J. C. R. Eckermann in the editor's historical introduction to the KGA I.12, XXVIII. The characterization of

Schleiermacher's remarks concerning the idea of God as tantamount to epiphenomenalism is Burkhard Gladigow's; see his "Friedrich Schleiermacher," 23.

11. G. L. Spalding to Schleiermacher, July 27, 1804; *Aus Schleiermachers Leben in Briefen*, vol. 3, 408. Cited in Redeker, *Schleiermacher: Life and Thought*, 77.

12. Schleiermacher's revision to the passage cited in part above are representative of his alterations elsewhere. In 1799 he wrote, "This is the proper measure of our religiousness: whether we have God as a part of our intuition depends on the direction of our imagination. In religion the universe is intuited; it is posited as originally acting upon us. Now if your imagination clings to the consciousness of your freedom in such a fashion that it cannot come to terms with what it construes as originally active other than in the form of a free being, then imagination will probably personify the spirit of the universe and you will have a God." (*On Religion*, 53.) In 1806 he revised this passage to read, "Universally, and here as well, what decides the worth of a person's religion is the way in which the deity is present to him in feeling, not the way in which he reproduces this, always inadequately, in the concept with which we deal now. If I do not pass judgment on your preferred practice of calling those who stand on this level but deny the concept of a personal god in general by Spinoza's name, I at least concede that this denial is not a decisive consideration against the presence of the deity in his feeling" (KGA I.12, 123; cf. *On Religion* [Oman], 97).

13. Here I follow Paul Capetz, who has observed that by way of a response to criticisms from Sack and others, in the second edition of the *Speeches* "the exposition is given a decidedly theistic cast and the word 'God' is inserted into the text in many places where 'universe' had originally appeared as the object of religious experience" (Capetz, *Christian Faith as Religion*, 123f.). The main difference between the first and subsequent editions of the *Speeches* that have attracted the lion's share of attention has, of course, been the incompletely carried out deletion of "intuition" (*Anschauung*) from Schleiermacher's discussion of the essence of religion. By 1909 Hermann Süskind could refer to an extended historical discussion of the difference between the editions (Süskind, *Der Einfluss Schellings*, 102ff.).

14. F. Chr. Schwarz, *Heidelbergische Jahrbücher* 5 (1812), 522f.; cited in Hjelde, *Die Religionswissenschaft und das Christentum*, 24.

15. The most extensive work of reconstruction in English since Niebuhr's *Schleiermacher on Christ and Religion* is contained in chapters 4 and 5 of Paul Capetz's *Christian Faith as Religion*. The concerns that motivate Capetz's project are, however, significantly different from my own in important respects.

16. On the controversies that unfolded at Halle prior to Schleiermacher's lifetime see Becker, "Pietism's Confrontation with Enlightenment Rationalism," 146–52, and Howard, *Protestant Theology*, 87–104. See Nowak, *Schleiermacher*, 32–42, for a discussion of the faculty at Halle during Schleiermacher's student years.

17. I refer here to the unpublished essays collected in vol. I.1 of the Schleiermacher KGA, in particular "Spinozismus," "Kurze Darstellung des spinozistischen Systems," "Leibniz," and "Über die Freiheit des Menschen." This last essay is discussed at length in chapter 1. Heino Falcke expressed a consensus among Schleiermacher scholars when he portrayed Schleiermacher as one dedicated to the project of "mediation" between not just religion and science but also a wide variety of ostensibly irreconcilable opposites: "spirit and reality, reason and history, freedom

and causality, subjectivity and positivity." Falcke, *Theologie und Philosophie der Evolution*, 4.

18. For descriptions of the origins of the *Speeches*, see KGA I.2, LIII–LX; Jack Forstman's foreword to *On Religion* (Oman), viiiff.; and Crouter's introduction to *On Religion*, xvi–xix. Ulrich Barth's discussion of the influences on Schleiermacher during the years prior to the composition of the *Speeches* is accessible and informative; see Barth, *Aufgeklärter Protestantismus*, 262–70.

19. See KGA I.6, 256, 338, and *Brief Outline on the Study of Theology*, 29.

20. In his summary of and responses to the contents of the first volume of *Where God and Science Meet*, Wildman notes that "I happen to agree with [Joseph] Bulbulia's (stated) assumption that supernatural beings do not interfere in natural processes. In my case, this is because I believe that supernatural beings do not exist (i.e., I am a religious naturalist)." Wildman, "Significance of the Evolution of Religious Belief," 268.

21. Slone, *Theological Incorrectness*, 14–23. Slone also discusses "transcendentalist" theorists of religion, placing Otto, Wach, and Eliade in this category (24). He does not discuss Schleiermacher.

22. Preus, *Explaining Religion*, x.

23. Ibid., xvf.

24. Ibid., xviii.

25. The high point of discussions connecting Schleiermacher to religious naturalism came, it seems to me, during the first "Schleiermacher renaissance" of the early twentieth century in the work of those associated with Ernst Troeltsch, such as Georg Wehrung, Hermann Mulert, and Hermann Süskind. Discussion in these works turned not around the concept of naturalism as such but rather around that of historicism; the connection between these is, however, an intimate one, as indicated by the citation from Süskind cited in note 107 this chapter. Richard Crouter, in his 1988 introduction to the *Speeches*, characterizes the young Schleiermacher as "a "religious naturalist" who subsequently accommodated these views to more orthodox beliefs" (*On Religion* [1988], 66). Useful essays that touch on the subject are Foreman, "Schleiermacher's 'Natural History of Religion,'" and Reynolds, "Religion within the Limits of History."

26. Byrne, *Natural Religion and the Nature of Religion*. In his first chapter Byrne distinguishes between four senses of "naturalism" in the deistic tradition. The first is natural religion vs. revealed religion or theology; the second, natural theology vs. civic or mythic theology; the third, natural religion vs. supernatural religion; and the fourth, natural in the sense of being universal, or grounded in human nature (7). For the sake of brevity I conflate Byrne's first and third types of naturalism, which combination Byrne attributed to the deists (8).

27. Ibid., 9.

28. Ibid., 8. Ivan Strenski follows Byrne on this point, commenting with reference to Byrne's treatment that "[w]hatever else they achieved, I take it to be a major victory for modern religious studies that the Deists established the intellectual bases of a comparative, naturalistic, academic study of religions." Strenski, *Thinking about Religion*, 29.

29. Byrne, *Natural Religion*, 9.

30. Ibid., 161.

31. Capps, *Religious Studies*.

32. Ibid., 11.

33. Ibid., 17.

34. Ibid., 13.

35. For examples of such evaluations of Schleiermacher's historical contribution that span the past century and more, see Gaß, *Geschichte der protestantischen Dogmatik*, vol. 4, 547; Mensching, *Geschichte der Religionswissenschaft*, 55f.; Wach, *Types of Religious Experience*, 13; Sharpe, *Comparative Religion*, 20f.; Arie Molendijk, introduction to *Religion in the Making*, 4f. Two in-depth explorations representative of the two historical "Schleiermacher renaissances" of the topic are Süskind, *Christentum und Geschichte bei Schleiermacher*, and Hjelde, *Die Religionswissenschaft und das Christentum*. Also useful is Herbert Richardson's essay collection *Friedrich Schleiermacher and the Founding of the University of Berlin*.

36. On Schleiermacher's role in the founding of the University of Berlin and the significance of his work for the relationship between theology and *Wissenschaft* see Richard Crouter, "A Proposal for a New Berlin University," in *Friedrich Schleiermacher: Between Enlightenment and Romanticism*, 140–68; Howard, *Protestant Theology*, chapter 3.

37. "I criticize Schleiermacher not because, like Hegel, he made religion into a matter of feeling, but rather only because as a result of theological bias he did not and could not come to draw out the necessary consequences of his standpoint, that he did not have the courage to recognize and accept that *objectively* God himself is nothing other than the *essence of feeling*, if subjectively feeling is the highest object of religion. In this respect I am so little opposed to Schleiermacher that he is on the contrary an essential buttress and the de facto confirmation of my claims, which are deduced from the nature of feeling." "Zur Beurteilung der Schrift 'Das Wesen des Christentums' " (1842) in Feuerbach, *Ludwig Feuerbachs Werke*, 211. Cited in part in Wagner, *Was ist Religion?* 95.

38. I discuss Karl Barth's criticisms of Schleiermacher on pp. 15f. below.

39. For discussion of the Hegelian "school interpretation" of Schleiermacher and its contemporary significance, see my "The Case of the Disappearing Discourse," 1–28.

40. Proudfoot, *Religious Experience*. The influence of Proudfoot's work on common understandings of Schleiermacher was evident even in the early 1990s. In a 1992 review essay Richard Crouter called attention to the sharp dichotomy between the degree of nuance, contextuality, and textual fidelity displayed by German scholarship and the lack of the same displayed by prominent representations of Schleiermacher in English. Part of the problem for Crouter lay in the fact that the main lines of academic discourse about Schleiermacher seemed not to be appropriately sensitive to developments in Schleiermacher scholarship. Observing that the work of Brian Gerrish had come to constitute a serious and historically well-informed body of work concerning Schleiermacher, Crouter went on to remark that "[i]t is at least likely, however, that recent North American understanding of Schleiermacher has been shaped not so much by Gerrish as by more general works that touch upon Schleiermacher as a way of taking their bearings in the setting of modern theology, the question of religious experience, or on behalf of a specific theological proposal" (Crouter, "Friedrich Schleiermacher: A Critical Edition," 24).

The works he then lists under this heading are George Lindbeck's *Nature of Doctrine* (1984), Proudfoot's *Religious Experience*, and Thiemann's *Revelation and Theology*. As my remarks above indicate, it seems to me that outside the work of Schleiermacher specialists and theologians, work on Schleiermacher in English still does not generally take into account the German scholarship, but, more important, of the three works to which Crouter refers it is fairly clearly *Religious Experience* that continues to have the greatest impact on the interpretation of Schleiermacher.

41. Proudfoot, *Religious Experience*, 2. It is important to note that Proudfoot did not invent the idea that Schleiermacher was interested in "protecting" religion; in 1941 Richard Brandt had advanced a similar claim in *The Philosophy of Schleiermacher*. See below, p. 140.

42. Proudfoot, *Religious Experience*, 3. Proudfoot was not very clear about the connection between Schleiermacher's account of religion and the later, explicitly "protectivist" theorists whom he criticized most directly. His practice of using the pronouncements of these later thinkers to exegete Schleiermacher at times verged on conflating his work with theirs. See in particular the digressions within his discussion of Schleiermacher into the work of James and Otto at pp. 7f. and Cassirer and Streng at pp. 26f.

43. For discussion of the degree of fit between Schleiermacher's and Otto's accounts of religion, see my "Schleiermacher and Otto on Religion." For a critical response to my arguments see David A. Smith, "Schleiermacher and Otto on Religion." Smith argues that, contrary to what I had claimed, on the issues of amenability to the explanation of religion in terms of natural causes or the possibility that God might intervene in the natural order "there is, in fact, nothing to distinguish these two thinkers" (295). Smith's essay appeared in print as the present volume was in the final stages of preparation. A direct reply to his arguments is in progress, but several of the crucial issues that he raises concerning the interpretation of Schleiermacher are also addressed in these pages, particularly in chapter 4.

44. Proudfoot, *Religious Experience*, xv.

45. Ibid., 53.

46. Ibid., 228.

47. Niebuhr, *Schleiermacher on Christ and Religion*.

48. Raschke, "Religious Experience," 620.

49. Sharf, "Buddhist Modernism," 229. See also Sharf, "Zen of Japanese Nationalism," 34f.

50. Masuzawa, *Invention of World Religions*, 328. It is not entirely clear whether Masuzawa endorses this project of "rounding up" varieties of cryptotheology and the cryptotheologians who practice it. If "we" were to successfully prosecute this "rounding up," she asks, "will we then have apprehended the right suspects? Or are we not failing to see a much larger, systemic network of discursive organization, of which the ones in custody are but low-level functionaries? Is the effort to prosecute these 'theological assumptions' for illegally traversing and thereby downgrading the science of religion, then, not like an attempt to punish some unknown evil still at large by burning a host of effigies?" On one construal of these remarks, Masuzawa is suggesting that the category of "right suspects" does not necessarily include any and all types of "cryptotheologian"; on another, however, the former category includes but

is not restricted to the latter, such that the project of purging the academy of corrupting influences will not be at an end when all of the cryptotheologians have finally been "rounded up" and properly dealt with.

51. Guthrie, *Faces in the Clouds*, 9.

52. Godlove, "Instability of Religious Belief," 49f. It is interesting that in a footnote Godlove cites Brian Gerrish's rejoinder to George Lindbeck's description of Schleiermacher in *The Nature of Doctrine*—specifically, Gerrish's remark that according to Schleiermacher "doctrines do not express a prelinguistic experience but an experience that has already been constituted by the language of the community" (Gerrish, "Review: The Nature of Doctrine," 90). Godlove says of this claim that "[t]he issue is controversial and, in any case, does not affect Proudfoot's treatment of the more influential *On Religion*" ("Instability of Religious Belief," 50n5).

53. Jantzen, *Power, Gender, and Christian Mysticism*, 311f. Jantzen has also explored Schleiermacher independently in "Could There Be a Mystical Core of Religion?"

54. Sharf, "Experience," 98. See also Sharf, "Zen of Japanese Nationalism," 34f., and "Buddhist Modernism," 229.

55. "In reaction to the eighteenth-century habit of reducing ('true') religion to morality, Schleiermacher and Otto fixed a theological notion of 'the sacred' that has been very durable until now: essential religion (which strongly implies 'authentic' religion), rooted in an apprehension of 'the holy,' is utterly prior to either conceptual or moral formulation and elaboration." Preus, *Explaining Religion*, 200. Preus does not refer to Proudfoot on this point, but *Religious Experience* does appear in his index.

56. See below, p. 27.

57. See, for example, McCutcheon, *Manufacturing Religion*, 60; *Insider/Outsider Problem in the Study of Religion*, 68, 128; *Critics Not Caretakers*, 4f.; "Critical Trends in the Study of Religion," 325.

58. Segal, "Religion as Interpreted rather than Explained: John Hick's *An Interpretation of Religion*," in *Explaining and Interpreting Religion*, 70.

59. This characterization is from William Adams Brown, who at the turn of the twentieth century presented Schleiermacher as arguing for the compatibility of the "speculative" and the "historic" in his understanding of Christianity: "Like every great systematic genius who has sought to combine in a single generalization elements of truth hitherto deemed irreconcilable, he has exposed himself to attack from both the right hand and from the left. His theological contemporaries reproach with having sacrificed too much Christian truth to the exigencies of a philosophical theory.... By his philosophical brethren, on the other hand, he is accused of weakness in retaining in his system much to which his speculative principles give him no right." Brown, *Essence of Christianity*, 172.

60. Farley, "Is Schleiermacher Passé?" 9; Niebuhr, *Schleiermacher on Christ and Religion*, 13. The partisan character of responses to not only Schleiermacher but also his "school" was noted in the nineteenth century. Cf. Frédéric Lichtenberger: "The school of conciliation, as it has been justly called, with its mediating theology, attaches itself directly to Schleiermacher. Its rights have been often ignored by the extreme parties who have had an interest in tracing a fantastic portrait of it, amounting even to a caricature which has been made for the purpose of depreciating it in the eyes of the public." Lichtenberger, *History of German Theology*, 467.

61. Crouter, "Friedrich Schleiermacher: A Critical Edition," 26.

62. Howard concludes his *Protestant Theology* with discussion of the 1923 correspondence between von Harnack and Barth (410–18). The text of the correspondence can be found in Rumscheidt, *Adolf von Harnack*, 85–106.

63. Karl Barth, *Theology of Schleiermacher*, 149.

64. Ibid., 153, 259f.

65. Ibid., 275, 277. Ted Vial makes this interrogation by Barth the framework of his investigation of the importance of worship for Schleiermacher's theology; see Vial, "Friedrich Schleiermacher on the Central Place of Worship in Theology."

66. Richard Crouter's "Friedrich Schleiermacher: A Critical Edition" provides a useful overview of the KGA project and incisive remarks about the state of Schleiermacher scholarship in 1992. Brent Sockness returned to the topic in 2003 in "The Forgotten Moralist: Friedrich Schleiermacher and the Science of Spirit," in particular pp. 324ff. His note 25 provides references to several discussions of the KGA by its editors.

67. Albrecht, *Schleiermachers Theorie der Frömmigkeit*, 1.

68. Nowak, *Schleiermacher*. For a selective overview of and engagement with trends in the German secondary literature during this period, see Ulrich Barth, "Schleiermacher-Literatur im letzten Drittel des 20. Jahrhunderts."

69. Sockness's "Forgotten Moralist" is an indispensable guide to the corpus of Schleiermacher's writings on ethics, which is fully conversant with the German literature. Robert Louden's introduction to the English translation of the later ethics lectures (*Lectures on Philosophical Ethics*, vii–xxx) is also helpful. The description of ethics as "the crux of Schleiermacher's philosophy" is Otto Braun's, cited in Louden, vii.

70. *On the* Glaubenslehre*: Two Letters to Dr. Lücke*; *On Freedom*; *Lectures on Philosophical Ethics*. Two texts by Schleiermacher on hermeneutics have also appeared in translation over the last generation: *Hermeneutics: The Written Manuscripts*, and *Hermeneutics and Criticism and Other Writings*. In addition to these texts a lengthy list of English translations produced by the Edwin Mellen Press since 1985 can be found in Lawler, Kinlaw, and Richardson, eds., *The State of Schleiermacher Scholarship Today*, ixnι. Terrence Tice's translation of Schleiermacher's *Brief Outline on the Study of Theology* has been indispensable for readers of English throughout this period.

71. Much of the interest in Schleiermacher among contemporary theologians is a result of Gerrish's influence. See his *Tradition in the Modern World*; *The Old Protestantism and the New*; *Prince of the Church*; *Continuing the Reformation*. A number or Richard Crouter's influential essays on Schleiermacher have been reprinted in *Friedrich Schleiermacher: Between Enlightenment and Romanticism*. Paul Capetz's *Christian Faith as Religion* reflects the concerns of contemporary theorists of religion to a greater extent than many other works on Schleiermacher and is particularly useful.

72. In this respect these more recent works stand in continuity with the classic twentieth-century, English-language discussions of Schleiermacher on religion. Richard Brandt's *Philosophy of Schleiermacher* (1941) was driven by its author's interest in the question of whether there is "some form of immediate knowledge in religious experience" that could provide access to "many of the things philosophers of religion are most interested in knowing" (viii). And Niebuhr's *Schleiermacher on Christ and Religion* (1964), although its core was a well-informed and perceptive analysis of

Schleiermacher's understanding of religion (and was one of the first texts in English to call attention to the importance of Schleiermacher's lectures on ethics), was framed as an investigation of his "theological style," carried out under the looming shadow of Karl Barth and oriented ultimately toward an assessment of the theological adequacy of Schleiermacher's Christology.

73. Crouter, "Friedrich Schleiermacher: A Critical Edition," 23.

74. See, for example, Damer, *Attacking Faulty Reasoning*, 20ff.

75. Welch, *Protestant Thought in the Nineteenth Century*, vol. 1, 2f.

76. Ibid., 68.

77. Ibid., 65. Welch preferred to avoid the standard practice of translating *schlecthin* as absolute; see 65n16.

78. Ibid., 66.

79. Ibid., 67.

80. McCutcheon, ed., *Insider/Outsider Problem*, 68. From McCutcheon's introduction to "The Autonomy of Religious Experience."

81. Ibid., 68.

82. Rendtorff, *Church and Theology*, 118.

83. Ibid., 25. This quotation is from Gaß, *Geschichte der protestantischen Dogmatik*, vol. 4, 435.

84. Rendtorff, *Church and Theology*, 113.

85. Ibid., 116.

86. Ibid., 122.

87. Ibid., 127, 122.

88. Rendtorff's work was preceded by three substantive investigations of this side of Schleiermacher's corpus: Samson's *Die Kirche als Grundbegriff der Ethik Schleiermachers*, Jørgensen's invaluable *Die Ethik Schleiermachers*, and Garczyk's *Mensch, Gesellschaft, Geschichte* (which Rendtorff did not reference). Rendtorff's work was followed closely by Spiegel's *Theologie der bürgerlichen Gesellschaft*. More recent examples are Falcke, *Theologie und Philosophie der Evolution*; Bernd Oberdorfer, *Geselligkeit und Realisierung von Sittlichkeit*, and Kumlehn, *Symbolisierendes Handeln*. Particularly useful recent essays on the subject are Firschung and Schlegel, "Religiöse Innerlichkeit und Geselligkeit"; Tyrell, "Religion: Das 'vollendetste Resultat der menschlichen Geselligkeit' "; and Cramer, "Die eine Frömmigkeit und die Vielen Frommen."

89. Grove, *Deutungen des Subjekts*.

90. "The investigation of Schleiermacher's philosophy of religion must therefore concentrate on his theory of subjectivity. However it should not be disputed that his religion-theoretical argumentations are, at the same time, absolutely tied to the communal; each religion is borne by a community according to Schleiermacher. [My] treatment, however, proceeds from the assumption that subjectivity cannot be derived from intersubjectivity and presupposes that this thematization of religion is independent and foundational. Here the emphasis will be on this thematization, while the intersubjective dimension of the concept of religion will not be pursued further." Grove, *Deutungen des Subjekts*, 4.

91. Proudfoot falls victim to this dynamic, for example, in arguing that the point of Schleiermacher's account of the formation of religious doctrines in *The Christian Faith* is to claim that not only spontaneous expressions of piety but also religious

doctrines, which are the product of reflection on these, are the result of a developmental process that is immune to nonreligious influences. According to Proudfoot, "Secondary religious language develops out of an attempt to understand or interpret the religious consciousness expressed in primary language. Though concepts are employed that have not been given directly in the religious consciousness or its primary expressions, it is in principle unaffected by speculative thought and judgments about the world"; Schleiermacher wanted "to show that the language of religious belief and doctrine emerges from [religious] affections without being contaminated by thoughts and claims about the world which might make it vulnerable to philosophical criticism or to contradiction by advances in knowledge." Proudfoot, *Religious Experience*, 32, 34.

92. *On Religion*, 25, 80.

93. Penner, "Interpretation," 58.

94. Ibid., 66.

95. Preus, *Explaining Religion*, 198.

96. *Insider/Outsider Problem*, 128. From McCutcheon's introduction to "Reductionism and the Study of Religion."

97. Dilthey, "Ideen über eine beschreibende und zergliedernde Psychologie," in *Wilhelm Dilthey gesammelte Schriften*, vol. 5 (Leipzig: Teubner, 1921), 143–44. Cited in Plantinga, *Historical Understanding in the Thought of Wilhelm Dilthey*, 33.

98. Dilthey, "Development of Hermeneutics," in *Wilhelm Dilthey Selected Writings*, 258, 260, substituting the German for Rickman's "sciences of man."

99. A number of recent discussions have called attention to the significance of this expansion of the hermeneutical paradigm by Dilthey in relation to Schleiermacher's own understanding. Besides the example of Gunter Scholtz (*Ethik und Hermeneutik*), see Fiorenza, "Religion," 26f.; Sockness, "Forgotten Moralist," 329ff.; Joy, "Beyond Essence and Intuition," 72ff.; and Joy, "Philosophy and Religion," 201.

100. Scholtz, *Ethik und Hermeneutik*. Sockness also calls attention to the early prominence of Schleiermacher's ethics in relation to contemporary representations; beginning with Dilthey, who himself worked with a broad range of Schleiermacher's texts, a process began whereby "the nineteenth-century image of Schleiermacher the ethicist [would] eventually recede behind the characteristically twentieth-century image of Schleiermacher the hermeneutician." Sockness, "Forgotten Moralist," 331.

101. Scholtz, *Ethik und Hermeneutik*, 86.

102. Ibid.

103. Scholtz called attention to the impropriety of reading Schleiermacher through the lens of the "crisis of historicism," which inaugurated the twentieth-century discussions of the *Geisteswissenschaften*—in no small part because of the anxieties motivated by the cultural relativism implicit in a thoroughgoing historicism. Scholtz argued that Schleiermacher's conception of *Ethik* was an attempt to unify two tendencies prominently displayed by Herder and Kant respectively: on the one hand an interest in the concrete facts of history and the characteristic human activities that constitute it, and on the other a drive toward systematicity and a desire to maintain a clear distinction between the "speculative-reasoned" and the "empirical-real." Ibid., 67ff.

104. For a diagrammatic representation of Schleiermacher's architectonic of the sciences see Geck, "Sozialethische und sozialpolitische Ansätze," 139.

105. I discuss Schleiermacher's conception of ethics at greater length in chapters 1 and 3.

106. Scholtz, *Ethik und Hermeneutik*, 75.

107. Cf. Süskind's digest of the results of Mulert's *Schleiermachers geschichts-philosophische Ansichten in ihrer Bedeutung für seine Theologie*: "The thought of historical continuity, i.e., the principle of the natural-causal explanation of every occurrence by the historical interconnection (*Zusammenhang*), was brought to bear by Schleiermacher even upon the investigation of Christianity, insofar as he both excluded the concept of supernatural miracle from the entire realm of Christianity and also allowed for nothing absolutely supernatural to be found in the appearance of Christ within history." Süskind, *Christentum und Geschichte*, 4.

108. The material discussed in this paragraph is treated in more detail in chapter 4; see pp. 141–43 below.

109. Wähner's review appeared in two sections in *Hermes oder kritisches Jahrbuch für Literatur*. This passage is from Stück 2, 289.

110. Ibid., 279; cited in part in Dunkmann, *Nachwirkungen*, 100.

111. Wähner, *Hermes*, 292; cited in Hjelde, *Religionswissenschaft*, 37.

112. See below, chapter 1 pp. 51–55.

CHAPTER 1

1. Neander, "Das verflossene halbe Jahrhundert," 6, 12f. The essay appeared serially in the issues for the year 1850 on pp. 3–14, 17–22, and 25–29.

2. Ibid., 13. Kurt-Victor Selge called attention to Neander's opposition to Schleiermacher's "inclination to determinism," citing this passage in part. See Selge, "Neander und Schleiermacher," 45.

3. Neander, "Das verflossene halbe Jahrhundert," 14.

4. CG2 §46.2; KGA I.13, 1, 269f. (173f.) In citing *Die christliche Glaube* I first give Schleiermacher's section numbers, distinguishing between the two editions with the labels CG1 and CG2; then provide the KGA page reference; then parenthetically provide the page reference to the English translation, *The Christian Faith*.

5. For an example see Robert Williams, who exposits "Schleiermacher's account of freedom" in the space of two pages in *Schleiermacher the Theologian*, 35f. Williams anticipates Jacqueline Mariña's recent work in attributing to Schleiermacher a doctrine of "qualified and limited" autonomy: "[W]hile freedom is a transcendental act, it is not concretely exercised *ex nihilo* or *de novo*, but always in a context of and in reciprocity with the social and natural orders of being" (ibid.). Williams's claims can be compared to those of W. H. Bruford, who wrote concerning the *Monologen* that "[Schleiermacher] never questions the control of the conscious mind over the body, or the freedom of the will, though he does not follow the more extreme Idealist philosophers and represent human conduct as unpredictable and completely non-determined. He understands the growth of character too well for that, giving due weight to the influence of heredity and past choices, as well as that of a man's friends and associates, and of the cultural tradition into which he was born" (Bruford, *German Tradition of Self-cultivation*, 81f.). It is worth noting that Bruford's and Williams's books predate both the appearance of the text of Schleiermacher's early essay on freedom in the KGA and Albert Blackwell's English translation.

6. The online *Stanford Encyclopedia of Philosophy* has useful entries on the topic of determinism (http://plato.stanford.edu/entries/determinism-causal/) and compatibilism (http://plato.stanford.edu/entries/compatibilism/) (accessed March 2009). A nineteenth-century discussion of the issue that ultimately comes down on the side of compatibilism and makes for a useful companion piece to Schleiermacher's "On Human Freedom" is Brentano, "Dispute between Determinism and Indeterminism," 222–71.

7. The abridged text of the essay is contained in Dilthey, *Leben Schleiermachers*, vol. 2 ("Denkmale"), 19–46.

8. See pp. 55–59 below.

9. Esselborn, *Die philosophische Voraussetzungen*, 8. For brief mentions of the issue see also Gaß, *Geschichte der protestantischen Dogmatik*, vol. 4, 542f., 594ff., and Zeller, *Geschichte der deutschen Philosophie*, 622.

10. The complete text is contained in the KGA I.1, 217–356. Following the publication of this volume of the KGA, its editor, Günter Meckenstock, documented the development of Schleiermacher's determinism through his engagement with the philosophies of Kant and Spinoza in his *Deterministische Ethik und kritische Theologie*.

11. *On Freedom*, trans. Albert Blackwell. A decade earlier Blackwell had written *Schleiermacher's Early Philosophy of Life* on the basis of the German manuscript.

12. For background on the composition of the essay see KGA I.1, liv–lviii; Blackwell, *On Freedom*, ii–v; Nowak, *Schleiermacher*, 52f.

13. For a historical overview of early modern compatibilist proposals see Sleigh, Chapell, and Della Rocca, "Determinism and Human Freedom."

14. See the postscript to ibid., 1269f.

15. For an account of this episode see Becker, "Pietism's Confrontation," 146–53.

16. George di Giovanni, *Freedom and Religion*.

17. See ibid., 5f.

18. On Weishaupt, see ibid., 44–47, 105; on Ulrich, 108; Jacobi, 108, 137–50. On Herder, see Timm, *Gott und die Freiheit*, 331–39.

19. Di Giovanni, *Freedom and Religion*, 122f.

20. Indeed, di Giovanni ruminates on "how much Schleiermacher's romantic pantheism . . . while often operating with idealistic language and idealistic distinctions, still found its intellectual home in the popular metaphysics of the late *Aufklärung*." Ibid., 292. Schleiermacher is not one of the figures whom di Giovanni investigates at length. He does speculate that Schleiermacher is perhaps best understood, along with Schelling, as a product of the "Spinozistic naturalism" of the late Enlightenment, due in part to the fact that he counted Eberhard as a mentor and in part to the fact that he "was a staunch defender of determinism in the metaphysical tradition of Ulrich or Weishaupt" (272, 341n9, 292). On a side note, di Giovanni's book offers us reason to be skeptical of Dilthey's claim that "On Human Freedom" was "for a long time the only consequential investigation [of freedom] from the side of determinism." Dilthey, *Leben Schleiermachers*, vol. 1, 138.

21. *On Freedom*, 29. Translations are Blackwell's unless otherwise noted.

22. Di Giovanni, *Freedom and Religion*, 205ff.

23. Schwarz wrote to Schleiermacher in his initial letter of November 9, 1800, "I have definitively stated wherein I cannot agree with the spirited author [of the *Speeches*]; and I had the feeling in doing so that this disagreement touches only on the

letter, and we are at one in the depths of our hearts. Some of my friends, above all the brave Professor Creuzer in Marburg, took objection to my remarks, and ever since these subjects have been interesting material for our discussions." Schleiermacher replied to Schwarz on March 28, 1801, "One more question: is the [given] name of this friend of yours, Creuzer, Leonhard? Several years ago one by that name interested me very much through a writing on the freedom of the will." Schwarz confirmed Creuzer's identity in his letter of reply. See Meisner and Mulert, "Schleiermachers Briefwechsel," 258, 265f.

24. Meckenstock, *Deterministische Ethik*, 127. For a discussion of Creuzer's essay, see di Giovanni, *Freedom and Religion*, 205–6.

25. *On Freedom*, 13f.

26. Ibid., 22.

27. Ibid., 21.

28. Ibid., 8.

29. Ibid., 10.

30. Ibid., 11.

31. Ibid., 25.

32. Ibid., 98.

33. Kant, *Critique of Pure Reason*, A446/B474, 484.

34. Ibid., 485. As Blackwell noted, a remark by Schleiermacher most likely written in 1789 indicates that he regarded Kantian transcendental freedom with incredulity: "transcendental freedom. Apparently, therefore, a faculty of causality without necessary connection with what has gone before. I have therefore certainly not misunderstood him." *On Freedom*, xi.

35. *On Freedom*, 28. In the KGA Meckenstock footnotes a passage from Wolff's *Vernünftige Gedanken von Gott, der Welt, und der Seele des Menschen* (which Blackwell helpfully carries over to his translation) that in essence presents the same argument.

36. *On Freedom*, 19f.

37. Ibid., 29.

38. Ibid., 38.

39. The position of this broader idea of universal determinism within the essay is an interesting one. It is not entailed by Schleiermacher's practical arguments; his explication of the intelligibility of our moral practices on the postulate of psychological determinism would hold even in the context of a principled agnosticism about whether causes that operate *outside* the human soul do so deterministically or indeterministically. And just such an agnosticism would seem to be required by Schleiermacher's practical approach since its point is to avoid mingling "the understanding's general laws concerning nature" (ibid., 13) with the concerns of practical reason. Nevertheless, Schleiermacher seems to have taken the view of the extrapersonal natural order as operating deterministically thoroughly for granted.

40. Ibid., 49.

41. Ibid., 42.

42. Ibid., 43.

43. Ibid., 84.

44. Ibid., 44.

45. Ibid., 81.

46. Ibid., 81.

47. Ibid., 82f.

48. Ibid., 122.

49. It is possible that Schleiermacher appropriated this idea from Leibniz. An essay by Robert Sleigh on Leibniz's doctrine of "moral necessity" highlights Leibniz's distinction between the "orders" of laws governing the behavior of bodies and mind respectively. As Leibniz wrote in his fifth letter to Clarke, "the natural forces of bodies are all subject to mechanical laws, and the natural forces of minds are all subject to moral laws. The former follow the order of efficient causes, the latter the order of final causes." See Sleigh, "Moral Necessity," 269.

50. *On Freedom*, 131.

51. Schleiermacher's remarks concerning his definition of free actions suggest some degree of awareness of the absurd conclusions that it entailed: "Just as we are justified in calling an action free that arises according to the law of the succession of ideas and initiates a series according to the law of motion, so too we are correct in calling an action free that arises according to the law of motion and initiates a series according to the law of the succession of ideas. To what extent and under what restrictions this latter case may be conceived as possible can be judged from the previous discussion and cannot be further developed here" (ibid., 133).

52. See below, chapter 4, pp. 159ff.

53. *On Freedom*, 12f.

54. Ibid., 66f.

55. Ibid., 71.

56. Ibid., 73.

57. Ibid., 81.

58. Ibid., 77.

59. According to Andreas Arndt, in Schleiermacher's early works the "feeling of freedom" "describes only a subjective-finite presupposition of moral judgment and activity but not the ground (*Grund*) of these itself. This [ground] only comes to light when the feeling of freedom is recognized and interpreted in respect to the determination of desire in the web of causal interrelations, at which Schleiermacher's intended reconciliation of freedom and determinism aims." Arndt, "Gefühl und Reflexion," 120.

60. The content of these lectures has appeared in several editions since Schleiermacher's death, with the best known being the edition of Ludwig Jonas in 1839 and Rudolf Odebrecht in 1942. Manfred Frank's two-volume Suhrkamp edition of the *Dialektik* (*Friedrich Schleiermachers* Dialektik) is based on the Jonas and Odebrecht editions. The most complete critical edition of the lectures appeared in 2002 as KGA II.10.1 and II.10.2. The history of Schleiermacher's lectures on *Dialektik* is described in the KGA II.10.1, VII–LVII. A list of the individual courses from which the surviving notes are drawn is found on pages XXVf. of the same volume.

61. KGA II.10.2, 138.

62. KGA II.10.1, 104ff. Peter Grove discusses Schleiermacher's deployment of the notion of a "relative antithesis" in both the *Ethik* and the *Dialektik*; see Grove, *Deutungen*, 378ff., 476f. Schleiermacher's introduction to the 1812/1813 ethics lectures makes use of the same device; see *Philosophical Ethics*, 5ff.

63. KGA II.10.2, 105.

64. KGA II.10.1, 100f.

65. Ibid., II.10.1, 138.

66. Ibid., II.10.1, 134.

67. KGA II.10.2, 218f.

68. Schleiermacher presented basically the same understanding of the relationship between freedom and necessity in his ethics lectures, albeit more briefly and less clearly than in the *Dialektik*. See in particular the final version of the introduction: *Lectures on Philosophical Ethics*, 160.

69. KGA II.10.2, 220.

70. KGA II.10.1, 258f.

71. KGA II.10.2, 236.

72. Ibid., 218f., emphasis in the original.

73. My discussion in this section is considerably informed by Julia Lamm's exploration of Schleiermacher's determinism in the *Speeches*; see *Living God*, 68–80.

74. *On Religion*, 5.

75. Ibid., 40; see above, p. 35.

76. *On Religion*, 102. Julia Lamm also cites this passage as a statement of Schleiermacher's adherence to a "complete determinism" in the *Speeches*; see Lamm, *Living God*, 71. In 1806 Schleiermacher revised this passage as follows: "Ethics (*Sittlichkeit*) depends, therefore, entirely on the consciousness of freedom, into whose realm falls everything which it produces; Piety, on the contrary, is not at all bound to this side of life, but stirs as well in the opposed realm of necessity, wherein no truly individual action appears." KGA I.12, 54.

77. See above, pp. 50, 54.

78. *On Religion*, 41.

79. Ibid., 59. Just prior to this statement Schleiermacher remarked, "You know that the manner in which each single element of humanity appears in an individual depends upon the manner in which it is limited or set free by the rest; only through this general conflict does each element in each individual attain a definite form and magnitude, and this conflict is sustained, in turn, only through the community of individuals and the movement of the whole."

80. Ibid., 40; see above, p. 35.

81. *On Religion*, 42.

82. See above, p. 8.

83. *On Religion*, 12.

84. Ibid., 104.

85. Schleiermacher, KGA I.12, 265. Another passage that Schleiermacher modified in 1806 is also of interest. In the first edition, defending the propriety of speaking of individual religious developments within an already-established religion, he says concerning the choice of a central intuition, "I hope you will not say that something natural or inherited could have an influence on that"; in the second edition this is modified to read, "I hope…that you will not at all see in this similarity a mechanical influence of the accustomed or inherited, but rather, as you do in other cases, recognize only a common determination (*Bestimmtsein*) from higher sources." *On Religion*, 105; KGA I.12, 268.

86. *On Religion*, 107.

87. Ibid.

88. Ibid.

89. The first edition of the *Monologen* is found in KGA I.3, 1–61, and the later editions in KGA I.12, 323–93. *Schleiermacher's Soliloquies*, translated by Horace Leland Friess is an English translation of the first edition with notes regarding Schleiermacher's revisions. The most useful discussion of the *Monologen* in English is Brent Sockness, "Schleiermacher and the Ethics of Authenticity."

90. Sockness, for example, describes "a sea-change in Schleiermacher's philosophy of life and moral outlook" between the years 1793 and 1800. Three aspects of the *Monologen* provide the principal evidence for this "sea change," the most relevant for my purposes being the fact that "a remarkable *defense* of freedom now appears, a quite radical freedom difficult, on my reading at least, to distinguish from the transcendental sort which 'On Freedom' was designed to refute." Sockness, "Was Schleiermacher a Virtue Ethicist?" 31. Ulrich Barth also espies in the *Monologen* an "almost Fichtean pathos of freedom" and notes concerning that text's celebration of the "beloved consciousness of freedom" that "such statements make it clear that Schleiermacher has traversed a long road in thinking since his first attempts on the subject of freedom, which were still entirely filled with sympathy for ethical determinism." Barth, *Aufgeklärter Protestantismus*, 311. John Crossley Jr. has also addressed the topic of freedom in the *Monologen*, but his position on the topic is difficult to assess; see note 107 this chapter.

91. Mariña, *Transformation of the Self*. I am grateful to Mariña for allowing me access to the manuscript version of her important book. I make use of her translations of the *Monologen* when reproducing passages that she cites from that work; elsewhere translations are my own and are labeled as such. One of the things at stake for Mariña in the question of whether Schleiermacher was a determinist is the question of whether religion can be "reduced to or explained in naturalistic terms alone"; she pronounces the view of Schleiermacher as "a determinist who believed religion could be thoroughly explained naturalistically" (which she attributes to me) as "certainly mistaken" (4n2). What for Mariña exempts religion from the fate of being so explainable is the fact that as she reads Schleiermacher, "religious experience has its origins in the transcendental conditions of subjectivity itself " and "is grounded in an absolute that transcends the self " (3f.). So far as I can see, this claim does not conflict with the postulate of determinism. It does, however, raise the issue of the role of Schleiermacher's various claims regarding the relationship between religious consciousness and God or the transcendent in his account of religion. I lay out my position on this subject in chapter 4, pp. 166–73.

92. KGA I.3, 12; cited in Mariña, *Transformation*, 128.

93. KGA I.3, 9; cited in Mariña, *Transformation*, 129.

94. KGA I.3, 10; cited in Mariña, *Transformation*, 128.

95. Mariña, *Transformation*, 128.

96. Ibid., 129. This claim itself requires the postulation of a change of position on Schleiermacher's part; earlier in the book Mariña documents Schleiermacher's extensive arguments against Kant, expressed in his early study essay *Spinozismus*, to the effect that "no equation allows itself to be made between identity of consciousness

and rational self-determination or independence from the mechanism of nature."
KGA I.1, 543; cited in Mariña, *Transformation*, 97.

97. KGA I.3, 10; cited in Mariña, *Transformation*, 129f.

98. Mariña, *Transformation*, 131f.

99. Ibid., 130. On the same page Mariña offers an illustration of the kind of freedom that she believes Schleiermacher had in mind: "To give an example from ethical life: the loveless actions of another can be received either as an affront or as a sign of the impoverished life of the other, and therefore as a call for help that must be met in the spirit of forgiveness. One is receptive to the world and to others, but the light in which those actions are received is the province of human freedom." It should also be noted that she also took account of Schleiermacher's characterization of necessity as "the determinate tone of the beautiful clash of freedoms," as well as his remark that "[f]reedom finds its limitation in another freedom, and whatever happens freely bears the marks of limitation and community" (KGA I.3, 10; cited in Mariña, *Transformation*, 132). As she reads these passages, "Schleiermacher does not here propose that we are *absolutely* free. Our freedom is curtailed by the material stuff of the world as well as by the freedom of other human selves" (132); "From the actual existence of other selves stems 'necessity,' that is, the curtailment of human freedom by what is genuinely other than the self. An infinite number of spiritual beings restrict the freedom through which the self can express itself" (133). Thus, on her view the freedom Schleiermacher embraced in this text is restricted in important but elusive respects.

100. KGA I.3, 10; cited in Mariña, *Transformation*, 130.

101. See below, chapter 4 note 34.

102. See above, p. 54.

103. Mariña, *Transformation*, 133.

104. In the letter that accompanied the submission of the *Monologen* to Brinckmann, Schleiermacher wrote, "I ask that you not criticize this little work, which—to my sorrow I confess it—arose in not quite four weeks too severely with respect to the language in the details, because I have not had time to come to the composure which is required of these finishing touches; but I would like to know how you are affected on the whole." KGA I.3, xxii. See also Sockness's description of the circumstances behind the *Monologen* in "Schleiermacher and the Ethics of Authenticity," 478–82.

105. Ungern-Sternberg, for example, saw the "feeling of necessity as the consciousness of the 'totality' of the self" as a common theme in both "On Human Freedom" and the *Monologen* and took the latter text's call to "be ever more that which you are" as a sign of the presence of the doctrine of necessity (Ungern-Sternberg, *Freiheit und Wirklichkeit*, 94). Richard Brandt remarked concerning Schleiermacher's talk of freedom in the *Monologen* that "it is precisely through an understanding of what he meant by this word that we can best appreciate the relationship between his determinism and his high valuation of social intercourse" (Brandt, *Philosophy of Schleiermacher*, 54, 134). Paul Siefert also saw no conceptual break between the *Speeches* and the *Monologen* on the subject of freedom: "This determination is no fetter (*Fessel*), otherwise the *Monologen* could not speak of freedom in straightforwardly

Fichtean tones. In fact, this binding makes free" (Siefert, *Theologie*, 136). See also note 111 this chapter regarding Jørgensen.

106. See above, p. 56. Siefert called particular attention to the relevant passage from the *Speeches* in discussing the commonalities between that text and the *Monologen*; see Siefert, *Theologie*, 135f.

107. John Crossley Jr., in "Ethical Impulse in Schleiermacher's Early Ethics," offers similar observations concerning the standpoint from which the *Monologen* was written, but it is not entirely clear whether his reading of the text is the same as mine or not. On the one hand Crossley fully acknowledges Schleiermacher's early embrace of determinism and claims that "[t]he relationship between freedom and necessity which Schleiermacher establishes to his satisfaction in 'On Human Freedom'…carries straight through the *Soliloquies* of 1800 and, indeed, straight through all his later lectures on ethics" (15). However, his description of this relationship as it operates in the *Monologen* is elusive. In discussing remarks by Schleiermacher on the "inward perspective" on the self, Crossley notes that "[t]he most striking aspect of these remarks is the clear connection of freedom with the development of the inner, spiritual life. Here Schleiermacher is not talking about freedom as the absence of causal compulsion, which is a freedom shared by all human beings within the framework of determination by the state of mind. Here he is talking about the freedom to alter one's state of mind, a freedom potentially open to anyone, but experienced only by those who turn their eyes inward" (16). Also, "The inner freedom one has to develop his or her character makes it possible for the individual actually to make an impression on the external world, which otherwise operates under laws of causal determination. From the vantage point of self-consciousness, the real world is perceived to be the inner world of free souls, not the external world of necessity" (20). Neither of these passages is entirely clear on the question of whether the free self-development of character also takes place of necessity, and certain turns of phrase seem to cut against this notion.

108. KGA I.3, XXII, 6.

109. Ibid., I.12, 326f.

110. See above, p. 50.

111. Jørgensen states, "Insofar as I myself am concerned and precisely the fact that within me an unfolding is occurring, I must therefore say that I belong to the high world of freedom.… But in the same instant, where I turn my action outwards towards the world and thereby enter into a relationship with it, in the way in which I admit myself into communality with that which is found in it, then do I indeed enter into the realm of necessity, where the eternal laws apply. Necessity is therefore posited outside of me, it is posited in the reciprocal affecting and community of all other individuals. I have then, in order to remain in the terminology of the *Dialektik*, concretized my action, changed it from the 'in itself' to the 'for itself,' and thereby subjected myself to the necessary succession which is always valid in 'coexistence.'" Jørgensen, *Ethik*, 160.

112. KGA I.3, 10, my translation.

113. KGA I.3, 11, my translation.

114. See, for example, *Philosophical Ethics*, 141–51, in particular 147. See also above, p. 52.

115. This locution is drawn from Schleiermacher's *Brief Outline on the Study of Theology*; KGA I.6, 337; *Brief Outline*, 27.

116. KGA II.10.2, 220.

117. *Philosophical Ethics*, 161, translation modified; *Ethik 1812/13*, 217.

118. *Philosophical Ethics*, 158.

119. Ibid., 157f.

120. Ibid., 158; *Ethik 1812/13*, 213.

121. The address is found in the KGA I.11, 431–51. A helpful English discussion of the address is George Boyd, "Schleiermacher's 'Über den Unterschied,' " 41–49.

122. KGA I.11, 433.

123. Ibid., 435.

124. Ibid., 446.

125. Ibid., 447. In discussing this essay Georg Behrens calls attention to Schleiermacher's resistance to the idea that the entirety of the natural order is governed by the "dead mechanism" observable within material bodies. Concerning the understanding of natural law presented in the address Behrens argues that "[n]ature, [Schleiermacher] thinks, must be conceived as a system in which higher principles of organization are not epiphenomenal with respect to the lower principles. The laws governing spiritual and even organic beings are irreducible to those governing elementary particles" (Behrens, "Order of Nature," 106). It is possible that Schleiermacher did hold that higher-order laws are irreducible to lower-order ones, although I can find no clear statement of this principle in his texts. If this was indeed his view, he would qualify as an emergentist about the capabilities of organisms and rational beings. There is, however, a tension between the position that the entirety of the nature system is governed by deterministic relationships of cause and effect (a position that Behrens attributed to Schleiermacher) and the idea of emergent orders of natural law that cannot be reduced to collections of lower-level laws.

126. KGA I.11, 447.

127. Ibid., 448.

128. Ibid.

129. Ibid., 448f.

130. Ibid., 449f.

131. See Brandt, *Philosophy of Schleiermacher*, 56ff., for discussion of the connection of this account to the philosophy of Schelling.

132. Boyd states: "The conclusion Schleiermacher drew from his description of an evolutionary process which produces human life is that within the single organic process and unity known as 'world,' moral law (laws of reason) is the designation for the determinative principles controlling that level of development which we distinguish as conscious/intelligent/rational, just as natural law (laws of nature) is the designation of the principles controlling all those aspects of the world that are not conscious." Boyd, "Schleiermacher's 'Über den Unterschied,' " 46.

133. Kant, *Religion within the Boundaries*, 47.

134. CG2 §66.2; KGA I.13,1 408 (273). Also, "Now if we imagine a state such that the flesh, that is the totality of the so-called lower powers of the soul, has a susceptibility only for the impulses which proceed from the locus of the God-consciousness, without being an independent motivating principle: then a conflict

between the two is not possible, but then we have then imagined a sinless state.... But so long as both have not yet become one in this sense, spirit and flesh exist as two opposed agencies; and insofar as the spirit presses towards that perfect unity, this state can only be appreciated as an incapacity of the same." KGA I.13, 1 407 (272).

135. CG2 §65.1; KGA I.13, 1 403 (269). I discuss Schleiermacher's conception of the divine causality in chapter 4, pp. 154f. The best discussion in English of Schleiermacher's understanding of evil in the *Glaubenslehre* is Robert Adams, "Schleiermacher on Evil."

CHAPTER 2

1. Seifert, *Theologie*, 88.

2. As Christian Albrecht puts it, the hermeneutical difficulty of the *Speeches* is such that the path that concentrates on the "principal theses" of religion's "original independence" and autonomy offers a relatively manageable project. See Albrecht, *Frömmigkeit*, 105ff. A different kind of response that has surfaced from time to time in the literature is to deny that a theory of religion can be distilled from this early text; see Grove, *Deutungen*, 254ff., for a brief survey of various responses to the problem of identifying such a theory in the *Speeches*.

3. Terence Tice, "Schleiermacher and the Study of Religion," in Richardson, *Friedrich Schleiermacher*, 66f. It is worth noting that the Oman translation of the *Speeches* greatly abetted the practice of disregarding all but the second speech by rendering its title, "Das Wesen der Religion," as "The Nature of Religion."

4. This procedure is far from novel. In 1901 Eugen Huber observed that in the *Glaubenslehre*, as well as in the *Speeches*, Schleiermacher vacillated between speaking of religion in a "narrow sense" and in a "broad sense," with the "narrow sense" referring roughly to religion's essence and the "broad sense" to actual, historical religion (Huber, *Die Entwicklung des Religionsbegriff*, 292). More recently Christian Albrecht has also distinguished three senses of religion in the *Speeches*, although his characterizations differ from mine: first, "the individual inclination of subjective consciousness (in the sense of 'religiosity')"; second, "the different empirically observable formations of religious community (*Gemeinshaftsbildungen*) (in the sense of 'positive religions')"; and third, "['religion'] occasionally serves, in an overarching sense, to describe a supra-individual, spiritual-cultural phenomenon (in the sense of the 'generally religious')." Albrecht, *Frömmigkeit*, 12. To reiterate a point from my introduction, my focus is on the second of these three senses of "religion."

5. *On Religion*, 22, 23, 26.

6. Indeed, the conflation between religion and religion's essence sometimes extends to the point that the grammatical specificity of the first passage cited here is overridden. A good example is found in Grove, who presents this passage ("religion's essence...is intuition and feeling") as "the famous definition of religion (*Religionsdefinition*) of the *Speeches*," claiming that here Schleiermacher lays out a "characterization (*Bestimmung*) of religion as intuition and feeling" (Grove, *Deutungen*, 273). Thus, Grove reads this passage, which is grammatically about religion's essence, as a claim about religion as such. In a sense my interpretation is a mirror image of Grove's: I read this passage according to its plain sense, as a claim about religion's

essence, but read the other cited passages, which are grammatically about religion, as advancing claims about religion's essence.

7. *On Religion*, 25, 73, 112.

8. Ibid., 96, 108, 111.

9. This state of affairs is clearly visible even in W. C. Smith's *Meaning and End of Religion*, a text known for its opposition to essentialism in the study of religion. Smith's criticisms of essentialism are, so far as I can see, encapsulated in his remark that "essences do not have a history. Essences do not change. Yet it is an observable and important fact that what have been called the religions do, in history, change" (Smith, *Meaning and End of Religion*, 143f.). Smith seems to regard the content of the notion of essence as self-evident; at least he says nothing about what sort of thing an essence was supposed to be according to the theorists who worked with the notion, nor about how the term functioned in their work. More recently, although Walter Capps titled the first chapter of his *Religious Studies: The Making of a Discipline* "The Essence of Religion," he never discussed the term "essence" in his text—not even in his discussion of Schleiermacher—and the term does not appear in his index. He did discuss what he terms the "first principle" of religion (also referred to as a sine qua non or religious a priori) as *"that without which religion would not be what it truly is"* (xviii). None of three recent, relatively high-profile collaborative reference works on the methodology of the study of religion (*Critical Terms for Religious Studies, Guide to the Study of Religion*, or *Routledge Companion to the Study of Religion*) consider "essence" to be a topic worthy of independent treatment, the historical importance of this notion for the field notwithstanding. Such mentions that are to be found in these works suggest roughly the same degree of familiarity with the notion as displayed by Smith.

10. For example, in the *Guide to the Study of Religion*, Gregory Alles opines that "it is doubtful that religion has an essence, that is, a common defining character that is everywhere the same" ("Exchange," in Braun and McCutcheon's *Guide to the Study of Religion*, 114). Talal Asad's brief references, in the first chapter of *Genealogies of Religion*, to "religion's essence," while they do reflect at least some of what was at stake for Schleiermacher (specifically, the question of religion's distinctness from politics), display the same brevity: "[T]he insistence that religion has an autonomous essence— not to be confused with the essence of science, or of politics, or of common sense— invites us to define religion (like any essence) as a transhistorical and transcultural phenomenon" (*Genealogies of Religion*, 28). Tomoko Masuzawa, in *The Invention of World Religions*, unpacks her phrase "unreconstituted religious essentialists" simply as referring to those who take "religion" to name "a category sui generis," an identification that brings no clarity to either locution (*Invention of World Religions*, 7).

11. Gelman, *Essential Child*.

12. Ibid., 277.

13. Ibid., 6. Gelman's discussion is not restricted to this generic form of essentialism: In fact, the introduction to her book provides one of the clearest and most useful discussions of the varieties of essentialism that I have encountered. Later in the book she hypothesizes that "essentialism is a species-general, universal, inevitable mode of thought—but that the form that it takes varies specifically according to the culture at hand, with the basic notion of essentialism becoming elaborated in each culture's complex theories of nature and society" (283).

14. For an example of a discussion that both reflects the association of essentialism with common sense and displays a marked lack of clarity concerning just what essentialism commits one to, see Stephan Fuchs, *Against Essentialism*, in particular 12ff. Gelman explicitly distinguishes the question of essentialism as a "habit of mind" from that of essentialism as a metaphysical doctrine and advances no claims about whether any form of essentialism is reflective of the structure of reality (Gelman, *Essential Child*, 10).

15. Locke, *Essay concerning Human Understanding*, 417. My discussion of the diversity of discussions of essentialism in analytic philosophy is based on Mike Rea's treatment in *World without Design*, 99–104.

16. So, for example, Diana Fuss defines essentialism as "a belief in the real, true essences of things, the invariable and fixed properties which define the 'whatness' of a given entity," a position that suggests "the idea that men and women, for example, are identified as such on the basis of transhistorical, eternal, immutable essences." Fuss, *Essentially Speaking*, xi. For a helpful survey of controversies surrounding the notion of "essence" within feminism and feminist theology, see Armour, *Deconstruction*, 16–22. A recent article on Edward Said by Irfan Khawaja focuses usefully on essentialism concerning *doctrines*. A subcategory of essentialism in general, essentialism about doctrines, according to Khawaja, involves claims in five areas: definitional identity, synchronic identity, diachronic identity, explanatory power, and logical implication (i.e., questions of what embracing a doctrine entails, regardless of whether those who embrace the doctrine realize it or not). Both Islam and Orientalism count as doctrines in Khawaja's sense of the term, and where Said's *Orientalism* was dedicated to a criticism of essentialism about Islam, Khawaja points out that Said explicitly embraced essentialism about Orientalism itself. Khawaja, "Essentialism, Consistency, and Islam."

17. My familiarity with the literature on the notion of essence suggests that it is primarily the legacy of Ernst Troeltsch that has kept interest in the subject alive in English. For discussions that are well informed and critical without being dismissive see Stephen Sykes, "Ernst Troeltsch and Christianity's Essence"; also Sykes, *Identity of Christianity*. Lori Pearson's *Beyond Essence* is a significant contribution to this literature. In German the best recent study of the notion of "essence" in Schleiermacher's work is Schröder, *Die kritische Identität*.

18. "What Does the 'Essence of Christianity' Mean?" was initially published in 1903 in *Die christliche Welt*, and Troeltsch substantively revised it in 1913 for republication among his collected works. A translation of the revised version by Michael Pye appears in Troeltsch, *Writings on Theology and Religion*, 124–79.

19. Troeltsch, *Writings on Theology and Religion*, 124, 129.

20. Ibid., 130, emphasis in the original.

21. Ibid., 141.

22. Ibid., 141, emphasis in the original.

23. Ibid., 144.

24. On this point see Huber, *Entwicklung*, 15ff.

25. *On Religion*, 24.

26. Ibid., 25, 34, 38f., 44.

27. For a useful discussion of the notion of "religious intuition" in the first edition of the *Speeches* see Grove, *Deutungen*, 290–306. Grove emphasizes that a

religious intuition for Schleiermacher has the character of an *interpretation* of ordinary experience; it is not intuition pure and simple but "*intuition of something as something, namely intuition of an individual thing as a depiction of the universe*" (295); emphasis in the original.

28. *On Religion*, 29, 35, 37f.

29. Ibid., 36, 54.

30. Ibid., 28.

31. Ibid., 45.

32. Ibid., 46.

33. Ibid.

34. Ibid., 29.

35. Ibid., 73.

36. Ibid.

37. Ibid.

38. Ibid., 48. Cf. also 96: "[W]hy should the inner, true church be one? It is so that each person may intuit and let the religion of another be imparted to him that he cannot intuit as his own and that was thought to be wholly different from it."

39. Ibid., 75.

40. Ibid., 50. In the early part of the third speech, Schleiermacher argues that religion, in the specific sense of a capacity to produce "intuitions of the universe," cannot be "taught." It should be clear, on the basis of the passages presented above, that this does not amount to the claim that religion cannot be communicated. I take his point to be that the communicative activities by which the ability to intuit is "awakened" cannot be *formalized* or *routinized* but requires the kind of flexibility and personal attention that only intimate fellowship can provide.

41. Ibid., 58.

42. Ibid., 75.

43. Ibid., 87.

44. Ibid., 75f.

45. Ibid., 76f.

46. In his introductory essay to Schleiermacher's lectures on ethics, Braun remarks that it was only around 1800 that Schleiermacher began to develop a sense of the necessity of community for the development of true individuality. Although this clearly emerges as a prominent theme in the ethics lectures in a way it does not in the *Speeches*, it seems clear to me that the *Speeches* clearly express the view that participation in religious community is required for religious formation or enculturation. See Friedrich Schleiermacher, *Schleiermachers Werke*, vol. 2, xff. Bernd Oberdorfer's *Geselligkeit und Realisierung von Sittlichkeit* further demonstrates that the social dimension of human life in general was critically important to Schleiermacher prior to his composition of the *Speeches* and has an important point of origin in Schleiermacher's exploration of Aristotle on the topic of friendship. Ted Vial also notes that the "formative" aspect of worship is a frequently overlooked aspect of Schleiermacher's thought; see Vial, "Friedrich Schleiermacher on the Central Place of Worship," 64f.

47. *On Religion*, 25f.

48. Metaphysics as Schleiermacher described it "classifies the universe and divides it into this being and that, seeks out the reasons for what exists, and deduces

the necessity of what is real while spinning the reality of the world and its laws out of itself." Ibid., 20.

49. Ibid., 27f.

50. Ibid., 86.

51. Ibid., 87. In his response to Sack's criticisms of the *Speeches* Schleiermacher expressed the same point in milder terms: "I have said clearly enough that I consider our church as presently constituted to be a double institution, dedicated in part to religion and in part to morality" (Blackwell, "The Antagonistic Correspondence," 119).

52. *On Religion*, 115. At greater length: "Judaism is long since a dead religion, and those who at present still bear its colors are actually sitting and mourning beside the undying mummy and weeping over its demise and sad legacy.... [Judaism] died when its holy books were closed; then the conversation with Jehovah with his people was viewed as ended; the political association that was linked to it dragged on in an ailing existence, and its external parts were preserved even longer still, the unpleasant appearance of a mechanical movement after the life and spirit had long since departed" (ibid.). For a discussion of Schleiermacher's conception of Judaism and its sources, see Joseph Pickle, "Schleiermacher on Judaism."

53. See especially *On Religion*, 70f.

54. CG2 §6 Zusatz; KGA I.13, 1 58 (29). See also the translators' footnote appended to this passage in the English edition. In fact, Schleiermacher's usage of the term in the first ten sections of the second edition does not entirely fit this description. There are indeed places where Schleiermacher appears to substitute "*religiös*" for his usual "*fromm*" for the sake of variety, as when he speaks of "*religiöse Erregungen*" and "*religiöse Gemeinschaft*" in §6. Some of the uses of "*Religion*" that do not clearly fit this description are formal terms (*Religionsphilosophie, Religionsgeschichte*); the consistent pattern of the remainder of his usage suggests that he found the term useful primarily in its broadest sense, as encompassing not only phenomena with a relatively immediate relationship to piety but also those that stand at some remove or in fact phenomena whose relationship to piety is not immediately evident. It is in this sense that he used the terminology "*religiöses Gebiet*," "*religiöse Sätze*" (§3), "*religiöses Leben*" (§6) and speaks of a particular "*Religionsform*" (§7–8), of "*Religion*" and "*Religionen*" (§7–10), of "*religiösen Symbolen*" (§8), and of "*religiösen Mysterien*" (§10).

55. Even otherwise careful readers sometimes present his account in this light. Richard Niebuhr puts the point thus: "Piety or religion is the name of the level of self-consciousness that is the most decisive of all." Niebuhr, *Schleiermacher on Christ and Religion*, 184. Throughout the book Niebuhr speaks of religion according to Schleiermacher as "a mode of self-consciousness." Both the conflation of religion and piety and attempts to maintain the distinction between them are in evidence in the German literature as well. Huber, for instance, presented this distinction as a corrective to D. F. Strauss's criticisms of Schleiermacher. According to Huber, Strauss missed the specific intentions of the *Glaubenslehre*, which "wanted not at all to define objective religion, but only subjective piety. Visible actions, cults, and organizations were not at all of interest. It defined only a spiritual fact in the life of the individual, not a communal fact." Huber, *Entwicklung*, 236. I think Huber overstated the case somewhat; while it is true that piety was a major locus of interest for Schleiermacher

in the *Glaubenslehre*, the entire project is oriented toward engagement with one aspect of outward religion, religious doctrine.

56. CG2 §6 Zusatz; KGA I.13, 1 58f. (29f.). Compare the first-edition version of this discussion in CG1 §12.3, KGA I.7, 1 42f.

57. CG2 §6 Zusatz; KGA I.13, 1 59 (30).

58. CG2 §4; KGA I.13, 1 32 (12).

59. The topic of "immediacy" in Schleiermacher's thought has been a topic of a great deal of discussion in the literature; useful treatments are found in Albrecht, *Schleiermachers Theorie*, 236ff., and Grove, *Deutungen*, 481–530 and 595ff. For my purposes the only pressing question in connection with Schleiermacher's appeal to "immediacy" is whether this appeal amounts to a claim of self-authentication or direct awareness of reality in general or God in particular. I discuss this topic in chapter 4, pp. 168ff.

60. CG2 §4.3; KGA I.13, 1 38 (16).

61. Cramer, "Die eine Frömmigkeit und die vielen Frommen," 333f.

62. CG2 §4.4; KGA I.13, 1 38f. (16).

63. I discuss the relationship between the content of the feeling of absolute dependence and the state of affairs of being in relation to God further in chapter 4, pp. 166–73.

64. CG2 §5.4; KGA I.13, 1 48 (22f.)

65. CG2 §5.1; KGA I.13, 1 42f. (19).

66. CG2 §5.3; KGA I.13, 1 46 (21).

67. CG2 §5.3; KGA I.13, 1 47 (22).

68. CG2 §5.3; KGA I.13, 1 46 (21). Compare the wording of the first edition: "no-one will be able to become conscious of an absolutely general feeling of dependence upon God, but rather always one referred to a particular condition." CG1 §10.5; KGA I.7, 1 37.

69. CG1 §16.1; KGA I.7, 1 55.

70. CG2 §4.4; KGA I.13, 1 39 (17).

71. CG2 §5 Zusatz; KGA I.13, 1 52 (25).

72. See §8 in the second edition, especially §8.2.

73. Schleiermacher seems not to be entirely consistent on this point. God-consciousness, for example, would seem to be a component of piety and indeed a fundamental component since (as Schleiermacher stated) it is only through the development of the God-consciousness that individuals become aware of their absolute dependence. But because God-consciousness makes reference to something other than the self, it does not accord with Schleiermacher's technical definition of "feeling." Thus, if God-consciousness is a component of piety, then piety is not entirely a matter of feeling. A remark by Schröder addresses this tension between the character of God-consciousness and its identification as an element of piety: "Since God-consciousness, as the intentional composition (*Fassung*) of religious feeling, emerges from reflection on pious feeling, it must be the 'most immediate reflection,' that is to say the 'most original representation' of religious consciousness, which must be defined as a kind of referentiality in which as yet no object is predicated." Schröder, *Die kritische Identität*, 33. In support of this reading Schröder cites two marginal notes that Schleiermacher appended to his discussion of the concept of God in the first

edition of *The Christian Faith*: "God only my reflection—but certainly the innermost within everything and most original," and "the religious doctrine of God is only an analysis of subjectivity" (KGA I.7, 3 22, 33). For my purposes the question of Schleiermacher's consistency on this point is relatively unimportant, as is the question of precisely where the boundaries of piety lie.

74. CG2 §3.4; KGA I.13, 1 26f. (8f.).

75. CG2 §3.4; KGA I.13, 1 29 (10).

76. CG2 §15; KGA I.13, 1 127 (76).

77. CG2 §6.2; KGA I.13, 1 55 (27).

78. CG2 §15.1; KGA I.13, 1 128 (77).

79. CG2 §15.1; KGA I.13, 1 128 (77).

80. CG2 §18.3; KGA I.13,1 142 (87).

81. I have discussed this topic further in "Schleiermacher's Theological Anti-Realism."

82. CG2 §16 Zusatz; KGA I.13,1 135 (82f.).

83. Indeed, Schleiermacher defended his identification of statements about the self as the "fundamental form" of Christian doctrines on precisely these grounds: "[I]t is clear that descriptions of human states of mind with this content can only be taken from the realm of inner experience, and that therefore in this form nothing alien can creep into the Christian doctrine of faith (*Glaubenslehre*), while expressions of qualities of the world can indeed be natural-scientific, and conceptions of divine modes of action purely metaphysical" (CG2 §30.2; KGA I.13,1 194 [126]).

84. *On Religion*, 25.

85. Ulrich Barth's comments on the methodology of the *Speeches* are relevant here. Barth characterizes Schleiermacher's approach as a "diagnosis of the times" (*Zeitdiagnose*), highlighting Schleiermacher's appropriation from the field of medicine of concepts such as "healthy" or "unhealthy." It is because it has this character that Schleiermacher's discussion "is in no way capable of attaining the level of plausibility of pure conceptual knowledge, let alone the exactitude of nomological cognition." Barth, *Aufgeklärter Protestantismus*, 269.

CHAPTER 3

1. Oberdorfer, *Geselligkeit*, 522.

2. For a complete accounting of Schleiermacher's activities during his early period see the KGA I.1 and I.2. Louden identifies the following essays as constituting Schleiermacher's early ethical corpus: "Notes on Aristotle: Nichomachean Ethics 8–9" (1788); "On the Highest Good" (1789); "On Human Freedom" (1790–1792); "On the Value of Life" (1792–1793); "Attempt at a Theory of Sociable Conduct" (1799) (Louden, viii–xvii). Louden does not identify a middle period in Schleiermacher's writings on ethics, and so includes the *Monologen*, the *Grundlinien*, and the *Brouillon* in the early period as well (xviii–xxiii).

3. Volume II.1 of the KGA, not yet published, will be dedicated to Schleiermacher's philosophical ethics. The most recent German edition of the Berlin ethics lectures is *Ethik (1812/13)*. *Lectures on Philosophical Ethics*, edited by Louden, is a translation of the Birkner edition. Citations from the Berlin lectures are drawn from

the Louden edition, with parenthetical page references to the Birkner edition; translations are those of Huish unless otherwise noted. I regularly substitute "ethical" for Huish's "moral" as a rendering of *sittlich* and "antithesis" for her "opposition" as a rendering of *Gegensaz* (*Gegensatz*).

4. The KGA I.11 contains the texts of Schleiermacher's academy lectures. Sockness calls attention to six of these in particular that bear on ethical themes: "On the Scientific Treatment of the Concept of Virtue" (1819), "Attempt at a Scientific Treatment of the Concept of Duty" (1824), "On the Difference between Natural Law and Moral Law" (1825), "On the Concept of the Permitted" (1826), and "On the Concept of the Highest Good" (presented in two parts in 1827 and 1828). Sockness, "Forgotten Moralist," 342.

5. *Die christliche Sitte nach dem Grundsätzen des evangelischen Kirche*, in *Friedrich Schleiermachers Sämmtliche Werke*, I.12, ed. Jonas et al. An updated critical edition is forthcoming as vol. II.5 of the Schleiermacher KGA. For an overview of the *Christliche Sittenlehre* see Eilert Herms, "Schleiermacher's Christian Ethics."

6. The first edition text of the *Monologen* is contained in the KGA I.3, the later editions in I.12. The *Grundlinien* is contained in KGA I.4.

7. The texts of the *Brouillon* are contained in *Werke, Auswahl in vier Bänden*, vol. 2, hereafter designated as *WA*. An English translation is by John Wallhauser, *Brouillon zur Ethik: Notes on Ethics (1805/1806); Notes on the Theory of Virtue (1804/1805)*. A helpful overview of the *Brouillon* is Wallhauser, "Schleiermacher's Brouillon zur Ethik, 1805/06." Citations of passages from the *Brouillon* are drawn from *WA*, and translations are my own unless otherwise noted.

8. See chapter 1, pp. 65–68.

9. *Brouillon*, *WA* 80.

10. KGA I.6, 257.

11. *Philosophical Ethics*, 5 (8).

12. The distinction between *Moralität* and *Sittlichkeit* will be most familiar to readers of Hegel, who also made this distinction a basis for his ethical writings. See Allen Wood, *Hegel's Ethical Thought*, in particular 195ff., and Terry Pinkard, "Virtues, Morality, and Sittlichkeit," in particular 226–229. I borrow the translation of *Sittlichkeit* as "ethical life" from Wood, although in some cases I render *Sittlichkeit* as "ethical character," particularly where it is predicated of features of human subjectivity or activity; see, for example, note 68 this chapter.

13. Scholtz, *Ethik und Hermeneutik*, 35; Sockness, "Forgotten Moralist," 343; Grove, *Deutungen*, 377.

14. This point was made more than once during the 1960s and in fact formed the starting point for the reflections of both Garczyk and Spiegel; see Garczyk, *Mensch, Gesellschaft, Geschichte*, 22; Spiegel, *Bürgerlichen Gesellschaft*, 16f.

15. So Nowak: "Since human beings were [for Schleiermacher] social beings, so that their ethical formation (*sittliche Gestaltwerdung*) did not extend to an (abstract) individual, ethics also had to encompass all social relations which would arise here in nature's becoming reasonable." *Schleiermacher*, 159.

16. *Philosophical Ethics* 8 (11), translation modified.

17. See Oberdorfer, *Geselligkeit*, in particular 23–77.

18. For an accessible discussion of the form-content distinction in Simmel's work, see Theodore Abel, *Systematic Sociology in Germany*, 19ff. The most prominent

point of contact between the work of Schleiermacher and Simmel has historically been the attention both of them dedicated to a particular social form, that of "sociability" (*Geselligkeit*). In a 1931 overview of German sociological theory, for example, Karl Dunkmann acknowledged Schleiermacher and Simmel as the two "masterful interpreters" of this social form (Dunkmann, "Soziologie der Religion," in *Lehrbuch der Soziologie und Sozialphilosophie*, 225). Indeed, between Schleiermacher's "Toward a Theory of Sociable Conduct" (1799) and Simmel's "Sociology of Sociability" (1910) there is an uncanny degree of resemblance, as Trutz Rendforff also noted (*Church and Theology*, 229). This essay can be found in *Georg Simmel on Individuality and Social Forms*, 127–40. Donald Levine's introduction to the volume is most helpful as an overview of Simmel's work on sociability; he also calls attention to Simmel's general reluctance to document his sources, which has made the task of tracing the influences on his work difficult. One 1938 article on the history of German sociology includes a diagram that charts direct lines of influence from Schleiermacher to Dilthey and Albert Schäffle, and (at the end of the nineteenth century) to Karl Dunkmann but not to Simmel ("Soziologie der Gegenwart in Deutschland," in *Deutscher Kulturatlas*, ed. Lüdtke and Mackensen, Bd. 5, Tafel 444 [1938]). Recently, however, Volkhard Krech has documented a fairly direct influence of Schleiermacher on Simmel's understanding of religion, including a set of more or less direct borrowings from *Christian Faith*; see Krech, *Georg Simmels Religionstheorie*, in particular 181–85.

19. See Tyrell, "Das Gesellige in der Religion," 35; Ulrich Barth, *Aufgeklärter Protestantismus*, 209ff. Christoph Dinkel makes points of comparison between Schleiermacher and Luhmann a persistent theme in *Kirche Gestalten*, crediting Michael Welker with drawing his attention to similarities between the two (see, e.g., 24, 108n23, 157n8, 264f.).

20. Simmel, "Problem of Sociology," in *Georg Simmel on Individuality and Social Forms*, 23. It might seem that seeing "society" as a term referring simply to the circles of association formed by individual persons is an idealist trope that contemporary scholars would be unlikely to embrace. But Bruce Lincoln understands "society" in much the same way, it seems: "Often…analyses of social institutions or systems of social organization pass for the analysis of society itself, and it is worth recalling that the elusive and ill-defined entity that we call society (from the Latin verb *socio*, to join or unite together, to associate) is basically a grouping of people who feel bound together as a collectivity and, in corollary fashion, feel themselves separate from others who fall outside their group." Lincoln, *Discourse and the Construction of Society*, 9.

21. This characterization is Peter Berger's; see his *Heretical Imperative*, 131.

22. So Martina Kumlehn, for example, speaks of the fourth speech as presenting for the first time "the empirical-functional definition of church community" which is characteristic of Schleiermacher's later theological writings. Kumlehn, *Symbolisierendes Handeln*, 112.

23. It is a commonplace that the biographical sources of Schleiermacher's conception of the "city of God" were his childhood experiences among the Moravians and his more recent participation in Berlin salon culture. The "city of God" combines the best features of both social contexts: on the one hand the sincerity and piety of the Herrnhutters, and on the other hand the delight in unfettered self-expression and creativity prized in the salons. See, for example, Spiegel, *Theologie*, 23, 226ff.; Nowak, *Schleiermacher*, 196f.

24. This essay was published anonymously in the *Berlinisches Archiv der Zeit und ihres Geschmacks* in January and February of 1799; the German text is found in the KGA I.2. An English translation by Jeffrey Hoover appeared as *Friedrich Schleiermacher's Toward a Theory*. My citations refer to the English translation, and translations are Hoover's. For a useful and interesting discussion of Schleiermacher's notion of "free sociability" as this was reflected in his friendship with Henrietta Herz, see William Rasch, "Ideal Sociability." Particularly useful is Rasch's distinction between "autonomy" from social relations as this notion is commonly attributed to Enlightenment thinkers and the more nuanced notion of "extrasocial spaces" explored by Schleiermacher (323ff.).

25. *Sociable Conduct*, 20.

26. Ibid., 21. Hoover translates *bürgerlich* as public rather than civic on the grounds that in the essay it seems to refer to any activity that takes place outside the home, that is, outside the private sphere (20n2).

27. Ibid., 24f.

28. Ibid., 28.

29. Ibid., 27f.

30. Ibid.

31. See below, p. 116.

32. See below, pp. 127ff.

33. *On Religion*, 75.

34. "It is plainly part of the perfection of a society that its members differ from one another as diversely as possible in their view of the object and their manner of treating it, since only in this way can the object be exhausted with respect to sociality and the character of the society fully developed." *Sociable Conduct*, 29f.

35. *On Religion*, 74.

36. So Oberdorfer: "Although religion cannot be the theme of conventional social conversation, where seriousness always appears connected with wit and steady exchange of speech and counterspeech dominates, while the 'intuition of the universe' is indeed an individual in such a strict sense that concerning it there can be no reasoning, but one of them can by its communication only be devoutly and without commentary accepted: so Schleiermacher thinks of true church as the hierarchy-free community for the reciprocal communication of such individual intuitions of the universe, which are in principle all of an equivalent dignity." Oberdorfer, *Geselligkeit*, 527.

37. *On Religion*, 79.

38. Ibid., 80.

39. Ibid., 86, 84.

40. Ibid., 81.

41. Ibid., 82.

42. Ibid., 84.

43. Ibid., 81.

44. Ibid., 85.

45. Ibid., 86f. Cf. also 85: "Would that even the most distant inkling of religion had ever remained foreign to all heads of state, all virtuosos and artists of politics!…For that has become for us the source of all corruption."

46. Ibid., 86f.

47. Ibid., 87.

48. Ibid.

49. Ibid.

50. Ibid., 90.

51. Ibid., 91. It should be recalled that the young Schleiermacher left the Moravian community at Barby over religious differences. His letters from the period and thereafter reveal that his departure was motivated in large part by the fact that his teachers prevented him from following his theological interests where these led him outside the formulations of their confession; that in hindsight, he regarded his departure as a major step in his own intellectual and spiritual development; that the resistance of some, in particular his father, to his independence of mind caused him great pain; and that in later years he looked back on his days with the Brethren with great fondness and in fact cited their communal practices with approval. It should be clear that the positions that I have attributed to him above speak to this episode in his life. If one reconstructs a picture of the ideal religious community on the basis of what Schleiermacher says in the *Speeches*, such a community would certainly have the piety, intimacy, and reverence of the Brethren—but would also have a tolerance and an openness to difference that might have allowed him to remain within the community while pursuing his own vision of Christianity.

52. Ibid., 88.

53. In his 1821/22 "Explanations" to the fourth speech, Schleiermacher noted that his earlier text voiced a preference for "smaller communions as against the great ecclesiastical institutions" and his particular concern that these be free from state control. In connection with his earlier vision of a number of "smaller and less definite" religious communities, he remarks, "When I first wrote this, America already seemed like a remarkably active stage, where everything took shape in such a way, and where on this account the freedom of religious life and of the religious community seemed to me more assured than anywhere else, our beloved fatherland not excepted. Since then this has continued to develop, and my intimation has been borne out. There, associations freely form and then dissolve again, smaller parts break free from a greater whole, and smaller wholes draw together to find a midpoint around which they might be able to form a greater unity." KGA I.12, 235.

54. See above, pp. 24–27.

55. In contrast to the Berlin lectures, the *Brouillon* is organized not by topics but by instructional hours.

56. Compare Schleiermacher's remarks on the same subject in the 1816/1817 Berlin lectures: "The opposition of good and evil means simply the setting against one another in each individual ethical domain of what is posited within it as the interrelatedness of reason and nature and what is posited as the separateness of the two." *Philosophical Ethics*, 157 (212).

57. *Brouillon*, WA 177. The remainder of the notes for the fifty-eighth hour concern the relationship of this claim to three competing definitions of religion; Schleiermacher reconciles each of these with his own claim by essentially restating them in the *Brouillon*'s technical vocabulary, evidence that suggests that he took his claim to comprehend each of these definitions. "It is said that 1) religion is immediate relation of the finite to the infinite. Now if the finite is nothing other here than reason

encompassed in the individual organization, then the infinite can be nothing other than the identity of reason with the totality of the real, and so the content of this formula is entirely the same. 2) In the same sense it is also said that religion is striving after reunification with the All. Now should this striving proceed from the identity of reason with organization, then its tendency cannot be destruction of organization; so only absolute community of these as a particular, delimited for itself, with the whole. 3) It is said that religion is community not with the world, but with God. But regardless of how one might set the two in opposition, God is always that in which the unity and totality of the world is posited. Therefore that which has been shown in fact amounts to community with God."

58. *Philosophical Ethics*, 155 (210).

59. Ibid., 158 (214).

60. "The functions of life are the formation (*Bilden*) of nature into an organ and the use of the organ for the activity of reason. There are no others besides these." *Brouillon*, WA 89.

61. See *Philosophical Ethics*, 168f. (231f.)

62. So, according to Sockness, in organizing activity "reason works to shape and organize its world, to transform nature into its instruments," and in symbolizing activity "reason stamps itself upon nature, as it were, converting it into its sign and symbol." "Forgotten Moralist," 344.

63. *Brouillon*, WA 88.

64. "To the individual we ascribe the character of nontransferability (*Unübertragbarkeit*). The adapted (*angebildet*) organ, insofar as it is the organ of particularity, cannot become that of another. Insofar as particularity remains in it, the cognition cannot similarly become another's living cognition." Ibid., 92.

65. On the continual circulation between organizing and symbolizing activity, see *Philosophical Ethics* 170ff (234f.); on the dialectical relationship between individuality and community see 181f. (247f.).

66. The term *ethical process* translates both *der ethische Prozeß* and *der sittliche Prozeß*. Both sets of terms are found and appear to be more or less interchangeable in the introduction to the 1812–1813 lectures; see ibid. 10f. (14f.).

67. "The concepts of person and personality are thus dependent solely upon the ethical domain, and on the manner of being individual and many within it; for the positing of others alongside oneself is as essential to the concept as is the distinguishing of oneself. The less an individual or a people is able to distinguish itself from others, the less personally developed it is in its ethical life (*Sittlichkeit*); the less it is able to posit and acknowledge others alongside itself, the less ethically developed it is in its personality." Ibid., 203 (274), translation modified.

68. "Self-consciousness which is sealed up inside personality is not an ethical act, because here reason stands under the power of nature; it can only become an ethical act by means of a reaction which supersedes that self-consciousness. It must become external in the form of cognition, in the same way as something objective does....The way in which self-consciousness becomes external to further the cognition of others is through depiction, and the ethical character (*Sittlichkeit*) of self-consciousness rests on the identical nature of the state of excitation and its depiction." Ibid., 22 (30), translation modified.

69. The passage cited in note 67 above continues, "There is no sense, however, in which the concept [of person] is restricted to individual human beings to such an extent that it can be applied to anything else only in a figurative sense; on the contrary, a family is a person and a people is a person in just the same way." Ibid., 203 (274f.).

70. For discussion of this scheme see Scholtz, *Ethik und Hermeneutik*, 36f., 129f.; Sockness, "Forgotten Moralist," 344f. A particularly useful diagrammatic representation of the forms of ethical activity in relation to Schleiermacher's "completed ethical forms" is found in Geck, "Sozialethische und sozialpolitische Ansätze," 136.

71. So, for example, Geck: "The sphere 'Church' is formed, in contrast [to that of the 'State'], by way of individual symbolization. It is the locus of a communication, which is in some way institutionalized, of a particular pious self-consciousness." Ibid., 137.

72. As Schleiermacher would put the point in 1816, "Thus, from individual self-consciousness to the collective consciousness of the human race, everything in ethical existence is an interaction of singleness and diversity, and thought and feeling are everywhere, and only external to each other in part; seclusion and communication are everywhere, and only relatively opposed to each other." *Philosophical Ethics* 191 (260), translation modified.

73. *Brouillon, WA* 156.

74. Ibid., 180.

75. Ibid., 176.

76. On this point Huber noted: "Now if intuition and feeling are distinguished as 'objective' and 'subjective' functions, it does not mean: intuition has an object to which it refers itself, while feeling proceeds entirely within the subject. Rather, feeling is also objective, in the sense that it has a *Gegenstand* [physical or actual object] as its *Objekt* [intentional object]. This follows from the fact that everything ethical, and thus also feeling, is a relation of reason to nature; it further follows that it can be called cognition." Huber, *Entwicklung*, 88.

77. "[T]he smallest domain of signification given to us is the consciousness enclosed in the body of each individual human being and mediated through it, so that self-consciousness is the most particular and non-transferable [aspect] of symbolizing activity. All feeling is in fact self-consciousness." *Philosophical Ethics* 191 (259).

78. This phrase is drawn from the final set of Berlin lectures, where Schleiermacher states this principle most clearly: "All in all, what we call feeling is the expression of reason in nature, just as thought is. It is an activity of life that has come to being in nature, but only because of reason, and this is true not only of ethical and religious feeling but also of bodily feeling, provided that it is posited as human, and as an entire moment of feeling. Feeling in itself is even less of an organ than thought, however, because it returns purely to itself. It is thus a definite expression of the way in which reason exists in this particular nature. For feeling, even of the very lowest kind, always expresses the effect that reason does or does not have within nature. And every feeling is always directed towards the unity of life, not towards something individual." Ibid., 190 (259), translation modified.

79. *Brouillon, WA* 98.

80. Ibid.

81. "But that seeking and desiring [of reciprocal communication] would always remain empty if feeling could not become known (*kund*) between one and the other. And in this, the relationship is the same as in the realm of thought. For feeling is also initially within consciousness, and given its particularity, its ethical character (*Sittlichkeit*) is conditioned upon the fact that its arising is at the same time its externalization (*Aeußerlichwerden*), and in that in this externalization it also becomes known (*kund*) to others; and this externalization of feeling is also to be seen as a consequence of the striving of reason to break through the confines of individuality, in order to be unified with itself, and to overcome once again the individuality (*Einzelwesen*) in which it is posited." *Philosophical Ethics* 197 (267), translation modified.

82. *Brouillon, WA* 180f.

83. Ibid., 181.

84. *Philosophical Ethics* 197 (267f.), my translation.

85. *Brouillon, WA* 100.

86. *Philosophical Ethics* 58 (77). Konrad Cramer has voiced skepticism concerning Schleiermacher's claim that feelings are "transmitted" between persons not as it were directly by a process of empathy but rather by way of mediation through the understanding of the feelings of another. Cramer takes particular exception to Schleiermacher's claim in §6.2 of *The Christian Faith* that the feeling of absolute dependence is first "awakened" through religious communication rather than experienced directly. "How is it supposed to be possible that some *feeling* is awakened in a subject *first* through the understanding of the expression of this feeling by another? Must one not, rather, recognize this feeling already on the basis of one's own inner experience, in order to identify a state of world as the expression of a particular feeling? How is one supposed to understand that another's expression allows a state of pain to come to external expression, if one does not know from one's own experience, for example through memory of one's own cases, what it means to have pains, and how a person himself expresses these when he expresses them?" Cramer, "Die eine Frömmigkeit," 333.

87. *Philosophical Ethics* 197 (268).

88. *Brouillon, WA* 101f.

89. *Philosophical Ethics* 200 (270f.), my translation.

90. Ibid., 201 (271). Also: "As the ethical is not completed in personality for itself, so also, personality is not given for itself, but only with its own way of becoming: namely, the difference between the sexes, likewise, and in the determinate form of race and nationality." Ibid., 60f. (80), my translation.

91. So, for example, Garczyk: "By 'climate' we understand any effects upon human beings which find expression in their bodily constitution and thereby also in the formation of their particular language, within particular large regions influenced by the same 'climate.' " *Mensch, Gesellschaft, Geschichte,* 210.

92. *Philosophical Ethics,* 201 (272), translation modified.

93. Ibid., 90 (120). As Schleiermacher used the term *schematism,* it seems to refer to structures that can be predicated of the members of a particular mass in general even if it is exemplified in no one of them perfectly. A schematism thus represents an unarticulated and underdeveloped commonality. For example, "Each

person is a unity of consciousness that is complete in itself. Thus, when reason produces a moment of cognition, it is produced as consciousness only for that person. What is produced under the character of schematism, however, is posited as having validity for everyone, and so in any one person being does not correspond to its character." Ibid., 48 (63f.).

94. Ibid., 89 (119).

95. Ibid., 91 (121).

96. Ibid., 90 (119).

97. Ibid., 91 (121).

98. "[T]here can hardly be a person in whom another should recognize no pious states of mind whatsoever that would be similar to his own to a certain degree, and who should be adjudged entirely immovable by him or incapable of moving him" (CG2 §6.3; KGA I.13, 1 56 [28]). This does not entirely answer the question of whether "preformation" can be overridden by socialization, but fairly clearly indicates a considerable flexibility of religious development even given the preexistence of some of the parameters of religion.

99. *Philosophical Ethics*, 91 (120).

100. Specifically, Schleiermacher introduced the postulate of "schematisms of feeling" to explain the difficulty of transposing bodies of religious communication (art) from one religious sphere to another: "It is always impossible to transfer the character of an artistic system into the domain of another religion; the most strenuous endeavors yield only lifeless results; whereas the poetry of a foreign people who nevertheless belong to the same religious unity can be appropriated quickly and easily." Ibid., 90 (120).

101. CG2 §9.1; KGA I.13, 1 75 (40).

102. *Philosophical Ethics*, 56 (75).

103. CG2 §15.1; KGA I.13, 1 128 (77). Mariña notes the appearance of this understanding of the relationship between thought and language as early as the *Monologen* of 1800. According to Mariña the *Monologen* describes a world that is "the common expression of free beings in communication with one another.... Furthermore, because of the social dimension of the world in which the self expresses itself and finds itself, the self comes to know itself in its relation to the socially constructed world. Hence the 'outer' empirical self is also, to a great degree, socially constructed." Mariña, *Transformation*, 134.

104. *Philosophical Ethics*, 194 (263). Schleiermacher advanced this claim in the context of a discussion of "faith," which as an ethical as opposed to a religious term signifies "the conviction underlying all action in this domain that each person's word is the same as his thought and that the thought which each person connects with a word that he has received is the same as the thought from which it proceeds in any other person." This is not, Schleiermacher claimed, something that can be known as a matter of general principle, but it is a premise of ethical activity generally. Ibid., 193f. (263).

105. Ibid., 197 (267).

106. In the *Brouillon* the externalization of such feelings takes the form of "tone, gesture, and most of all face, eyes" (*Brouillon, WA* 98); in the 1813 lectures Schleiermacher also states that "[e]very definite excitement of sensibility is

accompanied by tone or gesture as a natural means of expression" (*Philosophical Ethics* 54 [71]). Music figures centrally in Schleiermacher's *Christmas Eve* dialogue and in his lectures on aesthetics; see Scholtz, *Ethik und Hermeneutik*, chapter 9, in particular 212–25. The importance of music for Schleiermacher has been explored recently by Philip Stoltzfus; see his *Theology as Performance*, chapter 3, "Schleiermacher on Music as the Expression of Feeling and Mood."

107. *Philosophical Ethics*, 56 (74). Cf. also the *Brouillon*: "It is clear that the externalization of feeling just described is an element of great branches of the arts: the musical, the imitative (*mimisch*) and thereby also the plastic." *Brouillon*, WA 98.

108. *Philosophical Ethics* 57 (75).

109. Ibid., 92 (122), translation modified. Cf. the second edition of the *Brief Outline*: "Uplifting efficacy within the Christian cult is based predominantly on the communication of pious self-consciousness which has become thought, and there can be a theory for this only insofar as this communication can be regarded as art." KGA I.6, 425.

110. Ibid.; my translation.

111. The cult also provides a new principle for the development of social relationships and, perhaps most importantly for Schleiermacher, one that cuts across the boundaries established by extra-ecclesial social conditions. This is an expression of his claim that the social dynamic of religion should not follow the classifications of persons established by the family, state, or academy but should proceed according to the principle of "free sociability" informed by a religious interest. "In the church public worship must be absolutely popular, uniting all the classes, and then the more the religious interest predominates, the more social connections are formed on this basis, proceeding outward from public worship without being too precise about class boundaries." Ibid., 98 (130).

112. *Brouillon*, WA 196.

113. See chapter 4, pp. 153f.

114. See above, p. 107.

115. *Philosophical Ethics* 92 (122), my translation.

116. It is on this point in particular, according to Dinkel, that Schleiermacher's account of the "functional differentiation of society" anticipates the work of Niklas Luhmann; see Dinkel, *Kirche Gestalten*, 263ff.

117. *Philosophical Ethics*, 67 (89). Also: "Man and wife form a particularity in common which we may depict as a sphere within which and from which individual modifications develop and which are encompassed by it. The particularity in common is the character of the family; since the particularity of the two individuals is not strictly identical, it does not strictly constitute a unity, but a unity which bears multiplicity within it and will allow multiplicity to develop from it." *Philosophical Ethics* 66 (87).

118. *Brouillon*, WA 190.

119. Ibid., 196.

120. Schleiermacher's description of the dynamics of family life suggests that ethical roles change as families mature. For example, "Initially the parents themselves, as long as they are in their prime, during which time the children appear merely as *annexa*; then in both at the same time, as the children come into their prime and the parents continue in their maturity.... and finally in the children alone, for whom,

however, the parents have now become history and are beginning to die away." *Philosophical Ethics* 67 (89).

121. "A mass of families which has joined together to form a unity of type in the formative function is originally a horde; in this condition it is dominated by uniformity among those who exist alongside one another." Ibid., 71 (94).

122. In the 1812/1813 lectures Schleiermacher described tribe and nation as "smaller" and "larger unities" respectively, the difference between the two being the degree to which collective identity is determined by kinship. See ibid., 70, 78 (94, 104).

123. Ibid., 90 (119), translation modified.

124. "The essence of the state consists in the antithesis which emerges between authorities and subjects, however this comes about, and to that extent it stands in the same relation to the horde as conscious does to unconscious." Ibid., 71 (94f.), translation modified.

125. *Brouillon, WA* 192f.

126. "[M]odern [friendship] relates to the church like antique [friendship] to the state. The greater individuality first becomes clear within individuals, and these naturally come together as a unification of organs; the same individuality dwells in each but from different sides, and so they bind themselves to the first core of a greater organization. In this lies also the analogy to the school, although here this is immediately reciprocal; each in his manner of presentation becomes a teacher to the other." Ibid., 190.

127. Ibid., 196.

128. Ibid., 193. Schleiermacher appended a marginal note to this section that reads "the more the state leaves the family free, the more the church can arise."

129. *Philosophical Ethics* 71 (95).

130. Ibid.

131. Ibid., 91 (120).

132. Ibid., (121).

133. Ibid., my translation.

134. Ibid.

135. KGA I.6 281. I discuss the significance of this claim (in the expanded form in which it appears in the second edition of the *Brief Outline*) in chapter 6, pp. 185–196.

136. *Brouillon, WA* 193.

137. *Philosophical Ethics*, 85 (113), translation modified. Schleiermacher refers to this passage in discussing the church: "[W]hen the religious institutions which grow up out of this antithesis [between clergy and laity] also appear to be dependent upon the state, we should assess this in the same way" as in the case of the academy. *Philosophical Ethics* 90 (119), translation modified.

138. Ibid., 89 (119).

139. Ibid., 49 (65).

140. Cramer's skepticism about Schleiermacher's description of the process whereby "feeling" is transmitted from one individual to another leads him to a position that effectively undercuts Schleiermacher's claims about what makes religious tradition possible. Where Schleiermacher described the perpetuation of certain forms of feeling through religious communication as the basis of religious tradition, Cramer argues (not, if I understand him correctly, as an interpretation of Schleiermacher but in his own voice) that "[f]eelings, as feelings, cannot be learned.

Only their linguistic designations can and must be learned, namely through the understanding of their linguistic expression.... So Schleiermacher's thesis, that (even) religious consciousness becomes the basis of a community, must in the first instance mean something other than that an already existing religiously constituted community is the basis of a subject's becoming awakened to religious consciousness.... Intersubjectivity is also not the ground of subjectivity for Schleiermacher, the ground of the being of the subject. Rather, intersubjectivity is only, albeit at least, that for the sake of which the subject in his finitude wills (*das Worumwillen des Subjekts in seiner Endlichkeit*)." Cramer, "Die eine Frömmigkeit," 334.

141. Properly understood, then, Schleiermacher is not vulnerable to Talal Asad's criticism of Wilfred Cantwell Smith's understanding of "tradition." In Asad's words, "The tradition is thought of [by Smith] as a cognitive framework, not as a practical mode of living, not as techniques for teaching body and mind to cultivate specific virtues and abilities that have been authorized, passed on, and reformulated down the generations. Concrete traditions are not thought of as sound and visual imagery, as language uttered and inscribed (on paper, wood, stone, or film) or recorded in electronic media. They are not thought of as ways in which the body learns to paint and to see, to sing and hear, and to dance and observe; as masters who can teach pupils how to do these things well; and as practitioners who can excel in what they have been taught (or fail to do so). Yet such matters cannot be separated from the force and function of religious traditions—and so of religious experiences." Asad, "Reading a Modern Classic," 216.

142. *Philosophical Ethics* 93 (123f.). This citation spans three numbered paragraphs; I have removed Schleiermacher's paragraph numbers.

143. See Vial, "Schleiermacher and the State," 276ff.; and Raack, "Schleiermacher's Political Thought and Activity," 376–81. During the first "Schleiermacher renaissance" this episode of his career was the focus of Johannes Bauer's *Schleiermacher als patriotischer Prediger*; in 1966 Jerry Dawson examined Schleiermacher's political development during the first decades of the nineteenth century in *Friedrich Schleiermacher*. Reflections on this episode in Schleiermacher's career, with particular attention to the events of 1813, occupy two sections of Wolfes's *Öffentlichkeit und Bürgergesellschaft* (vol. 1, 209–373).

144. Heino Falcke, *Theologie und Philosophie der Evolution*, 4.

145. Hegel, *Faith and Knowledge*, 151f.

146. See note 53 this chapter.

CHAPTER 4

1. Translations of selections from the introduction to the first edition of *The Christian Faith* appear in Eric von der Luft, *Hegel, Hinrichs, and Schleiermacher*, 214–39.

2. On the Glaubenslehre, 64; KGA I.10, 351. Translations from the *Sendschreiben* will be those of Duke and Fiorenza unless otherwise noted.

3. In the second of his letters to Lücke Schleiermacher outlined his plans to reorganize the introduction to *The Christian Faith* and clarify the structure of his preliminary discussion of Christianity and dogmatics through the addition of section

headings. The problem with the first-edition version of the introduction, in his view, was that since it began with a definition of dogmatics, "The readers may therefore suppose that once this definition is given the dogmatics begins" and so mistakenly locate the contents of the remainder of the introduction within the science of dogmatics. As we will see below, the question of where dogmatics proper begins in *The Christian Faith* is exegetically important. If his revisions to the introduction were to prove successful, Schleiermacher noted, then "the proper task of the Introduction will have been met: it will be immediately evident how this particular theological discipline relates—as it must because of its scientific form—to the sciences in general. As it is now, the readers must find this relationship for themselves. I had hoped, of course, that my *Brief Outline* would have clarified this point, but the readers would then have to rely more than necessary on something other than my dogmatics itself." On the Glaubenslehre, 79f.

4. Brent Sockness, *Against False Apologetics*, and in particular the concluding chapter ("False Apologetics and Modernity: The Ambiguous Legacy of Schleiermacher's Eternal Covenant").

5. Ibid., 215.

6. One of the most important disagreements between Hermann and Troeltsch that Sockness presents has to do with the relationship of religion's essence to history. Both men, according to Sockness, were practitioners of the nineteenth-century search for the essence of religion, but "[w]hat Troeltsch regarded as a phenomenon of consciousness, history, and culture publicly available for the psychologist and historian of religion to describe, analyze, and categorize, and for the philosopher of religion (through epistemological and metaphysical inquiries) to validate and criticize, Hermann regarded as an entirely inward, incommunicable (*unübertragbar*), and ultimately mysterious 'event' or 'experience' (*Erlebnis*) of the individual subject accessible only upon introspection and moral self-examination." Troeltsch anticipated the contemporary consensus regarding appeals to "religious experience," it seems to me, when he charged that Hermann appropriated Schleiermacher's distinction between piety and scientific/philosophical knowledge "solely to avoid competition from metaphysics and retreat from all questions of *Weltanschauung* into an extremely subjective 'religious-ethical' interpretation of reality." Ibid., 207, 204.

7. Sockness does not develop his claim that Schleiermacher practiced both methods of keeping the eternal covenant. This is unfortunate, for such a development would likely have involved a clearer statement than he provides of just what in Schleiermacher's work is supposed to lend itself to Hermann's approach. The first alternative that he presents in the passage cited above is itself ambiguous and supports Hermann's project only on some interpretations. Is the distinctness of the "domain of faith or piety" from intellectual knowing such that this domain is off limits to scientific investigation and criticism? Is the resulting cognitive status of Christian doctrines such that there is no need to adjust their contents to the current state of the sciences? Only if Schleiermacher's texts answer these questions in the affirmative can it be said that they support Hermann's project. To answer them in the negative (as, indeed, I think they should be answered) makes it difficult to see how the first interpretation of the covenant that Sockness presents constitutes an alternative to the second.

8. Richard Brandt, *Philosophy of Schleiermacher*, 261f. It is worth noting that, according to his own confession, Brandt approached Schleiermacher's work in search

of an account of religious experience that would serve to authenticate the Christian religion—thus more in the spirit of Hermann and Otto than of Troeltsch. See Brandt, vii, and the introduction, n. 72.

9. See chapter 1, p. 63.

10. These terms are those of Brian Gerrish. According to Gerrish Schleiermacher's eternal covenant was "a kind of nonaggression pact: not, that is, a unification of Christian faith with scientific inquiry, but an agreement on the part of each to let the other go its way unhindered." *Continuing the Reformation*, 171. It will be apparent that my reading diverges from Gerrish's in significant respects.

11. For discussion of the political activities of the neopietists and their allies during this period see Bigler, *German Protestantism*, 53–155, and Howard, *Protestant Theology*, 51–77. Wolfes discusses the impact of the *Demagogenverfolgung* at length; see *Öffentlichkeit*, vol. 2, 133–270.

12. Birnker, "Der politische Schleiermacher," 145.

13. See Howard, *Religion and the Rise of Historicism*, 71–76, and *Protestant Theology*, 71ff. Where Wolfes claims that over the nine years of their acquaintance prior to 1819 Schleiermacher had "found a good friend" in de Wette, Howard resists the idea that de Wette was in some sense a protégé of Schleiermacher, noting his characterization of Schleiermacher's theology as "lax mysticism" and Schleiermacher's characterization of de Wette as "openly *neologisch*." Wolfes and Howard both note that the two men came to see each other as allies as a result of their mutual opposition to the rising tide of theological and political conservatism during the *Demagogenverfolgung*. See Wolfes, *Öffentlichkeit*, vol. 2, 143f., and Howard, *Protestant Theology*, 59ff.

14. Bigler, *German Protestantism*, 44, 30f., 36.

15. Howard, *Religion and the Rise of Historicism*, 74f.; cf. Wolfes, *Öffentlichkeit*, 157f.; Vial, "Schleiermacher and the State," 271.

16. KGA 1.12, 10.

17. Birkner, "Der politische Schleiermacher," 146; also cited in Wolfes, *Öffentlichkeit*, vol. 2, 167–71.

18. See Bigler, *German Protestantism*, 88–101, for discussion of Hengstenberg's early career and growing influence at Berlin. A particularly entertaining description of Hengstenberg's character and influence is found in Lichtenberger, *History of German Theology in the Nineteenth Century*, 212ff.

19. Wolfes, *Öffentlichkeit*, vol. 2, 259.

20. Bigler, *German Protestantism*, 90ff.

21. *On the* Glaubenslehre, 60, 67. In his discussion of the *Sendschreiben* Schröder emphasizes Schleiermacher's conviction that the view of the world as a self-contained "causal nexus" is incompatible with many traditional Christian claims: "The modern scientific worldview regarded the world as a nexus of causal effects which can be described by laws. Thereby the traditional-Christian belief in creation in its cosmological orientation is made obsolete," and thereby the reports of miracles in the New Testament are also rendered "in need of explanation (*erklärungsbedürftig*)." Schröder, *Die kritische Identität*, 18.

22. *On the* Glaubenslehre, 61.

23. Ibid., 60.

24. CG2 §3.1; KGA I.13, 1 21 (6). Mackintosh et al. render *das Wissen* as "scientific knowledge." The distinction that Schleiermacher invoked in this passage between "external orders" and the "affairs of piety" is almost certainly a reference to the distinction between *jus circa sacra* and *jus in sacra* commonly observed within German-speaking lands following the Protestant reformation. These terms denoted the features of religious life generally regarded as rightfully administered by the state and the church, with the former referring to general features of church governance and the latter to affairs of doctrine and religious practice. See Howard, *Protestant Theology*, 216ff.

25. *On the* Glaubenslehre, 64. Schleiermacher presented this "covenant" as a formula consistent with "building up both the church and science" and as a middle way between a pure empiricism that would "throw the origin of Christianity in with the infinite accumulation of experience and present it as raw material for science," on the one hand, and the approach of speculative theology, which "may safeguard it from natural science, but which will likewise set the rules and subject it to its general constructions" (63).

26. Ibid., 60.

27. KGA I.6, 337.

28. CG2 §28.1; KGA I.13, 1 183 (118).

29. A remark by James Brandt speaks to this dimension of Schleiermacher's work, albeit not specifically in reference to *The Christian Faith*: "Viewed from another perspective, Schleiermacher's contribution to the theological enterprise is his 'Christian naturalism,' his sense that the new and higher life of Christian faith is primarily a 'mode of being in the world' that lives and grows through the social and cultural medium of the church and is therefore open to investigation like any other phenomenon." James Brandt, *All Things New*, 146.

30. *On the* Glaubenslehre, 63.

31. I have discussed this topic at greater length in "Schleiermacher's Theological Anti-realism."

32. CG2 §46.2; KGA I.13, 1 270 (174). See chapter 1, p. 36.

33. CG2 §46; KGA I.13, 1 264 (170).

34. In her essay "Schleiermacher's Christology Revisited," Jacqueline Mariña presents the most extensive argument of which I am aware for the claim that Schleiermacher embraced an incompatibilist understanding of freedom in *The Christian Faith*. Mariña's case depends entirely on Schleiermacher's claim in §4 that "without a feeling of freedom a feeling of absolute dependence would not be possible." As she interprets this passage, "The feeling of absolute dependence arises out of our freedom or spontaneity, which is to say without such a feeling of freedom the God-consciousness could not develop. It is particularly insofar as we are aware of not being determined by intra-worldly or finite causes that we come to our awareness of our absolute dependence on God" (196). In my view her case rests on an identification of the "feeling of freedom" with an awareness of being free in an incompatibilist sense—as she puts the point, "our immediate knowledge of ourselves as free finite agents" (197)—an identification that she seems to take to be self-evident. I do not agree, and in chapter 1 I offer a different account of Schleiermacher's understanding of the "feeling of freedom" and its value as evidence for the nature of human agency.

My response to Mariña's argument for incompatibilism in *The Christian Faith* is implicit in the material that I present in this chapter, which so far as I can discern simply leaves no room for the idea that human activities are not determined by the workings of the *Naturzusammenhang* and, in theological perspective, by God's decree regarding its historical course. Indeed, it seems to me that the statement cited above that absolute dependence and natural-causal determinism are "the same thing merely regarded from different viewpoints" weighs quite heavily against Mariña's argument.

35. CG2 §47.1; KGA I.13, 1 278 (179).

36. CG2 §49.1; KGA I.13, 1 296f. (191).

37. CG2 §49.2; KGA I.13, 1 298 (192).

38. CG2 §49.1; KGA I.13, 1 297 (192).

39. Schleiermacher's discussion of omnipotence in §§55 and in particular his discussion of foreknowledge can also be cited as evidence for a compatibilist understanding of freedom. There Schleiermacher sided with theologians who view God's knowledge as productive rather than reactive, ruling out the possibility that what God knows about the activities of free creatures is posterior in the order of explanation to their volitions (hence ruling out Ockhamism). He also denied both that God knows any counterfactual states of affairs (unrealized possibilities) and that there are any actual states of affairs that God does not know about, ruling out both Molinism and any views that would deny God foreknowledge of the activities of free creatures. He also stated explicitly that there is no conflict between free will and divine foreknowledge. So far as I can see, compatibilism about freedom is the only way of making sense of these claims.

40. CG2 §46.1; KGA I.13, 1 265f. (171). This passage also seems to cut against Mariña's argument for incompatibilism in *The Christian Faith*; see note 34 this chapter.

41. "Now since the feeling of absolute dependence, regarded in itself, is entirely simple, and the concept of the same provides no ground for differentiation, we can only derive such a basis from the fact that each feeling must first unite with a sensible stimulation of self-consciousness if it is to fill a moment of time; these sensible stimulations, however, are to be regarded as infinitely various." CG2 §9.1; KGA I.13, 1 75 (40). Peter Grove says of this claim by Schleiermacher that it "stands in diametrical opposition to the occasional claim in the older literature that his later theory of religion implies a devaluation of the sensory and the temporal. It imputes to this an irreducible significance in religious consciousness." Grove, *Deutungen*, 577. Grove also points out that Schleiermacher noted, in the third edition of the *Speeches*, that his position in both the *Speeches* and the *Glaubenslehre* was "that this [religious] feeling can only become real in us when induced by the effects of individual things" and "that individual things cause (*veranlassen*) this feeling," a claim that according to Grove obscures important differences between the early and later texts. KGA I.12, 133f.; cited in Grove, *Deutungen*, 583.

42. CG2 §46.1; KGA I.13, 1 266 (172).

43. CG2 §45.2; KGA I.13, 1 262 (168).

44. CG2 §47.3; KGA I.13, 1 286f. (183f.). Schleiermacher diagnosed the tendency to seek supernatural explanations for events of religious import as a function of "human indolence": This tendency "naturally has its origins not in Christian piety, but

in a world-view which is confused but all too common in ordinary life, one which makes use of dependence on God only as a ground of explanation of the course of the world where the *Naturzusammenhang* is hidden, and thus mostly where something severed (*abgerissen*) from what went before and separated from its context appears either as a beginning or as something isolated." CG2 §38.2; KGA I.13, 1 228 (148).

45. CG2 §2.2; KGA I.13, 1 16 (3).

46. "By Ethics will be understood here the speculative presentation, running parallel to the natural sciences, of reason in its overall effectiveness. By Philosophy of Religion, a critical presentation of the different given forms of pious communities, insofar as in their totality they are the complete appearance of piety in human nature." CG2 §2 Zusatz; KGA I.13, 1 19 (5).

47. CG2 §3.1; KGA I.13, 1 20 (5).

48. CG2 §4.3; KGA I.13, 1 38 (16); §5.3, KGA I.13, 1 47 (22).

49. See Capetz, *Christian Faith as Religion*, 160–65, for a helpful discussion of Schleiermacher's method of identifying the particularity of Christianity.

50. CG2 §10.1; KGA I.13, 1 81 (44).

51. CG2 §11.3; KGA I.13, 1 97 (56). Schröder calls attention to the fact that Schleiermacher's presentation of the essence of Christianity in the first edition of *The Christian Faith* (in §18) is in certain respects clearer than the corresponding material in the second edition; see *Die kritische Identität*, 25, 43f. Cf. KGA I.7, 1 61ff.

52. CG2 §93.3; KGA I.13, 2 48 (382).

53. CG2 §93.3; KGA I.13, 2 44f. (382); cf. also §19.2, KGA I.13, 1 145 (89).

54. CG2 §15.2; KGA I.13, 1 129 (78).

55. CG2 §11.5; KGA I.13, 1 101f. (59).

56. Here I follow Mariña's claim that Schleiermacher's dogmatics is "an *internal* critique of faith whose two main principles of criticism are clarity and consistency," the touchstones of which procedure are the feeling of absolute dependence and the conviction that redemption has been accomplished in Jesus of Nazareth. In particular Mariña observes that Schleiermacher's analysis of Christian doctrines proceeds by asking the question "Given *that* redemption has been effected in us through Jesus Christ, what are the conditions for the possibility that such a redemption should have taken place?" "Schleiermacher's Christology Revisited," 185f., 190, emphasis in the original.

57. This is a point I emphasize in "Schleiermacher's Theological Anti-realism."

58. CG2 §§51–54; KGA I.13, 1 308–35 (200–19). On the divine causality see Bruce Boyer, "Schleiermacher on the Divine Causality"; Robert Adams, "Schleiermacher on Evil," in particular 563–65.

59. CG2 §51.1; KGA I.13, 1 309 (201).

60. CG2 §40.3; KGA I.13, 1 233f. (151f.).

61. CG2 §164, §164.1; KGA I.13, 2 494f. (723). Cited in Adams, "Schleiermacher on Evil," 575. Adams notes that, whereas here Schleiermacher advances claims about the divine teleology as a way of unpacking the contents of Christian piety, in places he speaks of an awareness of a "particular divine impartation" that is given through the consciousness of redemption. He remarks that "it may be that if he were pressed hard for the grounds of his hopes, he would simply appeal to a direct apprehension of the divine purpose in Christian consciousness of the efficacy of redemption" (576).

However, the passage from §80, to which Adams appeals in support of his claim that a "special divine impartation" is "experienced in redemption," seems to me rather to support the method of transcendental corroboration. The crucial sentence reads, "If we name the power of the God-consciousness in our souls 'grace'...and ascribe (*zuschreiben*) to it a particular divine impartation (*Mitteilung*)..." (KGA I.13, 1 488 [326]). This to me seems to be the language of postulation or interpretation rather than of direct apprehension.

62. CG2 §169; KGA I.13, 2 169 (735). I owe mention of this claim to Brent Sockness, who suggested it as an addition to a previous version of this list during a conference session in 2005.

63. CG2 §93.2; KGA I.13, 2 42 (377).

64. CG2 §93.2; KGA I.13, 2 42 (378).

65. CG2 §91.2; KGA I.13, 2 37 (372).

66. CG2 §93.2; KGA I.13, 2 44 (379).

67. CG2 §130.2; KGA I.13, 2 327 (600).

68. CG2 §130.4; KGA I.13, 2 331 (603).

69. CG2 §154.2; KGA I.13, 2 445 (689). Schleiermacher effectively stripped the notion of the "guidance of the Holy Spirit" of its supernatural trappings; in his usage it means nothing more than that the persons who were instrumental in the composition, redaction, and collation of the books of the New Testament were possessed of Christian piety. See the discussion of CG2 §130.

70. CG2 §88.2; KGA I.13, 2 23 (362).

71. CG2 §88.3; KGA I.13, 2 25 (364).

72. CG2 §87.3; KGA I.13, 2 20 (360).

73. CG2 §139; KGA I.13, 2 378 (638).

74. CG2 §142.2; KGA I.13, 2 401f. (656).

75. CG2 §142.2; KGA I.13, 2 402 (656).

76. *On the* Glaubenslehre, 64.

77. CG2 §10 Zusatz; KGA I.13, 1 90 (50). Mackintosh et al. render *nicht zu begreifen ist* as "cannot be explained."

78. CG2 §10 Zusatz; KGA I.13, 1 91 (51).

79. CG2 §10 Zusatz; KGA I.13, 1 92 (51f.).

80. The argument that follows here can be usefully read alongside Walter Wyman Jr.'s discussion in "Revelation and the Doctrine of Faith." Wyman understands Schleiermacher to maintain that the appearance of perfect God-consciousness in Jesus represents a "breach in the causal nexus," which stands in tension with his understanding of the divine causality and seems to agree with Troeltsch's diagnosis of a "residual supernaturalism" in this part of *The Christian Faith* (51, 60). I cite Gerrish's response to Wyman in note 89 this chapter.

81. KGA I.6 354; *Brief Outline*, 41.

82. KGA I.6 356f.; *Brief Outline*, 43.

83. KGA I.6 357; *Brief Outline*, 44. Schleiermacher's alteration of this part of the text for the second edition of 1830 amounts in the main to minor alterations and expansions. This final remark, however, is new in the second edition.

84. CG2 §13; KGA I.13, 1 106 (62).

85. CG2 §13.1; KGA I.13, 1 108 (63).

86. CG2 §13.1; KGA I.13, 1 107f. (62f.); emphasis added.

87. CG2 §13.1; KGA I.13, 1 108 (63).

88. CG2 §13.1; KGA I.13, 1 109f. (64).

89. So Brian Gerrish in response to Wyman's argument in "Revelation and the Doctrine of Faith": "What is supernatural about the appearance of the Redeemer is that it results, not from an unparalleled divine intervention in the flow of history, but from God's one eternal 'decree.' The decree to send Christ forth is one with the decree to create the human race. The supernatural in Christ is therefore not referred to a temporal act of God; it belongs rather to the timeless divine causality, in which creation and redemption coincide." Gerrish, "Errors and Insights," 82.

90. CG2 §88.4; KGA I.13, 2 26 (365).

91. CG2 §93.3; KGA I.13, 2 46f. (380f.).

92. CG2 §88.4; KGA I.13, 2 27 (365).

93. Barth, *Theology of Schleiermacher*, 205. Barth's reference here was to the second of Schleiermacher's *Sendschreiben*: "If science must admit the possibility that even now matter is beginning to form and to rotate in infinite space, then it must also admit that in the realm of spiritual life there is an appearance that we can only explain as a new creation, as the beginning of a higher development of spiritual life." *On the Glaubenslehre*, 64.

94. So Lichtenberger: "The School of Conciliation has been reprehended for introducing miracles into theology, while it yet at bottom participates in the general repugnance of the time for the supernatural. The truth is that it finds itself obliged to refer certain historical facts, and in particular the appearance of Christ, to a special intervention of God, and to the play of laws which it is still ignorant of." *History of German Theology*, 469.

95. CG2 §11.5; KGA I.13, 1 101f. (59).

96. CG2 §28.1; KGA I.13, 1 183 (118).

97. See introduction, p. 5.

98. CG2 §33; KGA I.13, 1 205 (133f.)

99. A related question is whether Schleiermacher's association of the "whence" of absolute dependence with God in §4 is to be understood as equivalent to the claim that God is the *cause* of the feeling of absolute dependence. For Schleiermacher to make such a claim would not, of course, amount to "proving" the existence of God; it would, however, make the existence of God a presupposition of his account of religion in the precise sense that this account would insist on a theistic causal explanation for the existence of the feeling of absolute dependence itself. Christian Albrecht addressed this question in *Schleiermachers Theorie der Frömmigkeit*, arguing that according to Schleiermacher's assertion of a *parallelism* between the feeling of one's own dependence and the feeling of the self as in relation to God, "all causal connection between God and the human feeling of dependence is ruled out: in no case may this formulation be misunderstood such that God is to be identified as the objectifiable, effective ground of the feeling of dependence—this misunderstanding turns the point of the exposition of the first three sections of the fourth paragraph of the CG2 completely on its head." Properly understood in fact, "The factual absoluteness of the consciousness of dependence is reflected straightaway in the fact that knowledge of its causal correlate is impossible." Albrecht, *Frömmigkeit*, 248f.

100. In *Continuing the Reformation* Gerrish discusses the historical fortunes of this accusation among the neoorthodox; as he summarizes Barth's narrative of the history of Protestant theology, in the wake of Schleiermacher "Feuerbach...showed how the transcendent reality of the theologians could now be viewed as an illusion, and Strauss showed what happens if you venture to read the New Testament as history. In sum, from merely human religious experience, Barth argued, you cannot get either to God or to the real Christ, and in the middle third of our century the theological world was widely, although by no means universally, dominated by his reading of Protestant history." Gerrish also noted Brunner's characterization of Schleiermacher's theology as "psychologism" and "agnostic expressionism" and Wobbermin's defense of Schleiermacher against this charge, which took the form of calling attention to similarities between the stances of Schleiermacher and Husserl in relation to religion qua object of inquiry: "[T]he givenness of God in the feeling of absolute dependence, Wobbermin pointed out, is something quite other than the inferential proof of God's existence that it has often been mistaken for." *Continuing the Reformation*, 173f.

101. Eric von der Luft, *Hegel, Hinrichs, and Schleiermacher*, 260. I have discussed this episode and the later history of the subjectivism charge in "The Case of the Disappearing Discourse," 7–10.

102. Ernst Troeltsch, "Half a Century of Theology," 59. A more recent echo of the kind of agnosticism or ambiguity indicated by Troeltsch comes from Cramer, who in 1984 published a groundbreaking essay interrogating the argument of §§3–4 of the second edition of *The Christian Faith*. Cramer's conclusion is worth quoting at length: "It was and is a task for Christian theologians to decide whether [his] definition of the original meaning of the term 'God' marks the point at which the theologian Schleiermacher reined in (*eingeholt*) the undertaking of Christian dogmatics as a second reformer in the stance of the consciousness of modernity, or rather the point from which the modern apostasy in theology and church took its point of departure. Schleiermacher's definition of the original definition of the name God does not break with the idea that God is something transcendent over against consciousness. For the 'whence' of our existence is something which is transcendent in relation to it, since it cannot be contained (*eingeholt*) within its structure. But Schleiermacher breaks absolutely with the idea of a *consciousness*-transcendent God. For the original meaning of the name God can only be explained as a function of insight into the structure of our consciousness itself. Without reference to the fact that *there is us*, the idea that *there is God* has no sense whatsoever. It is this *ambiguity* of this statement which must be of increased systematic interest not only for Christian theologians, but also for philosophers." Cramer, "Die subjectivitätstheoretischen Prämissen," 161, emphasis added.

103. Roberts, "Feeling of Absolute Dependence," 259ff.

104. Ibid., 262.

105. Ibid., 263.

106. Ibid., 264.

107. Thiemann, *Revelation and Theology*, 31.

108. Thiemann claimed that Schleiermacher was committed to the idea that "non-inferential experiences are direct, immediate, and *thus* self-authenticating"

(emphasis added) and argued that this principle was "established in his discussion of feeling as immediate self-consciousness and by the logic of his argument in paragraph 4 [of *The Christian Faith*]" (ibid., 29f.). But just where in §4 "self-authentication" appears or is implied he did not say, and I can find nothing in the argument that bespeaks the notion. So far as I can see, Thiemann was responding to the admittedly puzzling fact that Schleiermacher offered no argument for the veridicality of the feeling of absolute dependence while clearly assuming that it is veridical. The question of the relationship between the feeling of absolute dependence and belief in the existence of God continues to bedevil discussions of Schleiermacher; see, for example, Hueston E. Finlay, " 'Feeling of absolute dependence' or 'absolute feeling of dependence'?" Finlay challenges an earlier argument by Georg Behrens to the effect that Schleiermacher's appeal to an "absolute feeling of dependence" constitutes part of a proof of the existence of God that involves an intellectually dishonest grammatical "sleight of hand." In the same year Markus Mühling grappled with the same topic by way of a careful reconstruction of §4 of the *Glaubenslehre* ("Schleiermachers Gottesbeweis?"). Mühling observed at the outset the "winking (*augenzwinkernd*) and slightly heretical" character of his reconstruction, in that "this reconstruction recalls the form of a proof of God (*Gottesbeweis*), and Schleiermacher, as is generally known, did not intend this"; further, in order to generate a proof from §4, it is necessary to supplement Schleiermacher's arguments with premises he did not supply (ibid., 125). The crux of Mühling's comments concerning the distance between Schleiermacher's arguments and a proof of God's existence turns on the observation that Schleiermacher spoke not of "absolute receptivity" but of a "consciousness of absolute receptivity." Properly understood, "not only does Schleiermacher not provide a rational demonstration (*Aufweis*) that there is such a thing as [an absolute dependence or receptivity]; he also provides no phenomenal demonstration for this.... Thus §4 reduces to the proposition: 'there is an absolute self-consciousness that lies at the ground of temporal self-consciousness, which is determined as the consciousness (e.g., feeling) of absolute receptivity or dependence upon the non-objective' " (ibid., 128). This proposition Mühling further characterizes as a "mere assertion" rather than a claim supported by independent argument (ibid.).

    109. This refusal is articulated in §18.5 of the first edition and §11.5 of the second. The primary difference between the editions is that in the first Schleiermacher's refusal of the project of proving the truth or necessity of Christianity is obscured somewhat by his characterization of the adherence to Christianity which he expected of Christians as itself such a proof. The relevant passage in the first edition reads, "Thus here we refuse any other proof for the necessity and truth of Christianity besides that which each one bears within himself inasmuch as he is conscious that his own piety can assume no other form than this, and inasmuch as he feels himself satisfied in its historical and inward connection: and that is the proof of faith" (KGA I.7, 1 68). The language of the second reads, "We entirely renounce every proof for the truth or necessity of Christianity, and presuppose on the contrary that every Christian, before he involves himself at all with inquiries of this kind, already has the certainty within himself that his piety can take no other form than this" (KGA I.13, 1 102 [60]). Someone interested in defending Thiemann's assertion of "self-authentication" for Christian piety might find support in the language of the first edition, but to me it

seems fairly obvious that in the passage in question the final use of the term *proof* is a piece of rhetoric intended to mask Schleiermacher's abandonment of the traditional project of natural theology and that the language of the second edition expresses his position more accurately.

110. Gerrish, *Continuing the Reformation*, 208f., citing Thiemann, 69, 72. See also Gerrish's "Nature and the Theater of Redemption," 129–32, which represents the original appearance of his response to Thiemann. This aspect of Schleiermacher's theology stands, it seems, in need of continual restatement. See, for example, Philip Stolzfus, who calls attention to passages in which C. W. Christian and Claude Welch took pains to resist the "subjectivism" charge. Stoltzfus remarks that "[i]n each case, the author's desire is to assure the skeptical reader that the transcendental signifier—the 'objective reference' or 'something'—remains in place for Schleiermacher. But this assurance is precisely the game in which Schleiermacher did not want to engage." Stolzfus, *Theology as Performance*, 103.

111. *On the* Glaubenslehre, 40.

112. CG2 §33.3; KGA I.13, 1 210 (136).

113. It is on this point that Peter Grove's overall conclusion in *Deutungen des Subjekts* is most relevant for my project. Grove devotes attention in the final sections of his book to the relationship in Schleiermacher's later thought between *religious* and *philosophical* thought concerning God, the former articulated in *The Christian Faith* and the latter primarily in the *Dialektik*. Grove's diagnosis seems to me both correct and illuminating. Philosophical reflection delivers *objective* thought concerning God, which is, however, *undetermined* as regards content: God is described in the *Dialektik* as the "transcendent ground" of thinking but, qua transcendent, cannot be grasped in thought. Religious reflection, on the contrary, yields thought concerning God that is *rich in content* but merely *subjective*: Religious reflection, that is, attaches specific predicates to God (such as "creator" or "ordainer") and yet provides no guarantee of their truth. On Grove's view the relationship between philosophical and religious reflection within the overall corpus of Schleiermacher's thought is a complementary one, such that philosophy provides the metaphysical grounding that religion requires: "Schleiermacher's thesis of the distinction between metaphysics and religion, which is strongly emphasized in both his early and his later work, does not exhaust itself in the criticism of the admixture of the two, but includes just as much the refusal of their disconnection. The theoretical explication of religion and its interpretation needs metaphysics in order to be able to carry out an acceptable accounting of the thought of God." See Grove, *Deutungen* 591–618 and in particular 613–18; the citation is drawn from 618. There are two points that I believe should be emphasized in response to these claims by Grove. The first is that Schleiermacher's *omission* from the *Glaubenslehre* of the arguments for God's existence provided by the *Dialektik* seems to me to be deliberate and methodologically significant, and I comment on this in my text. The second is that if philosophical reflection can "objectively" justify the bare claim that there is a "divine whence," this justification cannot extend to specific predications concerning God and so cannot be used to provide a grounding for specifically Christian doctrines. It is also worth noting that in a recent essay Jeffery Kinlaw has challenged the idea that Schleiermacher's 'transcendent ground' argument should be regarded as a philosophical argument in favor of God's existence. According

to Kinlaw, to identify the 'transcendent ground' posited by Schleiermacher's argument with God is to "give a religious interpretation of one's original affectedness," and thus Schleiermacher is to be regarded not as a foundationalist but as a proto-pragmatist. Kinlaw, "Schleiermacher's Transcendent Ground Argument," 313.

114. CG2 §2 Zusatz 2; KGA I.13, 1 19 (5). On the "exoteric" nature of philosophy of religion for Schleiermacher, particularly as described in the *Brief Outline*, see Hjelde, *Religionswissenschaft*, 18–22.

115. *On the* Glaubenslehre, 78; KGA I.10, 374. These remarks were a response to F. H. C. Schwarz's review of the first edition of *The Christian Faith* and specifically to Schwarz's charge that Schleiermacher's attempt "to specify the correct position of Christianity within the totality of religious communities by comparing and contrasting it to other types of belief does not provide an adequate foundation for Christian dogmatics" (ibid.). Schleiermacher's response is in line with my claim that the question of the existence or nonexistence of God is a matter of indifference to the philosophy of religion, but one with which dogmatics and philosophy both concern themselves in different ways.

116. These terms are Schwarz's, which Schleiermacher cited with approval; *On the* Glaubenslehre, 78.

117. For a survey of these arguments, see Grove, *Deutungen*, 464–80; Frank, "Metaphysical Foundations"; and Kinlaw, "Schleiermacher's Transcendent Ground Argument."

118. What I have in mind here are places, of which there seem to me to be several within the introduction, where Schleiermacher anticipates or describes the standpoint "within" Christianity that, according to the above characterization, is the mark of dogmatics proper rather than of the philosophy of religion. The passage cited in note 109 this chapter is an example, as is the preliminary discussion of the "revelation" in Jesus discussed in section 4.3.4.

119. The discussion in question occurs in §36 of the first edition, which marks the opening of the doctrinal portions of the text; see KGA I.7, 1 124. In the 1822 *Dialektik* Schleiermacher also discussed the idea that the feeling of absolute dependence could be explained as an illusion in connection with the topic of religious feeling, which contains "the relationship of immediate self-consciousness to that which lies at the ground of all being and all affections." "We may explain this modification of immediate self-consciousness as we will," he observed, and even if it is nothing but "fiction or delusion (*Täuschung*)," still this state "expresses the striving of human beings to grasp the transcendental." KGA II.10, 2, 569f.

120. CG2 §32.2; KGA I.13, 1 203 (132). In the first edition Schleiermacher was clearer regarding the referent of "we," noting that "the one who bears pious feeling within himself cannot accept" the nonpious explanation of the feeling the "original feeling of dependence"; KGA I.7, 1 124.

121. My discussion of this part of the *Glaubenslehre* can be read as a response to Wayne Proudfoot's treatment of the same material in *Religious Experience*. Proudfoot regards Schleiermacher's rejection of the possibility that the feeling of absolute dependence might be illusory as constituting an argument, but a very bad one: "The nonreligious explanation is rejected on the grounds that it is not a proper elucidation of the religious consciousness. This argument, and the claim that the

feeling of absolute dependence is original, both appear to be designed to stave off criticisms of the belief that is assumed by the religious consciousness. The confusion between the proper description or elucidation of religious experience and its proper explanation is not unique to Schleiermacher, and we shall see that it plays a crucial role in the protective strategies that have been employed by some recent philosophers of religion" (39). Proudfoot neither observes a distinction between scientific disciplines within *The Christian Faith* nor considers the textual location of the passage in question to be worth noting; thus he takes the position Schleiermacher articulates in §32 as a statement of his position throughout the introduction as well.

122. CG2 §32.2; KGA I.13, 1 204 (133).

123. CG2 §32, §32.3; KGA I.3, 1 201, 204 (131, 133).

124. In §4 Schleiermacher claimed that reflection on the feeling of absolute dependence generates a "consciousness of God," that this consciousness is the proper referent of all talk of "an original revelation of God to man or in man," and thus that "in this sense one can indeed say that God is given to us in feeling in an original way." At least prima facie, these claims do not sit comfortably with my claim that Schleiermacher's discussion of Christianity does not assume the existence of supernatural entities such as God, for ordinarily we would not say that a person could be conscious of God if there were no such being and would not identify the purported consciousness of a nonexistent entity as a case of that entity's being "given to us." Nonetheless, it is certainly possible to interpret the notion of God-consciousness in a sense that does not presuppose God's existence. An ontological naturalist could easily agree with Schleiermacher that reflection on the feeling of absolute dependence (assuming it exists) can produce a state of awareness that *purports to be* about God, even if it is not actually about God (since, on that person's view, there is no such entity). Moreover, such a naturalist could also agree with Schleiermacher's claims that this state constitutes the real referent of talk of an "original revelation" of God in human consciousness and that it is in this precise sense that God is "given" to human beings, since for the naturalist these will be examples of the reduction of theological claims to claims about human psychology. So far as I can discern, nothing more than this—a willingness to exegete the phrase "consciousness of God" as referring to states of awareness that *purport to be* about God—is required to make the argument of §4 cohere with an ontologically naturalistic stance; and so far as I can see, nothing of the logic of Schleiermacher's argument is threatened by this reading.

125. Byrne, *Natural Religion and the Nature of Religion*, 242.

126. If the point of Byrne's passage is that anthropocentrism in the study of religion does not entail any metaphysical claims regarding the existence or nonexistence of those transcendent entities with which religions are concerned, Ivan Strenski arrives at a similar position from, so to speak, the opposite direction. In *Thinking about Religion* Strenski criticizes Russell McCutcheon, who on his reading "feels he needs to link his naturalist approach to religion with commitment to a naturalistic metaphysical ground." Strenski argues that McCutcheon "fails to realize that study of religion has no need of any such ideological or metaphysical foundations at all. . . . We don't need to decide whether or not religion really has a supernatural origin or not in order to go ahead and study it. Whether or not religion has a

supernatural origin, our human abilities to *know* are limited to the same restrictions in either case." Strenski, *Thinking about Religion*, 340.

CHAPTER 5

1. There is at least an initial plausibility to characterizing intuitions of the universe or the feeling of absolute dependence as "intrinsically religious." The implication would be that anyone who possesses either an intuition of the universe or the feeling of absolute dependence would thereby possess (something of) religion and thereby be (in some sense) religious, even in the absence of religious self-identification or any development out of this "essence." I suspect that Schleiermacher might endorse this view but find it to be an indifferent matter myself, as the "religion" described in such a case would lack most of the salient features of the broader phenomenon.

2. As I note in chapter 4, in *The Christian Faith* Schleiermacher's position that the "most immediate expression" of the feeling of absolute dependence—that is, the first product of reflection on that feeling—is "consciousness of God," which does not fit his definition of feeling. See above, chapter 4, n. 124.

3. The first of these passages is drawn from §8 in the first edition of *The Christian Faith*; see KGA I.7, 1 26. The second is common to the first and second editions (§8 and §3, respectively); see KGA I.7, 1 26 and KGA I.13, 1 20 (5).

4. It is this aspect of the structure of religion that explains Schleiermacher's autobiographical remark in the *Speeches* that "[r]eligion helped me when I began to examine the ancestral faith and to purify my heart of the rubble of primitive times. It remained with me when God and immortality disappeared before my doubting eyes." *On Religion*, 8.

5. See above, p. 89.

6. For the first edition see KGA I.2, 315; cf. *On Religion*, 114. For the later editions see KGA I.12, 283; cf. *On Religion* (Oman), 239.

7. *On Religion*, 114.

8. Ibid., 115.

9. KGA I.7, 1 61.

10. Hagenbach, *Encyklopädie und Methodologie der theologichen Wissenschaften* (Berlin: Weidmann'sche Buchhandlung, 1833), 5; cited in Howard, *Protestant Theology*, 318. Howard's translation.

11. *Kurze Darstellung* §160, §167; KGA I.6 383, 385f.; cf. *Brief Outline*, 62, 64. I have removed Schleiermacher's cross-references to §90 and §160.

12. Proudfoot, *Religious Experience*, 40.

13. Jantzen, *Becoming Divine*, 117.

14. McCutcheon, *Critics Not Caretakers*, 5.

15. "Since Christian piety arises in no individual independently and of itself, but only out of the community and in it: therefore there is adherence to Christ only in connection with an adherence to the community." CG2 §24.4; KGA I.13, 1 167 (106).

16. Schleiermacher, KGA 1.12, 265. See above, p. 58.

17. See above, p. 130.

18. See above, p. 158.

19. McCutcheon, *Manufacturing Religion*, 68. See also Jantzen, *Becoming Divine*, 75.

20. On this point see Wolfes, who has argued that "Schleiermacher, like no other Protestant theologian of his time, thought in political categories.... In fact Schleiermacher became an eminent political thinker precisely on the basis of his religious and theological self-understanding." Wolfes, *Öffentlichkeit*, vol. 2, 391.

21. KGA I.6, 281.

22. Ibid., 282.

23. Asad, *Geneaologies of Religion*, 28.

24. Ibid., 29. For a response to Asad's critique of Geertz see Schilbrack, "Religion, Models of, and Reality."

25. It is fairly clear that the grounds for this criticism of Asad's have to do with the fact that the distinction in question has a particular cultural and historical provenance and that applying it to Islam would involve the imposition of nonnative categories on Muslim traditions. Why this should lead to "failure," however, is not clear. Narrowly construed, the criticism is that the failure in question would be a failure to understand Muslim traditions. It would be somewhat difficult, however, to interpret Asad as arguing that no one can properly understand Muslim traditions who makes use of categories that are not internal to Muslim worldviews, for this would bring him perilously close to Geertz's position (see, for example, Geertz's essay "From the Native's Point of View"). This may nevertheless be the correct way to understand Asad; and if this is the case then I think his criticism does bear on Schleiermacher's account of religion, as indeed it bears on any account of religion that pretends to cross-cultural validity.

26. This same worry appears in the course of Timothy Fitzgerald's recent criticism of Bruce Lincoln's "Theses on Method." Fitzgerald reads Lincoln's Thesis 13, which claims that "[w]hen one permits those whom one studies to define the terms in which they will be understood...one has ceased to function as historian or scholar," as licensing the following sort of pronouncements: "If I say that you are a Mullah and that Mullahs are or ought to be 'religious,' and since I have also defined religious thinking as essentially different from secular political thinking, then it seems to follow from *Thesis 13* that if you act in a way which I define as 'political' then you are not a genuine Mullah, you are using religion for political ends. You are therefore a charlatan, a 'politician' pretending to be a 'religious' leader! And I will make sure that my knowledge about your real identity, defined according to my criteria and terminology, will be disseminated in English language books, journal articles and newspaper editorials, regardless of your Arabic or Urdu or Persian protestations! I operate from the ground of natural reason because I am a secular enlightened type, in touch with reality, able to represent the true order of things; I know the difference between the religious and the non-religious; and you are 'religious' and shall submit to my system of categorization whether you object to it or not!" Fitzgerald, "Bruce Lincoln's 'Theses on Method': Antitheses," 422f.

27. It is possible that Asad's claim that essentialism "invites us to separate [religion] conceptually from the domain of power" is also intended as a self-standing criticism in the sense that any approach to religion that invites such a separation is bad for reasons sufficiently self-evident that they do not need to be spelled out. However, for present purposes I take the claims presented in the passage I have cited above to represent his rationale for the badness of this "invitation."

28. For discussion of Schleiermacher's political sermons between 1808 and 1812 see Wolfes, *Öffentlichkeit*, vol. 1, 256–64. Wolfes cites, for example, the concluding passage from Schleiermacher's sermon titled "On the Proper Relationship of the Christian to His Authorities," preached in 1809: "Let our pious sense, then, be directed primarily to this subject: among us let…piety and loyalty go hand in hand; and let them form us ever more into a people devoted to our sovereign, harmonious among ourselves, sure and strong in the power of every good disposition." Wolfes, *Öffentlichkeit*, vol. 1, 260.

29. In his essay on the content and provenance of Schleiermacher's understanding of Judaism, Joseph Pickle argued in fact that "[t]he prophetic critic of intrusions of the state upon the Church accepts an internal and external view of Judaism that tied its essence to nationality" ("Schleiermacher on Judaism," 137). It seems to me that the "tie" of which Pickle speaks is a relatively loose one since Schleiermacher did not include reference to a particular political identity in his single attempt at characterizing the essence of Judaism. Pickle's essay is illuminating, however, regarding the prominence of questions about the political allegiances of Jews in turn-of-the-century Prussian discourse and Schleiermacher's response to these in his anonymously published *Briefe bei Gelegenheit der politisch-theologischen Aufgabe und des Sendschreibens jüdischer Hausväter*, composed immediately after the publication of the first edition of the *Speeches on Religion*.

30. KGA I.6, 339; cf. *Brief Outline*, 30.

31. See above, p. 128.

32. Proudfoot, *Religious Experience*, 45.

33. Proudfoot's claim that religious discourse could, within the general framework of Schleiermacher's understanding of religion, be understood as the product of the dynamics of external factors such as social class does not sit comfortably with his claim that Schleiermacher wanted "to show that the language of religious belief and doctrine emerges from [religious] affections without being contaminated by thoughts and claims about the world which might make it vulnerable to philosophical criticism or to contradiction by advances in knowledge" (ibid., 34; see introduction, n. 81). I am not certain how this tension is to be resolved.

34. Here I have benefited from two essays by Terrence Tice and Joseph Pickle: Tice's "Schleiermacher on the Scientific Study of Religion" and Pickle's "Promises of Positive Plurality."

35. For a contextually rich overview of the *Brief Outline* see Crouter, "Shaping an Academic Discipline: The *Brief Outline on the Study of Theology*."

36. So, for example, Dinkel: "A positive science exists only on the basis of excerpts from other scientific disciplines, which are independently worked into the positive science and are placed in connection to particular utilizations and interests." *Kirche Gestalten*, 41. The point that theology depends on other branches of science for its information concerning religion was not new in the edition of 1831 but informed the basic plan of the work in 1811 as well. This is in large measure because the *Brief Outline* originated as part of Schleiermacher's campaign to establish academic theology on a new and scientifically respectable basis within the new University of Berlin; according to Howard, it was in part a response to Fichte's charge that "all scientific material must be comprehended in its organic unity and interpreted in [a] philosophical spirit." See Howard, *Protestant Theology*, 310.

37. KGA I.6, 249f.; *Brief Outline*, 20.

38. KGA I.6, 329; *Brief Outline*, 20.

39. For discussion of Schleiermacher's distinction between historical, philosophical, and practical theology see Gerrish, "Friedrich Schleiermacher," 127–30; also Pannenberg, *Theology and the Philosophy of Science*, 250–55.

40. KGA I.6, 336; *Brief Outline*, 26.

41. KGA I.6, 353; *Brief Outline*, 41.

42. KGA I.6, 362f.; *Brief Outline*, 48.

43. KGA I.6, 377; *Brief Outline*, 58.

44. KGA I.6, 370; *Brief Outline*, 53.

45. KGA I.6 340f.; *Brief Outline*, 31. Thus ironically, it is apologetics that Proudfoot's description of what the study of religion could amount to for Schleiermacher most closely resembles.

46. Schröder in particular emphasizes the fact that Schleiermacher understood philosophical theology's task of identifying the particularity of Christianity as a species of "value-free" inquiry: Philosophical theology, "in accordance with its 'scientific content' (KD §37,16), is a critical discipline, and part of religion-historical research, which is free from practical interest. To this [type of] historical research, which is religion-theoretically reflective and independent of practical purposes, Schleiermacher assigns the task of determining what is particularly Christian." According to Schröder, "The epochal status of Schleiermacher's definition of essence consists... in *its reflective historicity*, which makes the essence of Christianity capable of being compared to that of other historical phenomena." Schröder, *Die kritische Identität*, 112f., 124f.

47. CG2 §2 Zusatz 2; KGA I.13, 1 19 (5). See also above, p. 171.

48. CG2 §7; KGA I.13, 1 60 (31).

49. KGA I.6, 335; *Brief Outline*, 25.

50. Hilgenfeld, "Die wissenschaftliche Theologie," 1, 11.

51. Ibid., 12f.

52. Ibid., 11.

53. Howard, *Protestant Theology*, 205.

54. Troeltsch, "Half a Century of Theology," 79.

55. There are, however, fairly substantial connections between Schleiermacher and Müller in particular. It is standard practice for discussions of Müller to call attention to his leanings in the direction of Romanticism in general; see, for example, Sharpe, *Comparative Religion*, 36f.; Strenski, *Thinking about Religion*, 69–72. Otto Gruppe claimed that Müller represents a continuation of the "evolutionary" line of investigation, which springs directly out of Schleiermacher's work, the line that "proceeds from the claim that the original religion arose in a veneration of the heavens and of heavenly manifestations" and "makes the metaphysical element of religion its point of departure." Gruppe, *Die greichische Culte*, vol. 1, 216f. Müller himself contested the claim, advanced by some readers of his first Gifford lectures, that his view was "some modified form" of the view of Schleiermacher and others that "the infinite can be known in the finite only, and that it should be known here always and everywhere." Müller, *Natural Religion*, 141.

56. Strenski, *Thinking about Religion*, 338, emphasis in the original. Strenski comments, "Such motivation does not, of course, justify or give added value to the

theories thus created. But recognizing that religious motives may inspire critical scientific thinking about religion as easily as might the desire to discredit religious viewpoints, should go some way toward closing the gap that yawns so widely today between religious believers and scientific skeptics" (339).

57. See above, p. 167, and my "Case of the Disappearing Discourse."

58. F. C. Baur, for example, described Schleiermacher's standpoint as the "standpoint of subjectivity" in his 1835 *Die christliche Gnosis* but a decade later acknowledged in his lectures on the history of Christian dogma that for Schleiermacher "the subjective [aspect] of the Christian consciousness has a further objective aspect as its presupposition: the religious community, the common life.... Therefore here it is a process which takes place outside of consciousness, in the objectivity of history." See my "Case of the Disappearing Discourse," 13–16.

59. Sockness, *Against False Apologetics*, vii.

60. Robert Morgan, "Ernst Troeltsch and the Dialectical Theology," 47–48; cited in Sockness, *Against False Apologetics*, 9.

61. Rudolf Otto, "Der neue Aufbruch," 137, emphasis in the original. This essay is an expanded version of Otto's "Wie Schleiermacher die Religion wiederentdeckte" ("How Schleiermacher Rediscovered Religion"). Discussion of Hermann's reading of Schleiermacher was added in the later version of the essay.

62. Ibid.

63. See above, p. 63.

64. See above, pp. 165f.

65. See above, p. 13.

66. Raschke, "Religious Studies."

67. Ibid., 132.

68. Ibid., 136.

69. Ibid.

70. Ibid.

71. Ibid., 136f.

72. Ibid., 137.

73. Ibid., 135.

74. Ibid., 136.

75. "Religious studies must wean itself rapidly from its love affair with descriptive pluralism and agree to certain normative and theoretical, if not strictly 'scientific,' standards. It must, as have other surviving disciplines, adhere to the canons of critical intelligence set forth at the opening of the modern age. Otherwise, the destiny of the field can be forecast without too much qualification. We all know what happened to Old Rome." Ibid., 138.

76. See above, p. 137.

77. James Brandt emphasizes the reformist dimensions of Schleiermacher's Christian ethics in the final chapters of *All Things New*. Brandt discusses under separate headings two aspects of the reformist impulse in Schleiermacher's work. The first of these has to do with the extent to which fidelity to Christianity requires activity directed at intervention in the broader social sphere. Under this heading Brandt identifies a number of discrete themes in the lectures on *christliche Sittenlehre*: "rejecting wars of aggression and the death penalty, slavery and the dehumanization of

workers, selfish nationalism, dueling and gambling, and calling for openness in society, mutuality and equality in fellowship between persons, and commitment to the reign of God as the absolute community of all with all" (130). The second involves Schleiermacher's "awareness of the changing, developmental character of the [Christian] tradition itself " and his commitment to the principle that "the tradition must change if it is to remain faithful to the intention embedded in its origin" (143). Brandt identifies both of these traits—as well as an "openness to insights from non-theological sources of knowing" (141)—as part of the inheritance of the Reformed ethical tradition.

78. See Bigler, *Politics*, 262ff.

79. This essay originally appeared in the *Journal of the American Academy of Religion* 65(2) (1997): 443–68. The following year responses to the piece appeared from Paul J. Griffiths and June O'Connor, with a reply from McCutcheon. O'Connor's piece constitutes a particularly thoughtful response to McCutcheon's position ("Response: The Scholar of Religion as Public Intellectual"). A revised version of McCutcheon's essay (to which my citations refer) appeared in McCutcheon, *Critics Not Caretakers*, 125–44. A shortened version appeared under the title "Critics Not Caretakers: The Scholar of Religion as Public Intellectual." A recent and quite useful examination of McCutcheon's stance is Michael Slater, "Can One Be a Critical Caretaker?"

80. McCutcheon, "Default of Critical Intelligence," 129.

81. Ibid., 135, 141.

82. Ibid., 135. Steven Engler calls attention to this aspect of McCutcheon's program in his review of McCutcheon's *Critics Not Caretakers*: "McCutcheon recommends no action beyond third-order description: issues of power and dominance are to be seen, not addressed." Engler, "Critics Not Caretakers: Redescribing the Public Study of Religion," 151.

83. McCutcheon, "Default of Critical Intelligence," 139. In this respect one essay cited by McCutcheon, Burton Mack's "Caretakers and Critics," makes for interesting reading when juxtaposed with McCutcheon's essay. The original version of "Caretakers and Critics," which McCutcheon cited, was read at Wesleyan in 1989; the essay was published in revised form in 2001, and it is to this later version that I refer. Mack, who counts himself among religion's critics rather than its caretakers, also laments the fact that "the academy has not learned how to share its knowledge with the generally enlightened non-specialist reader, and as for the society at large, it is just not attuned to the discourse of academics at all." However, Mack also acknowledges the fact that the public relevance of the critic of religion may not be immediately clear: "[W]hat good is our knowledge, anyway, if it no longer contributes to religious enlightenment, but rather to cultural critique?" "My answer," Mack responds, "would be that what we know is extremely important and could be very good news. The scholars and scribes of human societies have never found it easy to explain how it is that they know what they know. They have nonetheless had amazing authorization to mediate between the kings and the priests in the interest of rendering cultural critique. And they have always found a filtered way to let the secret out without detracting from the powers of the kings or the status of the priests." Mack's essay contains no suggestion that it would be improper for scholars of religion who

self-identify as critics rather than caretakers to adopt this "mediating" project—which resembles Schleiermacher's project more closely than does McCutcheon's—as their own. Mack, "Caretakers and Critics," 38.

84. Wiebe, "Reinvention or Degradation," 12.

85. Ibid.

86. Ibid., 13. Wiebe's concern that the theoretical character of the academic study of religion be kept free of contamination by practical, "religio-theological" interests forms a recurring theme in his *Politics of Religious Studies.*

87. Indeed, it can be stated fairly clearly that the issue of seeking practical, societal application of the results of academic work is not confined to religious studies. Consider a statement concerning the social sciences in general from the social and political psychologist Emanuele Castano: "In the end, theory-building in the social sciences is meant to improve the quality of our social life. That means that we have to draw some lessons, and, however immature our thinking on the issues is, we have to attempt to elaborate intervention strategies and suggest a research agenda that is not dictated only by our intellectual interests, but that also asks the cogent questions our research originated from as well as helped formulate." Castano, "On Glorifying the In-group," 165f.

88. McRoberts, in Ammerman et al., "2005 SSSR Presidential Address," 146. This address was a collaborative presentation by five scholars assembled by Nancy Ammerman.

89. See above, p. 175.

90. Robert Orsi's position on this question, as articulated in *Between Heaven and Earth,* is worthy of comment. On the surface Orsi opposes any attempts to distinguish between "good" and "bad" religion largely because of the tainted history that has attended such attempts among liberal Protestants. The conclusions Orsi draws from this history are fairly strong, as evidenced by his remark that "[we] may not condone or celebrate the religious practices of others . . . but we cannot dismiss them as inhuman, so alien to us that they cannot be understood or approached, only contained or obliterated (which is what the language of good/bad religion accomplishes, the obliteration of the other by desire, need, or fear)" (7f.). Orsi proposes religious studies in the mode of "disciplined attentiveness," predicated on "a disciplined suspension of the impulse to locate the other (with all her or his discrepant moralities, ways of knowing, and religious impulses) securely in relation to one's own cosmos" (198) and existing "in the suspension of the ethical" (203). Orsi's position can be contrasted with that of Talal Asad, who remarked in a 2001 essay, "In the case of religious movements in the part of the world I know best—the Middle East—there are certainly currents that are intolerant and destructive. But there are others that are different. These include movements that can be gradually assimilated in the form of political parties into the democratic processes familiar to us. But they also include developments that are creating new social forms for experience and aspiration that one hopes will help to reshape the idea of tolerance— tolerance neither as indifference nor as forbearance but as mutual engagement based on human interdependence." Talal Asad, "Reading a Modern Classic," 222.

91. Shortly after first writing this paragraph I encountered a similar sentiment from Wesley Wildman: "We probably all find religious phenomena intrinsically

fascinating, and we can certainly all see that religion is often a crucial factor in geopolitics, social change, and culture wars. We probably work in the hope that understanding will bring empathy and self-control, as it does so often in other facets of life. Some may go further and imagine that understanding religion may give us the power we need to eliminate it and to deliver its victims into humanistic enlightenment. Others might dream of a form of religion that can remain authentically spiritual while being fully aware of its evolutionary origins, social functions, psychological dynamics, and economic implications. Despite these discrepant motivations, cooperation seems feasible, and I think we can suspend our hidden and not-so-hidden social agendas for the sake of a quest for understanding." Wildman, "Significance of the Evolution," 228.

Bibliography

SCHLEIERMACHER TEXTS

Akademievorträge. Ed. Martin Rössler, with Lars Emersleben. Berlin: de Gruyter, 2002 (KGA I.11).
Aus Schleiermachers Leben in Briefen. Ed. Wilhelm Dilthey. 4 vols. Berlin: Reimer, 1858–1863.
Brief Outline on the Study of Theology. Trans. Terrence Tice. Atlanta: John Knox, 1966. Reprint, San Francisco: Mellen, 1988.
Briefwechsel 1799–1800. Ed. Andreas Arndt and Wolfgang Virmond. Berlin: de Gruyter, 1992 (KGA V.3).
Brouillon zur Ethik/Notes on Ethics (1805/1806). Trans. John Wallhauser. Lewiston, N.Y.: Mellen, 2003.
The Christian Faith. Trans. H. R. Mackintosh and J. S. Stewart. Edinburgh: T. and T. Clark, 1928. Reprint, 1989.
Der christliche Glaube nach den Grundsätzen der evangelischen Kirche im Zusammenhange dargestellt (1821–22). Ed. Herman Pieter. Berlin: de Gruyter, 1980 (KGA I.7, 1–3).
Der christliche Glaube nach den Grundsätzen der evangelischen Kirche im Zusammenhange dargestellt (1831–32). Ed. Rolf Schäfer. Berlin: de Gruyter, 2003 (KGA I.13, 1–2).
Ethik (1812/13). Ed. Hans-Joachim Birkner. Hamburg: Felix Meiner, 1990.
Friedrich Schleiermacher Dialektik. Ed. Manfred Frank. 2 vols. Frankfurt am Main: Suhrkamp, 2001.
Friedrich Schleiermachers Sämmtliche Werke. Ed. Ludwig Jonas, Alexander Schweizer, Friedrich Lücke, et al. 31 vols. Berlin: Georg Reimer, 1835–1863.
Hermeneutics and Criticism and Other Writings. Ed. and trans. Andrew Bowie. New York: Cambridge University Press, 1998.
Hermeneutics: The Written Manuscripts. Trans. James Duke and Jack Forstman. Atlanta: Scholars Press, 1977.

Jugendschriften 1787–1796. Ed. Günter Meckenstock. Berlin: de Gruyter, 1983 (KGA I.1).

Lectures on Philosophical Ethics. Ed. Robert Louden, trans. Louise Adey Huish. New York: Cambridge University Press, 2002.

The Life of Schleiermacher as Unfolded in His Autobiography and Letters. Trans. Frederica Rowan. 2 vols. London: Smith, Elder, 1860.

On Freedom. Trans. Albert L. Blackwell. Lewiston, N.Y.: Mellen, 1992.

On Religion: Speeches to Its Cultured Despisers. Trans. Richard Crouter. New York: Cambridge University Press, [1988] 1996.

On Religion: Speeches to Its Cultured Despisers. Trans. John Oman. Louisville: Westminster/John Knox, 1994.

On the Glaubenslehre: Two Letters to Dr. Lücke. Trans. James Duke and Francis Fiorenza. Atlanta: Scholars Press, 1981.

On the Highest Good. Trans. H. Victor Froese. Lewiston, N.Y.: Mellen, 1992.

On What Gives Value to Life. Trans. Edwina Lawler and Terence Tice. Lewiston, N.Y.: Mellen, 1995.

Schleiermachers Briefwechsel mit Johann Christian Gaß. Ed. Wilhelm Gaß. Berlin: Reimer, 1852.

Schleiermacher's Soliloquies. Trans. Horace Leland Friess. Chicago: Open Court, 1926. Reprint, 1957.

Schriften aus der Berliner Zeit 1796–1799. Ed. Günter Meckenstock. Berlin: de Gruyter, 1984 (KGA I.2).

Schriften aus der Berliner Zeit 1800–1802. Ed. Günter Meckenstock. Berlin: de Gruyter, 1988 (KGA I.3).

Theologisch-dogmatisch Abhandlungen und Gelegenheitsschriften. Ed. Hans-Friedrich Traulsen, with Martin Ohst. Berlin: de Gruyter, 1990 (KGA I. 10).

"Towards a Theory of Sociable Conduct." Trans. Jeffrey Hoover. *Friedrich Schleiermacher's Toward a Theory of Sociable Conduct and Essays on Its Intellectual-Cultural Context.* Ed. Ruth Drucilla Richardson. Lewiston, N.Y.: Mellen, 1995.

Über die Religion (2.–) 4. Auflage, Monologen (2–) 4. Auflage. Ed. Günter Meckenstock. Berlin: de Gruyter, 1995 (KGA I.12).

Universitätsschriften, Herakleitos, Kurze Darstellung des theologischen Studiums. Ed. Dirk Schmid. Berlin: de Gruyter, 1998 (KGA I.6).

Vorlesungen über die Dialektik. Ed. Andreas Arndt. Berlin: de Gruyter, 2002 (KGA II.10, 1–2).

Werke, Auswahl in vier Bänden. Ed. Otto Braun and Johannes Bauer, 2d ed. Aalen, Germany: Scientia, 1967.

SECONDARY LITERATURE

Abel, Theodore. *Systematic Sociology in Germany.* New York: Columbia University Press, 1929.

Adams, Robert Merrihew. *Leibniz: Determinist, Theist, Idealist.* New York: Oxford University Press, 1994.

———. "Schleiermacher on Evil." *Faith and Philosophy* 13 (1996): 563–83.

———. "Faith and Religious Knowledge." In *The Cambridge Companion to Schleiermacher,* ed. Jacqueline Mariña (2005), 35–51.

Albrecht, Christian. *Schleiermachers Theorie der Frömmigkeit: Ihr wissenschaftlicher Ort und ihr systematischer Gehalt in den Reden, in der Glaubenslehre und in der Dialektik.* Berlin: de Gruyter, 1993.

Ammerman, Nancy, Wendy Cadge, Milagros Peña, Robert D. Woodberry, and Omar
    M. McRoberts. "2005 SSSR Presidential Address: On Being a Community of
    Scholars—Practicing the Study of Religion." *Journal for the Scientific Study of
    Religion* 45 (2006): 137–48.
Antes, Peter, Armin Geertz, and Peter Warne, eds. *New Approaches to the Study of
    Religion: Regional, Critical, and Historical Approaches.* Berlin: de Gruyter, 2004.
Armour, Ellen T. *Deconstruction, Feminist Theology, and the Problem of Difference:
    Subverting the Race/Gender Divide.* Chicago: University of Chicago Press, 1999.
Arndt, Andreas. "Gefühl und Reflexion: Schleiermachers Stellung zur
    transzentendalphilosophie im Kontext der zeitgenössischen Kritik an Kant und
    Fichte." In *Transzendentalphilosophie und Spekulation: Der Streit um die Gestalt
    einer ersten Philosophie (1799–1807),* ed. Walter Jaeschke, 105–26. Hamburg:
    Meiner, 1993.
Asad, Talal. *Genealogies of Religion: Discipline and Reasons of Power in Christianity and
    Islam.* Baltimore: Johns Hopkins University Press, 1993.
———. "Reading a Modern Classic: W. C. Smith's *The Meaning and End of Religion.*"
    History of Religions 40 (2001): 205–22.
Barnard, G. William. "Explaining the Unexplainable: Wayne Proudfoot's 'Religious
    Experience.' " *Journal of the American Academy of Religion* 60 (1992): 231–56.
Barth, Karl. *Protestant Theology in the Nineteenth Century.* Valley Forge, Penn.: Judson,
    1973.
———. *The Theology of Schleiermacher: Lectures at Göttingen, Winter Semester of
    1923–24,* ed. Dietrich Ritschl, trans. Geoffrey W. Bromiley. Grand Rapids, Mich.:
    Eerdmans, 1982.
Barth, Ulrich. "Schleiermacher-Literatur im letzten Drittel des 20. Jahrhunderts."
    Theologische Rundschau 66 (2001): 408–61.
———. *Aufgeklärter Protestantismus.* Tübingen: Mohr Siebeck, 2004.
———, and Claus-Dieter Osthövener, eds. *200 Jahre "Reden über die Religion."* Berlin:
    de Gruyter, 2000.
Bauer, Johannes. *Schleiermacher als patriotischer Prediger: Ein Beitrag zur Geschichte der
    nationalen Erhebung vor hundert Jahren.* Gießen, Germany: Töpelmann, 1908.
Baur, Ferdinand Christian. *Vorlesungen über die christliche Dogmengeschichte,* vol. 3.
    Leipzig: Fues's (L. W. Reisland), 1865.
Beck, Lewis White. *Early German Philosophy: Kant and His Predecessors.* Cambridge,
    Mass.: Belknap Press of Harvard University Press, 1969.
Becker, George. "Pietism's Confrontation with Enlightenment Rationalism: An
    Examination of the Relation between Ascetic Protestantism and Science." *Journal
    for the Scientific Study of Religion* 30 (1991): 148.
Behrens, Georg. "Schleiermacher contra Lindbeck on the Status of Doctrinal
    Sentences." *Religious Studies* 30 (1994): 399–417.
———. "The Order of Nature in Pious Self-consciousness: Schleiermacher's
    Apologetic Argument." *Religious Studies* 32 (1996): 93–108.
———. "Feeling of Absolute Dependence or Absolute Feeling of Dependence? (What
    Schleiermacher Really Said and Why It Matters)." *Religious Studies* 34 (1998):
    471–81.
Beiser, Frederick C. *The Fate of Reason: German Philosophy from Kant to Fichte.*
    Cambridge, Mass.: Harvard University Press, 1987.

Berger, Peter L. *A Rumor of Angels: Modern Society and the Rediscovery of the Supernatural.* New York: Doubleday, 1969.

——. *The Heretical Imperative: Contemporary Possibilities of Religious Affirmation.* Garden City, N.Y.: Anchor, 1979.

Bigler, Robert M. *The Politics of German Protestantism: The Rise of the Protestant Church Elite in Prussia, 1815–1848.* Berkeley: University of California Press, 1972.

Birkner, Hans-Joachim. *Schleiermacher-Studien.* Berlin: de Gruyter, 1996.

Blackwell, Albert L. "The Antagonistic Correspondence between Chaplain Sack and His Protégé Schleiermacher." *Harvard Theological Review* 74 (1981): 101–21.

——. *Schleiermacher's Early Philosophy of Life: Determinism, Freedom, and Phantasy.* Chico, Calif.: Scholars Press, 1982.

Boyd, George. "Schleiermacher's 'Über den Unterschied zwischen Naturgesetz und Sittengesetz.' " *Journal of Religious Ethics* 17 (1989): 41–50.

Boyer, Bruce L. "Schleiermacher on the Divine Causality." *Religious Studies* 22 (1986): 113–24.

Brandt, James. *All Things New: Reform of Church and Society in Schleiermacher's Christian Ethics.* Louisville: Westminster/John Knox, 2001.

Brandt, Richard B. *The Philosophy of Schleiermacher: The Development of His Theory of Scientific and Religious Knowledge.* New York: Harper, 1941.

Braun, Willi, and Russell McCutcheon, eds. *Guide to the Study of Religion.* New York: Cassell, 2000.

Brentano, Franz. *The Foundation and Construction of Ethics,* ed. and trans. Elizabeth Schneewind. London: Routledge, 1973.

Brown, William Adams. *The Essence of Christianity: A Study in the History of Definition.* New York: Scribner's, 1902.

Bruford, W. H. *The German Tradition of Self-cultivation: "Bildung" from Humboldt to Thomas Mann.* New York: Cambridge University Press, 1975.

Byrne, Peter. *Natural Religion and the Nature of Religion.* London: Routledge, 1989.

Capetz, Paul. *Christian Faith as Religion: A Study of the Theologies of Calvin and Schleiermacher.* Lanham, Md.: University Press of America, 1998.

——. "Theology and the Non-theological Study of Religion: A Critical Assessment of Schleiermacher's Legacy." In *Schleiermacher und Kierkegaard,* ed. Cappelørn et al., 179–95 (2006).

Cappelørn, Niels Jørgen, Richard Crouter, and Theodor Jorgensen, eds. *Schleiermacher und Kierkegaard: Subjectivität und Wahrheit/Subjectivity and Truth.* Berlin: de Gruyter, 2006.

Capps, Walter H. *Religious Studies: The Making of a Discipline.* Minneapolis: Fortress, 1995.

Casanova, José. *Public Religions in the Modern World.* Chicago: University of Chicago Press, 1994.

Castano, Emanuele. "On Glorifying the In-group: Intergroup Violence, In-group Glorification, and Moral Disengagement." *Social and Personality Psychology Compass* 2 (2008): 154–70.

Clements, Keith. *Friedrich Schleiermacher: Pioneer of Modern Theology.* London: Collins, 1987.

Cramer, Konrad. "Die subjectivitätstheoretischen Prämissen von Schleiermachers Bestimmung des religiösen Bewußtseins." In *Friedrich Schleiermacher 1768–1834:*

Theologe–Philosoph–Pädagoge, ed. Dietz Lange, 129–62 (Göttingen: Vandenhoek and Ruprecht, 1985).

———. "Die eine Frömmigkeit und die vielen Frommen: Zu Schleiermachers Theorie der Vergesellschaftung des religiösen Bewusstseins." In *Schleiermacher und Kierkegaard*, ed. Cappelørn et al., 313–34 (2006).

Crossley, John, Jr. "The Ethical Impulse in Schleiermacher's Early Ethics." *Journal of Religious Ethics* 17 (1989): 5–24.

Crouter, Richard. "Friedrich Schleiermacher: A Critical Edition, New Work, and Perspectives." *Religious Studies Review* 18 (1992): 20–27.

———. *Friedrich Schleiermacher: Between Enlightenment and Romanticism.* New York: Cambridge University Press, 2005.

———. "Shaping an Academic Discipline: The *Brief Outline on the Study of Theology.*" In *Friedrich Schleiermacher: Between Enlightenment and Romanticism*, by Richard Crouter, 207–25 (2005).

Curran, Thomas H. "Schleiermacher wider die Spekulation." In *Internationaler Schleiermacher-Kongreß 1984*, ed. Selge, 997–1001 (1985).

———. *Doctrine and Speculation in Schleiermacher's* Glaubenslehre. Berlin: de Gruyter, 1994.

Damer, T. Edward. *Attacking Faulty Reasoning*, 2d ed. Belmont, Calif.: Wadsworth, 1987.

Dawson, Jerry. "Friedrich Schleiermacher on the Separation of Church and State." *Journal of Church and State* 7 (1965): 214–25.

———. *Friedrich Schleiermacher: The Evolution of a Nationalist.* Austin: University of Texas Press, 1966.

De Vries, Hent. *Religion: Beyond a Concept.* New York: Fordham, 2008.

De Vries, Jan. *The Study of Religion: A Historical Approach.* Trans. Kees Bolle. New York: Harcourt, Brace, and World, 1967.

Di Giovanni, George. *Freedom and Religion in Kant and His Immediate Successors: The Vocation of Humankind, 1774–1800.* New York: Cambridge University Press, 2005.

Dillenberger, John, and Claude Welch. *Protestant Christianity: Interpreted through Its Development.* New York: Macmillan, 1988.

Dilthey, Wilhelm. *Leben Schleiermachers.* 2 vols. Berlin: de Gruyter, 1970.

———. *Wilhelm Dilthey Selected Writings.* Ed. and trans. H. P. Rickman. Cambridge: Cambridge University Press, 1976.

Dinkel, Christoph. *Kirche Gestalten: Schleiermachers Theorie des Kirchenregiments.* Berlin: de Gruyter, 1996.

Dole, Andrew. "Schleiermacher and Otto on Religion." *Religious Studies* 40 (2004): 389–413.

———. "The Case of the Disappearing Discourse: Schleiermacher's Fourth Speech and the Field of Religious Studies." *Journal of Religion* 88 (2008): 1–28.

———. "Schleiermacher's Theological Anti-realism." In *Analytic Theology: New Essays in the Philosophy of Theology*, ed. Oliver Crisp and Michael Rea, 136–54 (New York: Oxford University Press, 2009).

Dorrien, Gary. *Soul in Society: The Making and Renewal of Social Christianity.* Minneapolis: Fortress, 1995.

————. *The Making of American Liberal Theology: Imagining Progressive Religion 1805–1900.* Louisville: Westminster/John Knox, 2001.

Duke, James O., and Robert F. Streetman. *Barth and Schleiermacher: Beyond the Impasse?* Philadelphia: Fortress, 1988.

Dunkmann, Karl. *Die Nachwirkungen der theologischen Prinzipienlehre Schleiermachers.* Gütersloh, Germany: Bertelsmann, 1915.

————. *Lehrbuch der Soziologie und Sozialphilosophie.* Berlin: Junker u. Dünnhaupt, 1931.

Durkheim, Emile. *The Elementary Forms of Religious Life.* Trans. Karen Fields. New York: Free Press, 1995.

Duttenhaver, Krista. "Relative Freedoms: The Influence of Spinoza on the Systems of Whitehead and Schleiermacher." *Schleiermacher and Whitehead: Open Systems in Dialogue,* ed. Christine Helmer, 93–117 (Berlin: de Gruyter, 2004).

Eckermann, Jakob Christoff Rudolf. "Über die Religion: Reden an die Gebildeten unter ihren Verächtern" (review). *Neue allgemeine deutsche Bibliothek* 56 (1801): 44–52.

Eckert, Michael. *Gott-Glauben und Wissen: Friedrich Schleiermachers philosophische Theologie.* Berlin: de Gruyter, 1987.

Engler, Steven. "Critics Not Caretakers: Redescribing the Public Study of Religion" (book review). *Journal of Religion* 84 (2004): 150–51.

Esselborn, Friedrich Wilhelm. *Die philosophische Voraussetzungen von Schleiermachers Determinismus.* Ludwigshafen, Germany: Biller, 1897.

Falcke, Heino. *Theologie und Philosophie der Evolution: Grundaspekte der Gesellschaftslehre Friedrich Schleiermachers.* Zürich: Theologischer Verlag, 1977.

Farley, Edward. "Is Schleiermacher Passé?" *Christian Faith Seeking Historical Understanding.* Ed. James O. Duke and Anthony L. Dunnavant. Macon, Ga.: Mercer University Press, 1997.

Feuerbach, Ludwig. *Ludwig Feuerbachs Werke in sechs Bänden,* ed. Erich Thies. Frankfurt am Main: Suhrkamp, 1975.

Finlay, Hueston E. " 'Feeling of Absolute Dependence' or 'Absolute Feeling of Dependence'? A Question Revisited." *Religious Studies* 41 (2005): 81–94.

Fiorenza, Francis Schüssler. "Schleiermacher and the Construction of a Contemporary Roman Catholic Foundational Theology." *Harvard Theological Review* 89 (1996): 175–94.

————. "Religion: A Contested Site in Theology and the Study of Religion." *Harvard Theological Review* 93(1) (2000): 7–34.

————, and Gordon Kaufman: "God." In *Critical Terms for Religious Studies,* ed. Taylor, 136–159 (1998).

Firschung, Horst, and Matthias Schlegel. "Religiöse Innerlichkeit und Geselligkit: Zum Verhältnis von Erfahrung, Kommunikabilität, und Sozialität unter besonderer Berücksichtigung des Religionsverständnisses Friedrich Schleiermachers." In *Religion als Kommunikation,* ed. Hartmann Tyrell, Volkhard Krech, and Hubert Knoblauch, 31–81. Würzburg: Ergon, 1998.

Fischer, Hermann. *Friedrich Daniel Ernst Schleiermacher.* Munich: Beck, 2001.

Fitzgerald, Timothy. *The Ideology of Religious Studies.* New York: Oxford University Press, 2000.

————. "Bruce Lincoln's 'Theses on Method': Antitheses." *Method and Theory in the Study of Religion* 18 (2006): 392–423.

Flood, Gavin. *Beyond Phenomenology*. London: Continuum, 1999.

Foreman, Terry Hancock. "Schleiermacher's 'Natural History of Religion': Science and the Interpretation of Culture in the Speeches." *Journal of Religion* 58 (1978): 91–107.

Forstmann, Jackson. *A Romantic Triangle: Schleiermacher and Early German Romanticism*. Missoula, Mont.: Scholars Press, 1977.

Frank, Manfred. "The Text and Its Style: Schleiermacher's Theory of Language." Trans. Helen Atkins. In *The Subject and the Text: Essays in Literary Theory and Philosophy*, ed. Andrew Bowie, 1–22. New York: Cambridge University Press, 1997.

————. "Metaphysical Foundations: A Look at Schleiermacher's *Dialectic*." In *Cambridge Companion to Schleiermacher*, ed. Jacqueline Mariña, 23–31 (2005).

Fuchs, Stephan. *Against Essentialism: A Theory of Culture and Society*. Cambridge, Mass.: Harvard University Press, 2001.

Funk, Robert. *Schleiermacher as Contemporary*. New York: Herder and Herder, 1970.

Fuss, Diana. *Essentially Speaking: Feminism, Nature, and Difference*. London: Routledge, 1989.

Gadamer, Hans-Georg. *Truth and Method*. Trans. Joel Weinsheimer and Donald Marshall. New York: Continuum, 1995.

Garczyk, Eckhard. *Mensch, Gesellschaft, Geschichte: F. D. E. Schleiermachers philosophische Soziologie*. Munich: UNI-Druck, 1963.

Gaß, Wilhelm. *Geschichte der protestantischen Dogmatik in ihrem Zusammenhange mit der Theologie überhaupt*. 4 vols. Berlin: Reimer, 1854–1867.

Geck, Albrecht. "Sozialethische und sozialpolitische Ansätze in der philosophischen und theologischen Systematik Schleiermachers." In *Sozialer Protestantismus im Vormärz*, ed. Martin Friedrich, Norbert Friedrich, Traugott Jähnichen, and Jochen-Christoph Kaiser, 133–46 (Münster: LIT Verlag, 2001).

Geertz, Clifford. "From the Native's Point of View: On the Nature of Anthropological Understanding." In *Local Knowledge: Further Essays in Interpretive Anthropology*, by Clifford Geertz, 55–70 (1983).

————. *Local Knowledge: Further Essays in Interpretive Anthropology*. New York: Basic Books, 1983.

Gelman, Susan. *The Essential Child: Origins of Essentialism in Everyday Thought*. New York: Oxford University Press, 2003.

Lüdtke, Gerhard, and Lutz Mackensen, eds. *Deutscher Kulturatlas*. Berlin: De Gruyter, 1938.

Gerrish, Brian. *Tradition in the Modern World: Reformed Theology in the Nineteenth Century*. Chicago: University of Chicago Press, 1978.

————. *The Old Protestantism and the New: Essays on the Reformation Heritage*. Chicago: University of Chicago Press, 1982.

————. *A Prince of the Church: Schleiermacher and the Beginnings of Modern Theology*. Philadelphia: Fortress, 1984.

————. "Friedrich Schleiermacher." In *Nineteenth-century Religious Thought in the West*, ed. Smart et al., 123–56 (1985).

————. "Review: The Nature of Doctrine." *Journal of Religion* 68 (1988): 87–92.

————. *Continuing the Reformation: Essays on Modern Religious Thought.* Chicago: University of Chicago Press, 1993.

————. "Errors and Insights in the Understanding of Revelation: A Provisional Response." *Journal of Religion* 78 (1998): 64–88.

Gladigow, Burkhard. "Friedrich Schleiermacher." In *Klassiker der Religionswissenschaft,* ed. Axel Michaels, 17–27. Munich: Beck, 1997.

Godlove, Terry. "The Instability of Religious Belief." In *Religion and Reductionism,* ed. Idinopulos and Yonan, 49–64 (1994).

Graby, James K. "Reflections on the History of the Interpretation of Schleiermacher." *Scottish Journal of Theology* 12 (1968): 283–99.

Graf, Friedrich Wilhelm. "Ursprüngliches Gefühl unmittelbarer Koinzidenz des Differenten." *Zeitschrift für Theologie und Kirche* 75 (1978): 147–86.

————. *Profile des neuzeitlichen Protestantismus,* vol. 1. Gütersloh, Germany: Gerd Mohn, 1990.

Gray, Marion W. *Prussia in Transition: Society and Politics under the Stein Reform Ministry of 1808.* Philadelphia: American Philosophical Society, 1986.

Grove, Peter. *Deutungen des Subjekts: Schleiermachers Philosophie der Religion.* Berlin: de Gruyter, 2004.

Gruppe, Otto. *Die griechische Culte und Mythen in ihren Beziehing zu den orientalischen Religion,* vol. 1. Hildesheim, Germany: Georg Olm, 1973.

Guenther-Gleason, Patricia Ellen. *On Schleiermacher and Gender Politics.* Harrisburg, Penn.: Trinity Press International, 1997.

Gundolf, Friedrich. *Romantiker.* Berlin-Wilmersdorf: Keller, 1931.

Guthrie, Stewart. *Faces in the Clouds.* New York: Oxford University Press, 1993.

Hagenbach, Karl Rudolph. *Über die sogenannte Vermittlungstheologie: Zur Abwehr und Verständigung.* Zürich: Meyer and Zeller, 1858.

————. *German Rationalism in Its Rise, Progress, and Decline.* Trans. Wm. L. Gage and J. H. W. Stuckenberg. Edinburgh: T. and T. Clark, 1865.

Harvey, Van A. "A Word in Defense of Schleiermacher's Theological Method." *Journal of Religion* 42 (1962): 151–70.

————. "On the New Edition of Schleiermacher's Speeches on Religion." *Journal of the American Academy of Religion* 39 (1971): 488–512.

————. "The Pathos of Liberal Theology." *Journal of Religion* 56 (1976): 382–91.

Haym, Rudolf. *Die romantische Schule: Ein Beitrag zur Geschichte des deutschen Geistes.* Berlin: Gaertner, 1870.

Hegel, Georg Wilhelm Friedrich. *Faith and Knowledge: Or, the Reflective Philosophy of Subjectivity in the Complete Range of Its Forms as Kantian, Jacobian, and Fichtean Philosophy.* Trans. Walter Cerf and H. S. Harris. Albany: State University of New York Press, 1977.

————. *Lectures on the Philosophy of Religion.* Trans. Peter Crafts Hodgson and Robert F. Brown. 1-vol. ed. Berkeley: University of California Press, 1988.

Hensgtenberg, Ernst Wilhelm. "Der Kunst- und Wissenschafts-Enthusiasmus in Deutschland als Surrogat für Religion." *Evangelische Kirchen-Zeitung* 69 (1828): 545–49.

Herder, Johann Gottfried. *Against Pure Reason: Writings on Religion, Language, and History.* Trans. Marcia J. Bunge. Minneapolis: Fortress, 1993.

Herms, Eilert. "Schleiermacher's Christian Ethics." Trans. and condensed by Jacqueline Mariña and Christine Helmer. In *The Cambridge Companion to Schleiermacher*, ed. Jacqueline Mariña, 209–28 (2005).

Hertel, Friedrich. *Das theologische Denken Schleiermachers untersucht an der ersten Auflage seiner Reden "Über die Religion."* Zurich: Zwingli, 1965.

Hilgenfeld, Adolf. "Die wissenschaftliche Theologie und ihre gegenwärtige Aufgabe." *Zeitschrift für wissenschaftliche Theologie* I (1858): 1–21.

Hinnels, John, ed. *The Routledge Companion to the Study of Religion.* London: Routledge, 2005.

Hjelde, Sigurd. *Die Religionswissenschaft und das Christentum: Eine historische Untersuchung über das Verhältnis von Religionswissenschaft und Theologie.* Leiden: Brill, 1994.

Hoover, Jeffrey. "The Origin of the Conflict between Hegel and Schleiermacher at Berlin." *Owl of Minerva* 20 (1988): 69–79.

Howard, Thomas Albert. *Religion and the Rise of Historicism: W. M. L. de Wette, Jacob Burkhardt, and the Theological Origins of Nineteenth-century Historical Consciousness.* New York: Cambridge University Press, 2000.

———. *Protestant Theology and the Making of the Modern German University.* New York: Oxford University Press, 2006.

Huber, Eugen. *Die Entwicklung des Religionsbegriffs bei Schleiermacher.* Leipzig: Dieterich'sche Verlagsbuchhandlung, 1901.

Hunsinger, George. "Truth as Self-involving: Barth and Lindbeck on the Cognitive and Performative Aspects of Truth in Theological Discourse." *Journal of the American Academy of Religion* 61 (1993): 41–56.

Idinopulos, Thomas, and Edward Yonan, eds. *Religion and Reductionism: Essays on Eliade, Segal, and the Challenge of the Social Sciences for the Study of Religion.* Leiden: Brill, 1994.

Jacobi, Friedrich Heinrich, and Marion Lauschke. *Über die Lehre des Spinoza in Briefen an den Herrn Moses Mendelssohn.* Hamburg: Felix Meiner, 2000.

Jantzen, Grace. "Mysticism and Experience." *Religious Studies* 25 (1989): 295–315.

———. "Could There Be a Mystical Core of Religion?" *Religious Studies* 26 (1990): 59–71.

———. *Power, Gender, and Christian Mysticism.* New York: Cambridge University Press, 1995.

———. *Becoming Divine: Towards a Feminist Philosophy of Religion.* Bloomington: Indiana University Press, 1999.

Jensen, Kipton. "The Principle of Protestantism: On Hegel's (Mis)Reading of Schleiermacher's Speeches." *Journal of the American Academy of Religion* 71 (2003): 405–422.

Jensen, Tim, and Mikael Rothstein, eds. *Secular Theories of Religion: Current Perspectives.* Copenhagen: Museum Tusculanum, 2000.

Jørgensen, Poul Henning. *Die Ethik Schleiermachers.* Munich: C. Kaiser, 1959.

Joy, Morny. "Beyond Essence and Intuition: A Reconsideration of Understanding in Religious Studies." In *Secular Theories of Religion*, ed. Jensen and Rothstein, 69–86 (2000).

———. "Philosophy and Religion." In *New Approaches to the Study of Religion*, ed. Antes et al., 185–217 (2004).

Junker-Kenny, Maureen. "Schleiermacher's Transcendental Turn: Shifts in Argumentation between the First and Second Editions of the Glaubenslehre." *New Athenaeum/Neues Athenaeum* 3 (1992): 21–41.

Kant, Immanuel. *Critique of Pure Reason.* Trans. Paul Guyer and Allen W. Wood. New York: Cambridge University Press, 1998.

———. *Religion within the Boundaries of Mere Reason and Other Writings.* Trans. Allen Wood and George di Giovanni. New York: Cambridge University Press, 1998.

Keller-Wentorf, Christel. *Schleiermachers Denken: Die Bewusstseinslehre in Schleiermachers philosophischer Ethik als Schlüssel zu seinem Denken.* Berlin: de Gruyter, 1984.

Kelsey, Catherine. *Schleiermacher's Preaching, Dogmatics, and Biblical Criticism: The Interpretation of Jesus Christ in the Gospel of John.* Eugene, Or.: Pickwick, 2007.

Khawaja, Irfan. "Essentialism, Consistency, and Islam: A Critique of Edward Said's *Orientalism.*" *Israel Affairs* 13 (October 2007): 689–713.

Kinlaw, Jeffery. "Schleiermacher's Transcendent Ground Argument." In *The State of Schleiermacher Scholarship Today,* ed. Edwina Lawler, Jeffery Kinlaw, and Ruth Drucilla Richardson, 295–313. Lewiston, N.Y.: Mellen, 2006.

Krech, Volkhard. *Georg Simmels Religionstheorie.* Tübingen: Mohr Siebeck, 1998.

Kumlehn, Martina. *Symbolisierendes Handeln: Schleiermachers Theorie religiöser Kommunikation und ihre Bedeutung für die gegenwärtige Religionspädagogik.* Gütersloh, Germany: Chr. Kaiser/Gütersloher Verlagshaus, 1999.

Lamm, Julia A. "The Early Philosophical Roots of Schleiermacher's Notion of Gefühl, 1788–1794." *Harvard Theological Review* 87 (1994): 67–105.

———. "Schleiermacher's Post-Kantian Spinozism: The Early Essays on Spinoza, 1793–94." *Journal of Religion* 74 (1994): 476–505.

———. *The Living God: Schleiermacher's Theological Appropriation of Spinoza.* University Park: Pennsylvania State University Press, 1996.

———. "Schleiermacher's Treatise on Grace." *Harvard Theological Review* 101 (2008): 133–68.

Lawler, Edwina, Jeffery Kinlaw, and Ruth Drucilla Richardson, eds. *The State of Schleiermacher Scholarship Today: Selected Essays.* Lewiston, N.Y.: Mellen, 2006.

Lichtenberger, Frédéric. *History of German Theology in the Nineteenth Century.* Trans. W. Hastie. Edinburgh: T. and T. Clark, 1889.

Lincoln, Bruce. *Discourse and the Construction of Society: Comparative Studies of Myth, Ritual, and Classification.* New York: Oxford University Press, 1989.

Lindbeck, George A. *The Nature of Doctrine: Religion and Theology in a Postliberal Age.* Philadelphia: Westminster, 1984.

Locke, John. *An Essay concerning Human Understanding.* Ed. Peter Nidditch. New York: Oxford University Press, 1975.

Luft, Eric von der. "A Reply to Professor Williams' Summary of My Ideas about Hegel's Reading." *Owl of Minerva* 14 (1982): 7–8.

———. "A Scholarly Note." *Owl of Minerva* 14 (1982).

———. *Hegel, Hinrichs, and Schleiermacher on Feeling and Reason in Religion: The Texts of Their 1821–22 Debate.* Lewiston, N.Y.: Mellen, 1987.

Luhmann, Niklas. "Differentiation of Society." *Canadian Journal of Sociology/Cahiers canadiens de sociologie* 2 (1977): 29–53.

Mack, Burton. "Caretakers and Critics: On the Social Role of Scholars Who Study
    Religion." *Bulletin of the Council of Societies for the Study of Religion* 30 (2001): 32–38.
Mackintosh, H. R. *Types of Modern Theology: Schleiermacher to Barth.* London: Nisbet,
    1937.
Mariña, Jacqueline. "Schleiermacher's Christology Revisited: A Reply to His Critics."
    Scottish Journal of Theology 42 (1996): 177–200.
———. "A Critical-interpretive Analysis of Some Early Writings by Schleiermacher on
    Kant's Views of Human Nature and Freedom." *Neues Athenaeum* 5 (1998): 11–31.
———. "Schleiermacher on the Philosopher's Stone: The Shaping of
    Schleiermacher's Early Ethics by the Kantian Legacy." *Journal of Religion* 79
    (1999): 193–215.
———. *The Cambridge Companion to Friedrich Schleiermacher.* New York: Cambridge
    University Press, 2005.
———. *Transformation of the Self in the Thought of Friedrich Schleiermacher.* New York:
    Oxford University Press, 2008.
Marshall, Bruce D. "Hermeneutics and Dogmatics in Schleiermacher's Theology."
    Journal of Religion 67 (1987): 14–32.
Martin, Wayne. "Transcendental Philosophy and Atheism." *European Journal of
    Philosophy* 16 (2007): 109–30.
Masuzawa, Tomoko. *The Invention of World Religions; Or, How European Universalism
    Was Preserved in the Language of Pluralism.* Chicago: University of Chicago Press,
    2005.
McCormack, Bruce L. "Revelation and History in Transfoundationalist Perspective:
    Karl Barth's Theological Epistemology in Conversation with a Schleiermacherian
    Tradition." *Journal of Religion* 78 (1998): 18–37.
———. "What Has Basel to Do with Berlin? Continuities in the Theologies of
    Schleiermacher and Barth." *Princeton Seminary Bulletin* 23 (2002): 146–73.
McCutcheon, Russell T. "A Default of Critical Intelligence? The Scholar of Religion as
    Public Intellectual." *Journal of the American Academy of Religion* 65 (1997):
    443–68.
———. *Manufacturing Religion: The Discourse on Sui Generis Religion and the Politics of
    Nostalgia.* New York: Oxford University Press, 1997.
———. *The Insider/Outsider Problem in the Study of Religion: A Reader.* London:
    Cassell, 1999.
———. "Critics Not Caretakers: The Scholar of Religion as Public Intellectual." In
    Secular Theories on Religion, ed. Jensen and Rothstein, 167–81 (2000).
———. *Critics Not Caretakers: Redescribing the Public Study of Religion.* SUNY series,
    Issues in the Study of Religion. Albany: State University of New York Press, 2001.
———. "Critical Trends in the Study of Religion in the United States." In *New
    Approaches to the Study of Religion,* ed. Antes et al., 317–43 (2004).
Meckenstock, Günter. *Deterministische Ethik und kritische Theologie: Die
    Auseinandersetzung des frühen Schleiermacher mit Kant und Spinoza, 1789–1794.*
    Berlin: de Gruyter, 1988.
———. "Die Wandlungen der 'Monologen' Schleiermachers." In *Schleiermacher und
    die wissenschaftliche Kultur des Christentums,* ed. Günter Meckenstock, 403–18.
    Berlin: de Gruyter, 1991.

————. "Schleiermachers Auseinandersetzung mit Fichte." In *Schleiermacher's Philosophy and the Philosophical Tradition*, ed. Sergio Sorrentino, 27–46. Lewiston, N.Y.: Mellen, 1992.

————. "Tracing the Development of the Schleiermacher Critical Edition (KGA)." *Zeitschrift für neuere Theologiegeschichte/Journal for the History of Modern Theology* 4 (1997): 169–76.

Meisner, Heinrich, and Hermann Mulert. "Schleiermachers Briefwechsel mit Friedrich Heinrich Christian Schwarz." *Zeitschrift für Kirchengeschichte* 53 (1934): 255–94.

Mensching, Gustav. *Geschichte der Religionswissenschaft*. Bonn: Universitäts Verlag, 1948.

Molendijk, Arie, and Peter Pels, eds. *Religion in the Making: The Emergence of the Sciences of Religion*. London: Brill, 1998.

Moretto, Giovanni. "The Problem of the Religious in the Philosophical Perspectives of Fichte and Schleiermacher." In *Schleiermacher's Philosophy and the Philosophical Tradition*, ed. Sergio Sorrentino, 47–74. Lewiston, N.Y.: Mellen, 1992.

Morgan, Robert. "Ernst Troeltsch and the Dialectical Theology." In *Ernst Troeltsch and the Future of Theology*. Ed. John Powell Clayton, 33–77. New York: Cambridge University Press, 1976.

Mühling, Markus. "Schleiermachers Gottesbeweis? Die (De/Re)konstruction subjektiver Selbstgewißheit und die Erkenntniß Gottes." In *Krisen der Subjectivität: Problemfelder eines strittigen Paradigmas*, ed. Ingolf Dalferth and Phillip Stoellger, 125–41 (Tübingen: Mohr Siebeck, 2005).

Mulert, Hermann. "Die Aufnahme der Glaubenslehre Schleiermachers." *Zeitschrift für Theologie und Kirche* 18 (1908): 107–39.

Müller, Friedrich Max. *Lectures on the Science of Religion*. New York: Scribner, Armstrong, 1872.

————. *Natural Religion: The Gifford Lectures Delivered before the University of Glasgow in 1888*. London: Longmans, Green, 1889.

Neander, August. "Das verflossene halbe Jahrhundert in seinem Verhältniß zur Gegenwart." *Deutsche Zeitschrift für christliche Wissenschaft und christliches Leben* 1 (1850): 3–14, 17–22, 25–29.

Niebuhr, Richard R. *Schleiermacher on Christ and Religion: A New Introduction*. New York: Scribner, 1964.

Nowak, Kurt. *Schleiermacher und die Frühromantik*. Göttingen, Germany: Vandenhoeck and Ruprecht, 1986.

————. *Schleiermacher: Leben, Werk, und Wirkung*. Berlin: de Gruyter, 2001.

Oberdorfer, Bernd. *Geselligkeit und Realisierung von Sittlichkeit: Die Theorieentwicklung Friedrich Schleiermachers bis 1799*. Berlin: de Gruyter, 1995.

O'Connor, June. "Response: The Scholar of Religion as Public Intellectual: Expanding Critical Intelligence." *JAAR* 66 (1998): 897–909.

Orsi, Robert. *Between Heaven and Earth: The Religious Worlds People Make and the Scholars Who Study Them*. Princeton: Princeton University Press, 2005.

Otto, Rudolf. "Wie Schleiermacher die Religion wiederentdeckte." *Die christliche Welt* 17(22) (May 28, 1903): 506–12.

————. *Naturalistische und religiöse Weltansicht*. Tübingen: Mohr Siebeck, 1904.

————. *Religious Essays: A Supplement to "the Idea of the Holy."* Trans. Brian Lunn. London: Oxford University Press, 1931.

———. "Der neue Aufbruch des *sensus numinis* bei Schleiermacher." In *Sünde und Urschuld und andere Aufsätze zur Theologie*. Munich: Beck'sche Verlagsbuchhandlung, 1932.

———. *Sünde und Urschuld und andere Aufsätze zur Theologie*. Munich: Beck'sche Verlagsbuchhandlung, 1932.

———. *The Idea of the Holy: An Inquiry into the Non-rational Factor in the Idea of the Divine and Its Relation to the Rational*. Trans. John Wilfred Harvey. London: Oxford University Press, 1952.

Pannenberg, Wolfhart. *Theology and the Philosophy of Science*. Trans. Francis McDonagh. Philadelphia: Westminster, 1976.

———. *Systematic Theology*, vol. 1. Trans. Geoffrey Bromiley. Grand Rapids, Mich.: Eerdmans, 1988.

Pauck, Wilhelm. *From Luther to Tillich: The Reformers and Their Heirs*. San Francisco: Harper and Row, 1984.

Pearson, Lori. *Beyond Essence: Ernst Troeltsch as Historian and Theorist of Christianity*. Cambridge, Mass.: Harvard University Press, 2008.

Penner, Hans. "Interpretation." In *Guide to the Study of Religion*, ed. Braun and McCutcheon, 57–72 (2000).

Perle, Johannes Helmut. *Individualität und Gemeinschaft im Denken des jungen Schleiermacher*. Gütersloh, Germany: Bertelsmann, 1935.

Pflüger, Christine. *Georg Simmels Religionstheorie in ihren werk- und theologiegeschichtlichen Bezügen*. Frankfurt am Main: Peter Lang, 2007.

Pickle, Joseph. "Schleiermacher on Judaism." *Journal of Religion* 60 (1980): 115–37.

———. "Promises of Positive Plurality: How Comparative Religion Could Have Been Studied in Schleiermacher's University of Berlin." In *Friedrich Schleiermacher and the Founding of the University of Berlin*, ed. Richardson et al., 83–119 (1991).

Pinkard, Terry. "Virtues, Morality, and Sittlichkeit: From Maxims to Practices." *European Journal of Philosophy* 7 (1999): 217–38.

———. *Hegel: A Biography*. New York: Cambridge University Press, 2000.

Plantinga, Theodore. *Historical Understanding in the Thought of Wilhelm Dilthey*. Toronto: University of Toronto Press, 1980.

Preus, James S. *Explaining Religion: Criticism and Theory from Bodin to Freud*. New Haven: Yale University Press, 1987.

Proudfoot, Wayne. *Religious Experience*. Berkeley: University of California Press, 1985.

———. "Symposium on Schleiermacher's *On Religion: Speeches to Its Cultured Despisers*." *Harvard Divinity Bulletin* 24(3) (1995): 10–13.

Pummer, Reinhardt. "*Religionswissenschaft* or Religiology?" *Numen* 19 (1971): 91–127.

Raack, Richard C. "Schleiermacher's Political Thought and Activity, 1806–1813." *Church History* 28 (1959): 374–90.

Rasch, William. "Ideal Sociability: Friedrich Schleiermacher and the Ambivalence of Extrasocial Spaces." In *Gender in Transition: Discourse and Practice in German-speaking Europe, 1750–1830*, ed. Ulrike Glaxton and Marion W. Gray, 319–39. Ann Arbor: University of Michigan Press, 2006.

Raschke, Carl. "Religious Studies and the Default of Critical Intelligence." *Journal of the American Academy of Religion* 54 (1986): 131–38.

———. "Religious Experience" (review). *Journal of the American Academy of Religion* 55 (1987): 620–22.

Rea, Michael. *World without Design: The Ontological Consequences of Naturalism.* Oxford: Clarendon, 2002.

Redeker, Martin. *Schleiermacher: Life and Thought.* Trans. John Wallhauser. Philadelphia: Fortress, 1973.

Rendtorff, Trutz. *Church and Theology.* Trans. Reginald Fuller. Philadelphia: Westminster, 1971.

Reynolds, Thomas. "Religion within the Limits of History: Schleiermacher and Religion—a Reappraisal." *Religion* 32 (2002): 51–70.

———. "Reconsidering Schleiermacher and the Problem of Religious Diversity: Toward a Dialectical Pluralism." *Journal of the American Academy of Religion* 73 (2005): 151–81.

Richards, Jay Wesley. "Truth and Meaning in George Lindbeck's *The Nature of Doctrine.*" *Religious Studies* 33 (1997): 33–53.

Richardson, Herbert, ed. *Friedrich Schleiermacher and the Founding of the University of Berlin: The Study of Religion as a Scientific Discipline.* Lewiston, N.Y.: Mellen, 1991.

Richardson, Ruth Drucilla, ed. *Schleiermacher in Context: Papers from the 1988 International Symposium on Schleiermacher at Herrnhut, the German Democratic Republic.* Lewiston, N.Y.: Mellen, 1991.

Roberts, Robert C. "The Feeling of Absolute Dependence." *Journal of Religion* 57 (1977): 252–66.

Roy, Louis. "Consciousness according to Schleiermacher." *Journal of Religion* 77 (1997): 217–32.

Rumscheidt, Martin. *Adolf von Harnack: Liberal Theology at Its Height.* London: Collins, 1989.

Runzo, Joseph. *Reason, Relativism, and God.* London: Macmillan, 1986.

Rupp, George. *Culture-Protestantism: German Liberal Theology at the Turn of the Twentieth Century.* Missoula, Mont.: Scholars Press, 1977.

Samson, Holgar. *Die Kirche als Grundbegriff der Ethik Schleiermachers.* Zürich: Zollikon, 1958.

Schilbrack, Kevin. "Religion, Models of, and Reality: Are We through with Geertz?" *Journal of the American Academy of Religion* 73 (2005): 429–52.

Scholtz, Gunter. *Ethik und Hermeneutik: Schleiermachers Grundlegung der Geisteswissenschaften.* Frankfurt am Main: Suhrkamp, 1995.

Scholz, Heinrich. "Analekta zu Schleiermacher." *Zeitschrift für Theologie und Kirche* 21 (1911): 293–314.

Schröder, Markus. *Die kritische Identität des neuzeitlichen Christentums: Schleiermachers Wesensbestimmung der christlichen Religion.* Berlin: de Gruyter, 1994.

Schurr, Johannes. "Fichte's 'Bestimmung des Menschen' und Schleiermachers 'Monologen': Dokumente eines Umbruchs?" *Vierteljahrsschrift für wissenschaftliche Pädagogik* 55 (1979): 317–28.

Scott, Charles E. "Schleiermacher and the Problem of Divine Immediacy." *Religious Studies* 3 (1968): 499–512.

Segal, Robert. *Explaining and Interpreting Religion: Essays on the Issue.* New York: Peter Lang, 1992.

Selge, Kurt-Victor, ed. *Internationaler Schleiermacher-Kongreß 1984.* Berlin: de Gruyter, 1985.

———. "Neander und Schleiermacher." In *Schleiermacher und die wissenschaftliche Kultur des Christentums*, ed. Günter Meckenstock, 33–50 (Berlin: de Gruyter, 1991).

Sharf, Robert. "The Zen of Japanese Nationalism." *History of Religions* 33 (1993): 1–43.

———. "Buddhist Modernism and the Rhetoric of Meditative Experience." *Numen* 42 (1995): 228–83.

———. "Experience." In *Critical Terms for Religious Studies*, ed. Taylor, 94–116 (1998).

Sharpe, Eric. *Comparative Religion: A History*. New York: Scribner's Sons, 1975.

Sherman, Robert. "Isaak August Dorner on Divine Immutability: A Missing Link between Schleiermacher and Barth." *Journal of Religion* 77 (1997): 380–401.

Siefert, Paul. *Die Theologie des jungen Schleiermacher*. Gütersloh, Germany: Gütersloher Verlagshaus, 1960.

Simmel, Georg. *Georg Simmel on Individuality and Social Forms*. Ed. Donald Levine. Chicago: University of Chicago Press, 1971.

Slater, Michael. "Can One Be a Critical Caretaker?" *Method and Theory in the Study of Religion* 19 (2007): 332–42.

Sleigh, Robert, Jr. "Moral Necessity in Leibniz's Account of Human Freedom." In *Metaphysics and the Good: Themes from the Philosophy of Robert Merrihew Adams*, ed. Samuel Newlands and Larry Jorgensen, 252–71 (New York: Oxford University Press, 2009).

———, Vere Chappell, and Michael Della Rocca. "Determinism and Human Freedom." In *The Cambridge History of Seventeenth-century Philosophy*, ed. Daniel Garber and Michael Ayers, vol. 2, 1195–1278 (New York: Cambridge University Press, 1998).

Slone, D. Jason. *Theological Incorrectness*. New York: Oxford University Press, 2004.

Smart, Ninian, John Clayton, Steven Katz, and Patrick Sherry. *Nineteenth-century Religious Thought in the West*. 3 vols. New York: Cambridge University Press, 1985.

Smith, David A. "Schleiermacher and Otto on Religion: A Reappraisal." *Religious Studies* 44 (2008): 295–313.

Smith, Wilfred Cantwell. *The Meaning and End of Religion*. Minneapolis: Fortress, 1991.

Snow, Dale Ebert. "F. H. Jacobi and the Development of German Idealism." *Journal of the History of Philosophy* 23(3) (1987): 397–416.

Sockness, Brent. *Against False Apologetics: Wilhelm Herrmann and Ernst Troeltsch in Conflict*. Tübingen: Mohr Siebeck, 1998.

———. "Was Schleiermacher a Virtue Ethicist? *Tugend* and *Bildung* in the Early Ethical Writings." *Zeitschrift für neuere Theologiegeschichte* 8 (2001): 1–33.

———. "The Forgotten Moralist: Friedrich Schleiermacher and the Science of Spirit." *Harvard Theological Review* 96 (2003): 317–48.

———. "Schleiermacher and the Ethics of Authenticity: The *Monologen* of 1800." *Journal of Religious Ethics* 32 (2004): 477–517.

Sorrentino, Sergio. "History and Temporality in the Debate between F. C. Baur and Schleiermacher." *Schleiermacher's Philosophy and the Philosophical Tradition*. Ed. Sergio Sorrentino, 111–32. Lewiston, N.Y.: Mellen, 1992.

Spiegel, Yorick. *Theologie der bürgerlichen Gesellschaft: Sozialphilosophie und Glaubenslehre bei Friedrich Schleiermacher*. Munich: Kaiser, 1968.

Spiegler, Gerhard E. *The Eternal Covenant: Schleiermacher's Experiment in Cultural Theology.* New York: Harper and Row, 1967.

Spinoza, Benedict de. *A Spinoza Reader: The Ethics and Other Works.* Ed. and trans. Edwin Curley. Princeton: Princeton University Press, 1994.

Stephenson, Gunther. "Geschichte und Religionswissenschaft im ausgehenden 18. Jahrhundert." *Numen* 13 (1966): 43–79.

Stoltzfus, Philip. *Theology as Performance: Music, Aesthetics, and God in Modern Thought.* New York: T. and T. Clark, 2006.

Strenski, Ivan. *Thinking about Religion: An Historical Introduction to Theories of Religion.* Malden, Mass.: Blackwell, 2006.

Süskind, Hermann. *Der Einfluss Schellings auf die Entwicklung von Schleiermachers System.* Tübingen: Mohr, 1909.

———. *Christentum und Geschichte bei Schleiermacher: Die geschichtsphilosophischen Grundlagen der Schleiermacherschen Theologie.* Tübingen: Mohr, 1911.

Sykes, S. W. "Ernst Troeltsch and Christianity's Essence." In *Ernst Troeltsch and the Future of Theology.* Ed. John Powell Clayton, 139–71. New York: Cambridge University Press, 1976.

———. *The Identity of Christianity: Theologians and the Essence of Christianity from Schleiermacher to Barth.* Philadelphia: Fortress, 1984.

Taylor, Mark C., ed. *Critical Terms for Religious Studies.* Chicago: University of Chicago Press, 1998.

Thandeka. *The Embodied Self: Friedrich Schleiermacher's Solution to Kant's Problem of the Empirical Self.* Albany: State University of New York Press, 1995.

Thiemann, Ronald F. *Revelation and Theology: The Gospel as Narrated Promise.* Notre Dame: University of Notre Dame Press, 1985.

Thrower, James. *Religion: The Classical Theories.* Washington, D.C.: Georgetown University Press, 1999.

Tice, Terrence. *Schleiermacher Bibliography: With Brief Introductions, Annotations, and Index.* Princeton: Princeton Theological Seminary, 1966.

———. "Schleiermacher on the Scientific Study of Religion." In *Friedrich Schleiermacher and the Founding of the University of Berlin,* ed. Richardson et al., 45–82 (1991).

———. "Schleiermacher's 'Highest Intuition' in Landsberg (1794–1796)." In *Schleiermacher in Context: Papers from the 1988 International Symposium on Schleiermacher at Herrnhut, the German Democratic Republic,* ed. Richardson, 18–42 (1991).

Timm, Hermann. *Gott und die Freiheit: Studien zur Religionsphilosophie der Goethezeit.* Frankfurt am Main: Klostermann, 1974.

Troeltsch, Ernst. "Schleiermacher und die Kirche." In *Schleiermacher der Philosoph des Glaubens: Sechs Aufsätze,* 9–35. Berlin-Schöneberg: Buchverlag der "Hilfe," 1910.

———. "Empiricism and Platonism in the Philosophy of Religion: To the Memory of William James." *Harvard Theological Review* 5 (1912): 401–22.

———"Half a Century of Theology: A Review." Trans. Robert Morgan. In *Writings on Theology and Religion,* ed. Morgan and Pye, 53–81 (1977).

———. *Writings on Theology and Religion.* Ed. and trans. Robert Morgan and Michael Pye. Atlanta: Knox, 1977.

Tyrell, Hartmann. "Das Gesellige in der Religion: Soziologische Überlegungen im Anschluß an Schleiermachers 'Vierte Rede.' " In *Reden über die Religion—200 Jahre nach Schleiermacher: Eine interdisziplinäre Auseinandersetzung mit Schleiermachers Religionskritik*, ed. Friedrich Huber, 30–49. Wuppertal, Germany: Foedus, 2000.

———. "Religion: Das 'vollendetste Resultat der menschlichen Geselligkeit.' Perspektiven einer Individualitätskultur im Verhältnis von Religionstheorie und Gesellschaftstheorie." In *200 Jahre "Reden über die Religion*," ed. Barth and Osthövener, 79–99 (2000).

Ungern-Sternberg, Arthur von. *Freiheit und Wirklichkeit: Schleiermachers philosophischer Reifeweg durch den deutschen Idealismus.* Gotha, Germany: Klotz, 1931.

Vial, Ted. "Friedrich Schleiermacher on the Central Place of Worship in Theology." *Harvard Theological Review* 91 (1998): 59–73.

———. "Schleiermacher and the State." In *The Cambridge Companion to Friedrich Schleiermacher*, ed. Mariña, 269–85 (2005).

Waardenburg, Jean Jacques. *Classical Approaches to the Study of Religion: Aims, Methods, and Theories of Research.* The Hague: Mouton, 1973.

Wach, Joachim. *Types of Religious Experience.* Chicago: University of Chicago Press, 1951.

Wagner, Falk. *Was ist Religion? Studien zu ihrem Begriff und Thema in Geschichte und Gegenwart.* Gütersloh, Germany: Mohn, 1986.

Wähner, Friedrich. "Die christliche Glaube nach dem Grundsätzen der evangelichen Kirche im Zusammenhange dargestellt von Dr. Friedrich Schleiermacher" (review). *Hermes oder kritisches Jahrbuch für Literatur* (1824), Stück 2, 275–344; Stück 3, 214–74.

Wallhauser, John. *Brouillon zur Ethik.* Two books in one edition: *Notes on Ethics (1805/1806)* and *Notes on the Theory of Virtue (1804/1805).* Lewiston, N.Y.: Mellen, 2003.

———. "Schleiermacher's 'Brouillon zur Ethik,' 1805/06." In *Schleiermacher in Context.* Ed. Ruth Drucilla Richardson, 109–31. Lewiston, N.Y.: Mellen, 1991.

Ward, Keith. *Religion and Revelation: A Theology of Revelation in the World's Religions.* Oxford: Clarendon, 1994.

Welch, Claude. *Protestant Thought in the Nineteenth Century.* New Haven: Yale University Press, 1972–1985.

Welker, Klaus Eberhard. *Die grundsätzliche Beurteilung der Religionsgeschichte durch Schleiermacher.* Leiden: Brill, 1965.

Wiebe, Donald. *The Politics of Religious Studies: The Continuing Conflict with Theology in the Academy.* New York: St. Martin's, 1999.

———. "The Reinvention or Degradation of Religious Studies? Tales from the Tuscaloosa Woods." *Reviews in Religion and Theology* 11 (2004): 3–14.

Wildman, Wesley J. "The Significance of the Evolution of Religious Belief and Behavior for Religious Studies and Theology." In *Where God and Science Meet: How Brain and Evolutionary Studies Alter Our Understanding of Religion*, ed. Patrick McNamara, vol. 1, 227–72 (Westport, Conn.: Praeger, 2006).

Williams, Robert R. *Schleiermacher the Theologian: The Construction of the Doctrine of God.* Philadelphia: Fortress, 1978.

———. "A Scholarly Note?" *Owl of Minerva* 14 (1982): 9–10.

Willich, Ehrenfried. *Aus Schleiermachers Hause.* Berlin: Reimer, 1909.

Wintsch, Hans Ulrich. *Religiosität und Bildung: Der Anthropologische und bildungsphilosophische Ansatz in Schleiermachers Reden über die Religion.* Zürich: Verlag Zürich, 1967.

Wobbermin, Georg, Theophil Menzel, and Daniel Sommer Robinson. *The Nature of Religion*. New York: Crowell, 1933.

Wolfes, Matthias. "Public Sphere and Nation State: Friedrich Schleiermacher's Political Practice." Trans. Brent Sockness. In *Schleiermacher's 'To Cecilie' and Other Writings by and about Schleiermacher*, ed. Ruth Drucilla Richardson, 197–204 (Lewiston, N.Y.: Mellen, 2001).

———. *Öffentlichkeit und Bürgergesellschaft: Friedrich Schleiermachers politische Wirksamkeit*. 2 vols. Berlin: de Gruyter, 2004.

Wood, Allen. *Kant's Moral Religion*. Ithaca: Cornell University Press, 1970.

———. *Hegel's Ethical Thought*. New York: Cambridge University Press, 1990.

Wyman, Walter E. *The Concept of Glaubenslehre: Ernst Troeltsch and the Theological Heritage of Schleiermacher*. Chico, Calif.: Scholars Press, 1983.

———. "Revelation and the Doctrine of Faith: Historical Revelation within the Limits of Historical Consciousness." *Journal of Religion* 78 (1998): 38–63.

Zeller, Eduard. *Geschichte der deutschen Philosophie seit Leibniz*. Munich: Oldenbourg, 1875.

Index